The Congressional Experience

THIRD EDITION

David E. Price

Westview
PRESS

A Member of the Perseus Books Group

TRANSFORMING AMERICAN POLITICS

Lawrence C. Dodd, Series Editor

Dramatic changes in political institutions and behavior over the past three decades have underscored the dynamic nature of American politics, confronting political scientists with a new and pressing intellectual agenda. The pioneering work of early postwar scholars, while laying a firm empirical foundation for contemporary scholarship, failed to consider how American politics might change or recognize the forces that would make fundamental change inevitable. In reassessing the static interpretations fostered by these classic studies, political scientists are now examining the underlying dynamics that generate transformational change.

Transforming American Politics brings together texts and monographs that address four closely related aspects of change. A first concern is documenting and explaining recent changes in American politics—in institutions, processes, behavior, and policymaking. A second is reinterpreting classic studies and theories to provide a more accurate perspective on postwar politics. The series looks at historical change to identify recurring patterns of political transformation with in and across the distinctive eras of American politics. Last and perhaps most important, the series presents new theories and interpretations that explain the dynamic processes at work and thus clarify the direction of contemporary politics. All of the books focus on the central theme of transformation—transformation in both the conduct of American politics and in the way we study and understand its many aspects.

BOOKS IN THIS SERIES

Transforming American Politics

Copyright © 2004 by Westview Press, A Member of the Perseus Books Group

Hardcover edition first published in 1992 in the United States of America by Perseus Books.

Paperback edition first published in 2000 by Westview Press.

Find us on the world wide web at www.westviewpress.com

Westview Press books are available at special discounts for bulk purchases in the United States by corporations, institutions, and other organizations. For more information, please contact the Special Markets Department at the Perseus Books Group, 11 Cambridge Center, Cambridge, MA 02142, or call (800) 255-1514 or (617) 252-5298, or e-mail special.markets@perseusbooks.com.

Cataloging-in-Publication data is available from the Library of Congress.
ISBN 0-8133-4262-7 (paperback)

The paper used in this publication meets the requirements of the American National Standard for Permanence of Paper for Printed Library Materials Z39.48–1984.

10   9   8   7   6   5   4   3   2   1

For Lisa, Karen, and Michael

Contents

Figures and Tables

Figures

Table

Preface to the First Edition

To write a book in the midst of congressional service is an improbable undertaking, and I am indebted to many people for their help and encouragement. I would never have considered such a project without the urging of series editor Larry Dodd. The many hours that he subsequently spent critiquing the manuscript helped me immensely. Gene Conti, Don DeArmon, Paul Feldman, Ferrel Guillory, and Mac McCorkle each read all or most of the manuscript and offered valuable suggestions for improvements. For help with specific chapters, I am indebted to Saul Shorr, Mark Mellman, and Ed Lazarus (Chapter 2); Gay Eddy, Joan Ewing, John Maron, and Rachel Perry (Chapter 10); and Robert Seymour (Chapter 11).

An earlier version of Chapter 8 appeared in *Challenges to Party Government* (Carbondale: Southern Illinois University Press, 1992); I am grateful to the editors of that volume, John White and Jerome Mileur, and to David Rohde for their suggestions. Chapter 11 is adapted from my Sorensen Lecture of February 13, 1990, at the Yale University Divinity School. I wish to thank Andrew Sorensen for his sponsorship of this annual lecture and Dennis Thompson for his helpful comments. I am also indebted to Don DeArmon, Paul Feldman, and Michael Malbin, who encouraged and helped me to pause and record my early impressions of the House of Representatives. Bill Keech and Barbara Sinclair made certain I saw relevant current work in political science. For help in tracking down and assembling data, I thank Roger Davidson, Walter Oleszek, David Beck, Maria McIntyre, and Kevin Levy.

Sally Maddison (Wooten) has been the keeper of the manuscript, producing endless revisions with extraordinary competence and good humor. It has also been a pleasure to work with the staff at Westview Press: senior production editor Libby Barstow, copyeditor Joan Sherman, editorial assistant Rachel Quenk, and acquisitions editor Jennifer Knerr, who saw the potential of this project early on and offered encouragement throughout.

Finally, I owe far more than the usual acknowledgment to my wife, Lisa, and our children, Karen and Michael. I am thinking not merely of their patience with the diversion and preoccupation this book occasioned but also of their role in the story it tells. Their efforts have made my "congressional experience" possible, and their attitudes have made it a positive experience for our family. The dedication of this volume is only a token of my indebtedness and gratitude to them.

David E. Price
March, 1992

Preface to the Second Edition

As I was preparing to write the preface to this second edition, I asked my wife, Lisa, if she would still describe writing such a book in the midst of congressional service as an "improbable undertaking." Yes, she answered emphatically, adding that the improbability is compounded when one is also moving (as we were in 1998–1999) to a new house across town! I cannot disagree with that view, and I am happy once again to record my gratitude for her tolerance and support.

I am indebted to series editor Larry Dodd for urging me to pick up the story where I had left it in 1992 and for once again preparing a thoughtful and helpful critique of the manuscript. Mac McCorkle, Billy Moore, and Thomas Bates each read several chapters and offered useful suggestions, while Rose Auman, Richard Kogan, Tom Kahn, Bill Laxton, and Paul Feldman provided valuable feedback on individual chapters and case histories. For help in assembling specific information and source material, I am grateful to Jean-Louise Beard, Cathy Chesney, Gay Eddy, Tracy Lovett, Sandra Massenburg, Robyn Winneberger, Mark Harkins, Darek Newby, Catherine Baker, Dale Caldwell, Amy Childs, John Friedman, Bill Boesch, John Aldrich, Alan Secrest, Saul Shorr, Charles Johnson, David Reich, and Scott Olson.

Darek and Patty Newby prepared the manuscript with great efficiency and care. My daughter, Karen Price, assisted in preparing the index. It has again been a pleasure to work with the staff at Westview Press; I particularly want to thank executive editor Leo Wiegman and project manager Jane Olivier.

I assume responsibility, of course, for any errors of fact or interpretation that remain. But there are far fewer of these than there would have been without the counsel of these friends and colleagues, and their interest and help have greatly encouraged me to see this "improbable undertaking" through.

David E. Price
June 2000

Preface to the Third Edition

This third edition of *The Congressional Experience* appears four years after the second, cutting in half the time between the first two editions. But bringing the story forward has been no less challenging, for those four years have seen portentous changes in our country's fiscal and foreign policies and in the context of congressional service. I welcome the chance to interpret these developments and am grateful to Westview Press and the readers and users of earlier editions for providing the warrant for an updated account.

I want to thank Mac McCorkle, Richard Kogan, Jim Davis, Jean-Louise Beard, and Bridget Lowell for helpful review of this edition's new material. I am indebted to Rose Auman, Darek Newby, Eric Sapp, Elizabeth Kirkland, Elizabeth Gottschalk, Marian Currinder, Catherine Liao, Lee Hamilton, Don Wolfensberger, Walter Oleszek, Raleigh Myers, Kayla Drogosz, and Sophie Hayford for help in assembling information and data. Portions of the revised Chapter 8 were first presented at the Miller Center of the University of Virginia; I am grateful to Kenneth Thompson, William Lee Miller, and others at the Center for their hospitality and useful comments.

Catherine Baker prepared the manuscript competently and carefully, and Jessica Forrest helped complete the index. At Westview I particularly want to thank executive editor Steve Catalano and, again, series editor Larry Dodd. Project editor Iris Richmond and copyeditor Chrisona Schmidt saw the book through production in a cooperative and remarkably efficient fashion.

My wife Lisa again facilitated and encouraged the project in various ways. No member of Congress would survive in the job, much less perform it effectively, without an extensive support system—starting with family and friends and including staff, colleagues and collaborators, political supporters and attentive constituents. I am fortunate that my support system has been strong and resilient, and I am hopeful that those who have been part of it will see this book as their story as well as mine, a token of my indebtedness and gratitude.

David E. Price
June 2004

1

Introduction

On November 4, 1986, I was elected to the U.S. House of Representatives from the Fourth District of North Carolina, a five-county area that at the time included the cities of Raleigh, Chapel Hill, and Asheboro. Many thoughts crowded in on me during election night, but one of the most vivid was of a the spring evening in 1959 when I had first set foot in the part of North Carolina I was now to represent. At the time, I was a student at Mars Hill, a junior college in the North Carolina mountains a few miles from my home in the small town of Erwin, Tennessee. I had taken an eight-hour bus ride from Mars Hill to Chapel Hill to be interviewed for a Morehead Scholarship, a generous award that subsequently made it possible for me to attend the University of North Carolina (UNC). I was awed by the university and nervous about the interview. Thinking back on some of the answers I gave ("Would you say Cecil Rhodes was an imperialist?" "I believe so."), I still marvel that I won the scholarship. But I did, and the next two years were among the most formative and exciting of my life.

I went north in 1961 to divinity school and eventually graduate school and a faculty appointment in political science, all at Yale University. But the idea of returning to the Raleigh–Durham–Chapel Hill area of North Carolina continued to tug at me, particularly as I decided on a teaching career and thought about where I would like to put down personal and academic roots. Fortunately my wife, Lisa, also found the idea agreeable, despite her budding political career as a member of the New Haven board of aldermen. Therefore, when I received an offer to join the political science faculty at Duke University and help launch what is now called the Terry Sanford Institute of Public Policy, I jumped at the opportunity. In mid-1973, we moved with our children (three-year-old Karen and one-year-old Michael) to Chapel Hill. Though we were delighted with the community and the job and saw the move as a long-term one, I would have been incredulous at the suggestion that within fourteen years I would represent the district in Congress.

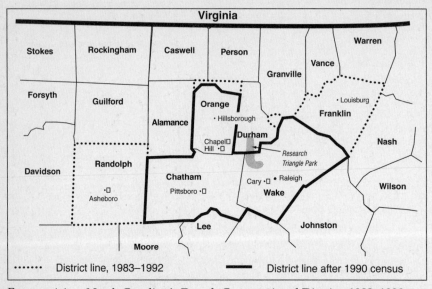

FIGURE 1.1a   North Carolina's Fourth Congressional District, 1983–1998.

The Fourth District has been redrawn three times since I was first elected (see Figures 1.1a and 1.1b). After the 1990 census, statewide population growth dictated expanding North Carolina's House delegation from eleven to twelve, and growth concentrated in our part of the state required a reduction in the geographic spread of the Fourth District, from five counties to three. The new district was more compact than the old and more Democratic, although not sufficiently so to withstand the electoral tide of 1994. After losing that election and staging a comeback in 1996, I faced another redistricting as the North Carolina General Assembly responded to a court order to correct alleged racial gerrymandering. The target of the order was the Twelfth District, a majority black district that wound through the Piedmont from Durham to Charlotte. However, legislators chose to redraw the entire congressional map, providing the Fourth District with almost one-third new constituents. This gave me all or part of five counties, now including the city and county of Durham and excluding central portions of Raleigh and territory to the east.

This configuration lasted for only two election cycles, since the 2000 census revealed the Fourth District was 147,000 residents above the new norm (619,000) for North Carolina's districts. The state gained a thirteenth congressional seat, and sizable portions of Wake County as well as the Fourth District part of Person County were transferred to the new district.

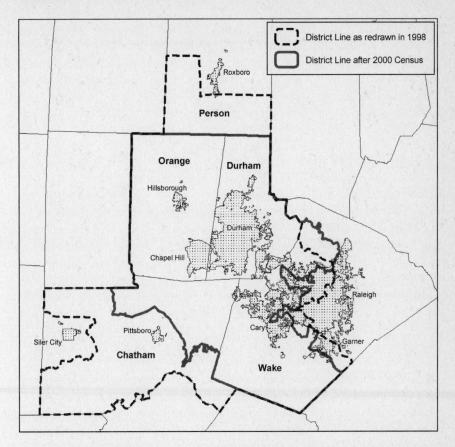

FIGURE 1.1b   North Carolina's Fourth Congressional District, as redrawn in 1998.

The Fourth District currently centers on the cities of Raleigh, Cary, Durham, and Chapel Hill and includes Research Triangle Park, a monument to synergy among high-tech industries, research universities, and the state and federal governments. The area has experienced rapid economic and population growth and widespread suburbanization, although some small-town and rural areas remain in all four counties. African Americans comprise 21 percent of the district's population, and increasing numbers of people with Chinese, Indian, Latin American, and other ethnic backgrounds have been drawn to the area. The 2000 census pegged the Hispanic population at 5 percent, a fourfold increase over the past decade.

Politically the district is 49 percent Democratic by voter registration and 31 percent Republican. Some 20 percent of the voters are registered as "unaffiliated" and many more than that are independent in their voting habits. The addition of Durham in 1997 increased the district's Democratic tilt, but this was largely offset when the more Democratic parts of Raleigh and Wake County were transferred to the neighboring Second and Thirteenth Districts. The Fourth remains a "swing" district, a partisan battleground in national, state, and many local elections.

Several of the district's counties were represented in the distant past by Nathaniel Macon (1791–1815), North Carolina's only Speaker of the U.S. House of Representatives. For the first two-thirds of the twentieth century, the eastern part of the present Fourth District was represented by two men: Edward W. Pou (1901–1934), who chaired the House Rules Committee, and Harold D. Cooley (1934–1967), flamboyant chairman of the House Agriculture Committee. Carl Durham, who represented the district's western counties from 1939 until 1961, chaired the Joint Committee on Atomic Energy. Such extended periods of service, with attendant seniority in the House, have become less common in our part of North Carolina since the departure of Durham and Cooley. Heightened partisan competition has produced more frequent turnovers in congressional seats. Members have also become less intent on House careers, sometimes resigning to seek other political offices. And the drawing and redrawing of district lines following the Supreme Court's reapportionment decisions have destabilized traditional electoral coalitions and rendered elections less predictable.[1] When I was sworn in on January 6, 1987, I became the Fourth District's third representative in as many terms.

By the time I ran for Congress, I had amassed a good deal of political experience. Senator E. L. ("Bob") Bartlett (D-Alaska) hired me as a summer intern in 1963, and I returned to his staff as a legislative aide for the four succeeding summers, eventually doing interviews out of his office for a doctoral dissertation on the Senate. After moving back to North Carolina, I worked actively in local politics, managed a couple of congressional districts (including the Fourth) in Jimmy Carter's 1976 presidential campaign, and took leaves from Duke in 1980 and 1984 to serve as executive director and then chairman of the North Carolina Democratic Party. But these were diversions, albeit increasingly serious ones, from a primary career in teaching and research. By 1986 I had studied, taught, and written about Congress, among other subjects, for twenty years.

Among some voters—and occasionally among congressional colleagues—my academic background has been a barrier to be overcome. But not for most. My district, it is claimed, has the highest number of

Ph.D.'s per capita of any comparable area in the country. Representing an area that boasts six institutions of higher education, the Research Triangle Park, and retirement communities populated by people of substantial accomplishment, I have remarkably literate constituents. I sometimes reflect ambivalently on this as I contemplate the piles of well-reasoned letters on every conceivable issue that come into my office. Yet the electoral advantages are considerable. During my first campaign, we polled to test public reactions to my academic affiliation and background, expecting to downplay them in the campaign. Instead, we found highly positive associations and ended up running a television ad that featured me in the classroom!

It was, I suppose, in light of my dual background as an academic and a political practitioner that I was asked to contribute reflections on my first term in office to the 1989 edition of *Congress Reconsidered*.[2] I was reluctant at first, pressed for time and uncertain of the value of the exercise, but I was challenged by the idea of giving an account of congressional operations that would combine personal experience with the sort of generalization and analysis characteristic of political science. My story and the stories of other people and events would be told not mainly for their own sake but as a way of showing how the U.S. Congress works. The article that I produced formed the core of the first edition of this book, which extended through the midpoint of my third term (1991–1992). The second edition took the story forward to the 106th Congress (1999–2000), and the present edition extends it to the 108th (2003–2004). The chapters to follow will address getting elected (and unelected and then reelected); adjusting to life in Congress and finding a niche in the House; policy entrepreneurship; the politics of appropriations, the budget, and foreign affairs; party operations and White House relations; and serving the district.

Topics that were familiar to me as an academic—the place of religion in politics, the ethics of public service, and the critique of Congress as an institution—have taken on particular interest during my years in office, and in later chapters I will offer some reflections on them. These are areas where ideas are often used as weaponry more than as a means to enlightenment, and I will try to nudge these discussions in a more productive direction.

The period covered in this volume was a contentious and challenging time for Congress and the country. It extends from the waning of Ronald Reagan's presidency, through George H.W. Bush's one term and Bill Clinton's two, into the fourth year of George W. Bush's tenure. It was a time of momentous change in world politics, spanning the end of the cold war and the collapse of communism in Russia and Eastern Europe, allied interventions in Bosnia and Kosovo, two U.S.-led wars against

Iraq, the terrorist attacks of September 11, 2001, and the subsequent offensive against al Qaeda and international terrorism. At home, it was at first a period of tepid economic performance and a deepening recession (1990–1991), followed by a decade-long economic recovery and, after 2000, a pronounced economic downturn. The boom years of the 1990s were especially evident in districts like mine, but so was the downturn, which particularly affected the high-tech and telecommunications sectors. Intertwined with these trends as both cause and effect was a federal budget crisis with $250 billion deficits "as far as the eye could see" giving way in the mid-1990s to declining deficits and even modest budget surpluses but then, in the George W. Bush administration, abruptly returning to red ink and mounting debt.

It was also a period of political turbulence, with neither party clearly dominant, in my district or in the nation, and citizens expressing considerable dissatisfaction with politics and politicians. Democrats controlled the House, Senate, and White House for two unstable years (1993–1994), as did the Republicans after the 2002 elections. But the norm during these years was divided party control, with the Republican control of the presidency and Democratic control of both houses of Congress that obtained from 1987 to 1992 reversing itself after 1994. During the eight terms covered in this volume, I served under four House Speakers—Democrats Jim Wright and Tom Foley and Republicans Newt Gingrich and Dennis Hastert. Wright and Gingrich resigned amid ethics charges and political turmoil during a period that also spanned President Reagan's Iran-Contra scandal and President Clinton's impeachment.

The reputation of Congress, never Americans' favorite political institution, reached historic lows during these years, and House members often found it politically profitable to run for Congress by denigrating and running against the institution. Gingrich and his self-styled Republican revolutionaries came to power in 1994 largely on the strength of a harsh institutional critique. They in turn became the targets of public cynicism and distrust as their revolution overreached and began to falter. "Congress bashing" often crowded out more reasoned and relevant judgments about individual and institutional performance. My hope in this book is to encourage and facilitate more useful assessments by conveying a sense of how Congress works and beginning to raise some of the right evaluative questions.

But first things first. Recalling the dictum of former House Speaker Tip O'Neill that "all politics is local"[3] (at least most of the time, I might add, in light of 1994), I will begin with an account of how I came to run for Congress and managed, with the help of a great many people, to get elected.

Notes

1. See David E. Price, "Roll Call: A Congressman Looks Back at Those Who Went Before," *Raleigh News and Observer*, July 30, 1989, p. 1D.

2. David E. Price, "The House of Representatives: A Report from the Field," in Lawrence C. Dodd and Bruce I. Oppenheimer, eds., *Congress Reconsidered*, 4th ed. (Washington, D.C.: Congressional Quarterly Press, 1989), chap. 17.

3. Thomas P. O'Neill, *Man of the House* (New York: Random House, 1987), chap. 1. "You can be the most important congressman in the country, but you had better not forget the people back home. I wish I had a dime for every politician I've known who had to learn that lesson the hard way. I've seen so many good people come to Washington, where they get so worked up over important national issues that they lose the connection to their own constituents. Before they know it, some new guy comes along and sends them packing" (p. 26).

2

Getting Elected

The University of North Carolina at Chapel Hill has an elaborate student government and a tradition of lively campus politics. The years I was there, 1959–1961, were particularly active because of the civil rights movement. The sit-ins that began at a Greensboro lunch counter in February 1960 rapidly spread across the state, and many students became involved in efforts to desegregate restaurants, theaters, and other public accommodations. The movement awakened my political consciousness and channeled my campus involvement. I was president of the Baptist Student Union at a time when campus religious groups were among the most active proponents of change, and my main achievement as a member of the student legislature was the narrow passage of a resolution urging Chapel Hill merchants to desegregate their businesses.

I knew a number of campus politicians who were reasonably certain that they would someday be governor, senator, or at the very least a member of Congress. I did not regard such expectations as realistic for myself and had other career interests I wanted to pursue. But those years were politically formative in a number of respects. I began to realize that, by conviction, I was a Democrat, despite an East Tennessee background that predisposed me in the opposite direction. I came to admire political leaders like Adlai Stevenson, John F. Kennedy, and North Carolina's young governor, Terry Sanford. Most of the new ideas and responses to social problems seemed to be coming from Democrats; the Eisenhower-era Republican Party, by contrast, seemed cautious and complacent. Like others in my student generation, I discovered that communities and political institutions could respond positively to pressures for change. The Vietnam and Watergate generations that followed had a far difference experience. A spark was lit that later led me, in addition to whatever else I was doing, to involve myself in local politics and community affairs.

During my years of graduate study and teaching in New Haven, my political activities ranged from canvassing for the Johnson-Humphrey ticket in 1964, to returning to Tennessee in 1970 to organize campus groups and get-out-the-vote operations in Sen. Albert Gore's last reelection campaign, to helping my wife win a seat on the New Haven board of aldermen.[1] On returning to North Carolina in 1973, she and I became active with the Democratic Party. Today, when someone gives me the line about how closed and conspiratorial politics is, I sometimes respond with a description of our first party precinct meeting, less than a month after arriving in Chapel Hill. My wife emerged from that meeting as precinct chairwoman and I as a member of the precinct committee—an outcome that said more about the state of local party organization than about anything we said or did.

I had already ventured into North Carolina politics from a distance the year before, working with a friend from the Gore campaign to lay the groundwork for Senator Edmund Muskie's presidential primary effort in the state. I still regard the collapse of the 1972 Muskie campaign as especially unfortunate and fateful, considering the directions in which George McGovern's nomination took the Democratic Party and Richard Nixon's subsequent election took the country. In 1976, after I had permanently returned to North Carolina, friends from the Muskie campaign recruited me to manage two congressional districts (including the one I now represent) in Jimmy Carter's bid for the presidency. In 1980 I was asked to take a year's leave from my teaching position at Duke University to serve as executive director of the North Carolina Democratic Party. This tour of duty put me in the thick of statewide politics and introduced me to state senator Russell Walker of Asheboro, who was serving as state party chairman and who has been my most valued mentor and role model in politics.

During these years, I also became a friend and political ally of North Carolina's governor, Jim Hunt, a young progressive whose main causes were education and economic development. Hunt also took an active hand in party affairs. In 1981 he was named by the Democratic national chairman to head the party's Commission on Presidential Nomination, charged with undertaking a complete review of the nomination process and devising needed changes in party rules.[2] Hunt recruited me as his staff director. The assignment struck me as both politically important and academically interesting, offering an opportunity (realized only in part) to alter the "reformed" Democratic presidential nomination process in ways that might restore some of the strength lost by the organized party and its convention. What I did not foresee was how this stint in Washington and the acquaintances I struck up with party leaders would prove useful if I decided to run for office myself.

In 1984 Hunt asked me to take another leave from teaching to return to the state Democratic Party as a full-time professional chairman. I accepted readily, for this was the event we had all been waiting for—the marathon Senate race between Hunt and incumbent Sen. Jesse Helms, the television commentator–turned–politician who was the Senate's most visible champion of right-wing causes. Many had thought, quite justifiably, of the 1970 race between Gore and William Brock as a momentous one with national implications, but it paled in comparison to the Hunt-Helms contest. The 1984 race produced expenditures of $26.4 million (Senator Helms's $16.9 million campaign was the most expensive Senate campaign in U.S. history until he broke his own record in 1990) and focused national and international attention on North Carolina. Our state party spent an unprecedented $2 million and organized a massive voter-contact and mobilization effort.

The results were bitterly disappointing. Helms, aided by Ronald Reagan's national landslide, won with 52 percent of the vote. This "sent a signal throughout the world," the senator told his supporters on election night, "that North Carolina is a God-fearing, conservative state."[3] Behind these code words, I saw a devastating setback for the hopes and aspirations that had first brought me into politics and for the progress we had begun to make in North Carolina.

Our Senate loss was intensified by the loss of the governorship and three Democratic House seats. One of these was in the Fourth District, where six-term Democratic incumbent Ike Andrews was defeated by Bill Cobey, a former athletic director at the University of North Carolina who had close ties to Helms's organization, the National Congressional Club. I was deeply stung by these defeats and in the following weeks thought a great deal about how they might be reversed. For the first time, I seriously entertained the prospect of becoming a candidate myself. By spring, I had made my decision: I was running for Congress.

The First Campaign

It was my work as state party chairman that first led others to think seriously of me—and led me to think of myself—as a potential candidate. The job's traditional elements (organizational work in the counties, fundraising, voter-contact, and turnout operations) reached a new level of intensity and put me in touch with hundreds of party activists. The position attained a new level of public visibility as I held dozens of press conferences and took the lead in challenging and refuting the opposition. It was no longer a behind-the-scenes job, and the experience and exposure it offered were ideal preparation for a congressional candidacy.

Still, I had not expected the Fourth District seat to turn over, and it took a while for me to get comfortable with the idea of actually running instead of supporting another candidate, or making politics a full-time vocation rather than a sporadic engagement. My wife, Lisa, became more and more enthused at the idea. Her political interests had always been strong. She grew up in a family of New Deal Democrats in the Washington suburbs, and her college experience with civil rights was similar to my own. When I first met her during one of my Washington summers, she was a social worker in a War on Poverty job training agency. Later she was elected to the board of aldermen in New Haven and shared my political interests in North Carolina.

To run for Congress in what was certain to be an expensive, difficult race gave us both pause, and I had seen enough political families to know that I would never run without my wife's full support. We had searching conversations with friends and family and two congressional couples whom we respected. Our teenage children were growing increasingly independent, and I had earned a sabbatical year at Duke; this would let me draw half my salary and (barely) get by financially. But the ultimate question was whether we wanted to do this, knowing how much work and sacrifice it would require but also sensing how exciting and rewarding it could be. Without too much agonizing, we decided that the answer was yes. It was a commitment my wife took very seriously, and she has been intensely active, both behind the scenes and in public, in each of my seven campaigns.

Our discussions also involved a group of friends who, once the decision to run was made, became the "Wednesday night group," an inner circle that remained central to the entire effort. We met weekly to discuss campaign strategy, parcel out key contacts and tasks, and bolster one another's morale. This group was a fertile source of campaign ideas, good and bad. (One scheme for bringing attention to my race, mercifully abandoned, would have had me staging a Lawton Chiles–style walk from Liberty in the western part of the district to Justice, a community in the east!) Our group included several young attorneys with whom I had been associated in politics, a government affairs official from Duke, and an old college friend and his wife, who was an active local realtor. The campaign manager was Randolph Cloud, a veteran of several local campaigns who had worked with me as get-out-the-vote coordinator for the state party in 1984. We later added a deputy manager, Michelle Smith, who, despite limited political experience, proved to be an exceptionally quick study. This was fortunate, for the leadership of the campaign was thrust on her when Cloud left after the primary.

My decision to run was prompted in part by the realization that 1986 represented a window of opportunity that might not open again. The odds nationally of defeating an incumbent were low; the general election success rate for incumbents seeking reelection had fallen below 92 percent only once since 1966. But North Carolina had been something of an exception to this pattern. Close contests and incumbent defeats had become fairly common since the 1960s, particularly in western districts (where both parties historically had strong bases) and in Piedmont and urban–suburban districts (where split-ticket voting was on the increase, with GOP candidates often benefiting from national trends). My district, the Fourth, had displayed considerable volatility—voting for Governor Hunt over Senator Helms by 14,282 votes in 1984, for example, but at the same time giving President Reagan a 46,552-vote margin in his victory over Walter Mondale. Congressman Andrews had lost to Bill Cobey by fewer than 3,000 votes.

The district's volatility and Cobey's narrow win suggested that he could be beaten in 1986. I felt that he had won because of factors peculiar to 1984—the presidential landslide and Andrews's personal vulnerabilities—and that Cobey's beliefs and background put him considerably to the right of modal opinion in our part of the state. The Fourth District was by no means "Helms country," despite the fact that the senator lived in Raleigh. Yet Cobey stood out, even in comparison to the other North Carolina Republican members, in his ties to the Helms organization and in his decision to firmly align himself with the most conservative group of House Republicans, the so-called Conservative Opportunity Society, once he got to Washington. He seemed an uneasy fit for the district and was likely to be especially vulnerable in 1986, his first try for reelection—before he had a chance to fully reap the advantages of incumbency and in a year when there would be no Republican presidential coattails.

In firming up my decision to run, I talked with a number of elected officials and other political leaders in the district, including several who, I thought, might consider running. Some had advantages that I lacked, such as living in Wake County (the district's largest), enjoying greater name recognition, having stronger financial ties, and so forth. I learned that a race was out of the question for most of the possible contenders. Because I saw few advantages in deferring or holding back, I decided to make an early, firm announcement of my intent to run, which I did at the time of the county Democratic conventions in April, over a year before the May 1986 primary. Although this probably helped limit the proliferation of candidates, the primary field eventually expanded to four. Wilma Woodard, a well-known state senator from Wake County, was generally considered to be the front-runner.

Most members of our Wednesday night group had worked together in the Hunt campaign and had taken from that experience the idea of blending the "old" politics and the "new." We believed strongly in the politics of personal contact; I began to steadily call on people who could be helpful and to attend every party gathering or community function I could find. Since traditional voter-contact and fund-raising functions now required high-tech backup, we moved early to establish a computer capability and to contract for direct mail services. We also assumed from the beginning (long before we had the money to pay for it) that we would have an extensive media campaign. Hard-hitting television ads had come early to North Carolina, thanks largely to Senator Helms and the National Congressional Club, and had reached saturation levels in 1984. Television had been a major factor in Cobey's unseating of Andrews, and we assumed more of the same would be necessary if we were to shake loose the new incumbent.

We decided to seek outside professional assistance in three areas: media, polling, and out-of-district fund-raising. My status as a challenger having no money and facing three primary opponents meant that the better-known Washington consultants took little interest in me. But I had my own prejudices against these operators in any case, stemming from my experience with the Hunt campaign. I had heard far too much pontification from media and polling experts based, it seemed to me, on thin survey data and a deficient "feel" for the state. I felt at the time that if I ever ran, I would want consultants who were young and lean and hungry and wanted to win as badly as I did. So we looked to smaller, independent operators who seemed personally compatible and likely to give my campaign their personal attention. Fortunately we found a team that was willing to work with us during the lean times with confidence that better-funded campaigns might follow.

As media consultant we chose Saul Shorr of Philadelphia, whose use of humor and instinct for the clever counterpunch especially appealed to me. For polling we engaged Mark Mellman and Ed Lazarus, who had gotten their start in 1982 as Yale graduate students helping elect Bruce Morrison to Congress; by 1985 they were well on their way to being established nationally. For fund-raising we chose Linda Davis, a North Carolinian who was successfully freelancing in Washington as head of her own small consulting firm. This proved to be a compatible team and a durable one as well, holding together through 1986 and several subsequent elections.

I maintained my full teaching schedule through the end of 1985 while campaigning extensively. I scheduled dozens of meetings with political and community leaders, as attested to by a couple of notebooks filled with descriptions of these personal conversations. I considered it a major breakthrough when people such as the preeminent Democratic fund-raiser in my district and a respected black city council member in Raleigh agreed to help me. I also attended countless community functions and visited the small-town business districts and suburban malls, ideally with a local supporter to introduce me. But a rude awakening came in February 1986, when we could finally afford to take our first poll. Despite a year of personal campaigning and considerable prior exposure as state party chairman, my name recognition among Democrats had reached only 11 percent. I was headed for a second-place primary finish.

What changed all that was television. The kind of campaigning one does in small towns and rural areas is not sufficient to reach many people in a growing district like mine—people who may be new to the area, whose community roots do not go deep, whose political contacts are few, and who receive most of their political information through television. Fortunately, four out of my five counties were in a single media market, but the market was the second most expensive in the state, and my campaign was struggling financially.

By April 1986, we had raised $155,000, a sum that, though respectable for a challenger running in a contested primary, is inadequate to run an extensive television campaign. I did, however, have some fund-raising advantages. I had more contacts and more credibility in Washington circles than would have been true for most challengers, and I cultivated potential donors carefully, calling on them personally and sending them a steady flow of information about the campaign—particularly coverage suggesting I might win. Yet these efforts would not fully pay off until I had proved myself in the primary. I received early endorsements and contributions from a number of labor organizations, which had reasons to oppose both the incumbent and my major primary opponent. An endorsement by Raleigh's major black political organization was critical organizationally but less so financially. Other groups, like doctors and teachers, contributed to my main primary opponent because of help she had given them in the state legislature. Mainly, the organized groups and political action committees (PACs) stayed out of the primary. Their rule of thumb is generally to support incumbents if they have been reasonably receptive to the group's concerns. After all, the percentages suggest that the incumbents will survive, and their organization will need to deal with them in the future. But even issue-oriented, Democratic-leaning PACs that had good reason to like me and oppose the incumbent were unwilling to help me until I had survived the primary and could show that I had a good chance to win in November.

I have undertaken few ventures as difficult and discouraging as raising money for the primary campaign. Our trademark became "low-dollar" fund-raisers, to which a host or group of sponsors would invite their circle of friends and associates. These events were profitable politically as well as financially, but with net receipts per event of $500 to $2,500, the dollars added up slowly. (I seldom had the heart to tell sponsors of such events that their labors would underwrite the purchase of one prime-time, thirty-second television spot.) We sent mail appeals to party activists and to lists of donors from the 1984 Senate campaign and then periodically resolicited those who had already given. I spent a lot of time personally approaching potential large contributors, with mixed success. My wife and I shed our inhibitions and contacted our Christmas card lists from years past, our professional colleagues at home and across the country, and far-flung family members. Finally we did what we had said we would never do—we took out a $45,000 second mortgage on our home.

With all of this, the campaign was able to buy $75,000 worth of television time during the three weeks before the May primary, going $80,000 in debt. We also spent $20,000 on radio spots, an underestimated medium that boosts name familiarity (especially when one can play on a name like Price). Our sixty-second "name familiarity" radio ad mentioned my name no less than fifteen times:

> [Background: Marching band music throughout]
>
> WOMAN: What's the cheering about?
> MAN: Oh . . . Price for Congress.
> WOMAN: There's a Price for Congress?
> MAN: (Laughing) No . . . not a price for Congress—David Price for Congress.
> WOMAN: Oh . . . David Price.
> MAN: Yeah, David Price. He's putting some real decency back into North Carolina politics.
> WOMAN: No mudslinging or name-calling?
> MAN: Uh-uh, not David Price. Just straight talk about the issues . . . like improving education, reducing the federal deficit.
> WOMAN: Hey, this Price is going up in my book.
> MAN: Come on! Listen to David Price's background. He's been an educator most of his life, like his parents; he was a Morehead Scholar at Carolina, earned a divinity degree and later his Ph.D. in political science.
> WOMAN: Sounds priceless.
> MAN: David Price teaches government at Duke University. He's a nationally known expert on how Congress works. Price was chairman of North Carolina's Democratic Party and Jim Hunt chose him to direct a national committee to reform the presidential nominating process. He's really experienced!
> WOMAN: Hmm? That's quite a Price.
> MAN: An honest Price.
> WOMAN: David Price . . .
> MAN: for Congress.

Needing to make a forceful impression in a fluid primary situation on limited resources, we decided to produce three low-budget television ads.

One featured quotes from my recent endorsement by the *Raleigh News and Observer*, the district's most prominent newspaper. The two ads that we ran most heavily showed me talking about one major theme: the need to straighten out North Carolina politics, stop mudslinging, and deal with the real issues again. We knew from polling and campaign experience that this was a powerful theme, drawing on people's negative memories of the 1984 Senate race and their reactions to the nasty 1986 Senate Republican primary then underway. But it wasn't until the primary results came in that we realized just how right we had been. I received 48 percent of the vote, and Senator Woodard, who polled 32 percent, elected not to call for a runoff.

Fund-raising for the general election was a continuing struggle but paid richer dividends. We spent $550,000 in the fall campaign, including $300,000 for television airtime. This permitted a more diversified ad campaign: "soft" biographical spots in September and more forceful, issue-oriented spots in October. Some of the issue ads dealt with the incumbent's record: I had to take him on directly to give voters sufficient grounds for distinguishing between the two of us, but in a way consistent with my own injunctions about getting North Carolina politics on a more positive, issue-based footing. The ads therefore focused on three areas—Social Security, African famine relief, and farm credit—that illustrated the incumbent's isolation from mainstream members of both parties in terms of his roll call voting and featured me looking into the camera and saying that I would have voted differently.

We were able to afford more polling after the primary. The most important message the polls conveyed concerned the incumbent's vulnerability: Although he enjoyed considerable personal popularity, there was a sizable gap between the number of voters who recognized his name and those who gave him a high job performance rating or were firmly committed to vote for him. The early "horse race" numbers were inconclusive, primarily measuring the gap in name familiarity, but they documented a narrowing of that gap over the months of the campaign; the incumbent's lead dropped from 21 percentage points in July to 10 points on October 4 and 1 point on October 26. But the only poll that actually showed me ahead was the election itself, when I received 56 percent of the vote—the highest percentage by which any challenger in the nation defeated an incumbent in 1986.

Television was the major factor in this result, but other campaign efforts played a part as well: organizing and personal campaigning in small towns and rural areas, voter-contact and turnout operations undertaken in conjunction with party and other organizations, and canvassing and literature drops that utilized hundreds of volunteers and helped raise the campaign's visibility. Cobey was damaged when the press headlined a "Dear Christian

Friend" letter he had sent to individuals on a mailing list compiled by the religious right, encouraging the faithful to support him lest he be replaced by "someone who is not willing to take a strong stand for the principles outlined in the Word of God." Although our polling did not detect any measurable impact from this letter, my surmise is that it helped by generally raising the visibility of the race and framing a key issue for some groups (e.g., white-collar suburbanites) that I needed to reach. Finally, we were helped by the year's electoral trends—the absence of presidential coattails and a return to the fold by enough Democrats to produce senatorial victories across the South, including former governor Terry Sanford's win in North Carolina.

I will never forget the exhilaration of election night 1986, and neither will my family and the friends who had lived and breathed the campaign for almost two years (see Figure 2.1). My father, who had been featured in one of Saul Shorr's best spots, came from Tennessee to help work the polls and was shocked to be greeted on election night as a television celebrity. We had talked a great deal during the campaign about "recapturing our politics" and "turning North Carolina around," and on that night, it seemed to have happened, dispelling the dark clouds of 1984. We also felt we had succeeded in our announced strategy of combining the old and new politics, integrating traditional organizing techniques and lots of personal campaigning into an effort that was well financed, professionally managed, and media smart. We felt confident about the future, but if we thought it would be ours without a fight, we had the election night comments of the state Republican chairman to ponder: The Fourth District, he opined, had just elected another one-term congressman!

Getting Reelected

I knew that the Republicans were likely to target my seat in 1988—my first reelection try, when the presidential and gubernatorial races on the ballot might be expected to give them an advantage. It became clear by mid-1987 that the most likely challenger was Tom Fetzer, a thirty-three-year-old protégé of Senators John East and Jesse Helms who had spent virtually his entire working life as a political operative, including several positions with the National Congressional Club. The more moderate wing of the GOP had apparently agreed not to challenge his nomination. I had mixed feelings about this. My district was relatively unsympathetic to Senator Helms, and a Congressional Club affiliation could be used effectively against an opponent. At the same time, I knew what having an opponent from that quarter was likely to mean in terms of the money he could raise and the negative tone of the campaign. As it turned out, I was not proven wrong on either count.

FIGURE 2.1 Election night, 1986. To my right is my nephew, Bob Shepherd, and concealed behind me are my sister, Mary Anne Combs, and her other son, Steven Shepherd. To my left are my wife, Lisa; my brother-in-law, Sam Combs; our son, Michael; our daughter, Karen; my father, Albert Price; Nell Benson, wife of our finance chairman; and campaign manager Michelle Smith.

In the early months of 1987, we retired the $80,000 debt from the previous year and began planning the 1988 effort. Fund-raising was easier for me as an incumbent but was still a struggle, both because of the amounts required (my 1988 campaign eventually cost over $900,000) and my district's history of modest giving and the weakness of my ties to potentially large donors. Knowing that the campaign would be long and demanding and not wanting to divert my congressional staff, I recruited as campaign manager an outside professional, Mike Davis, whom I had come to know well when he was deputy manager of Hunt's 1984 campaign. I escaped

primary opposition and kept most of my personal appearances in a congressional mode, officially kicking off the campaign only after Labor Day
1988. By then, we had held dozens of organizational meetings and fund-
raisers, both in the district and in Washington, and campaign headquarters had been open for four months, eventually accommodating a paid
staff of seven and numerous volunteers.

Blessed for the first time with an adequate campaign budget, we produced a series of television spots touting my work on consumer protection,
education, home ownership, agriculture, and cutting bureaucratic red tape
for constituents. We ran the ads heavily throughout September and October, while carefully planning ways to counter the opposition attack that
was sure to come. Fetzer ran generic anti-Congress material in September,
but we got some clues as to what would follow when the firm conducting
his early September poll called one of our campaign workers, thus providing us a list of the various negative messages that were being tested.

On September 30, we learned what the thrust of Fetzer's message
would be: taxes. The ad he first aired that day went as follows:

ANNOUNCER: Liberal politicians. False promises.
[Audio clips from Price appearances in 1986, identified by script on
    screen]
QUESTIONER: Mr. Price, under what circumstances would you sup-
    port a federal tax increase?
DAVID PRICE: [1.] I would not support a federal tax increase, and
    I've said repeatedly that I would not . . .
[2.] I do oppose a tax increase . . .
[3.] We're not going to reduce that deficit by tax increases . . .
ANNOUNCER: False promises. In his first year David Price voted to
    increase taxes four different times.
[Visual: newspaper headline, "Democrats Seek Billions in New Taxes"]
David Price: False Promises. Liberal Votes.

Viewers attentive to past North Carolina campaigns could note certain
Congressional Club trademarks in the ad, such as the pseudo-documentary
use of snippets, generally out of context, purporting to show not only that
the opponent differed on the issue but that he was dissembling and opportunistic.

Our counterpunch was already taped, and we had it on the air in a day:

ANNOUNCER: In recent days, we've seen TV ads that distort the
    record of our congressman, David Price. We know the ads are paid
    for by the Tom Fetzer Campaign . . .

But who is Tom Fetzer?

[Script on screen, synchronized with audio]

Tom Fetzer has spent most of his adult life working for Jesse Helms's
 Congressional Club or its candidates.

In fact, Fetzer actually headed the Club's operations.

We've seen Congressional Club tactics before . . .

The distortions . . .

The negative campaigning . . .

The mudslinging.

[Audible stamp of universal "NO" symbol (circle and slash) on these
 words]

Will we allow ourselves to be "Clubbed" again?

Subsequently, although my negative ratings went from 9 percent to 15
percent between our early September and early October polls, Fetzer's
negatives increased far more, from 12 percent to 31 percent. This pointed
up one of Fetzer's strategic mistakes—his failure to give the voters positive information about himself. By running mainly negative material, first
against Congress and then against the incumbent congressman, he failed
to identify himself positively and thus left himself vulnerable to my definition. Moreover, his ads served to validate his identification with the
Congressional Club and its notorious campaign tactics. Our ads "framed"
his ads, so that when viewers saw the latter, they got not only a negative
message about me but also a negative impression of him, his associations,
and his tactics.

Fetzer aired several variations of his message on taxes in the early
weeks of October, a message reinforced by the "no new taxes" pledge featured in George H.W. Bush's presidential campaign. As far as I could tell,
the allegation that I had voted to "increase taxes four different times" was
based on a strained interpretation of a series of budget resolution and
"reconciliation" votes (see Chapter 7). By mid-October, Fetzer was relying
heavily on ten-second zingers that reduced the message to even simpler
terms:

ANNOUNCER: [Script on screen synchronized with audio]

How liberal is David Price?

He voted to increase taxes an average of $700 per family.

Too liberal—that's David Price.

Naturally I found all this highly frustrating, and my first impulse was
to run an ad that set the record straight. We therefore cut a spot that featured me looking into the camera and saying:

I'm David Price. My opponent, Tom Fetzer, is distorting my record.

But the facts are clear. I have never voted to raise your tax rates.

Tom Fetzer is actually criticizing me for supporting a bipartisan deficit reduction agreement that closed tax loopholes and cut spending by more than 36 billion dollars.

President Reagan asked me to vote for it.

Tom Fetzer is assuming voters won't know the difference between increasing taxes and tightening loopholes.

Let's stop the distortion and stick to the facts.

As it turned out, we never ran this ad. Despite my impulse and the urgings of supporters to answer my opponent's charges, I became convinced that it would play into his hands. We would then be debating his issue. He might excerpt a clip from my ad and do a response to the response, appearing to refute it. Viewers might then perceive a bewildering array of charges and countercharges that seemed somehow to implicate me. And in the meantime, my own positive message would have been lost.

Consequently we settled on a second "framing" ad, one that rolled a long list of issues down the screen. It reminded viewers that Fetzer had run an almost totally negative campaign, distorting my record but not telling them where he stood on much of anything. This kept the focus on his campaign tactics while reinforcing the Congressional Club association, without moving the campaign to his chosen turf—taxes. Meanwhile, all through October, we continued to mix in my positive ads on education, housing, and so forth. The strategy worked very well; our late October polls showed my favorability ratings again picking up, and I finished with a 58 percent win.

It was reassuring to me and my campaign staff to be able to neutralize the well-financed attack ads that we had known were coming. Our confidence had been shaken by the failure of the Hunt campaign to mount an effective defense in 1984 and by Michael Dukakis's stunning helplessness against George Bush's prison furlough/pledge of allegiance campaign in 1988. But we prepared carefully and developed a strategy that, at least in 1988, proved quite effective: (1) Lay out a compelling positive message, focusing on issues or character traits that voters care about, and never let yourself get more than temporarily diverted from that message. (2) Make campaigning itself an issue, tapping into the negative feelings that most people have about distortions and personal attacks (regardless of the fact that those same people may also be influenced by such ads). (3) Frame the opposition's ads, so that when viewers see them they are drawing as many conclusions about your opponent as about you. (4) Do not let damaging attacks go unanswered, but beware of answering point for point in a way that puts you on your opponent's turf. (5) Do all this in a straightforward and truthful manner, so that you are not and do not appear to be descending to your opponent's level.

Our 1988 experience was not an entirely reliable guide to the campaigns that followed. What changed was not the negative attacks—I have yet to draw an opponent who ran more than a few scattered positive ads—but the political context. As public cynicism about politics and politicians deepened, it became more difficult to move public opinion with positive messages or neutralize an opponent's negative characterizations. My 1990 campaign thus posed challenges that went beyond the lessons of 1988 and raised warnings of more serious problems to come.

The Third Campaign

Some expected 1990 to be an easier year. After all, they reasoned, the presidential race would not be on the ballot, another two years in office would have enhanced my standing in the district, and my solid 1988 win would discourage potential challengers. These factors did help; I went into the 1990 race, for example, with favorability ratings and vote-to-reelect numbers 10 points above what they had been in 1988. But one potential challenger would not be deterred: John Carrington, a wealthy, self-made businessman who, failing a second try for statewide office in 1988, announced that he might bid for Congress next.

Carrington's electoral career provides an extreme example of what can result when moneyed candidates are coupled with weak parties. He moved from New Jersey to North Carolina in 1976 but never even registered to vote until he decided to run for lieutenant governor eight years later. In both that race and his 1988 run for secretary of state, he dominated a weak Republican primary field and captured the nomination solely on the basis of a television campaign financed out of his own pocket. Carrington came remarkably close to winning in the general election (46 percent in 1984; 48 percent in 1988), aided by strong Republican showings at the top of the ticket. He was actively embraced by the Republican Party organization for the first time in 1990. They had no one else to run against me, and in Carrington they saw a candidate who would pay his own way. By concentrating his considerable resources in one media market, he might win or at least do considerable damage to me. In contrast to Fetzer's 1988 challenge, the Congressional Club played little part in this campaign. Senator Helms had his own race to contend with, and although Carrington's positions and tactics were often indistinguishable from the Club's, he was not close to the organization.

Although we had known throughout my first term what we were likely to face in 1988, we were unsure of Carrington's intentions until he actually filed in early 1990. Even then, it was hard to know what we were up against. Normally an opponent's Federal Election Commission (FEC) reports indicate the candidate's breadth of support and the scale of the campaign he or she is likely to mount. In Carrington's case, the FEC reports were useless. They revealed very little support, but his campaign potential was nonetheless immense, limited only by his willingness to spend. As it turned out, the $500,000 he had given to each of his previous campaigns was not a very reliable guide to what he was willing to do in 1990; he would contribute over $800,000 toward total campaign expenditures of $891,000.

We hoped to run a less elaborate and less expensive campaign than we had in 1988. We opened headquarters later and cut back the size of the paid staff. We also made greater use of resources at hand. My administrative assistant (chief of staff), Gene Conti, took a leave of absence to manage the campaign, and my press secretary and two other staff members also took leaves at appropriate times to gear up the campaign operation. But Carrington's willingness to spend and the harshness of his television attacks helped ensure that it would not be a low-key political year. The overall political climate was negative, with Congress and the president mired in a highly visible budget battle until late October and Congress bashing reaching a fever pitch. We therefore invested as much in polling as we had in the previous two campaigns combined. It was a good investment, for it let us spot trouble early and step up our campaign efforts accordingly. In the end, we spent a total of $698,000 and bought as much television time as we had in 1988. So much for the scaled-back campaign!

Early in the summer, Carrington began to run ads on radio and cable television attacking Congress as an institution, adding over-the-air television after Labor Day. But he repeated Fetzer's mistake of failing to use any material introducing or defining himself. His early ads consequently did little to boost his favorability numbers or dispel the relatively high unfavorability ratings he brought from his previous campaigns. Nor did his early ads do any discernible damage to me. This changed in late September, when he switched from generic anticongressional ads to spots attacking me personally. But even then, he was in a poor position to pick up the slack; although he could make some people think less of me, he gave them no reason to vote for him.

The damage inflicted by his ads nonetheless concerned us a great deal. Carrington threw various accusations at me, but his most persistent theme was that I was in the pocket of the savings and loan (S&L) industry and was to blame for a debacle that was going to cost every American taxpayer thousands of dollars. My 1987 vote in the Banking Committee for one short-term recapitalization plan for the S&L insurance fund rather than another (a question on which the two main S&L industry associations were divided) was portrayed by Carrington as a capitulation to the industry that brought about the entire disaster. My overnight trip to address the southeastern S&L trade association on a consumer protection bill that I was pushing through the Banking Committee was presented as a reward for my vote—a "paid vacation on Captiva Island." One ad even featured an unflattering picture of me with dollar signs superimposed over my eyes.

There was so much error and distortion that it was hard to know where to begin a counterattack. Drawing on our 1988 experience, our first response ad attempted to frame Carrington's message, reminding viewers of the kind of tactics he had used in his past failed campaigns:

ANNOUNCER: John Carrington has a track record.
[Copy on screen tracks audio, with newspaper editorials in background]
When John Carrington ran for secretary of state, and lost, an editorial said, "John Carrington's campaign has spent a fortune on mean-spirited commercials."
When John Carrington ran for lieutenant governor, and lost, an editorial said, "John Carrington's campaign has consisted largely of negative commercials that unfairly distort the record of his opponent."
Now against David Price, John Carrington is at it again with the same negative campaign tactics.
[On screen: "The Carrington record speaks for itself."]
You'd have thought that John Carrington would have learned by now.

But 1990 was not 1988. The political climate was far more hostile to incumbents, and negative attacks were harder to discredit. Carrington's unfavorability numbers, already relatively high, continued to rise in early October, but my vote-to-reelect and job performance numbers were eroding more rapidly. Clearly we needed to fight back with something more potent. In particular, we needed to deal with the S&L accusations, and my impulse to rush out and set the record straight was even stronger than in 1988. However, we still understood the pitfalls of a point-for-point response and instead decided on an ad that drew on a local newspaper editorial and showed that I had answers to the charges. More importantly, it let me tell of the initiatives I had taken to address the S&L problem:

ANNOUNCER: [Copy of editorial on screen] John Carrington is distorting David Price's record on savings and loans. A recent editorial called Carrington's charges "ill-founded."

DAVID PRICE [Into camera]: Let's get to the facts. I wrote the law
that prevents corrupt savings and loan executives from writing
themselves big bonus checks and I sponsored legislation to require
the attorney general to go after the savings and loan crooks.
ANNOUNCER: A clean campaign. A congressman fighting for you.
Reelect David Price.[4]

The more direct, forceful ad helped stop the slippage our October 17
poll had revealed. Within a week, the horse race numbers had leveled off
at around 43 percent for me and 25 percent for Carrington. But my favorability and job performance ratings continued to slip. Though we knew
this was as much the function of the negative media coverage Congress
was then getting as of Carrington's ads, we also recognized the continuing need to frame his message. He gave us an unexpected assist as we
were preparing copy for our late October ads, acknowledging to a reporter that his attack ads were "a garbage way of running a campaign."[5]
We were on the air within three days, first with an ad documenting via
newspaper copy what Carrington had said about his own campaign and
then with an ad that featured me looking at one of his ads on a television
monitor and turning to comment on it:

[Clip from Carrington ad on TV monitor]: "David Price voted to let
them keep gambling with your money."
ANNOUNCER: Here's what John Carrington says about the TV ads
he's running: "This is a garbage way of running a campaign, but
it's the only way." [Quote superimposed on screen, with monitor
still showing]
DAVID PRICE [pointing to monitor, then looking into camera]: Mr.
Carrington calls his own ads garbage, but he's wrong to think this
is the only way to run a campaign. For four years now we've
shown that a positive, clean campaign can address real issues.
Please join me in saying no to John Carrington's distortions.

Our successive efforts to neutralize Carrington's attacks represented a
continuation of our 1988 strategy but with modifications necessitated by
the huge quantity of his ads, the sharply personal nature of his attacks,
and the stormy political climate that threatened damage to all incumbents. The same was true of the positive ads we used to open our television campaign in early September and ran throughout the two-month
campaign. We again stressed my work on middle-class issues like education and housing but dropped the pictures of me bustling around Washington. Although I have steadfastly refused to run for Congress by

running against Congress (see Chapter 12), 1990 was not a good year to stress one's credentials as an "insider," no matter how essential those skills might be in producing the results that voters care about. Consequently we hearkened back to my first campaign when, as a challenger, I set out to "turn North Carolina politics around," even using a clip from an early 1986 spot in my first ad for 1990. In discussing education, we reminded viewers that I was not a career politician. I had taught for seventeen years before coming to Congress, we stressed, which had given me a fresh perspective on the issues.

The 1990 campaign was far more frustrating than previous ones. I felt besieged, both personally and as an incumbent; Congress was taking a beating in the media; and the ads being run against me went far beyond anything I had experienced before. I felt helpless as I watched from afar, stuck in Washington as the budget battles dragged on. But my wife, my campaign manager, and others filled in for me very well. Our volunteers put in long hours on the phones, in the neighborhoods and headquarters; our contributors came through with the funds for stepped-up media buys; and our polling and media consultants monitored the situation daily and kept us on the offensive.

Our October 27 poll confirmed that the turnaround we had detected on October 22 was genuine; my vote-to-reelect numbers were on the way back up, and Carrington's unfavorable numbers had actually overtaken his favorables. I finished with a 58 percent win, closely replicating our 1988 result. Our team felt hugely relieved and vindicated on election night, although the occasion was marred when Harvey Gantt's spirited challenge failed to unseat Senator Helms.

For the moment, we had defied a national trend that saw the average victory margin of incumbents decline by almost 5 points. For fifty-three members, their 1990 reelection margin was their lowest ever, and for another fifty-seven it was their lowest since their first election.[6] Nationally, six Democratic members and nine Republican members were defeated by challengers; those numbers would have been higher had the parties anticipated the strength of anti-incumbent sentiment in time to recruit strong teams of challengers and finance them well. But the trend was unmistakable, fueled by increasingly negative public perceptions of Congress and frustrations at the governmental gridlock and partisan wrangling exemplified by the protracted 1990 budget battle (see Chapter 7). Because control of government was divided between the parties and the blame for failure diffused, these sentiments were limited in their electoral impact. It would not be until 1994, when they found a clear partisan target, that their devastating potential, both for me and for the Democratic Party in the House, would become fully evident.

Notes

1. My experiences in Tennessee led to an effort to measure the electoral effect of voter-contact activities and a conviction that such activities should be an integral part of state and county party operations. See David E. Price, "Volunteers for Gore: The Evolution of a Campaign," *Soundings,* Spring 1971, pp. 57–72; and David E. Price and Michael Lupfer, "Volunteers for Gore: The Impact of a Precinct-level Canvass in Three Tennessee Cities," *Journal of Politics,* May 1973, pp. 410–438.

2. *Report of the Commission on Presidential Nomination* (Washington, D.C.: Democratic National Committee, 1982), p. 1. For an account of the commission's efforts and rationale, see David E. Price, *Bringing Back the Parties* (Washington, D.C.: Congressional Quarterly Press, 1984), chaps. 6–7.

3. Quoted in William D. Snider, *Helms and Hunt: The North Carolina Senate Race, 1984* (Chapel Hill: University of North Carolina Press, 1985), p. 203.

4. My first reference was to my amendment, initially added to the Financial Crimes Prosecution and Recovery Act of 1990 in the Banking Committee and eventually included in the Crime Control Act of 1990, to authorize regulators to disallow extravagant severance payments (golden parachutes) to the executives of failing financial institutions. The second reference was to the Savings Association Law Enforcement Improvement Act of 1990, an effort to step up prosecution of S&L fraud.

5. Van Denton, "Carrington Bombards Airwaves Hoping to Oust Price," *Raleigh News and Observer,* October 23, 1990, p. 1A.

6. *Congressional Quarterly Almanac* 46 (1990): 903.

3

Defeat and Return

The 1992 election proved to be the lull before the storm in the Fourth District and across most of North Carolina. Nationally the anti-institutional sentiment and anti-incumbent voting evident in 1990 intensified. This was effectively promoted by Newt Gingrich, whose election as House Republican whip in 1989 had heralded a newly confrontational style of minority leadership. Gingrich had relentlessly pressed the case against Speaker Jim Wright, forcing his resignation amid ethics charges. Although the so-called House Bank scandal, which identified a few members abusing the banking services of the House payroll office while many more got burned by its lax accounting practices, involved members of both parties, Gingrich and the self-styled Gang of Seven conservative Republicans used it in the period leading up to the 1992 election to indict "corrupt" Democratic leadership.

To these anti-institutional stirrings were added the effects of the post-1990 congressional redistricting and the discontent stirred up by a weak economy. The result was the departure of the largest number of House incumbents since 1948. Fifty-two members, many of them anticipating electoral trouble, retired; nineteen were defeated in primaries, and sixteen Democratic and eight Republican incumbents were defeated in the general election.[1] The partisan impact was blunted. Divided government still presented multiple targets for voter ire, and Bill Clinton's strength in the presidential race helped hold the net Democratic loss of House seats to ten. This hardly provided a mandate to Democrats as they assumed control of both the presidency and Congress for the first time in twelve years, but it fell short of the Democratic losses many had anticipated.

Very little of this turbulence was apparent in the Fourth District. The main impact of redistricting in North Carolina was the election of two African American members, the first since the turn of the century. Several traditionally Democratic districts were weakened by the removal of loyal partisan voters, but the effects would not be evident until 1994. The Fourth District was made marginally more Democratic when it was pared from five counties to three, although the loss of traditionally Republican Randolph County to the west was soon to be offset by Republican gains in the fast-growing Raleigh suburbs (see Figure 1.1a, p. 2).

Not knowing what sort of opposition to expect, we raised $185,000 in 1991 to discourage Republicans from targeting the district and prepared to run a campaign similar to the 1990 effort. I retained the same team of consultants and arranged for administrative assistant Gene Conti again to take a leave to manage the campaign. As it turned out, the Republicans mounted only a token effort.[2] Lavinia "Vicky" Goudie, a Republican activist who had been appointed executive secretary of the State Board of Cosmetic Art Examiners, filed for the seat when other prospective candidates did not and ran a minimal campaign on a $12,000 budget.

I naturally scaled back my campaign efforts, but I was aware of some lingering negative associations in voters' minds from the 1990 campaign and an escalating anti-incumbency sentiment nationwide. I was determined to take nothing for granted. We maintained a full schedule of campaign appearances and ran two weeks of television ads, featuring my legislative efforts on education and technical training. In the end, I secured 65 percent of the vote, with Goudie's 34 percent representing the Republican hard core and little more.

Election night was again marred by a Senate loss, as Terry Sanford fell before the sharp attacks of Lauch Faircloth. (Ominously, Faircloth carried Wake County, which made up 83 percent of my district.) But North Carolina's House delegation reached a high-water mark of eight Democrats and four Republicans. This set the stage for what I experienced as one of my most enjoyable and productive (if also most contentious) terms in office. But it was not to last; in fact, the 8 to 4 ratio was precisely reversed as North Carolina's House delegation, largely insulated from the turbulence of 1992, felt the full force of the gathering storm in 1994.

The Revolution Hits Home

One of the earliest and surest signs that the 1994 campaign season was going to be different was the growing anger and disruption at my community meetings. The mix of issues ranged from gays in the military to abortion to taxes and spending. But the anti-Clinton, anti-Democratic, and antigovernment rhetoric, as well as the attacks to which I was subjected, reached an intensity that I had never experienced and was not certain how to handle. Some of this was organized by local religious right and antitax groups, and many were clearly utilizing information picked up from talk radio, which was attracting a larger and larger audience nationally and locally. My staff (and my wife) began to question whether we should continue to hold open meetings. But I disliked the idea of letting our adversaries shut us down. Although I was concerned that these raucous sessions were leaving me looking beleaguered, I was also drawing considerable praise from many of those attending the meetings and from the press for continuing to hold open discussions and not responding in kind. We began asking local law enforcement to cover the meetings, modified the format (not very successfully) to gain more control over the agenda, and forged ahead with a full schedule. We thus had a constant reminder of the hostility toward the Democratic Congress that was rising across the country and ample evidence that incumbents like me were unlikely to escape the anti-institutional ire.

It soon became clear that the Republicans were going to contest the Fourth District seat more strongly than they had in 1992. Growing Republican organizational strength was evident in 1993, as my opponent from 1988, Tom Fetzer, was elected mayor of Raleigh in a well-funded campaign. At about the same time, a group of Republican leaders announced that they had recruited a young businessman, Rob Romaine, to run against me. But they soon learned that Raleigh's retiring police chief, Fred Heineman, also had his sights on the GOP nomination. Heineman was a native of New York City who had put in twenty-three years on the NYPD before Raleigh recruited him as its chief in 1979. He ran into some turbulence in his later years as chief, particularly in relations with the black community, and plotted a retirement strategy that included switching his party registration to Republican in 1993 and entering the race for Congress. Although he undertook this largely on his own, he had some advantages over Romaine: name familiarity from his years as chief and identification with the fight against crime, which was rapidly shaping up as a dominant national issue. Some Republican leaders who resented the Romaine kingmakers decided to give Heineman their backing. Heineman eked out a 243-vote victory on May 3 in a low-turnout primary that gave little indication of the Republican mobilization to come.

My benchmark poll, taken in late June, contained clear warning signs. President Clinton, who won 47 percent of the district's presidential vote in 1992 (compared to George Bush's 39 percent and Ross Perot's 14), had slipped in popularity; he now polled below Senator Helms, for whom the Fourth had always been a problem. The percentage of voters rating me favorably had drifted to 47, while my "unfavorables" had jumped to 27 percent and my job rating was relatively weak. These numbers clearly reflected the more general negative assessments voters were giving Congress and incumbent officeholders, but that offered little reassurance. In fact, it pointed up the obstacles my campaign and I were likely to face in trying to turn them around single-handedly.

The "horse race" numbers were 46 percent for Price, 32 percent for Heineman, and 22 percent undecided, reflecting slippage in the number of voters committed to my reelection as well as the fact that Heineman started with higher name recognition than any of my previous opponents had. When respondents were given personal profiles and sample campaign pitches from the two of us, the gap narrowed further. And when they were asked what issues concerned them most, government waste and crime trumped education, home ownership, and transportation, the issues with which I was most strongly identified.

In the meantime, the 103rd Congress had grown more and more contentious. Republicans unanimously opposed and relentlessly criticized Clinton's 1993 deficit reduction plan, exaggerating its tax increases and belittling its spending decreases (see Chapter 7). Throughout 1994, leaders of the GOP and the religious right collaborated in bringing to the fore issues such as abortion and gay rights in order to activate their electoral base (see Chapter 11). The politics of health care dominated the 1994 congressional session, as Democrats struggled to modify and move along Clinton's complicated, comprehensive national plan and Republican opposition became more vociferous. My mid–1994 poll revealed that my constituents viewed my performance on taxes, the budget, and health care negatively and still regarded the budget deficit and wasteful spending as unaddressed issues. They also registered strongly negative reactions to "President Clinton's health care plan," although the numbers were reversed when they were asked about the plan's actual contents (requiring employers to provide insurance and increasing cigarette taxes).

Nationally Republicans were finding "that it was virtually impossible to overreach in attacking Washington or the federal government."[3] They portrayed Clinton's anticrime legislation as weak and pork laden and won a major victory on August 11, 1994—with the help of an improbable left–right coalition of Democrats, some opposed to the bill's expansion of the death penalty and others to its ban on assault weapons—defeating the rule governing debate on the House-Senate conference report. I regarded this as the single most politically damaging vote of the legislative session.[4] It was reversed ten days later after mostly marginal changes in the bill. But by then the Republicans, with the help of their allies in talk radio, the National Rifle Association, and other groups, had driven home their negative views of the crime bill and of Democratic management of the Congress with large numbers of voters. The episode killed what little prospect remained for action on health care reform, which in turn emboldened the Republicans to kill (most often by use of the filibuster in the Senate) campaign finance reform, lobbying reform, hazardous waste cleanup, and almost everything else that would have let the president and congressional Democrats claim success.

It was at first unclear how much Heineman would be able to capitalize on the national turmoil. His fund-raising got off to a slow start, and national and state GOP leaders regarded the Fourth District as a second-tier race, surpassed by four other North Carolina seats as a pickup prospect. But toward the end of the campaign, as it became clear that a national victory might be in the offing, the national party pumped more than $60,000 into Heineman's campaign. Overall, he raised $265,000, a modest amount for a challenger but enough to be on television for most of October and, under the circumstances of 1994, to solidify his name recognition as a crime fighter and catch the wave of anti-Washington, anti-Democratic sentiment.

I knew that my campaign would need to go well beyond my 1992 effort. Gene Conti, my former administrative assistant who had managed my 1990 and 1992 campaigns, had taken a position in the Clinton administration. I therefore went back to the 1988 model of recruiting a campaign manager from outside and brought Tim Tompkins, who had worked in Terry Sanford's Senate campaign, on board in August. By then, our fund-raising, which eventually produced $676,000, was well underway. I kicked off my campaign officially with the usual cross-district tour on September 7, and we planned four weeks of television ads. After the Democratic leadership gave up on getting anything more from the 103rd Congress and adjourned on October 8, I had almost five weeks to campaign full-time in the district.

We faced a difficult dilemma in formulating my television message and had ample reason to second-guess ourselves in the course of the campaign. The profile and the positions I had featured in past campaigns were devalued in the context of 1994, as were the district-related benefits I had managed to secure on the Appropriations Committee. Our challenge was to frame my message so that it was relevant to the values and concerns on voters' minds while maintaining continuity with my past appeals and denying Heineman the ability to define the agenda. My biographical ad, for example, featured photos of my parents and captions pointing out that I was "the son of two small-town schoolteachers" and had earned a divinity degree. "My parents taught me to do my best and to do my part," I said in a script that I wrote personally, to show the moral context in which I placed public service:

> Lisa and I have stressed hard work and personal responsibility with our own children Our country still depends on strong faith and strong families. And

while government can open up opportunities, we won't solve our problems until people take responsibility for their own actions and each one of us pitches in and does our part.

I also ran an education ad focusing on school safety and funding I had obtained for a North Carolina program to discipline young offenders. Another ad touted legislation I had cosponsored to strengthen child-support enforcement: "Our government can't pay for everything. We've got to restore personal responsibility. It's the key to making our country stronger."

The greatest challenge was the crime issue, which was clearly on voters' minds. My credentials as an active proponent of the 1994 crime bill were genuine, and on specific provisions where Heineman and I differed (e.g., community policing and the assault weapons ban) he had shifted away from his earlier support and the public seemed to agree with me. We therefore produced an ad that put me on camera pointing out these differences and noting that Heineman's "own police force has failed to endorse his candidacy." The ad's captions referenced the endorsements I had received from the local and national Fraternal Order of Police. Heineman responded with an ad featuring a retired police officer attesting to his character and protesting that police departments did not endorse candidates. Although I had not said that they did, I regretted giving him the opening. And we had ample reason to reflect on whether we should have raised the crime issue in the first place; it was clearly Heineman's turf. His identification as police chief and the negative publicity surrounding the Clinton crime bill put him in a strong position to ridicule the bill and my support for it (another of his ads featured much-maligned "midnight basketball" recreation programs for at-risk youth) and to slough off criticisms of his specific positions.

Heineman, like my previous opponents, failed to run biographical or other positive ads. But the omission hurt him less because he was reasonably well-known and the political climate was not conducive to positive messages. His ads attacked me on issues ranging from the death penalty to health care to the line-item veto. The ads frequently linked me to Clinton and always contained a tag line tying me to the unpopular institution of Congress. For example, one zinger managed, in ten seconds, to distort both my position on Clinton's health care plan and the plan's effects:

Congressman Price supported Clinton's health care plan to increase spending and taxes.

[On screen: revolving pictures of Clinton and Price, then captions: $700 BILLION SPENDING; 27% TAX INCREASES]

> To change Congress, you've got to change your congressman. Vote Heineman for change.
>
> [On screen: picture of Heineman with captions: FOR CHANGE. HEINEMAN FOR CONGRESS]

We became sufficiently concerned about Heineman's last-minute ads and mailings to add a refutation of his charges on Social Security and the balanced budget amendment to our mix of ads in the campaign's last week.

Heineman said little about the much-touted GOP Contract with America, which he had signed in September. He was nonetheless in a position to benefit from Republicans' successful "nationalizing" of the election as a protest against Democratic liberalism and all things governmental. The advent of unified Democratic control of Congress and the White House had provided a clear partisan target for the voter anger that had been building since 1990.[5] I began hearing alarming reports from Democratic colleagues across the country and from my media consultant, Saul Shorr, and others working with imperiled candidates. A tidal wave was coming. The only question was how large and encompassing it would be and what, if anything, campaigns like mine could do about it.[6] Heineman's television message was less pervasive, with fewer dollars behind it, than Carrington's had been in 1990, but we had similar worries about a political climate that made it difficult to get my message through and neutralize my opponent's attacks. We took hope when our late October polls seemed to show my vote solidifying and Heineman's attacks not moving my "favorables" down very much. But election day told another story. The tidal wave swept across North Carolina with special severity, and in the Fourth District I fell short by 1,215 votes.

Turnout was exceptionally low, even for a nonpresidential year. Heineman, in winning, received 11,500 fewer votes than had Vicky Goudie in her 34 percent showing in 1992. Heineman and I together received 17,000 fewer votes than I had received in 1992. The main effect of the antigovernment fever and the negative tone of the campaign was not the mobilization of hitherto inactive voters but rather voter apathy and withdrawal. Heavily Democratic areas were particularly affected. The 1990 redistricting, which contributed significantly to North Carolina's other three Democratic House turnovers, had an indirect effect on my race: Raleigh's African American representative in the state House had been placed in a safe, single-member district. Republicans had the good sense to refrain from filing an opponent against either him or Wake County's popular black sheriff, thus making it more difficult to mobilize voters in those precincts. The absence in North Carolina of a Senate or other major competitive statewide race was also important; nationwide comparisons suggested that this not only depressed turnout but also helped make House Democrats the victims of voter ire that otherwise might have been directed at more prominent targets.[7]

I greeted voters until the polls closed and approached election-night headquarters with an ominous feeling. Turnout was especially low in central Raleigh and Chapel Hill precincts, and poll workers reported seeing busloads of voters brought in from conservative churches. It became apparent as the first returns came in that I was in trouble, running well behind in suburban precincts where I had once lost narrowly or broken even. Orange and Chatham County numbers trickled in later, but they were not enough to make up the difference.

I had already begun to formulate what I would say if I lost. As the results became clear, my family and I went to the hotel ballroom, which offered a funereal contrast to the joyous election nights of years past. "We have fought the good fight," I said to assembled friends and campaign workers. "We can be proud of what we have stood for, and nothing that has happened tonight should lead us to cynicism or despair." I tried hard that night and in the ensuing weeks to follow my own advice.

The nationwide results were stunning, with thirty-four House Democratic incumbents defeated and an additional net shift of eighteen open seats to the Republicans. North Carolina was hit especially hard, with party control of one-third of our twelve U.S. House seats turning over and Republicans gaining control of the state House of Representatives with a 60 percent gain, from forty-two seats to sixty-seven. My wife and I became accustomed to being called or stopped on the street by people expressing their shock and chagrin, some admitting they had not voted and a few even telling me that they had voted Republican as a protest but would not have done so had they known I was in trouble! I also received hundreds of supportive letters. Despite the feeling they sometimes prompted that I was reading my own obituary, I will forever treasure them. They helped me determine to stay in the fight.

My staff and I had to pull ourselves together quickly. We return to Washington for a brief lame-duck session to pass legislation implementing the General Agreement on Tariffs and Trade (GATT) and to pack up eight years' worth of papers and records. Within two months, I was back in the classroom at Duke University, at first teaching seminars on Congress and eventually my previous courses in ethics and public policy and modern American political thought. I felt welcome at Duke and valued the chance to get back in touch with my former career and friends I had seen too infrequently. I was determined to find time for reflection, but I knew that I would need to make and announce a decision about my political plans within a few months. I engaged in considerable soul-searching, analyzed the loss, and sought advice about how it happened and whether I should try to reverse it. I closely followed national and local political developments and discussions. They left little doubt that 1996 would be a hard-fought election, determining whether 1994 was an aberration or whether it marked a longer-lasting partisan and ideological realignment; whatever hopes Democrats had for a comeback would depend critically on districts like the Fourth.

Comeback

During the spring and summer of 1995, I moved steadily toward a decision to run. I was not certain how I would react as the reality of my loss sank in psychologically. But I found that the determination and defiance I had felt during the congressional struggles of 1993–1994 did not fade. If anything, they intensified. I was at the peak of my capacity to serve, and it seemed unthinkable to let 1994 be the last word personally or politically. My wife strongly agreed with these sentiments.

Because my defeat had been so unexpected and so close, I faced no opposition within the Democratic Party and benefited from the widespread expectation that I could reverse the outcome. I was not so sure, as I witnessed the extraordinary energy and discipline with which the new House majority enacted most elements of the Contract with America. (The Contract proved far more important in shaping Republican purpose and cohesion in the 104th Congress's first hundred days than it had in the campaign.) Nonetheless I firmed up my decision to run, and as both the House leadership and Heineman began to stumble, that began to look more and more like a winning proposition.

The first Republican blunder to gain widespread attention in my district was the attempt to gut environmental regulation by attaching seventeen legislative "riders" to the FY 1996 Veterans Administration, Housing and Urban Development, and Independent Agencies (VA-HUD) appropriations bill. The bill proposed to cut Environmental Protection Agency (EPA) funding by 33 percent and limit the agency's authority to regulate matters such as emissions from industrial facilities and oil refineries, raw sewage overflows, arsenic and radon in drinking water, and cancer-causing substances in processed foods. The issue was highlighted and the GOP leadership embarrassed on July 28, 1995, when fifty-one Republicans (not including Heineman) broke ranks and joined with most Democrats in deleting the riders. Republican leaders managed to reverse the vote three days later, leaving an impression of environmental extremism and creating "a wedge issue Democrats would use through the 1996 campaign."[8]

Heineman had already received publicity in the district for his uncritical support of Gingrich's Contract (ranking first in the North Carolina delegation) and for his overnight reversal on the question of cop-killer bullets on the Judiciary Committee, supposedly at the behest of the National Rifle Association via the Republican leadership. He took a harder hit on the environmental issue, since the VA-HUD bill he supported not only contained the EPA cuts and antiregulatory riders but also omitted funding for a new EPA research center in the Research Triangle Park, which I had helped get off the ground and which he had claimed credit for supporting (see Chapter 6).[9]

None of this compared, however, with the criticism and ridicule that followed a comment he made to a *Raleigh News and Observer* reporter in an interview for an October 21 feature story. Following up on a remark Heineman had dropped in an earlier discussion with the newspaper's editorial board, the reporter asked where his congressional salary and police pensions (totaling some $184,000 per year) placed him on the income scale. Heineman responded:

> That does not make me rich. That does not make me upper-middle class. In fact, that does not make me middle class. In my opinion, that makes me lower-middle class. . . .
>
> When I see a first-class individual who makes $80,000 a year, he's lower middle class. When I see someone who is making anywhere from $300,000 to $750,00 a year, that's middle class. When I see anyone above that, that's upper middle class.[10]

My first reaction to the comments, which appeared in a sidebar to the feature piece, was bewilderment. But the next day, at two of the neighborhood gatherings I had scheduled to talk politics and explore my candidacy, I found people talking of little else. Biting editorials and editorial cartoons soon appeared; a local radio station ran a "Hiney-thon," inviting listeners to fax dollar bills to their impoverished congressman. Democrats from minority leader Dick Gephardt on down had a field day on the House floor, purporting to find in Heineman's remarks "a unique window onto the Republican worldview."

In the meantime, I had announced my firm intention to run. Plotting my course with Mac McCorkle, a close friend and an original member of the 1986 Wednesday night group who was now in business as a policy and message consultant, I began in midsummer to schedule neighborhood gatherings, asking friends to invite neighbors of all political persuasions to meet for open-ended discussions. I gained a great deal of insight from these meetings as to how Washington appeared from the Fourth District and how the new House leadership was misreading its mandate. I declared my candidacy in early October in a letter to 8,000 supporters and contributors. This letter brought in an astounding $80,000 in contributions, three times more than I had ever raised with a single mailing. I also began spending numerous hours each week in a small campaign office calling larger donors. Here too the response was encouraging; by the time I filed in January, I had raised $215,000 and was well on my way to what became a $1.17 million campaign.

I decided to bring on a new pollster, Alan Secrest, who was known for his unblinking worst-case analyses and for coordinating closely with campaign media and message operations. McCorkle and I searched extensively for a campaign manager and were fortunate to enlist Joe Goode, a senior analyst with Greenberg Research who was in North Carolina because of his wife's graduate study and was intrigued by the challenge of hands-on campaign management. By late spring, we had a core campaign staff of seven and many committed volunteers. In some ways it felt like the first campaign. I was on the trail every day after my teaching duties ended in May; this time it was Heineman who was alternately stuck in Washington or catching grief at town meetings, trying to persuade voters that his party really wasn't cutting Medicare. I was well aware of the advantages of incumbency that he now enjoyed, but I found it liberating and invigorating to be the challenger again. I was less defensive, more adversarial, free to go on the offense in developing and delivering a message. I also had far more time and energy for retail politics. We held dozens of low-dollar, friends-and-neighbors functions that were as much outreach events as they were fund-raisers, and my door-to-door neighborhood walks became a hallmark of the campaign.

We took our benchmark poll in January. This was after fiscal year 1996 budget talks between the president and congressional leaders had collapsed and Republicans had borne most of the blame for the accompanying government shutdowns (see Chapter 7). But we were still apprehensive about what we might find and uncertain how much damage from 1994 remained. We were therefore relieved to find that I led Heineman in the horse race numbers, 47 to 38 percent, although the result owed more to negative views of Heineman than to positive views of me. Heineman had been hurt by negative reactions to Gingrich and the Republican Congress but was also carrying some heavy individual baggage. Many voters from the groups I most needed to reach were strongly offended by his "middle class" gaffe, including working-class and less-educated respondents who were tempted to vote Republican by cultural and social issues. On various measures, my numbers were considerably better than his (e.g., a 45–32 positive-negative rating, compared to Heineman's 38–40 and Gingrich's 32–57), but they nonetheless showed that we had a great deal of work to do.

In early September, when Heineman was already running television ads and I was set to begin my own, two events occurred that altered both the pace and the content of the campaign. Heineman suffered a perforated intestine and underwent emergency surgery. And Hurricane Fran hit central North Carolina, creating widespread devastation and displacing politics with more immediate concerns. We canceled most campaign events for two weeks, pitching in with community relief and cleanup efforts. Heineman briefly cut back on his ads, which at that point were attacking me on the Medicare issue. I delayed the beginning of my television campaign by a week and then ran only an introductory biographical spot that stressed my educational background and advocacy.

We knew, however, that I could not safely let Heineman's attacks go unanswered, and we were well aware of his greatest point of vulnerability. Therefore, during the last week in September, with Heineman out of the hospital and his ad campaign back in full swing, we unveiled "Earth to Fred":

> "MISSION CONTROL": Earth to Fred. Come in, Congressman. [Video shows flight through space, passing by planets and stars]
> ANNOUNCER: It's amazing. Fred Heineman actually said "middle-class" people make between $300,000 and $700,000 a year. [Text with *Business Week* citation superimposed on space shots]
> MISSION CONTROL: Fred, are you there?
> ANNOUNCER: And Heineman claims his $180,000 a year income makes him, quote, lower middle class. [Text with *USA Today* citation superimposed]
> MISSION CONTROL: Earth to, ah, Fred, over.
> ANNOUNCER: Fred Heineman: He's out of touch with average families here. Way out. [Video of space flight continues]
> MISSION CONTROL: Earth to Fred. Come in!

This ad effectively countered everything Heineman threw at me. His Medicare ad featured a film clip from my cable show that cut me off in midsentence and left the impression that I was eager to cut Medicare. This ad attempted to neutralize the damage he was suffering from Republican budget cutbacks as well as AFL-CIO issue advocacy ads, which focused sharply on Medicare. But his main efforts to bring down my numbers reached back to the anti-institutional and antitax themes of 1994. His ads not only attacked me for raising taxes, raising my own pay, and "bouncing checks in the bank scandal" but also accused me of breaking promises or lying about each. "Now you remember why we voted him out," one of them added. And then the tag line that almost all of Heineman's ads contained: "David Price. Too liberal then. Too liberal now."

As in previous races, we polled carefully and wrestled with the dilemma of whether and how directly to respond. We cut an ad directly addressing the House bank allegations but elected not to run it when a late poll showed Heineman's ad doing less damage than we feared.[11] We ran ads criticizing Heineman's votes on Medicare and the antienvironmental riders, with frequent references to "Newt Gingrich's Congress" and "Newt Gingrich's plan." But nothing worked as well as "Earth to Fred," and voters called to complain when we took it off the air. We returned to the ad and to a variant that linked his views on the income scale to his willingness to cut student loans ("It's not just what Heineman says. It's how he votes.") throughout October.

I ended up spending more than $455,000 on television airtime over a seven-week period, and Heineman spent a like amount from his overall budget of $980,000. There was a strange contrast between his pervasive presence on television and his virtual absence from the campaign trail. North Carolinians were familiar with this pattern from Jesse Helms's Senate campaigns, but in Heineman's case it was difficult to know how much was deliberate strategy and how much the result of his illness. Despite a dozen or more invitations, we never had a debate or joint appearance. He began in October to attend fund-raisers and Republican meetings but declined all opportunities to engage face-to-face. "We just don't have enough time to prep the chief [the title Heineman preferred]. He doesn't have time to study," said his campaign spokesman in an ill-advised explanation of his boss's cancellation of a TV debate. This selectivity in scheduling led to widespread editorial criticism and, in several cases where the sponsor chose not to cancel the forum, gave me the opportunity to present my policy views and make a point about responsiveness and open campaigning.

My election-day margin of 54–44 percent (with 2 percent going to the Libertarian candidate) varied little from the polls we had taken in January and throughout the year. Our postelection poll showed a shift for the better in my favorable-unfavorable numbers to 54–34, compared to Heineman's 42–45. But it also suggested that the main effect of the campaign had been to solidify preexisting voter inclinations. As in 1994, there was a great deal of oppositional voting; just as Heineman had persuaded voters to "fire Congress" and me in the process, a number of voters had now elected to fire him. Among those who voted for me, 51 percent described their vote as mainly pro-Price, 30 percent as mainly anti-Heineman, and 19 percent as both or not sure. Anti-Heineman voters reported a strong receptivity to portrayals of the incumbent as both "out of touch" and "too close to Newt Gingrich and his extremist agenda." Among Heineman voters, 54 percent described their vote as mainly pro-Heineman, 29 percent as mainly anti-Price, and 17 percent as both or not sure, and our poll suggested that Heineman's portrayals of me as dishonest and "too liberal" had taken their toll. It had been a rough campaign in which getting any traction with a positive message was difficult; it left both of us bruised and me with the challenge of solidifying my positive credentials in the eyes of my constituents as I returned to office.

Beyond the Fourth District, election night revealed mixed results. Bob Etheridge, formerly North Carolina's Superintendent Of Public Instruction, recaptured the neighboring Second District for Democrats, but the other two House seats that had turned over in 1994 remained in Republican hands, leaving our delegation divided 6–6. Harvey Gantt's second attempt at unseating Senator Helms failed, and President Clinton lost North Carolina while winning nationally, although both Gantt and Clinton narrowly carried the Fourth District. Nationally the 1996 election continued a pattern of what James Ceaser and Andrew Busch called "losing to win": Republicans winning Congress in 1994 by virtue of their loss of the presidency in 1992 and Democrats winning the presidency in 1996 largely in reaction to their congressional loss of 1994 and what it produced.[12] Although the Republicans lost ground in the House, they did not lose control. I was one of sixteen Democrats defeating a Republican incumbent; in too many cases, Gingrich's stumbles and the show of Republican vulnerability had come too late for Democrats to recruit strong challengers. Overall, the net Democratic gain was only nine seats, with most of the 1994 Republican freshmen hanging on and the GOP picking up a number of conservative seats, especially in the south, where senior Democrats had retired. This left the House narrowly divided at 228–206 (plus one independent) and guaranteed another intense battle for control two years hence.

The 1996 campaign was our strongest grassroots effort since 1986, and our election night celebration was the largest and most raucous since that first win. The outcome was never in doubt. Turnout, boosted by the presidential race, was relatively high all over the district and the early returns from Wake County precincts showed me running far ahead of 1994. I

FIGURE 3.1   Election night, 1996. Displaying a well-worn shoe. Photo from *Herald-Sun* (Durham, N.C.). Reprinted with permission.

ended up with a 51.2 percent win in Wake, which I had lost with 45.1 percent in 1994, and I scored 56.7 percent in Chatham County and 68.4 percent in my home county of Orange. In acknowledging victory, I held up a well-worn shoe as a symbol of our grassroots effort (Figure 3.1) and gave my heartfelt thanks to family, staff, and volunteers for a wonderful team effort that had accomplished exactly what we set out to do.

Campaigning in Clinton's Shadow, 1998

The air of celebration from the 1996 election lingered for weeks, as I continued neighborhood walks to thank voters, held receptions to thank volunteers, and planned for my January 7 swearing-in. With a staff drawn from my previous terms of service and our campaign organization and with a promise from the Democratic leadership to place me back on the

Appropriations Committee, I hoped to pick up where I had left off two years before, despite the fact that I was now in the minority. In the early months of 1997 there was a period of bipartisan cooperation that contrasted sharply with the previous Congress and enabled me to do more than I might have anticipated as a minority member. But I also knew that there would be little respite for me at home politically and that I was likely to face a strong challenge in 1998. My 1996 win was substantial enough to remove me from the top tier of most vulnerable incumbents. But I was in the next tier, and there was a candidate in the wings waiting to take me on: Tom Roberg, a software executive who had been chairman of the Wake County Republican Party during its 1994 heyday and had considerable potential to finance his own campaign.

It was also clear that I would be defending a substantially redrawn Fourth District. The Supreme Court on June 13, 1996, had declared North Carolina's black-majority Twelfth District unconstitutional. Not until a judicial panel's early August ruling were we certain that the 1996 election would be held on schedule and in our existing districts. But the North Carolina General Assembly was bound to draw a new Twelfth District (and in the process to alter the surrounding districts) in advance of the 1998 election. This it did in the spring of 1997 in a fashion that gave the Fourth District almost one-third new territory. That plan itself was challenged and then modified; it was not until a year later that we were certain that the Fourth District boundaries drawn in 1997 would hold for the fall election. But I knew that we would not be returning to the three-county district in which I had run since 1992, and I began to move around Durham County on the assumption that it would become part of the Fourth District.

Redistricting performed major surgery on the Raleigh–Wake County portion of my district (see Figure 1.1b, p. 3). Some 44 percent of the county went to the Second District, including the state Capitol complex and the Democratic-leaning precincts where many of my loyal voters and volunteers lived. Durham was a compatible addition that largely compensated for the loss, though not without hard work. I knew Durham County well from living next door, teaching at Duke University, and working in the Democratic Party. Durham residents had seen my television ads and my cable call-in show for years, and I already had a contributor base there, mainly drawn from the Duke community. The county had numerous active political groups accustomed to endorsing candidates and working in campaigns, including a large and relatively well-organized African American community. Most of these activists were Democratically inclined and ended up welcoming me warmly. Yet it was a challenge to touch the bases and establish a level of comfort and confidence, particularly in the context of the politics of impeachment, which came to dominate much of 1998.

We planned a campaign comparable to 1996 in both financing and structure. I again brought in a campaign manager from outside, Chris Chwastyk, who had successfully managed Chet Edwards's (D-Texas) 1996 campaign. We eventually employed a core staff of eight, including Jean-Louise Beard who took a leave from my Washington staff to direct fund-raising. We set and eventually raised a campaign budget of more than $1.2 million. Our headquarters in Cary and Durham became bases for extensive volunteer and field operations, including phoning, mailing, neighborhood literature drops, and get-out-the-vote efforts. We also continued the neighborhood walks and low-dollar, outreach-oriented fund-raisers that had proved so successful in 1996.

We were acutely aware of the parallels between 1994 and 1998: another nonpresidential election year with the potential for depressed turnout, with the outcome determined by the most angry or intense voters. But we also were aware of the pitfalls of "fighting the last war" when circumstances in fact had changed. The atmosphere of my community meetings was much as I remembered it prior to the 1993–1994 turbulence, and my first poll, taken in March 1998, confirmed a remarkable turnaround in attitudes about the country's direction. Between 1994 and 1996, at least in the Fourth District, voters had shifted not so much in their level of discontent or their tendency to opposition voting as in the object of their discontent, with Newt Gingrich and the Republican Congress becoming a major target. But when, in 1998, we asked the standard question as to which way respondents thought the country was heading, 53 percent said the right direction, with only 29 percent disagreeing—compared to 28 percent right direction and 53 percent wrong just two years before. We also found that education was back in its accustomed position as the Fourth District's top-rated issue, although the linkage between me and that issue in the voters' minds was relatively weak. These findings helped shape our media strategy: We would frame a positive message, introducing me in terms of my educational background and specific recent achievements such as the Education Affordability Act (see Chapter 6).

The poll contained a mixed message for my 1998 prospects. Whether as a result of the generally improved political climate or of impressions I had made as an incumbent, my positive-negative ratings showed a marked improvement, from 54–34 to 58–19. I prevailed in the trial heat, 50–23, but this owed much to Roberg's lack of name familiarity and revealed that more of the electorate than we would have liked was "in play." Roberg did not have any obvious points of vulnerability—certainly nothing like Heineman's "middle class" comments—but neither did I: The bank/pay raise charges that Heineman had pounded home registered weakly, as did other criticisms we anticipated Roberg might make. But this finding was overtaken by events, as President Clinton's Monica Lewinsky scandal deepened and Roberg decided to make it the centerpiece of his campaign.

Roberg began in early August with light television and more substantial radio buys. "At home David Price talks like a moderate," the main television ad began, "but in Washington, Price votes with the liberals." The ad went on to cite votes "against reforming the IRS tax code" (worded to confuse my vote against a Republican proposal to scrap the entire tax code, without specifying any reforms or alternative provisions, with the vote on Internal Revenue Service reform, which I and virtually every other member supported); "for the largest tax increase in history" (presumably the 1993 deficit reduction plan; see Chapter 7); and "against [the constitutional] amendment to protect the flag." In the meantime, on August 17, Clinton acknowledged his relationship with Lewinsky before a Washington grand jury. On September 9, Independent Counsel Kenneth Starr delivered his report recommending impeachment to the House. Within a few days, Roberg had a new ad on the air:

ANNOUNCER: Where do you stand, Congressman Price? [Video: picture of Price with text superimposed]

Bill Clinton has admitted lying to us. [Clinton picture appears alongside Price]

Leading newspapers, including the *Durham Herald-Sun*, *USA Today*, and the *Winston-Salem Journal*, have called for Bill Clinton's resignation. [Banners from these papers swoop up, covering Price picture]

And Tom Roberg has called for Bill Clinton's resignation. [Color photo of Roberg covers Clinton]

This is not the time to be silent, Mr. Price. Where do you stand? [Price photo, text superimposed]

Tom Roberg for Congress, for conservative leadership. [Text on screen]

We viewed Roberg's attack with trepidation, for I was picking up a great sense of anger and disillusionment with the president, not only from expected sources but also from Democrats, even at my own fund-raisers. The poll we took on September 8–10 verified that Bill Clinton was not the only one sustaining damage; my trial heat numbers had slipped to 45–27. More ominously, Clinton's positive-negative numbers had taken a tumble (from 45–46 in March to 36–52) and mine with them (from 58–19 to 50–30), with my slippage concentrated among white Democrats and independents.

I expressed my moral outrage at Clinton's behavior in repeated public statements, while recognizing the need to reserve official judgment until all the facts were in and chastising Roberg for using the situation for his own political gain. My polls confirmed that a large majority of voters agreed with this approach, although they were not of one mind about resignation or impeachment. I decided to begin my television campaign as originally planned, with an engaging "School Play" ad featuring children and conveying information about education legislation I had pushed. Despite the Clinton mess, I knew that voters were still basically in an optimistic mood and receptive to a positive message; the need we had earlier identified to link me more strongly to education remained. "School Play" did this quite nicely while giving viewers a respite from the television clutter surrounding other campaigns and the Lewinsky scandal.

A major test loomed, however, as the House prepared to vote on October 8 on whether and in what fashion to carry the impeachment inquiry forward. Republicans proposed an open-ended inquiry in both content and duration, while Democrats wished to limit the inquiry to the material referred by Starr and end it by December 31. As I will explain in Chapter 8, I did not see this vote (unlike the impeachment votes to follow) as a matter of high principle, and I believed that either Clinton or Speaker Gingrich could have offered a compromise and "defused" the vote to their eventual advantage. As it became clear that a compromise was not going to happen, I discussed how to handle the vote with staff, campaign advisers, and district political leaders. After I supported the Democratic alternative and it failed, should I then vote for the Republican plan, knowing that a "no" vote would be portrayed by my opponents as opposition to any inquiry whatsoever?

The results from our early October poll were available the day before the vote, but they mainly underscored the dilemma I faced. The poll contained good news: My positive-negative numbers were becoming unlinked from Clinton's and were moving in the right direction, and the trial heat was looking better as well. But the poll also suggested that almost half of the electorate could be influenced in their vote by how I voted on the impeachment inquiry. Among that same group, approximately half would be more likely to vote for me and half less likely, no matter how I voted!

As the hour of the vote approached, I became more and more convinced that after voting for the limited inquiry I should then vote against the open-ended version. The more I thought about it, the less I wanted to be fighting on two fronts simultaneously. Roberg and other opponents of the president would attack me in any case. Did I really want to have to defend myself among loyal Democrats and supporters of the president as well? I gave particular attention to Durham in this connection and consulted with leaders there—not just because a large number of Durham voters opposed impeachment, but because these were new constituents who were taking their measure of me and whose wholehearted support I very much needed.

Almost immediately I came to see the vote as both right on the merits and more helpful than harmful politically. I felt comfortable and confident in explaining it and was put on the defensive far less than I expected. As anticipated, Roberg reacted quickly with a radio ad: "Congressman Price stood up for Bill Clinton and voted against an impeachment inquiry . . ." But he got little traction from the issue, as my next poll (and no doubt his as well) showed. Opinions as to whether Clinton should resign had actually shifted in the president's favor (from 42–53 on October 6 to 37–56 on October 19). When respondents were asked whether Price or Roberg could be better trusted "to do the right thing when it comes to Bill Clinton," my earlier 32–28 advantage increased to 39–30, with a particularly dramatic shift from 23–32 to 36–20 among white independent voters. We thus continued to run positive ads, adding to our education message a testimonial from a breast cancer victim required to leave the hospital immediately after her mastectomy (which the Patients Bill of Rights would change) and a "protect Social Security" message featuring senior citizens. Our only ad "answering" Roberg did not deal with the president at all but placed Roberg's positions on school construction and HOPE scholarship tax credits in juxtaposition with mine.

Roberg's campaign budget of $453,000, to which he personally contributed $180,000, was not as large as we had expected. But with the help of the National Republican Congressional Committee (NRCC), he was able to buy $354,000 worth of over-the-air and cable television time and another $52,000 on radio. This compared favorably with my $427,000 media budget, almost all of it spent on over-the-air television. Still, his message did not work. He never bothered to introduce himself and what he was for; he spread his ads over thirteen weeks, often in buys too scattered to penetrate; and his attempt to tie me to Clinton's troubles was not well received by most voters. After that fizzled, he had very little message left.

In late October, Roberg announced that he was severing ties with his consulting firm, apparently in disagreement with their recommendation that he run even harder-hitting ads in the campaign's closing weeks. His ads then returned to the more familiar themes of Social Security and taxes. In public forums, he attempted to turn the "negative campaigning" tables on me, criticizing fliers I had mailed that bluntly compared our positions and records on education and Social Security. In rebuttal, I explained and documented the charges I had made and expressed amazement that he would make such complaints after running 5,000 negative ads against me.

My victory margin was 57–42 percent. Durham performed impressively at 67.8 percent as did my home county of Orange at 70.2 percent, but I was just as proud of almost breaking even in the Fourth District portion of Wake County (48.2 percent), given the hand I had been dealt in redistricting. Election night brought a strange mixture of exhilaration and relief, for this had been a campaign of ups and downs, and we had often felt at the mercy of events beyond our control. The dreaded repeat of 1994, which for a time the president's troubles seemed likely to produce, did not materialize. Turnout rebounded from the abnormally low levels of four years before, increasing from 38 percent of registered voters in 1994 to 45 percent in 1998, although it was still far below presidential-year levels. The negative correlation at the precinct level between the Price vote and turnout percentages improved somewhat (from –.50 to –.44). But the greatest difference was simply in my share of the vote. This owed less to the substitution of new precincts for old (the areas added from Durham, Person, and northern Orange counties were only slightly more favorable than the areas lost in Wake and western Chatham) than to an overall improvement in performance. In Cary, for example, my percentage went from 41.7 in 1994 to 49.4 in 1998.

Nationwide, the 1998 elections produced little change in the margins of party control in Congress but a much greater upheaval politically, because Democratic performance far exceeded predictions and expectations. North Carolina delivered an important Senate turnover for Democrats as John Edwards defeated Lauch Faircloth in a tight race that helped boost enthusiasm and turnout for all of us on the ticket. But the overall partisan balance in the Senate remained the same at forty-five Democrats and fifty-five Republicans. In the House, only six incumbents were defeated, but five of these were Republicans; eleven open seats turned over, of which Democrats won six.[13] While this left Democrats on the short end of a 223–211 alignment in the House, we were within six seats of gaining control. The outcome was stunning not only in light of the expected impact of the Clinton scandal but also in its reversal of historic patterns. Not since 1934 had the party holding the White House gained seats in a midterm election, and not since 1822 had this happened during a president's second term. Clearly Republican reliance on Clinton's problems—particularly the decision by

Gingrich and NRCC chairman John Linder (R-Georgia) to put almost $10 million into a media blitz highlighting the scandal during the campaign's last week—had been a major miscalculation. Three days after the election, Gingrich, facing a serious challenge within House Republican ranks, announced his resignation as Speaker.

The Clinton scandal had a negative impact on a number of Democratic races by discouraging potentially strong candidates from running and by requiring the Democratic Congressional Campaign Committee (DCCC) in the critical weeks after August 17 to shift attention and resources away from promising challengers and open-seat candidates to races like mine, where incumbents suddenly looked imperiled. One case in point was North Carolina's Eighth District, where Mike Taylor, an underfinanced Democrat running for the seat vacated by Bill Hefner, lost by only 3,378 votes. Neither did the election head off impeachment. Although I and many others at first expected the outcome to encourage a compromise, it actually made impeachment more likely by creating a leadership vacuum among House Republicans that pro-impeachment zealots were all too eager to fill (see Chapter 8).

The 2000 and 2002 Campaigns

The opponents I faced after Tom Roberg—Cary councilman Jess Ward in 2000 and political newcomer Tran Nguyen in 2002—were not well-known, raised little money, and received minimal help from the Republican Party. I still faced a substantial and growing straight-ticket Republican vote in Wake County and mounted an extensive voter-turnout effort in the heavily Democratic parts of the district. But for the first time I was able to forgo television advertising, which enabled us to cut campaign costs by half but may have limited my margins among independent and moderate Republican voters.

Our March 2000 poll revealed a substantial incumbency advantage. Optimism about the country's direction remained high (50–27), and my favorability rating, 56–24, was close to where it had been before the attack ads of 1998. We faced some uncertainty, however. Despite their generally upbeat view of the economy, Fourth District voters expressed a 46–42 percent preference for the Republican nominee, Governor George W. Bush, over Vice President Al Gore in the presidential race. Although Jess Ward remained largely unknown, we were concerned that he, as an African American elected official from Wake County, might pick up support beyond the hard-core Republican base.

As it turned out, such threats never materialized. My 78–7 percent lead over Ward among black voters in March increased to 84–3 by September.

Ward raised $41,000 and maintained a rather casual campaign schedule. In the meantime, we polled carefully and assembled a campaign operation that could deal with whatever challenges might emerge. Jean-Louise Beard took a leave from my congressional staff to manage the campaign, and Terrance Taylor, who had proved his mettle as an organizer when we first campaigned in Durham County in 1998, took charge of field operations.

We raised $686,000 over the two-year cycle and again invested heavily in efforts to turn out African American and core Democratic voters. Our mail program and my personal schedule—still featuring door-to-door walks in suburban neighborhoods—also targeted swing voters and recent arrivals. Our decision not to buy television time freed me to offer more financial help to congressional candidates in swing districts in North Carolina and elsewhere. I often pointed out to supporters how much closer I could come to the job that I wanted to do and they wanted me to do if I were part of a Democratic House majority.

My winning majority was 62 percent, again led by Durham and Orange Counties (74 and 72 percent respectively). Gore carried the district by three points while losing North Carolina overall, 43–56 percent. Nationally the election could hardly have been closer. The Senate was left divided exactly in half, a balance that tipped toward Democrats a few months later when Senator James Jeffords (R-Vermont) became an independent. Democrats netted two additional House seats but not the seven needed to regain the majority. And the presidential race went into overtime: Gore won the popular plurality by almost 540,000 votes, but the electoral vote was in doubt as recounts were started and stopped in Florida over a five-week period. Ultimately the U.S. Supreme Court intervened with a 5–4 ruling, overturning the Florida Supreme Court's dictate that a statewide recount be completed and effectively declaring Bush the winner.

An irony of the post-2000 partisan standoff in Congress was that it was produced by the cumulation of mainly noncompetitive House races. This pattern, as well as the steepness of the hill we Democrats had to climb to regain the majority, was reinforced by the redistricting that followed the 2000 census. The number of likely safe seats for both parties rose, while population shifts toward southern and western states provided an increment of eight Republican-leaning districts.

The Fourth District was a mixed case. The district had grown more rapidly during the 1990s than any other in North Carolina and had to be reduced in population by 147,000. Meanwhile, North Carolina's overall growth had resulted in the state's being assigned a thirteenth district, which could most easily be carved out of the Triangle area. Any desire I had for a more Democratic district, and any inclination the Democrats who controlled the General Assembly might have had to draw such a district, were tempered by the realization that if the three Triangle area districts (Fourth, Second, and new Thirteenth) were each to have the prospect of electing a Democrat, none of us could be greedy. The new Fourth District was thus given a contour roughly equal to the old in terms of Democratic performance. Much of the area that had supported me strongly—Orange, Durham, and northeast Chatham counties—was retained. But 41 percent of Wake County remained in the Fourth, comprising 42 percent of the district's population and its area of most likely rapid growth (see Figure 1.1b, p. 3). The few Democratic areas that had remained after the 1997 redistricting were mainly transferred to the Thirteenth, leaving the Fourth District portion of Wake County with 43 percent Republican, 22 percent unaffiliated, and only 35 percent Democratic registered voters.

In many respects, including the 61 percent margin of victory, my 2002 race tracked 2000. Durham County weighed in at 73 percent and Orange at 72, but the impact of redistricting was evident as I carried the district's Wake County precincts by fewer than 1,000 votes amid a tide of straight-ticket Republican voting. The neighboring districts remained in the Democratic column, with Bob Etheridge gaining reelection in the Second and Brad Miller, who had headed the redistricting effort in the North Carolina Senate, winning in the new Thirteenth.

My opponent, Tran Nguyen, a well-spoken but inexperienced and little-known newcomer, filed for election virtually unannounced on the last day of the filing period and managed to raise only $7,869. We raised $702,000 over the two-year cycle and went beyond our 2000 effort considerably in helping promising congressional candidates in North Carolina and across the country and in organizing local get-out-the-vote operations on behalf of the entire ticket.

The 2002 campaign was managed by Anna Tilghman, who had headed up our fund-raising in 2000, and field operations were again directed by Terrance Taylor. We again targeted Durham for intensive voter-contact work, knowing that turnout required special attention with neither a presidential nor a gubernatorial election on the ballot. We worked closely with Erskine Bowles in his race to succeed Senator Helms, but even with a 51–48 percent win in the Fourth District, Bowles lost by nine points to Elizabeth Dole statewide. As in 1992 and 1993, the Wake County results sent up a storm signal: Dole carried the county handily, in the Fourth District precincts and beyond, and Republicans swept most local races.

Nationally the 2002 outcome reflected once again the even partisan division of the electorate. But the shifts that did occur were highly significant, tipping control of the Senate back to the Republicans and adding five seats to the Republican House majority. Republicans, like Democrats in 1998, broke from the historical pattern of midterm losses for the president's party, ending at three the streak of elections since 1996 that had produced Democratic gains in the House. Redistricting helped determine this outcome, but more important was the change in the national political climate after the September 11, 2001, terrorist attacks. The president's popularity had soared, and he capitalized on it by campaigning vigorously and repeatedly on behalf of key House and Senate candidates. The administration escaped the consequences of the slowing economy and the financial scandals affecting Enron and other companies as the political focus shifted to national defense and foreign policy issues, where Republican credibility was stronger. As Gary Jacobson concluded, "Had the terrorist attacks not occurred, Bush's overall approval rating would have remained much closer to his rating on the economy, and if standard midterm referendum models are to be believed, this alone might have cost Republicans control of the House."[14]

In 2002, as in past campaigns, we polled carefully, this time working with Fred Yang of the Garin-Hart-Yang Research Group. Underneath the surface similarities, the surveys revealed an election dynamic that differed considerably from 2000. The increased salience of foreign policy issues was evident, for example, but those issues did not pull the Fourth District electorate in a single direction. By our September 30, 2002, survey, the national consensus that had formed around the post–9/11 antiterrorism offensive and the war in Afghanistan was beginning to fracture over the president's determination to invade Iraq, with or without the support of key allies. The situation was reminiscent of October 1998, when the pivotal House vote loomed on authorizing the impeachment inquiry. In October 2002, the pivotal vote was an open-ended authorization for the president to employ military force in Iraq (see Chapter 9). As in 1998, there was an alternative resolution that many other Democrats and I supported: a proposal written by Rep. John Spratt (D-South Carolina) authorizing the president to use armed force to protect weapons inspectors and undertake U.N. enforcement actions but requiring him to come back to Congress if he wished to invade Iraq unilaterally. I was more certain than I had been in 1998 that, after voting for the alternative proposal and seeing it fail, I would oppose the main motion. But the issue had excited passions in my district comparable to impeachment, and the vote, coming less than a month before the election, seemed likely to have a major—if not totally predictable—political impact.

As in 1998, our poll revealed some political peril no matter which way I voted. Respondents divided closely (43 percent in favor, 46 percent opposed) on the question of a U.S. invasion to remove Saddam Hussein from power; the balance shifted to 77–17 if the United Nations supported the action. When asked to choose between a hypothetical Democrat who opposed invasion "at this time" and a Republican who wanted to give President Bush the authority he requested, the opponent of invasion prevailed by six percentage points (47–41). Then came the October 10 vote: I chose not to vote quietly but to publicize my work on the Spratt alternative and my arguments for voting no on the main motion. Yang found a greater awareness of my vote among my constituents than was true in the districts of any of the other members for whom he was polling.

Our October 15 poll showed my constituents favoring by 55–40 percent the resolution I had opposed. But when given the gist of the Spratt resolution and told that I had supported it, 59 percent (including 31 percent of those who favored the president's request) expressed their approval. Meanwhile my positive "feeling thermometer" score went from 61 to 74 percent among Democrats, while my negative score went from 21 to 29 among undecided voters and 23 to 30 among independents. We concluded that, while the war vote had perhaps shaved my margin among these latter groups, it had also helped energize my Democratic base.

Our polls also revealed a striking shift since 2000 in the mood of the electorate. The optimistic "right direction" numbers from two years before (50–27 in one poll, 57–30 in another) abruptly reversed, with 37 percent believing the nation was headed in the right direction and 50 percent choosing "wrong track." When asked about "this part of North Carolina," given the state's job losses and budget woes, constituents reversed themselves even more starkly, from 67–23 in 2000 to 33–50 in 2002. Thus the optimistic readings characteristic of the 1998 and 2000 election cycles seemed headed in the pessimistic direction of 1994 and 1996, although this time the discontent was concentrated on the left rather than the right. Less clear was whether the recent trend toward status-quo elections might also be reversed. In 2002, any negative drag on Republicans as the party presiding over the national economy was largely overcome by the president's popularity and the ascendance of foreign policy and security concerns. But if the jobs did not come back and the president's management of foreign policy and the military began adding to the discontent rather than neutralizing it, then the ramifications in 2004 could be momentous indeed.

Campaign Reform

The nine campaigns I have weathered, in addition to my previous work as a state party chairman and political scientist, have left me with a few thoughts on campaign reform. Partly because of my political science background, I was drawn into media commentary during the 2000 Florida recount. In mid-November, when it seemed that Congress might be confronted with two competing sets of Florida electors sending conflicting electoral certificates to Washington, I introduced a resolution requiring the archivist of the United States, the official responsible for coordinating the functions of the Electoral College, to inform the House of preparations he was making to receive lists of qualified electors from the states and any challenges to their legality.[15] I was appalled when the Supreme Court cut off the Florida recount, and as the 107th Congress got underway, I resolved to salvage some election reform from the debacle.

My own preference would have been to abolish the Electoral College or to modify its workings substantially, for example, by giving a fifty-vote electoral bonus to the winner of the popular vote. But most reform efforts aimed at the more immediate problems with voting equipment and election procedures that the Florida experience had highlighted. My contribution to this agenda was the Voting Improvement Act (H.R. 775), which I introduced along with Steny Hoyer, ranking Democrat on the Committee on House Administration, on February 28, 2001. The bill would have provided funds to states and localities to replace punch card voting systems, the least reliable among systems commonly in use, and proposed creation of a federal commission to develop a model election code for the states.

With memories of Florida still fresh, the possibilities for bipartisan cooperation were unclear, even to repair obvious flaws. Many Republicans were wary lest reform efforts shed a negative light on the 2000 outcome; Democrats had no desire to settle for halfway measures, which would imply the Florida problems and abuses were less than serious. Many of us criticized Speaker Hastert for refusing to appoint a special committee on reform equally divided between the parties, but his negative decision had a silver lining: it freed minority leader Dick Gephardt to appoint an all-Democratic committee that could be much bolder in its critique and its agenda for reform. I was named as one of eight vice chairs of the committee, which held six hearings across the country and issued a comprehensive reform proposal.[16]

In the end, election reform became one of the few areas of bipartisan achievement for the 107th Congress, largely through the efforts of Hoyer, Chairman Bob Ney (R-Ohio) of the Committee on House Administration, and their Senate counterparts. The Help America Vote Act (H.R. 3295), signed by the president on October 29, 2002, retained the punch card machine buyout from the Voting Improvement Act, as well as the commission to oversee work on a model election code. In addition, it set national elections standards (e.g., requiring states to provide voters with a means of checking and correcting errors in casting their ballots and to furnish a "provisional" ballot when a voter's eligibility was in doubt) and authorized grants to help the states meet those standards.

In beginning this book with accounts of my nine election and reelection efforts, I have perhaps risked giving an impression of life in Congress as an endless sequence of campaigns. The remainder of the book will provide perspective on campaigning relative to other congressional duties. For all but about three months of the twenty-four-month election cycle, I am involved in congressional more than campaign activities. That, I believe, is how constituents prefer it, and most campaigns would be hard-pressed to improve on the typical schedule maintained by members of Congress in their districts to reach out to voters and let them know what the member is about.

Still, we are never far from the next election; I often tell supporters that they never need to remove their bumper stickers. Is the two-year term too short? It would be a rare House member who has not on occasion looked enviously at the Senate with its six-year terms. But the House is the body of government constitutionally designed to be most sensitive to currents of public opinion, and recent history has frequently seen voters applying what many saw as a "corrective" to presidential outcomes and policies in House races two years later: 1966 comes to mind, as do 1974, 1982, and, indeed, 1994. I am not an unbiased observer. A trend of this sort in North Carolina in 1986, following the wipeout of Democrats in 1984, helped first elect me to the House, and I was again fortunate, in trying to recapture the Fourth District seat in 1996, to face a turnaround time of only two years.

The most serious criticism of the two-year cycle is that it requires nonstop fund-raising. But that is less a criticism of two-year terms than it is of the financial demands of politics. Despite their longer terms, senators often are as fully and continually preoccupied as House members with the quest for dollars. I am neither fond of nor particularly adept at fund-raising, but I have raised $7.6 million in nine campaigns, outdoing my opponents in every campaign except John Carrington's largely self-financed effort in 1990. I have needed this money (and obviously should have raised and spent more in 1994) to defend myself in a sometimes hostile environment and get my message out as I challenged two well-financed incumbents.

The main factor driving these campaign expenditures is television. I have probably worked harder than most candidates at keeping the politics of personal contact alive. I believe in it and will continue to do it. But as I survey the vast, rapidly growing suburban tracts around Raleigh and throughout my district and as I ask myself how I am going to reach them, there is no answer that does not lead back to television. This is the medium that most people attend to; it is their main source of political information. And the most effective format by far is the well-conceived, well-produced thirty-second ad.

This greatly complicates the task of controlling campaign costs. In a system biased in many ways toward incumbents, television is often the most effective tool that a challenger has. I share the misgivings that many have expressed about how much money a serious race for Congress requires, the good people that this eliminates from participation, and the constant preoccupation with fund-raising it requires. But if we want campaigns that reach and raise the awareness of the vast majority of the community, we must come to grips with the unique power of television, and that means big money.

There is a place in campaign reform for spending limits to prevent excesses of the kind we have seen in several U.S. Senate races in North Carolina. But such limits must be high enough to permit full and effective campaigns and they must be supplemented by other measures if we are to relieve fund-raising pressures, encourage a healthy diversity of funding sources, and level the playing field for incumbents and challengers. Measures worth considering include a "floor" of public funds that would match small individual contributions and be financed by an expansion of the tax checkoff system (or perhaps by a fee on PACs and large contributors); a restoration of the tax incentives for small contributors that existed prior to 1986; limits on the percentage or cumulative amount of contributions that candidates can receive from PACs; requirements that television time be offered free or at reduced rates; and strengthened incentives for voter engagement with state and local political parties.

In the meantime, however, campaign finance laws already on the books have been rendered largely ineffectual by the efforts of candidates, parties, and interest groups to create and exploit loopholes, often aided by court and Federal Election Commission rulings. Legislation to close two of the largest loopholes—by eliminating the unlimited, largely unregulated contributions to parties known as soft money and requiring unions, corporations, and nonprofits to pay for advertisements that advocate the election or defeat of specific candidates with regulated political action committee (PAC) funds—finally passed in 2002. Sponsored by Chris Shays (R-Connecticut) and Martin Meehan (D-Massachusetts) in the House and John McCain (R-Arizona) and Russ Feingold (D-Wisconsin) in the Senate, the bill also dealt with self-financed candidates in one of the few ways left open by the courts, raising the limits on permitted contributions to their opponents.

In 1998 and 1999, the Shays-Meehan legislation cleared the hurdles erected by the House Republican leadership and passed by substantial votes, only to fall to Senate filibusters. In the 107th Congress, President Bush's opposition was added to the mix. But so was the collapse of the Enron Corporation, amid revelations of the company's political contributions and influence, and that was sufficient to prompt the necessary 218 members to sign a discharge petition forcing the bill onto the floor despite leadership opposition. Our margin of victory was 240–189, and this time the Senate went along, 60–40. The president signed the bill on March 27, 2002, pointedly refusing to stage the usual signing ceremony.

The battle then shifted to the courts, first to a special district court panel and then to the U.S. Supreme Court. As a long-time cosponsor of the Shays-Meehan legislation, I joined with Michael Castle (R-Delaware) in organizing a bipartisan group of twenty-five members to submit an amicus curiae brief defending the bill. With the help of law professors Charles Tiefer of the University of Baltimore and Richard Briffault of Columbia University, we stressed the continuity of Shays-Meehan's loophole closings with past, legally sanctioned attempts at regulation. We particularly argued that reducing the parties to "mere conduits for the flow of big soft-money contributions" to be expended by candidates and their operatives, far from strengthening parties, "hollowed out" and marginalized their traditional organizational functions.[17] Finally, in a 5–4 ruling on December 10, 2003, the Supreme Court upheld the major provisions of the law.[18]

Campaign reform is not just about money; most people are equally troubled by the nastiness and distortions in campaign advertising. The thirty-second ad format is made to order for oversimplification and personal attacks. Even when responsibly used, its limitations as a vehicle for serious campaign communication and debate are severe. Candidates and parties need to restore the vitality of pretelevision modes of communicating—targeted mail, tabloids, voter-contact activities—and encourage television and radio formats that go beyond the thirty-second ad. Certainly any proposal for free or reduced-rate television time should address the format as well as the cost of the ad. And there has long been a need to strengthen the "disclaimers" whereby the candidates and organizations running ads identify themselves—often with a postage stamp–size picture and tiny print on the screen.

I took on the disclaimer issue in 1997 when I introduced what I termed (with apologies to Tammy Wynette) a "Stand by Your Ad" bill. The idea was to require candidates (or interest group representatives) to appear briefly, full-screen, identifying themselves and acknowledging that they approved and paid for the ad the viewer has seen or is about to see.[19] This strengthened disclaimer would not regulate the content of the body of the ad but, in requiring a more explicit assumption of personal responsibility, could help deter reckless charges and distortions. I worked with Representatives Shays and Meehan to include "Stand by Your Ad" in their bill from 1999 through the 2002 House-Senate conference, and its major elements remained in the bill the president signed. We were careful to point out in our amicus brief that these provisions simply strengthened requirements already in law. The Supreme Court agreed, specifically upholding the enhanced disclaimer in its decision.[20] In the meantime, I took great satisfaction in seeing presidential candidates "stand by their ads" as they began running commercials in the 2004 campaign.

It is no simple matter, given the strictures of the First Amendment, to devise regulations that encourage fairness and truthfulness in advertising. "Stand by Your Ad" should help, empowering voters to identify and punish campaign tactics of which they disapprove. For the foreseeable future, we are going to have to live with the dominance of thirty-second ads. Making their contents more accurate and more relevant to the decisions voters face will depend less on regulation than on the kinds of appeals that viewers choose to reward and on the ethical responsibility that candidates and their consultants choose to assume.

Notes

1. The resulting 93 percent reelection rate for incumbents who were on the November ballot thus considerably "overstated the security enjoyed by incumbents." See James Ceaser and Andrew Busch, *Upside Down and Inside Out: The 1992 Elections and American Politics* (Lanham, Md.: Rowman & Littlefield, 1993), p. 144.

2. The first edition of Paul S. Herrnson, *Congressional Elections: Campaigning at Home and in Washington* (Washington, D.C.: Congressional Quarterly Press, 1995), featured my 1992 campaign as "typical of those assembled by most shoo-in incumbents." In particular, see the accounts of the campaign's organization and fundraising, pp. 70–71, 137–139. Needless to say, Herrnson's second and third editions (1998 and 2000) treated the Fourth District as an example of a different sort!

3. Dan Balz and Ronald Brownstein, *Storming the Gates: Protest Politics and the Republican Revival* (Boston: Little, Brown, 1996), p. 253.

4. See the accounts in Balz and Brownstein, *Storming the Gates*, pp. 45–46, 91–94, 193–197; and E. J. Dionne Jr., *They Only Look Dead: Why Progressives Will Dominate the Next Political Era* (New York: Simon & Schuster, 1997), pp. 143–146.

5. See the analysis in Gary C. Jacobson, "The 1994 House Elections in Perspective," in Philip A. Klinker, ed., *Midterm: The Elections of 1994 in Context* (Boulder: Westview, 1996), chap. 1; and Jacobson, "Divided Government and the 1994 Elections," in Peter F. Galderisi, ed., *Divided Government: Change, Uncertainty, and the Constitutional Order* (Lanham, Md.: Rowman & Littlefield, 1996), chap. 3.

6. "In this political season of voter discontent, the four-term congressman is running for re-election as if he has never run before, logging 12-hour days on the campaign trail. . . . 'Any candidate who is not polling, who is not working very hard, is divorced from reality.' Price said. 'This is a year when you have to watch it very carefully.'" James Rosen, "Dogged Price Does Homework, Pursues Goals," *Raleigh News and Observer,* October 29, 1994, p. 16A.

7. Robert E. Orme and David W. Rohde measured this at my suggestion and confirmed the predicted effects. "Presidential Surge and Differential Decline: The Effects of Changing Turnout on the Fortunes of Democratic House Incumbents in 1994" (prepared for delivery at the annual meeting of the American Political Science Association, Chicago, 1995).

8. Linda Killian, *The Freshmen: What Happened to the Republican Revolution?* (Boulder: Westview, 1998), p. 134; also see David Maraniss and Michael Weisskopf, *"Tell Newt to Shut Up!"* (New York: Simon & Schuster, 1996), pp. 91–93.

9. See, for example, the following editorials: "The Case of the 'Cop-Killer Bullets,'" *Washington Post,* June 17, 1995, p. A16; "Heineman's Peculiar Retreat," *Raleigh News and Observer,* June 21, 1995, p. A10; and "Environmental Setback," *Raleigh News and Observer,* August 8, 1995, p. A8.

10. James Rosen, "Heineman Says He's Not Middle Class," *Raleigh News and Observer,* October 21, 1995, p. A14. On the circumstances of the interview and subsequent reactions, see Rosen, "Heineman Comments Cause Flap," *Raleigh News and Observer,* October 26, 1995, p. 1A.

11. "Fred Heineman is not telling the truth," this ad stated. "As a newspaper 'ad watch' now confirms, David Price's checks did not bounce and David Price did not misuse any money at the House bank." For the ad watch cited, which dealt with various Heineman charges, see Joe Dew, "Heineman Hits Price over House Bank Scandal," *Raleigh News and Observer,* October 24, 1996, p. A3.

12. Ceaser and Busch, *Losing to Win: The 1996 Elections and American Politics* (Lanham, Md.: Rowman & Littlefield), 1997, p. 145.

13. The 395 members returned to office in 1998 were the most for any midterm House election in history. The number of incumbents defeated (6) tied the record for least change in any midterm, and the total number of seats switching party control (17) set a new low. Incumbents in both parties enjoyed an average vote gain of 2.6 percentage points over 1996. "That voters did opt for the status quo in 1998 is beyond question." Gary Jacobson, "Impeachment Politics in the 1998 Congressional Elections," *Political Science Quarterly,* Spring 1999, p. 32. The results, Jacobson argued, were compatible with the election's underlying conditions—few exposed Democratic incumbents (thanks to earlier losses), a strong economy, and a Democratic president with high job-approval ratings: "about what we would expect if no one had ever heard of Monica Lewinsky" (p. 36).

14. Gary C. Jacobson, "Terror, Terrain, and Turnout: Explaining the 2002 Midterm Elections," *Political Science Quarterly,* Spring 2003, pp. 6–7.

15. H.Res. 667, 106th Congress. See the accompanying remarks in the *Congressional Record,* daily ed., November 14, 2000, pp. E2101–2.

16. Special Committee on Election Reform, Democratic Caucus, *Revitalizing Our Nation's Election System* (Washington, D.C., 2001).

17. Reps. Castle and Price et al., Brief of *Amici Curiae, Mitch McConnell et al. v. Federal Election Commission et al.,* U.S. Supreme Court, August 5, 2003, pp. 15–16. See also the more extensive refutation of the party-weakening argument by a distinguished group of academic specialists: Norman J. Ornstein et al., Brief of *Amici Curiae, McConnell v. FEC,* U.S. Supreme Court, August 5, 2003.

18. *McConnell et al. v. Federal Election Commission et al.,* slip opinion 02–1674, December 10, 2003.

19. H.R. 1541, 105th Congress; H.R. 227, 106th Congress; H.R. 156, 107th Congress. The proposal was adapted from a bill initiated by North Carolina lieutenant governor Dennis Wicker and passed in modified form by the General Assembly in 1999.

20. See Castle and Price Brief, pp. 26–30; *McConnell v. FEC,* p. 147, upholding section 311 of the law.

4

Getting Adjusted

"It was like being dropped into the jungle and having to learn to survive," a freshman senator told Richard Fenno after his first year in office. "Gradually, you cut out a little place for yourself, a clearing in which you can live."[1] I would not have given quite as dramatic a description of my first year, perhaps because my staff work in the Senate, my years of studying congressional policymaking, and my previous work in national politics had taught me what to expect. Still, the adjustments confronting any new member are profound: from campaigning to organizing legislative and constituent services offices, from the expectations and demands of one job or profession to those of another, from hometown family life to the bifurcated existence of an airborne commuter. I will describe some of these transitions in the present chapter and then turn, in Chapter 5, to the further task described by Fenno's senator: finding a niche within the institution, cutting out "a clearing in which you can live." I will concentrate on my entry with the class of 1986 but will also refer to my experience as a "recycled" freshman after the 1996 election. Though all senators and representatives make these adjustments, they vary a great deal in how they do so and in how happy, confident, and productive they are as they "move from involvement in running for office to involvement in running the country."[2]

Getting Started

Veteran House members can recall numerous horror stories of the trial-and-error process by which they were "oriented" to the institution. That process has been eased considerably, although not completely, by new member sessions that are held before the Congress formally convenes. Both party caucuses organize several days of orientation a few weeks after the election in conjunction with the party sessions that elect leaders and adopt rules for the new Congress. My first trip to Washington as a member-elect and my first encounter with my future colleagues came on

December 1, 1986. We plunged immediately into a series of briefings on everything from ethics to setting up an office to survival techniques for families, as well as the receptions and dinners at which the leaders and prospective leaders of the House welcomed us to Washington.

"The orientation process has emotional ups and downs that compare fully with the campaign," I wrote in a journal I kept during the early weeks of the 100th Congress. "Most new members seem to come in with euphoria from election night still lingering, full of campaign stories. But a sense of relief and satisfaction at simply being here quickly becomes mixed with anxiety about all there is to be done and about one's own status in the unfolding order of things." The new member comes from the electoral arena into another arena, which is equally political and equally challenging, though not identical in the skills it requires or the behavior it rewards—the arena of House politics.

After the party-sponsored sessions, most members of our class from both parties then traveled to the Kennedy School of Government at Harvard University for a week of lectures and discussion focused on major issues. Many in my class also took advantage of a supplementary orientation, held in Williamsburg in January, that was organized by the Brookings Institution, the American Enterprise Institute, and the Congressional Research Service of the Library of Congress. I found these sessions very rewarding. They furnished a common background on various issues and an introduction to the workings of Congress—far preferable to being left to just sink or swim after the formal session begins. The orientation weeks also helped establish a strong bond among members of the entering class, an easy accessibility and familiarity that would be replicated more slowly and irregularly as we took our place among our seniors in the House.

The orientation process had its ups and downs in later years, as the confrontational style associated with Newt Gingrich took hold among House Republicans. Some Republicans began complaining that the Kennedy School sessions did not give sufficient weight to conservative views, and with their encouragement the Heritage Foundation in 1992 began offering an alternative orientation that abandoned any pretext of ideological balance. The Republican class of 1994 withheld participation from the Kennedy School program, forcing its cancellation, and went en masse to the Heritage orientation, the highlight of which was a dinner speech by radio talk show host Rush Limbaugh. By the time I returned with the class of 1996, the Kennedy School had worked with Republican leaders to reinstate a bipartisan program, which thirty-two Democrats and only six Republicans attended. Although I did not go to Harvard and participated only selectively in other orientation activities, I was struck by how much more limited the early contacts across party lines were than those I had experienced ten years before. That is a regrettable loss, both for individual members and for the institution.

The classes I entered with in 1987 and 1997 were both relatively small and politically diverse. I was one of the few in both groups who had defeated an incumbent; most had been elected to open seats (i.e., seats without incumbents) on the basis of factors peculiar to their districts. In 1996 I was part of a modest Democratic trend reducing the Republicans' margin of control. But in most respects the cohorts of 1986 and 1996 contrasted with such large, landmark classes as the post-Watergate influx of 1974 (with its reform-minded Democrats who immediately began rewriting House rules and deposing aged and unpopular committee chairmen) and the 1994 class of "revolutionary" Republicans. Our classes were not totally conventional; the 1986 group, for example, contained such well-known personalities as civil rights hero John Lewis (D-Georgia), basketball star Tom McMillen (D-Maryland), and Fred Grandy (R-Iowa) from television's *Love Boat*. But both groups included relatively large numbers of experienced politicians and few who had simply ridden a national tide to victory.

As our 1986 class entered the House, there was a relatively quiet changing of the guard in House leadership. Majority leader Jim Wright of Texas was not challenged in his race for the speakership, and neither was Tom Foley of Washington in his move from majority whip to majority leader. In the only contested leadership race, Tony Coelho (D-California), to whom many members felt indebted by virtue of his energetic chairmanship of the Democratic Congressional Campaign Committee, defeated two other contenders for the post of majority whip. Coelho was beginning his fifth term; his selection, like the reelection of sixth-termer Dick Gephardt of Missouri to head the Democratic Caucus, showed how accessible the leadership ranks had become to aggressive younger members.

The only contest that put new members on the spot was a challenge to Armed Services chairman Les Aspin (D-Wisconsin). I wrote in my journal of feeling that we "had walked into a blood feud," the background of which we barely understood. Like most freshmen, I was singled out for intense conversations by Aspin and each of his three rivals; one Steering and Policy Committee member even tied his willingness to help me obtain my preferred committee assignments to a vote for one of the challengers. But such heavy-handedness was exceptional. I chose to keep my own counsel in the race, seeing little to be gained by declaring for one candidate or the other, and I never suffered any ill effects of which I was aware. As it turned out, Aspin's critics had enough support to force a vote in the caucus but not enough to put a majority behind any one of his opponents.

In 1996 there were even fewer intraparty contests, partly because we Democrats were now in the minority and the stakes were lower. This time I

worked actively to elect my friend John Spratt (D-South Carolina) as ranking Democrat on the Budget Committee. Henry Gonzalez (D-Texas), the
aging, increasingly erratic ranking Democrat on the Banking Committee,
managed to fend off a challenge to his leadership. The 1994 electoral upheaval had produced the defeat of Speaker Tom Foley in Washington State,
but otherwise House Democrats had kept their top leadership team in
place. These jobs were uncontested in 1996: Gephardt for minority leader,
Dave Bonior (D-Michigan) for minority whip, and Vic Fazio (D-California)
for caucus chair. Interestingly, this top leadership team was considerably
more senior than that chosen in 1986, although the creation of several additional deputy whip positions made room for less senior and more ethni-
cally diverse members in leadership ranks.

Setting Up Shop

My experience in Senator Bartlett's office, where the needs of Alaskans
were attended to very carefully, impressed on me the importance of having a competent, energetic staff and a well-managed office.[3] I learned the
same lesson in a less positive way through campaign experiences with a
couple of senators who had reputations for poor constituent services and
slack staff operations—reputations that proved hard to shake and very
damaging politically. I therefore devoted a great deal of time to staffing
decisions in the three months following my election.

I decided to ask my campaign manager, Michelle Smith, who also had
some Hill experience, to come to Washington as my administrative assistant (chief of staff). She and I were given a tiny cubicle in which to interview prospective aides and handle calls and letters until permanent office
space could be assigned. We immediately confronted thousands of pieces
of mail that had accumulated since the election, with no possible way of
responding until mid-January. But two items—requests for me to back an
American Airlines application for a London gateway from Raleigh-
Durham Airport and letters opposing the start-up of a nuclear power
plant in my district—had arrived in such volume that we decided to use
an outside mail house to send these responses before we set up our office.
Unfortunately the mail house confused the two lists, sending several
hundred power plant responses to people who had written about the airport! Consequently we were more than ready to get our own house in order when the day finally came to move into my assigned office.

Freshmen are at the bottom of the list when it comes to selecting offices,
but I didn't do too badly in the drawing to determine the order in which
we new members would choose. I ended up in the Longworth House Of-

fice Building, the middle of the three House office buildings in terms of location and age. The main drawback of my office was that its three rooms were not adjacent; the third room was an annex on another floor. I had to live with this deficiency until I was able to choose another office at the beginning of my third term.

I deployed my staff in a fashion that has become rather common in the House, setting up several district offices and locating most constituent service functions there. The main district office in Raleigh included a district manager, two field representatives, two casework specialists to assist constituents in dealing with federal agencies, and two persons who alternated between receptionist and clerical duties. We also established one-person constituent service offices in Asheboro and Chapel Hill.

In Washington, I recruited Gene Conti, a longtime friend who had worked for eight years at the Office of Management and Budget and the Treasury Department, as legislative director. He became chief of staff after Michelle Smith left to attend law school. I also named an office manager, who oversaw everything from computer operations to my personal schedule; an assistant legislative director, who helped me handle committee work; a press secretary; a computer operator; a receptionist; and three legislative assistants, who covered specific projects but mainly helped us cope with the flood of mail on pending issues.

My allowance for staff salaries in 1987 was just over $400,000. I was well aware of the need to hire relatively senior people with Washington experience for the top positions. For most other staff positions I hired younger people hoping to gain in experience and exposure what I couldn't pay them in dollars. Some came to the congressional staff from the campaign staff, and most had helped in some fashion with the campaign. Although I did not make it an absolute condition, every staff member, as it developed, had some past or present North Carolina connection.

My appointment to the Appropriations Committee in 1991 required a major reorganization of staff responsibilities. It also entitled me to an additional allowance for staff, which I used to add a slot and also, for the first time in four years, to give the staff decent raises in pay. My fourth term brought further changes as I gained enough seniority to move into the Rayburn Building, an early-1960s behemoth that is the least attractive of the three House office buildings externally but has larger suites that are more easily outfitted with modern equipment. I obtained an appointment to the Budget Committee in addition to Appropriations, which brought with it another increase in my staff allowance. Gene Conti, whose background was in budgeting, took on the budget duties himself. Eventually (few appointments were made quickly in the Clinton administration) he left to become Deput Assistant Secretary of Transportation for budget. His duties as chief of staff were assumed by my longtime legislative director, Paul Feldman, with whom I had worked since he joined my first campaign as a gradate student at Duke.

I had remarkably little staff turnover during my first four terms, but after my 1994 loss, staff members moved, retired, or took other positions. Although I was able to bring back several key staff members when I returned to the House in 1997, three-fourths of my staff was new. As chief of staff I chose Billy Moore, who had held that position for Jim Chapman (D-Texas), a colleague from the class of 1986 who had just retired. I brought eight people onto the Washington and district staffs who had proved their mettle during the 1996 campaign. My seniority (I was considered a fifth-term member for purposes of office selection) still entitled me to a Rayburn suite, but my Appropriations slot no longer brought with it any additional staff allowances. The Republicans, on assuming control of the House in 1995, had eliminated the second of the add-on staff positions for appropriators, which was a reasonable cost-cutting move. But they had also denied the first add-on staff position to those on the bottom third of the committee's seniority ladder, which did not make sense, since those were the members who had least access to subcommittee staff and thus needed extra help the most.

With the advent of the 106th Congress (1999–2000), I advanced far enough up the Appropriations ladder to again obtain a staff allowance, and my reappointment to the Budget Committee produced an additional increment. This made it possible for me to offer better compensation to my three senior staff members who were doing appropriations and budget work. I also added a district office in Durham, retaining the aide who had run the office for Rep. Mel Watt when Durham was in his district. When Billy Moore left for the private sector after the 2000 election, I asked Jean-Louise Beard, who had worked her way up from computer operator to senior appropriations aide, to succeed him as chief of staff.

Overall, my staff of seventeen full-time members and one half-time member is about the same size as the one I had in 1987, but it is more experienced, better compensated, and far more focused on appropriations issues. The caseload in the district offices has grown larger and more diverse in ways I will later describe (Chapter 10). We have tried to maintain an ethic of responsiveness to constituents in dealing with legislative inquiries as well as casework and have utilized an annual retreat, regular staff meetings, weekly reports, and other devices to foster accountability and communication among our four offices. At our 1999 retreat we formalized a "mission statement" that encapsulates the goals that successive chiefs of staff and I have pursued through eight terms:

- I want to help build a community—in North Carolina and the nation—where people have a sense of expanding opportunity and common purpose, nurtured in high-quality schools, safe neighborhoods, good housing, accessible health care, and security for old age.
- I want to help make government an instrument of our common purpose by being an activist legislator, encouraging staff entrepreneurship, developing and pushing clear funding priorities, actively engaging my constituents, advocating for those who need help, and conducting myself and running our office in a way that builds confidence and solidifies support.

Family and Career

As my wife and I first weighed the decision to run, we talked with two couples, who described the quite different ways they coped with the demands congressional life placed on their families. One family lived in Washington, and the member made sporadic weekend trips back to the district; the other family lived in the district, to which the member returned every weekend. Although each couple claimed that their arrangement worked satisfactorily and though we knew that roughly equal numbers of members chose each pattern, we never doubted what would be best for us: to keep our main residence in Chapel Hill. This decision spared us the rigors of the Washington real estate market and the family upheavals attendant on moving. I rented an apartment on Capitol Hill, walked to work, and settled into a pattern of heading for the airport after the final vote was taken on the House floor each week, usually late on Thursday afternoon.

We chose this option partly because of the easy commute—two hours and fifteen minutes door to door, with several nonstop flights each day—and because my political situation required maximizing my presence in the district. It also suited our family situation, since a move would be difficult for our teenage children. Although relocating to the Washington area would have been relatively comfortable for my wife, who grew up there, she preferred the idea of frequent visits to the capital rather than moving our primary residence there. As it turned out, the visits were not frequent, thanks to the soaring cost of airline tickets and to my wife's demanding jobs, first as assistant to the mayor of Chapel Hill and then as executive director of North Carolinians Against Gun Violence.

The fact that we already were familiar with Washington and had a number of friends in the area made our decision easier, for we had less to lose by not electing to live there. We have missed out on a certain amount of social and family contact with my colleagues. But even members who live in Washington travel to their districts frequently, and there is far less weekend socializing than there used to be. And the wear and tear of weekly commuting is not overwhelming, once a routine is established. In fact, I have found that compartmentalizing my life works rather well. When I am in Washington, usually on Tuesday through Thursday or Friday, I generally work fifteen-hour days, staying at my office into the night. But when I head for home, I concentrate on district matters and family life. I can't imagine that it would work as well in reverse: dragging home late when Congress is in session and then heading for North Carolina on the weekends, leaving the family behind. But these are highly personal decisions, and if our children had been at a different stage or if my commute had required multiple connecting flights, the options might have looked very different.

Becoming a member of the House also alters the roles and routines associated with one's previous career. I took a special interest, naturally, in Fenno's interview with a freshman senator who had been a college professor. "Life in the Senate," he said, "is the antithesis of academic life."[4] I would not put it quite that way, since this viewpoint exaggerates the orderliness and tranquillity of modern academic life and underestimates the extent to which one can impose a modicum of order on life in the Congress. Still, few jobs present as many diverse and competing demands as does service in Congress.

Consider, for example, my schedule for three rather typical days at the end of March 2004, reprinted here with the deletion of some individual names and the addition of few explanatory notes (Table 4.1). This was at a time of the year when appropriations hearings were in full swing and many groups in North Carolina, ranging from postal supervisors and insurance agents to doctors, health research advocates, and soybean growers, were making their annual visits to Washington, generally in conjunction with meetings of their national associations. I began the week with a visit to a corporate research facility in Research Triangle Park and flew to Washington a few hours earlier than usual to attend the Enlarging Ceremony at the White House for new NATO members. The week's party meetings included one of the minority leader's periodic lunches for caucus members, the regular Democratic Caucus and whips meetings on Wednesday and Thursday morning respectively, and a dinner discussion organized by Steering and Policy Committee cochair Rosa DeLauro (D-Connecticut). I presided over the weekly meeting of the Democratic Budget Group and then dropped by an Aspen Institute breakfast to discuss the No Child Left Behind education program; that same topic was the focus of a luncheon the North Carolina State Board of Education organized and asked our delegation to attend.

TABLE 4.1   Typical Member's Daily Schedule

Monday, March 29

9:30 A.M.	Meet with North Carolina Farm Credit representatives
10:30	Plant Tour, BASF Plant Science Center, Research Triangle Park
1:30 P.M.	Flight to Washington
2:45	Meet briefly with several members of the North Carolina Chapter of the National Association of Postal Supervisors
3:40	Attend NATO Enlarging Ceremony on the White House South Lawn, welcoming seven former Soviet-bloc states
4:45	Meet with North Carolina representatives of the National Association of Health Underwriters
6:30	Votes on House floor

Tuesday, March 30

10:00 A.M.	Homeland Security Appropriations Subcommittee hearing: Under Secretary for Science and Technology, Dr. Charles McQuery
11:30	Meet with son of constituent to discuss job opportunities on the Hill
1:00 P.M.	"Leader's Lunch" with minority leader, Nancy Pelosi, for members
2:15	Meet with NC members of the Parkinson's Action Network
2:45	Meet with members of the N.C. Soybean Growers' Association.
3:00	Meet with NC members of the Communications Workers of America
3:30	Meet with members of the North Carolina Medical Society
4:00	Meet with six members of the American Chamber of Commerce in Egypt
4:30	Meet with Dr. Amitai Etzioni on possible Communitarian Network forum
6:30	Receptions: Communication Workers of America, Rep. Gene Taylor

Wednesday, March 31

8:00 A.M.	Democratic Budget Group with Democratic Budget Committee staff substituting for Sen. Kent Conrad. Topic: GOP Budget Resolution
8:30	Aspen Breakfast: Katie Haycock of Children's Defense Fund on implementation of "No Child Left Behind" legislation
9:00	Democratic Caucus
10:00	Homeland Security Appropriations Subcommittee hearing: Admiral Thomas Collins, commandant of the United States Coast Guard
11:00	Meet briefly with student representative from UNC Dental School
11:15	VA-HUD Subcommittee hearing: Secretary of Veterans Affairs Anthony J. Principi
12:00 P.M.	State Board of Education luncheon with North Carolina Delegation
1:00	Continue VA-HUD Subcommittee hearing: Veterans Affairs
3:00	Meet with employees of member firms of the American Electronics Association, including Cree in Durham
3:30	Meet with a young physician at Duke, here for the American Medical Association's legislative conference
4:00	Meet with representatives of the Association Executives of NC
5:30	Speak on budget on House floor during Special Orders
7:30	Dinner for Caucus members at the home of Rep. Rosa DeLauro with David Cay Johnston, author of *Perfectly Legal*

Appropriations Subcommittee hearings involved key officials and required considerable time and attention, as did my steady, sometimes overlapping, schedule of meetings with North Carolina groups. And the schedule does not capture the numerous trips to the House floor for votes, the phone calls, and the media interviews and staff conferences scattered throughout the day.

This schedule lists only events I actually attended; others were covered by staff when I was detained in hearings or when roll call votes were called on the House floor. The schedule also reflects the general rules my staff and I follow to keep life from getting even more hectic. In general, I talk with groups about pending legislation only when there is a North Carolina connection; most Washington groups are well aware that their delegations need to include at least one representative from the district. I also generally skip receptions at the end of the day unless constituents will be there or a colleague asks me to attend.

This sheer busyness in Washington, as well as at home (see Chapter 10), surpasses what almost all members experienced in their previous careers and requires specific survival techniques. Most important, you must set priorities—separate matters in which you want to invest considerable time and energy from those you wish to handle perfunctorily or not deal with personally.[5] Confronted with two or three simultaneous subcommittee hearings, a member often has a choice: pop in on each of them for fifteen minutes or choose one and remain long enough to learn and contribute something. It is also essential to delegate a great deal to staff and to develop a good mutual understanding within the office about what requires the member's personal direction and attention. But there are no management techniques that can make a representative's life totally predictable or controllable or can convert a congressional office into a tidy bureaucracy. A member (or aide) who requires that kind of control—who cannot tolerate, for example, being diverted to talk to a visiting school class or to hear out a visiting delegation of homebuilders or social workers—is in the wrong line of work.[6]

My previous career has influenced my adaptation as a member of Congress in many ways. Certainly my previous study and staff experience helped me undertake specific policy initiatives (which I will describe in Chapter 6). I naturally gravitated toward education and research issues, and felt well equipped by both background and temperament for the work on the Appropriations and Budget Committees. Stylistically I have been fastidious about what goes out of the office under my name. I spend far more time than the average member reviewing and editing mail, and I have found it difficult to delegate speechwriting to staff. I tell myself that much of this personal attention is required by the remarkable volume, diversity, and erudition of the correspondence that my district produces. But the habits and standards (and the streak of compulsiveness) I developed during my years in academic life also play an important role.

My background also has predisposed me toward an activist, but selective and specialized, legislative style. Speaker Sam Rayburn used to distinguish "show horses" from "workhorses" in the House, while expressing his clear preference for the latter. Today, the norms of specialization, apprenticeship, and deference that once held show horse behavior in check have weakened considerably, and even self-effacing workhorses must pay more attention to courting the media and building public support. But the rough stylistic distinction still holds, and the workhorse label is one that most Appropriations members would claim for themselves and would apply to the committee.[7] This has been my own preferred style. There is still something of the student in me, with an urge to master the assignment at hand, and the committee system continues to encourage and reward this sort of behavior. In my early terms, I concentrated on a limited number of initiatives, mostly in my committee areas, on which I could work in a concerted fashion. This was a sensible strategy for a junior member, but it also stemmed from my preference, rooted in prior experience, to focus on a manageable number of projects and operate from a substantial base of knowledge. I gradually became more involved in efforts to pass or amend bills from outside my committee areas on the House floor. But most of my work in recent years, in addressing both district needs and national priorities, has been channeled through the Appropriations Committee where, most of the time, value is still placed on the workhorse virtues of careful preparation, practicality, and a spirit of accommodation.

For many members, the transition from the campaign trail to congressional life is as jolting as any career change.[8] I found the shift emotionally dramatic but not especially problematic. Some of the issues I highlighted in my first campaign led to specific legislative initiatives. I proposed, for example, to repeal the requirement for a second national repository for high-level waste in the Nuclear Waste Policy Act (my district had been identified as a possible site for this repository). The continuity was stronger in later campaigns, after I secured committee assignments that let me pursue initiatives in housing, education, research, and transportation, and developed a legislative record to talk about. My campaign experience (recall that my ads made a great deal of Bill Cobey's isolation on key votes from both Democrats and Republicans in the North Carolina delegation) made me more sensitive to the few instances when I later found myself voting with a small minority. I never got myself into binds as some of my colleagues did when, in the course of their campaigns, they got pressed into taking "the pledge" to never, ever raise anyone's taxes. But, especially as Tom Fetzer's campaign was warming up, I was wary of votes that might be construed as reversals of position or might provide material for thirty-second ads. I have gradually gotten more relaxed about this, realizing that no amount of caution can prevent an opponent's media consultants from finding something on which to base an outrageous ad, that most of these ads can be effectively countered, and that it is simply intolerable to have one's life and work dominated by memories of the last (or fears of the next) campaign.

I will argue in this book's final chapter that a deep and dangerous gap has opened up between campaigning and governing in our country—a gap that inspires public cynicism and threatens democratic accountability. My experience with "hot-button" attack politics in North Carolina and my decrying of its irrelevance to the "real problems of real people" over the years have made me especially concerned to maintain the continuity between what I say in campaigns and what I do as a House member. But there will always be a certain tension between campaigning and governing, and that tension can be positive and productive, as well as distracting and debilitating. For me, the move from academic life into a congressional campaign was as great an adjustment as moving from the campaign to Congress. I have found that certain instincts and sensitivities bred in campaigns are of continuing use in the Congress, sometimes acting as a counterweight to my inclination simply to do a workmanlike job on the task before me. Traditional congressional norms, reinforced in my case by my career background, encourage members to choose a few matters for specialization and to work persistently, mainly out of the limelight, to shape policy or obtain funding in these areas. But constituents expect their representatives to be their voices and votes on the full range of governmental matters, and members cannot realistically expect constituents to understand and appreciate their policymaking efforts if they do not make the effort to interpret, even dramatize, them. In these respects, the sensitivities and skills acquired in the campaign are of continuing relevance.

That, at least, is the way it has worked for me. My background in teaching and research has proved serviceable in many ways. Fortunately for me, I was forced out of those routines for a demanding twenty-month campaign and developed the broad-gauged knowledge of national issues, the sensitivity to constituency needs and views, and the ability to communicate that was required by that effort. This does not mean that I want or need a John Carrington throwing $900,000 at me every two years! But I believe that, for much of what the contemporary member of Congress needs to do, the experience and exposure offered by recurring campaigns, far from being diversions, are absolutely essential.

Notes

1. Richard F. Fenno Jr., "Adjusting to the U.S. Senate," in Gerald C. Wright Jr., Leroy N. Rieselbach, and Lawrence C. Dodd, eds., *Congress and Policy Change* (New York: Agathon, 1986), p. 142.

2. Fenno, "Adjusting to the U.S. Senate," p. 123.

3. A 1990 survey found that fifty-four House members and fourteen senators had earlier served on congressional staffs. "One Out of Eight Sitting Members Was Once a Staffer, Survey by Roll Call Finds," *Roll Call*, May 28, 1990, p. 3.

4. Fenno, "Adjusting to the Senate," p. 126.

5. On this point, Fenno's ex-professor seems to agree: "You need to establish a set of priorities. . . . Don't let yourself be a piece of cloth pulled at from every side. Don't let yourself unravel." "Adjusting to the U.S. Senate," p. 128.

6. Presumably it would not suit journalist Fred Barnes, who, in a profile of John Hiler (R-Indiana), concluded that "the daily routine of House members is mindlessly hectic and stupefyingly dull." See Barnes, "The Unbearable Lightness of Being a Congressman," *The New Republic*, February 15, 1988, p. 19. Barnes provided an enlightening account of Hiler's schedule in Washington and at home, but it was apparently beyond his comprehension that a member could find visiting a local nursing home or addressing Jaycees interesting or worthwhile. Barnes is not alone in this attitude among Washington-based journalists; his amazement is shared, for example, by George Will in his account of the retirement of Don Pease (D-Ohio): "A Good Job Gone," *Washington Post*, national weekly ed., November 25, 1991, p. 29.

7. For an attempt to operationalize the show horse–workhorse typologies and discuss the conditions of their occurrence, see James L. Payne, "Show Horses and Work Horses in the United States House of Representatives," *Polity*, Spring 1980, pp. 428–456. Payne found that the orientations are indeed distinctive, with few members ranking high on both "legislative work" and "publicity" indexes. He also found evidence that "being a show horse pays off electorally" and is far less costly than it once was in terms of advancement within the House.

8. One of Fenno's senators, for example, was having trouble settling down to work in Washington. Having stressed in his campaign that his opponent had lost touch with home, he now lived in mortal fear that the same would be said about him. Therefore he continued "immersing himself in his home state and avoiding the work of the Senate." See Fenno, "Adjusting to the U.S. Senate," pp. 130–131.

5

Finding a Niche

My first extended conversation with the new Speaker of the House, Jim Wright, occurred during orientation week, one month after the 1986 election. We met to discuss committee assignments. Although U.S. House committees neither enjoy the autonomy nor receive the deference they did thirty years ago, they are still quite powerful relative to the status of committees in most of the world's legislative bodies. The legislative division of labor in the House follows the lines of standing committee jurisdictions, and committee assignments largely determine the focus of a member's legislative and oversight efforts.

I understood the importance of being assigned to desirable committees, and I knew how much the new Speaker was likely to have to do with that decision. One of the critical House reforms of the 1970s removed the committee assignment function for Democrats from the Democratic members of the Ways and Means Committee, where it had resided since 1911, and placed it in the party's Steering and Policy Committee. That committee had thirty-three members in 1986, including the Speaker and other top party leaders, twelve representatives elected by the regional party caucuses, and eight at-large members appointed by the Speaker. This arrangement obviously enhanced the leadership's role in committee assignments—depending in part on how forceful the Speaker was in making his preferences known. Those who knew Jim Wright expected him to be forceful indeed.

Wright had visited my district once during the campaign. My memory of the visit related mainly to the relief I felt when it was over. Wright's staff had told us on very short notice that he would be coming on a Saturday afternoon, when, as luck would have it, both the University of North Carolina and North Carolina State had home football games. Our thought, in throwing together a fund-raising barbecue, was less of the money we could raise than of how we could get enough people together to convince our guest we were not dying on the vine. This we barely were able to do. Unfortunately Wright punctured his leg on a wire protruding from the seat of my station wagon as I drove him to the airport. My embarrassment exceeded his injury, but it was the kind of day that seems much funnier in retrospect than it did at the time.

Memories of this encounter notwithstanding, Wright was cordial but non-committal about my prospects when we met in Washington in December 1986. I approached the conversation with some trepidation. I knew better than to request one of the three "exclusive" committees—Appropriations, Ways and Means, and Rules, termed exclusive because their members were required to drop all other standing committee assignments—for they were virtually off-limits to first-term members. There is intense competition for these powerful positions, and party and committee leaders ordinarily wish to take the measure of a member before placing him or her in such a critical spot. A story had circulated among our class about a freshman who had been filmed for a television feature as he made his initial rounds. He had told Speaker O'Neill of his desire to be appointed to Appropriations, Ways and Means, or Rules, and the camera had caught the Speaker as his eyes rolled heavenward. So I knew what not to request. But the assignment I most wanted—to the Energy and Commerce Committee—also seemed likely to be out of reach, and I was uncertain how hard to press my case before falling back on a second choice.

I had a particular personal interest in Energy and Commerce. My time with Senator Bartlett had involved extensive work with the Senate Commerce Committee, of which he was a senior member, and my academic work had included a general study of both the House and Senate Commerce Committees and an examination of the House Committee's oversight role.[1] The Energy and Commerce Committee, moreover, had an exceedingly broad jurisdiction—health, communications, energy, the environment, consumer protection, transportation, and securities and exchanges—much of it vitally important to North Carolina and to my district in particular. Former North Carolina representatives James Broyhill, a Republican, and Richardson Preyer, a Democrat, had risen to ranking positions on the committee, but by 1987 the state had no Energy and Commerce member and had not had a Democratic member for six years.

My problem was that Energy and Commerce had become almost as sought after as the exclusive committees by virtue of the increasing salience of its jurisdiction and the success of its chairman, John Dingell (D-Michigan), in carving out an assertive and expansive role for it. (In fact, it was designated an exclusive committee by the Democratic leadership a few years later.) When I began to talk with party leaders about my committee assignment possibilities, I was advised to push (up to a point) for Energy and Commerce. My state's needs and my own credentials were unusually strong, and even if I did not make it, I could leave a powerful impression for possible future reference. But I was also advised that many second- and third-term members would be putting in strong bids and that I should be prepared to indicate a backup choice. If I held out too long, I was cautioned, I might end up without any desirable alternative.

I received no encouragement from Wright, suggesting that the rumors were probably true that he and Chairman Dingell, who was also on the Steering and Policy Committee, were prepared to endorse three members, none of whom was a freshman, for the available Energy and Commerce slots. At the same time, I was disconcerted to see that some other freshmen still seemed to regard Energy and Commerce as a good possibility; I wondered what Wright had told them that he had not told me. (None of them, however, ended up getting the assignment.) I decided it was time to shift to plan B, to settle on a realistic backup choice and let my alternative preferences be known.

Banking, Science, and Small Business

Although I was not initially drawn to the Banking Committee, after looking at the available alternatives and how they fit my own interests and the state's needs, I concluded that it was the most attractive backup possibility. North Carolina is a major banking state, and the committee seemed poised to tackle important banking issues in the 100th Congress. The committee also is responsible for housing policy, an area in which I had some experience and considerable interest. In addition, I decided that the most desirable choice by far as my second or "nonmajor" committee would be Science, Space, and Technology, a panel of obvious importance to the educational institutions and research enterprises of central North Carolina.

I, like most new representatives, called on the Steering and Policy Committee members one by one. It was not clear to what extent Wright would try to call the shots for assignments beyond the exclusive committees, Budget, and Energy and Commerce. For many of the remaining committees, the leadership might have no overriding preference and, in any case, leadership control was not absolute. So freshmen seemed well advised to seek out Steering and Policy members, to get acquainted and make as strong a case as possible for suitable assignments.

My regional representative on Steering and Policy, Butler Derrick of South Carolina, agreed to nominate me for the Banking and Science vacancies. On the day of the meeting, I anxiously awaited his call, having finished my round of visits without a sure sense of how I would fare. As it turned out, I received both assignments but by a rather circuitous route. The initial balloting for Banking slots was complicated by the late entry of members who had missed out on other assignments, and I failed to obtain a seat by one vote. Then I was the first member chosen for the available seats on Science, no doubt as a consolation prize. But two additional Banking slots were later added as part of an agreement with the Republicans, and I obtained one of them.

Some weeks later, after all assignments had been made, I was offered a temporary, one-term assignment on a second nonmajor committee, Small Business, presumably because the leadership saw this committee as relevant to my district and felt that such an assignment might enhance my reelection prospects. I accepted the post eagerly, for Small Business was a possibility to which I had been drawn from the beginning.

These three assignments—Banking, Science, and Small Business—were as strong a combination as I could realistically have hoped for, and I made good use of each one. The Banking Committee presented the greatest challenge in several respects: the complexity of its subject matter; the number of major policy questions on the agenda; the intricacy of committee politics, both internally and in relation to outside groups; the depth of its leadership difficulties, which continued despite a change in committee chairs in 1989; and, increasingly, the political perils associated with the policies under its care, especially savings and loan (S&L) regulation. To my surprise, however, the Banking Committee proved most amenable to my own legislative projects. In my first term, I concentrated on sponsorship of a consumer protection bill, the Home Equity Loan Consumer Protection Act. In my second term, I took a more active hand in the committee's two major legislative efforts, the S&L reform bill and the 1990 housing bill, adding several of my own amendments to each. I will describe some of these initiatives in the next chapter.

The Science and Small Business Committees are less torn by conflicting interests than is Banking. Their histories feature promotion and advocacy for American scientific leadership and the well-being of small businesses, respectively. These missions have often attracted like-minded members to the committees and helped mute partisan conflict. Especially on the Science Committee, however, this tradition of advocacy began in the 1980s to run up against the painful choices necessitated by budget constraint. The space station, the ill-fated superconducting supercollider, healthy National Science Foundation budgets—the Science Committee historically and often effectively had said, "We want it all." The trade-offs were difficult to make, and as the committee faced the necessity of setting priorities, its bipartisan promotional consensus came under increasing strain.

On both Science and Small Business, I concentrated initially on securing compatible subcommittee assignments, preferably under young, aggressive subcommittee chairmen who would pursue an expansive agenda and would welcome my participation. Such criteria are often more important than the subcommittee's precise jurisdiction, for the subject matter lines are rather ill defined and an aggressive chairman generally has wide latitude in exploring policy questions of interest. For example, I was able to secure the cooperation of Chairman Doug Walgren (D-Pennsylvania) in bringing our Science, Research, and Technology Subcommittee to my district for a day of hearings on workplace literacy—examining the knowledge and skills required in the high-tech workplace. I then used the subcommittee as a base for developing a legislative proposal to improve curricula and teaching methods in science, mathematics, and advanced technical training in community colleges (see Chapter 6).

I also made good use of the one-term Small Business assignment. The full committee held hearings in my district on government and military procurement, asking how small and local businesses could be included in that process more effectively, and I used my committee position to help secure a full-time Small Business Administration procurement officer for the state. Representative Dennis Eckart's (D-Ohio) Antitrust Subcommittee also came to the district, exploring the availability and costs of liability insurance for small businesses.

Such experiences confirmed the compatibility of my committee assignments with my own policy interests and the needs and concerns of my district. But such compatibility is not always self-evident; considerable effort and initiative are required to ensure that the fit is a good one and results in productive activity.

Pursuing Appropriations

Although I was reasonably content with my committee assignments, I hoped to move to one of the more powerful and prestigious panels early in my career. This would let me accumulate seniority on the new panel and avoid giving up a great deal of seniority on Banking and Science. At first I saw Energy and Commerce as my most likely move, but I gradually began to shift my sights to Appropriations.

Energy and Commerce was still appealing and North Carolina needed majority representation there. But in 1989 a Republican from our state delegation, Alex McMillan was appointed, curtailing the urgings from constituency and other groups for me to seek an appointment. And the case I could make to Steering and Policy Committee members for regional equity became weaker after two Democrats from our four-state Steering and Policy region were appointed to Energy and Commerce.

The main reason for my change, however, was that Appropriations, which had not been a possibility for me as a freshman, was simply a more attractive assignment. With its control over the federal government's discretionary expenditures, Appropriations has far more power than any other committee in shaping and setting priorities for federal activity, although its power is constrained by the budget process and by pressure to keep the budget deficit under control. But in a time of scarcity and constraint, it is all the more important to have a seat at the table when the spending decisions are made.

North Carolina already had a senior Appropriations member—Bill Hefner, chairman of the Military Construction Subcommittee. Hefner was an effective inside player many of us depended on for help with district-related projects. But the balance that counts in allocating committee seats is not only among states but also among Steering and Policy regions, and on that basis, my argument was very strong. Although our region—which then included North Carolina, South Carolina, Georgia, and Tennessee—was tied for first in its number of House Democrats, it was one of the few regions with only two Appropriations members (most had three and several had four). Fortunately our regional representative on the Steering and Policy Committee, Butler Derrick, was a forceful advocate, and he promised to help me with whatever committee move I wanted to undertake.

Late in 1988, Derrick, Hefner, and I went to talk with Speaker Jim Wright about my committee assignment prospects. Wright was not inclined to leave Steering and Policy decisions (or much of anything else) to chance, and he had already let it be known that he wanted one of the two Appropriations slots coming open at the beginning of the 101st Congress to go to his fellow Texan, Jim Chapman. (The other was bound to go to the New England region, which would be reduced to one seat with Edward Boland's retirement.) We assured the Speaker that we had no desire to challenge that decision, but we also reminded him of my personal credentials and of our region's underrepresentation and indicated that I would be seeking the next Appropriations seat that came open. Although he said that I could be assured of serious consideration for that slot, he promised nothing more specific.

As it turned out, the next Democratic vacancy occurred in March 1990 when Rep. Daniel Akaka of Hawaii was appointed to the Senate after the death of Sen. Spark Matsunaga. By then, Wright had resigned. Tom Foley, the new Speaker, was less inclined than Wright to dictate Steering and Policy decisions, at least on early midterm appointments like this one. The result was a wide-open race for the seat. I decided to run and run hard, for the race, in addition to providing one new member for Appropriations, was likely to establish a presumption as to who might get future seats, based on a show of strength in this round.

A number of other members saw it the same way, including some who were senior to me (Marcy Kaptur of Ohio, Peter Visclosky of Indiana) and some from my own class (David Skaggs of Colorado, Nancy Pelosi of California). Of the other members considering the race, one who was from my region especially concerned me. A region had recently forfeited an otherwise strong claim to a major committee seat because two members from the region ran, thus giving Steering and Policy members a perfect excuse to vote for neither of them. Thus it was important to establish that I was the candidate who had our region's endorsement. Derrick's vocal backing helped, as did a unanimous letter of support I secured from the Georgia delegation. Eventually my potential rival withdrew.

Since the beginning of the 101st Congress, I had been casually visiting with Steering and Policy members, letting them know of my eventual interest in whatever opened up on Appropriations. Now I greatly accelerated that activity. My staff and I kept records of each contact, distinguishing among those promising first-ballot support, those promising later-ballot support if their preferred candidate was eliminated, and those merely expressing good wishes. Individuals in the latter group ranged from one supporter of a rival who assured me he had "nothing against me" and seemed to think I should be relieved to hear it, to some who were genuinely uncommitted. I asked a number of colleagues to speak on my behalf to Steering and Policy members whom they knew well, and in several instances this helped produce commitments. What I did not do was ask any person or group outside the House to intercede on my behalf. Most members consider Steering and Policy deliberations, like leadership contests, to be an internal affair, and outside entreaties might well hurt more than help.

Kaptur won the vacant seat. Although she was not a leadership favorite, she benefited from a concerted effort by Midwestern members (anticipating a loss of seats in the 1991 reapportionment) to shore up their representation. In addition, Jim Wright had given her a promise that was allegedly more specific than the ones he had given to me and others (this swayed mainly the Texas members). And there was the fact that Appropriations contained few women. It was a close contest that required four ballots to resolve. My six first-ballot votes were enough to put me in second place, and I held that position throughout, surviving until the last ballot. It was a stronger finish than most had predicted, and I felt encouraged because I had strengthened my position for the next round at the beginning of the 102nd Congress. But I knew that the ground could shift over the coming months and that next time the leadership might do more to shape the decision. I therefore continued to talk to Steering and Policy members, especially the top party leaders. Most of what I heard encouraged me.

Running for Appropriations was an intense and, on the whole, enjoyable experience. I got to know a number of senior members better, and a good deal of camaraderie developed among most of us who were competing. We mostly knew what commitments of support each other had, and what we did not know before the balloting we figured out by comparing notes afterward. Most Steering and Policy members had been careful in what they promised, but for those who had made inconsistent promises to several of us or who had not delivered on their pledges, the secret ballot concealed very little.

Resignations produced two Democratic vacancies on Appropriations for the 102nd Congress, and the slight shift in the balance of party strength in the House produced by the 1990 elections was sufficient to let the leadership add two more Democratic seats (combined with one new seat for the GOP). This resulted in four Democratic vacancies—good news for those of us lining up for the race. The leaders also decided to make their preferences for Appropriations and other top committee assignments known this time, and fortunately I was on the list.

The Steering and Policy decisions were made during the presession organizational meetings in December 1990. Larry Smith (D-Florida), a late entry who was beginning his fifth term, led the balloting. I was second, followed by Pelosi and Skaggs. Visclosky fell short with a fifth-place finish, but the leaders promised him their support for the next vacancy to occur. It was therefore a happy outcome, accommodating all of us who had made a serious run for the midterm vacancy. Having survived a rougher than expected 1990 reelection contest, I was gratified to see this exercise in internal House politics turn out successfully as well. Although I had been working at it for a long time, I realized that I was fortunate to secure an Appropriations seat as early as the beginning of my third term. I was not forfeiting a great deal of seniority on Banking or Science, and I was getting on the all-important seniority ladder on Appropriations at a relatively early point, in advance of a number of anticipated 1992 retirements.

I nonetheless gave up the Banking and Science assignments with mixed feelings. Appropriations would offer more influence on a broader range of policies, but the initiatives I could take would be less visible and more incremental in nature. During my first two terms, I had been able to use committee hearings, especially the five we held in the district, to publicize issues that needed attention and to involve North Carolinians who had a stake in those issues. I had also steered initiatives in consumer protection, housing, and science education through my committees and on to final

passage. Now I would need to find new channels for working on such issues and for interpreting what I was doing for my constituents. But I
knew that the Appropriations assignment was likely to open far more
doors than it closed. Beyond that, there were certain characteristics of my
former committees that I would not miss at all. This occurred to me force-
fully in February 1991 as the House Banking Committee wrangled over a
bill to authorize additional borrowing by the Resolution Trust Corporation, the agency responsible for the S&L cleanup. The committee spent
eight hours loading the bill down with amendments, only to defeat the
measure at the end of the day. It was a good time, Nancy Pelosi and I
agreed, to have left the Banking Committee!

Most appropriations work is done in subcommittees, and senior members jealously guard their positions on these panels, for subcommittee
chairmanships on the Democratic side (Republicans have different procedures) are based on subcommittee, rather than full committee, seniority.
The subcommittees are kept small—most contained ten members in the
102nd Congress—and members are allowed to lock in or "grandfather"
two of their previous subcommittee assignments as each new Congress
begins. At first, it seemed that the four new Democratic members, myself
included, might have very little to choose from because subcommittee
chairs resisted enlarging their panels and a new Democratic slot was
added only to two subcommittees, Defense and Agriculture. But the
availability of the Defense slot induced a middle-ranking member to give
up his grandfathered rights in order to claim it. This set up a chain reaction down the seniority ladder, with each new member being assigned to
at least one of the more sought after subcommittees.

The other new members and I gathered all the information we could
and carefully plotted how the bidding for slots was likely to go. My first
choice was the Subcommittee on Veterans Affairs, Housing and Urban
Development, and Independent Agencies (VA-HUD), which appropriated in both the housing and National Science Foundation areas where I
had worked hardest for the past four years. Higher-ranking committee
members were unlikely to drop their assignments for this vacancy, but
Marcy Kaptur, who ranked just ahead of our group in committee seniority, would likely claim it. As I considered the available vacancies and the
likely preferences of those ahead of me in the order of bidding, it became
clear that I could secure a seat on the Subcommittee on Transportation
and that a seat on Agriculture and Rural Development would still be
available to me in the second round of bidding.

These highly desirable subcommittees allowed me to work on matters
important to my district—airport development, highways, intercity
mass transit planning, agricultural research, nutrition, rural housing—

and put me in a position to broker the interests of other members as well. Additional possibilities opened up in the 103rd Congress: I elected to hold on to the Transportation Subcommittee, where I was gaining seniority rapidly because of retirements, and I picked up a new second subcommittee with an expansive and diverse jurisdiction, Commerce, Justice, State, and Judiciary (C-J-S).

With the support of party and committee leaders, I also gained assignment to one of the Budget Committee seats reserved for Appropriations members. This was one of the few second assignments members of the "exclusive" Appropriations and Ways and Means Committees could hold; the architects of the budget process had provided for such representation as a way of limiting the independence of the Budget Committee. Ways and Means Democrats tended to assign their most senior members to the positions, but Appropriations members could pursue them more freely. I welcomed the assignment as a way of combining macro and micro approaches to the budget—first considering overall fiscal policy in the context of the annual budget resolution, focusing on the economy and the nation as a whole, and then getting down to particular expenditures and policy priorities in the appropriations bills, with a highly specific focus on North Carolina's needs.

Appropriations Regained

When I was contemplating a comeback effort in 1995, I sought and received assurances from the minority leader, Dick Gephardt, as well as other party leaders, that I would be first in line for reappointment to the House Appropriations Committee. I was well aware that my appropriations accomplishments had been devalued in the political context of 1994, when government was demonized and all spending caricatured as "pork barreling." We had filmed an ad touting my achievements for the district but barely ran it. I also watched with dismay as Speaker Gingrich and the Republican leadership pressed the Appropriations Committee into service of the "revolution," demanding deep funding cuts and insisting that legislative riders be included on appropriations bills.[2] This threatened the tradition of bipartisan comity that had given the committee solidarity, credibility, and strength, both in the House and in relation to the executive. But I still felt strongly that Appropriations was where I wanted and needed to be.

I had found Appropriations work challenging and satisfying. Constituents I had worked with on major projects—from the planned Environmental Protection Agency lab in the Research Triangle Park (RTP) to highways and mass transit to numerous research enterprises—were among the first to urge me to run again. And there were good reasons to expect, particularly as the Republican leadership overreached and the political tables turned, that the committee would regain strength. Republican control of the House might not continue. But if it did, Appropriations would still be one of the better places for a minority member to be.

Seven Democratic Appropriations slots were opened up by retirements in 1997, more than enough to accommodate me and the five Democrats who had served a term on the committee in 1993–1994 but had been bumped when the shift in party control reduced the number of Democratic seats. Although the number of vacancies removed any potential conflict between me and the members who had been waiting during the previous Congress to reclaim their seats, it did not resolve a more subtle question: What seniority ranking would we have within the committee? This was important in determining the order in which we would bid for subcommittees. In promising displaced members a speedy return to the committee, party leaders apparently didn't consider the possibility that a member like myself, with four years of committee service compared to two years for the others, might return at the same time.

I naturally argued that my four years should trump their two, and I had strong supporters on the Steering Committee (colleagues whose loyalty I will long remember).[3] But that view did not prevail, so I ended up five slots below where I would have been had I headed the new cohort and eleven slots below my former position.

In the short run, ironically, this situation led to an improved subcommittee assignment. I had assumed that I would get back on Transportation; there were three vacancies, and it seemed likely that one would be left even when the bidding got around to me. But as the bidding proceeded, one member after another chose Transportation, shutting out that possibility. As I anxiously scanned the board to see what alternatives remained, I was astounded to find that a slot on VA-HUD was still available. I claimed it gleefully. This was the subcommittee I had most wanted six years before, and with many district interests in housing, veterans affairs, research, environmental protection, and other policy areas, it was still my best prospect. The Transportation Subcommittee, meanwhile, had been devalued as the money available for specific projects had been cut back, and it was to be devalued further as the Transportation Equity Act of 1998 permanently shifted large areas of transportation funding authority to the authorizing committee. Had a Transportation slot been available to me, I likely would have accepted it, for state and local officials and transportation advocates were counting on my being there. As it turned out, I was freed to take on a new assignment that was ultimately more valuable for me and the state, and I was able to work from the full committee, with the help of friends who remained on Transportation, to fund key transportation items as well.

With the reduced number of seats for the minority and my reduced seniority, I had no hope of reclaiming C-J-S as my second subcommittee. I thus chose Treasury–Postal Service instead and decided to stick with the choice in the two succeeding Congresses. This was partly because of its attractive jurisdiction, which included most Treasury Department and White House operations, and also because of the subcommittee's small size, which let members like myself gain seniority and the potential for leadership relatively quickly. As it turned out, this strategy failed, for reasons I could hardly have anticipated. In the aftermath of the 9/11 terrorist attacks, twenty-two federal agencies were gathered into the new Department of Homeland Security. At the beginning of the 108th Congress, House Appropriations chairman Bill Young (R-Florida) gained the assent of the House leadership to reorganize Appropriations subcommittees to conform to the change. A new Homeland Security Subcommittee was formed, and the Treasury-Postal and Transportation Subcommittees, both of which had lost major pieces of jurisdiction to the new subcommittee, were combined into a new Transportation-Treasury Subcommittee.

In the meantime, I was preparing to serve as ranking Democrat on Treasury-Postal while Steny Hoyer (D-Maryland) took a leave from that position to become Democratic whip. While the normal Democratic practice was to honor subcommittee seniority, the full committee's ranking Democrat, Dave Obey (D-Wisconsin), decided that the members of the Treasury-Postal and Transportation Subcommittees should be placed in a single pool and allowed to bid, in order of full committee seniority, for slots on either of the two new panels. This placed me at a decided disadvantage, compounding the effects of the decision on my full committee ranking made six years earlier. I ended up as second-ranking Democrat on Homeland Security, a desirable assignment but a disappointment in terms of my earlier expectation to be a ranking member.

I also rejoined the Budget Committee, encouraged by the ranking Democrats on both Appropriations and Budget to pursue a vacancy that opened midway in the 105th Congress. On Budget, much more than on Appropriations, being on the minority side contrasted with my earlier experience. The Budget Committee's main responsibility—producing a budget resolution early in each session—is a highly partisan exercise. The minority is limited to offering an alternative resolution (if it wishes) and futilely proposing a few amendments to the majority resolution to highlight policy differences. Moreover, my return to the committee in 1998 coincided with an effort to deemphasize the budget process by Republican leaders, who faced serious internal divisions and were tempted to use the budget resolution to highlight a political message (tax cuts, large but nonspecific cuts in spending) rather than furnish a realistic blueprint for subsequent action (see Chapter 7). Chairman John Kasich (R-Ohio), increasingly preoccupied with his budding presidential campaign, convened few hearings. I continued to invest a good amount of time and staff work in budget issues. Because ranking Democrat John Spratt and the Democratic leadership were serious about the task of crafting an alternative resolution, I still enjoyed my part in "big picture" deliberations. But other Democrats and I were on the outside of the committee's decision process, and the overall role and stature of the committee in the House were clearly slipping.

Informal Groups and Caucuses

Although members give primary attention to their committee assignments, most also affiliate with some of the more than 250 caucuses and other informal member organizations that have sprung up in the House since the mid-1970s.[4] This proliferation reflects the array of constituent interests with which members are dealing and their need to find outlets and form alliances beyond the committee and party systems.

Informal caucuses have sometimes been criticized for dissipating members' energy and contributing to the fragmentation of the House. When Republicans reorganized the House after the 1994 election, they took aim at these caucuses, particularly the twenty-eight designated legislative service organizations (LSOs) that were allowed to pay staff with moneys transferred from members' office accounts and, in many cases, occupy space in House office buildings. Critics, with considerable justification, saw partisan motives in the abolition of LSOs. Speaker Gingrich and the new majority were trying to consolidate power and shut down alternative sources of information and advocacy, and the most dramatic effect was on the Congressional Black and Hispanic Caucuses, both predominantly Democratic in membership. Although a number of LSOs were weakened, only three disbanded entirely and most were reconstituted as congressional member organizations, which meant that members' aides could work part-time on caucus matters. Overall, the number of caucuses is now more than double its mid-1990s level, and it is Democrats more than Republicans who are most often heard complaining about staff allocations being used to support interest group advocacy.

I am currently affiliated with some thirty caucuses and informal groups. Most of them (e.g., caucuses on eye disease research and treatment, biomedical research, diabetes, Parkinson's disease, heart disease and stroke, community health centers, the National Guard and Reserves, textiles, and older Americans) have been organized to demonstrate support for legislative or funding initiatives; they seldom meet. Others, however, require more time and involvement from at least some of their members and can extend members' reach significantly. I can illustrate this by describing how five organizations have worked for me.

The Congressional Sunbelt Caucus was a regional, bipartisan LSO that unfortunately was destroyed by the "reforms" of 1995. In my early terms, the caucus provided an important outlet, through task forces, member briefings, and a pooling of staff resources, for my interests in workplace literacy, infant mortality, and other issues of special relevance to the South. Under the direction of Rep. Hal Rogers (R-Kentucky) and myself, its affiliated think tank, the Sunbelt Institute, commissioned a study on workforce needs in the region and the education and training programs required to meet them. This complemented work I was doing on the Science Committee and helped lay the groundwork for the Scientific and Advanced-Technology Act of 1992 (see Chapter 6).

As a member whose committee assignments have focused almost exclusively on domestic affairs, I have relied on caucuses to extend my knowledge and involvement in foreign and defense policy. My longest-standing membership of this kind is in the Congressional Study Group on Germany, an informal organization of 138 House members and 37 Senators interested in German and European affairs, which I helped found in 1987 and chaired in 1990. I have also been active in the House Caucus on India and Indian Americans, encouraged in part by the interest of the growing number of Indian Americans in my district. Founded in 1993, this caucus now numbers 174. I will discuss in Chapter 9 the parliamentary exchanges and other activities these caucuses have facilitated.

I have also worked with two groups composed of Democratic House members but outside the party's formal organization—the New Democrat Coalition (NDC) and the Democratic Budget Group. The NDC is a new and improved version of the Mainstream Democratic Forum (1990–1996) and is loosely affiliated with the Democratic Leadership Council (DLC), a national organization of elected officials and other Democratic leaders who have attempted to inspire serious policy debate within the party and maintain its broad middle-class appeal. Most NDC members regard themselves as moderates, but the group is more loosely organized and more diverse ideologically than the more conservative Blue Dog Coalition. The NDC has now grown to 74 members. More than half of the freshman Democratic classes of 1996, 1998, and 2000 affiliated, which says a great deal about the suburban and/or swing districts most of us come from, the kind of districts Democrats must capture to gain control of the House.

During the second Clinton administration, the NDC played an important role in the House on issues like trade and the budget, where it was often closer to the White House position than the Democratic leadership was. But the NDC rarely attempts to mobilize its members on specific votes. It functions more as a clearinghouse for member projects and a forum for discussing both pending and longer-term issues, sometimes with guest experts. The group has a regular Top o' the Week session early in the work week and organizes additional discussions and briefings, often with representatives of high-tech firms, internationally oriented businesses, and others interested in its work.

The Democratic Budget Group was organized by freshman Democrats Buddy MacKay (D-Florida) and Tim Penny (D-Minnesota) in 1983 as the Reagan-era budget deficits began to escalate. I became a regular participant immediately after coming to the House in 1987 and was made the group's cochair in 1989, after MacKay left the House to run for the Senate. I resumed the cochairmanship on returning in 1995, this time in partnership with Earl Pomeroy (D-North Dakota).

All Democratic members are invited to Budget Group sessions at 8:00 A.M. on Wednesdays, and a large percentage of them drop in at one time or another. The attendance at a typical weekly meeting is around eighteen members plus an audience of some thirty staff. The sessions particularly attract party moderates and others concerned about the fiscal challenges facing the country. We have never organized the group formally or mobilized on behalf of a particular position, and it is not a power base for any person or faction, which is one reason it has worked so well. Our focus is usually budget related, but in recent years, responding to a desire for more open and candid discussions than is typical of official party meetings, we have ranged more widely, including, for example, several sessions on national security and foreign affairs.

Budget Group guest speakers during the Clinton administration included Office of Management and Budget (OMB) directors Frank Raines and Jack Lew, Treasury secretaries Robert Rubin and Larry Summers, National Economic Council chairman Gene Sperling, and U.S. Trade Representatives Mickey Kantor and Charlene Barshefsky. During the George W. Bush presidency we have frequently heard from these and other Democratic officials in "exile" as well as experts from the Brookings Institution, the Center on Budget and Policy Priorities, and other think tanks. We also often hear from our own committee and party leaders about pending and prospective House business. I have found the Budget Group's discussions as enlightening and free of posturing as any in the House, which is why I have participated enthusiastically and have gladly contributed to the group's leadership.

Finally, a word about our state delegation. North Carolina's House delegation currently consists of six Democrats and seven Republicans. We are not formally organized and do not have regularly scheduled meetings. Howard Coble, a Greensboro Republican, became our "dean," or most senior member, in 1999, and I became the most senior Democrat. We have occasionally convened delegation meetings to share information, and I have more often called meetings of Democratic members to discuss redistricting and other home-state political and legislative matters. The delegation meets with the governor, state cabinet secretaries, university presidents, or other state leaders when they come to Washington. We frequently come together for luncheons or receptions organized by groups from the state, such as community college trustees, university cancer center researchers and patients, independent insurance agents, and agricultural extension leaders.

Our Democratic delegation met with some frequency among ourselves and with Clinton administration officials to discuss federal appointments, particularly over the six years (1993–1998) when the state had no Democratic senator. With or without formal meetings, I see North Carolina colleagues, particularly Democratic colleagues, on the floor daily, exchange information and opinions with them, learn how they are inclining on matters before us, and discuss projects in which we are jointly involved.

Sometimes all members from the state or a region within the state join to express an opinion or make a request, for example, urging the Pentagon to leave the Army Research Office in the Research Triangle Park or backing a bid for an international route by an air carrier from one of the state's major airports. Through most of 1997, our staffs worked with Governor Jim Hunt's Washington office and with each other to coordinate requests to various agencies for relief and repair after Hurricane Fran, which turned out to be a warm-up for the more intensive efforts that followed Hurricane Floyd and the attendant floods in 1999. We frequently count on well-situated members to carry the ball for the rest of us, for example, Transportation Committee members trying to secure a more favorable formula for the return of Highway Trust Fund moneys to the state, Agriculture members seeking a fair pricing policy for dairy farmers in our region, or appropriators obtaining funding for harbor dredging, rail corridor improvements, wilderness area purchases, or other projects of statewide significance. Often (but not always) these patterns of reciprocal assistance extend across party lines.

The state delegation's role as a reference group is especially important in roll call voting. The party cue is often compelling, of course, and on some votes a member may want to know how other members from the committee of jurisdiction are voting, how members identified as experts on the issue are inclined, and so forth. But on any vote involving a significant division of opinion, I generally check the voting board to see how at least some of my North Carolina Democratic colleagues are recorded. That is a way of double-checking my intended vote, looking for an impact on the state or another consideration that I may have missed. If I am in a minority among my fellow North Carolinians on a given vote, I want to make certain I know what I am doing.

During my eight terms, the collegiality of the North Carolina delegation has fluctuated. I will later describe (Chapter 6) a rift that occurred in 1993, when our new senator decided to oppose a major federal project in RTP that had hitherto enjoyed bipartisan support. I also noticed a decline in collegiality on returning to the House in 1997. This was partly a function of the reduction of our Democratic contingent to six and the departure of several colleagues from both parties with whom I had a great deal in common. It also reflected the greater polarization in the House as a whole. I was surprised when two North Carolina Republican colleagues came into my district in 1998 to campaign for my opponent—something I had never done and had never known North Carolina's members from either party to do.

In general, however, our state delegation has avoided the animosity and conflict that some other delegations display and has maintained relatively high levels of collegiality and cooperation. No one understands or cares about home like one's home state colleagues, and cordial, cooperative relationships within a delegation can be a tremendously important personal and political resource for a member. I am fortunate that, by and large, it has worked that way for me.

Notes

1. David E. Price et al., *The Commerce Committees* (New York: Grossman, 1975); Price, "The Impact of Reform: The House Commerce Subcommittee on Oversight and Investigations," in Leroy N. Rieselbach, ed., *Legislative Reform* (Lexington, Mass.: Lexington Books, 1978).

2. See David Maraniss and Michael Weisskopf, *"Tell Newt to Shut Up!"* (New York: Simon & Schuster, 1996), chap. 7; and John H. Aldrich and David W. Rohde, "The Republican Revolution and the House Appropriations Committee," *Journal of Politics,* February 2000, pp. 1–33. Aldrich and Rohde documented the

tactics Republican leaders used to gain control of the appropriations process, the increased partisan polarization of committee markups and floor proceedings, and the continuing tensions among Appropriations leaders, Republican Party leaders, and conservative members of the GOP Conference. They failed to note, however, that even in 1995 and certainly thereafter, most Appropriations sub-committees still assembled their bills with substantial bipartisan input.

3. Democrats split the Steering and Policy Committee into two committees in 1995, with the Steering Committee in charge of committee assignments. Minority leader Nancy Pelosi rejoined the two in 2003.

4. The count in 2003 was 267, excluding caucuses with only a Senate presence. "Caucuses and Their Members Make Up a Large Contingent," *Congressional Quarterly Weekly*, September 27, 2003, pp. 2379–88. See the discussions in Alan K. Ota, "Caucuses Bring New Muscle to Legislative Battlefield," *Congressional Quarterly Weekly*, September 27, 2003, pp. 2334–41; and Susan Webb Hammond, "Congressional Caucuses in the 104th Congress," in Lawrence C. Dodd and Bruce I. Oppenheimer, eds., *Congress Reconsidered*, 6th ed. (Washington, D.C.: Congressional Quarterly Press, 1997), chap. 12.

6

Policy Entrepreneurship

"The President is now the motor in the system," wrote a distinguished political scientist in the mid-1960s; "the Congress applies the brakes."[1] My staff work in the Senate during those years, when I was also casting about for a doctoral dissertation topic, led me to question this particular piece of conventional wisdom. It also put me in a good position to observe committee politics and build on studies of congressional committees being pioneered by Richard Fenno, Ralph Huitt, and others.[2] I wrote a dissertation (later published as *Who Makes the Laws?*) that delineated congressional and executive roles on thirteen major pieces of domestic legislation during the 89th Congress (1965–1966) and focused especially on the three committees handling the bills in the Senate.[3] I found the congressional role in legislation to be significant, even for major administration initiatives at the height of President Lyndon Johnson's Great Society program. But the congressional role varied a good deal at different stages of the legislative process and depended significantly on the incentives, opportunities, and resources present in various committee settings.[4]

In searching for the sources and conditions of congressional policy initiatives, I soon came to focus on the emerging phenomenon of "entrepreneurship" among senators and their aides. During the 1960s public opinion seemed to underwrite an expansive governmental role. The institutional folkways that had inhibited legislative activity down through the ranks of the Senate were beginning to erode, and a new breed of activist senators exemplified by Hubert Humphrey, Joseph Clark, Philip Hart, Edmund Muskie, and Jacob Javits were beginning to make their mark. I particularly stressed the importance of entrepreneurship in congressional staffs—a continual search for policy gaps and opportunities, a job orientation that stressed the generation and promotion of policy initiatives designed to heighten the public visibility of the senator and his or her leadership role in the chamber. Senate committees like Commerce or Labor and Public Welfare (later renamed Labor and Human Resources) became hotbeds of legislative innovation, and the development of an entrepreneurial orientation on the part of members and aides was a critical element in the productivity of these committees in the 1960s and beyond.[5]

Policy entrepreneurship was slower to emerge in the House, where the size of the body placed greater restrictions on most members' independence and impact. Their electoral fortunes turned more on constituent services and district relations and less on media exposure than was true for most senators. But House members also faced a changing political environment that increasingly left them on their own electorally. An important element in this change, as I will show in Chapter 8, was the decline of political parties. Members faced voters who were less inclined to support them on partisan grounds alone, just as party organizations were becoming less effective in communicating with and mobilizing the electorate. Party decline, together with the rise of television as the dominant news and campaign medium, thus gave members incentives to seek a higher public profile. For many representatives, especially those from districts where public awareness of and concern for national policy questions were high, policy entrepreneurship was a promising means to that end.

The desire for a more prominent policy role was a powerful motivation behind the House reforms of the 1970s, which for the most part parceled out authority and resources to subcommittees and individual members. These changes, in turn, encouraged policy initiatives down through the congressional ranks, although the fragmentation of power, ironically, also made it more difficult for the House to handle conflict and bring legislative initiatives to fruition.

The 1980s saw a waning of entrepreneurial activity. A few figures are suggestive: In the 97th Congress, during the first two years of the Reagan administration, the number of public laws enacted dropped to 473, the lowest since World War II. The volume of committee hearings tapered off somewhat after the peak years of the 1970s and reached a postwar low in 1986.[6] A number of factors contributed to this decline—shifts in the political climate that seemed to reduce public support for legislative activism, the advent of an administration hostile to much policy innovation, and, most important, constraints imposed by the budget crisis on new policy departures, especially those that cost money. Still, the distribution of authority and resources in both the House and Senate gave large numbers of members opportunities for legislative entrepreneurship. Many members continued to find it advantageous, as they considered both their electoral prospects and their standing within Congress, to establish active policy-making roles for themselves.

I came to the House with some entrepreneurial experience (I had handled the Radiation Protection Act of 1967 for Senator Bartlett, who was its chief Senate sponsor), some awareness of the conditions of successful activism, and strong personal and political motivations to develop such a role for myself. At the same time, I faced certain constraints, first as a junior member expected to concentrate on my committee assignments and defer to committee leaders and later as a member of the Appropriations Committee ineligible for a seat on an authorizing committee. I will discuss in this chapter several initiatives that I managed, under contrasting circumstances, to push to passage. I will first describe two kinds of endeavors from within the Banking Committee: the passage of a free-standing bill of limited scope and the formulation of amendments to a major committee bill. Second, I will describe three education initiatives I undertook from outside the committees of jurisdiction. Finally I will give some examples of the use of appropriations to further policy objectives.

The Home Equity Loan
Consumer Protection Act

My arrival on the Banking Committee with an eye out for entrepreneurial opportunities coincided with the rise of home equity loans as a hot new financial product. The Tax Reform Act of 1986 had terminated income tax deductibility for interest on most consumer loans and credit card accounts, but it had left deductibility in place for loans secured by one's home. In response, home equity loans—second mortgages that ordinarily had a variable interest rate and an open line of credit up to a substantial portion of the value of the house—were vigorously marketed, and many consumers (including me) found them attractive and advantageous. This aggressive marketing and the possibility that, with a rise in interest rates, borrowers might find themselves in over their heads with their homes at risk made certain basic consumer protections desirable. Yet these loans were subject to little advertising regulation and, under the Truth in Lending Act, were treated as an open-end product, like a credit card, rather than as a closed-end product, like an adjustable-rate or fixed-rate mortgage. Consumers could be given considerably less information than would be required in the case of other loans secured against their homes, and even this information might be provided only after they had paid nonrefundable fees or closing costs. It seemed obvious that home equity loans should be subject to disclosure requirements at least as stringent as those that applied to other mortgages. And my committee assignment gave me a good position from which to work on a measure to accomplish this.

Having discovered a promising policy gap and feeling anxious lest other members might be getting similar ideas, I hurried to draft a bill and to circulate a "Dear Colleague" letter inviting other members to join me as cosponsors. My staff and I solicited suggestions from several consumer and banking groups and, most importantly, from the staff of the Federal Reserve Board, which was already working on new regulations for the timing and content of disclosures for adjustable-rate mortgages. One critical early decision was to make this primarily a disclosure bill. Although it went beyond what most industry associations preferred, it fell short of the consumer groups' wish lists. I made this decision on the merits of the case. I did not want to place regulations on home equity loans that went far beyond what was required of comparable products; nor did I want to see these loans increased in price or made less available. At the same time, however, I wanted the bill to attract a broad base of political support. An alternative approach would have been to introduce a much more extensive bill, with the idea of compromising later if necessary. In fact, Rep. Charles Schumer (D-New York) subsequently introduced such a home equity loan bill, to the applause of the consumer groups. But I chose to draft a bill that I thought could pass and that came close to what I thought Congress finally should produce. This approach paid off: No potential opponents got too upset, and the bill attracted a bipartisan group of twenty-three original cosponsors, including the chairman and ranking Republican member of the House Banking Committee.

Frank Annunzio (D-Illinois), chairman of the Banking Committee's Subcommittee on Consumer Affairs and Coinage, scheduled hearings on the bill for October 6, 1987. He and his staff were wary of possible attacks by consumer groups, who had begun rather noisily to object to my initial draft. However, it was clear that the industry groups (which, like the consumer groups, had formed an informal coalition for purposes of negotiation and lobbying) would resist adding substantive restrictions on home equity loans to the disclosure and advertising regulations contained in my bill. It was not difficult to imagine lenders deciding to oppose the bill; their success in defeating interest-rate caps on a related credit card bill by a large margin suggested that they might be able to do the same if the home equity bill were amended to contain such restrictions. Moreover, they could assume that if Congress was unable to act, the Federal Reserve Board would promulgate regulations they could live with. I was eager to keep both groups at the table because I knew that the disaffection of either would break up the coalition of members who had joined in sponsoring the bill and would make its passage far less likely.

At the House subcommittee hearings, I identified several areas where I thought the bill could be strengthened and substantive restrictions should be considered: limiting the ability of a lender to arbitrarily manipulate the interest rate, for example, and tightly restricting the lender's right to call in a loan or change its terms. Fortunately the consumer groups also chose to focus on such potential areas of abuse, rather than push hard for the kind of broad limits on the terms of home equity loans contained in the Schumer bill. Despite this, our negotiations grew contentious and came close to breaking down. We got a revised bill reported out of subcommittee only by promising all concerned that they would get another crack at it before the full committee undertook its final revisions.

In the meantime, the Senate Banking Committee's Subcommittee on Consumer Affairs, under the leadership of Chairman Christopher Dodd (D-Connecticut), took up the home equity issue, using my bill and Schumer's as the basis for a day of hearings on November 18, 1987. The committee leadership later decided to append a home equity loan disclosure provision to their bill repealing the Glass-Steagall Act and expanding bank powers—Senate Banking's most ambitious legislative project in the 100th Congress—which passed on March 30, 1988. Home equity legislation had not originated in the Senate, and the home equity title that the Senate approved was a hastily drawn proposal. Nonetheless, this temporary shift to the Senate of the negotiations among industry and consumer groups served us well on the House side: The prospect of immediate floor action forced everyone to reveal their bottom lines in short order, and we were able to use the Senate language to resolve several difficult issues that were slowing our progress toward full committee markup in the House.

The House Banking Committee approved the Home Equity Loan Consumer Protection Act by a unanimous vote on May 19, 1988, and the House passed the bill by voice vote on June 20. Although I was happy to see the measure pass the Senate expeditiously as part of the bank powers legislation, I wanted to pass it as a separate bill in the House, where the prognosis for the bank powers bill was far less hopeful and home equity's prospects could be harmed if it became entwined in the conflicts surrounding the broader measure. This strategy, supported by the full committee's ranking Republican member as well as Chairman Fernand St. Germain (D-Rhode Island), preserved both options—taking home equity to a House-Senate conference as part of the larger bill or passing it as a freestanding measure if the bank powers bill failed.

This proved to be a wise strategy, for the bank powers legislation ran into major obstacles in the House. However, both the chairman and the ranking Republican of the Senate Banking Committee, who were also the chief proponents of the bank powers bill, were reluctant to pass home equity separately because they believed it enhanced the broader bill and improved their chances for getting it approved. It was only after the prospects for bank powers were seen as completely hopeless that separate passage of home equity could even be discussed. By then, though, time was so short that the only feasible approach was for the Senate to pass the House's freestanding home equity bill and send it directly to the president, thus making further House action or a House-Senate conference on the bill unnecessary.

My legislative director, Paul Feldman, and I spent many hours during the closing days of the session working with allies that included several House members and aides as well as industry and consumer lobbyists, trying to secure Senate passage. The task was complicated by the fact that the Senate was conducting its business essentially by unanimous consent in the waning hours. Any one member could block approval, and several placed holds on the home equity bill, hoping to use it as a vehicle or bargaining chip for proposals of their own. The Senate committee staff worked all day on October 21 to accommodate as many of these members as possible and finally, at 2:00 A.M., got home equity to the floor as part of a package of three bills. With one hour remaining before final adjournment of the 100th Congress, the Home Equity Loan Consumer Protection Act passed the Senate by voice vote and was on its way to the White House.

The home equity case suggests several conditions that facilitate and shape policy entrepreneurship in the House. In the first place, the committee environment was a relatively favorable one. The chairmen of both the subcommittee and the full committee stood to benefit if the Banking Committee was regarded as active and productive in the consumer protection area. Both were generally permissive and helpful with respect to member initiatives in this area, particularly with nonthreatening junior members like myself. These committee leaders handled certain other areas of their jurisdiction quite differently, encouraging initiatives and sharing power much less readily. But in the consumer protection area, leadership style and the effective decentralization of the committee fostered entrepreneurship and gave it a fair chance of success.

The committee's mode of partisanship also had a positive effect. Though House Banking Committee members frequently experienced severe conflict and committee leaders often failed to manage conflict well, these divisions shifted from issue to issue and often cut across party lines. There was a tradition of cross-party collaboration on discrete measures on which I could draw in introducing and refining the home equity bill.

The political conditions surrounding the home equity issue were also favorable.[7] The bill spoke to a problem of growing public salience, one that promised recognition and reward to legislators who addressed it. In addition, the issue was not saddled with the kind of debilitating conflict that would have discouraged legislative involvement. Members could see this as a consumer protection measure with considerable potential public appeal without worrying that support of the bill would draw them into serious conflicts with outside groups or their colleagues.

The relevant "interested outsiders" had good reasons for adopting a constructive, cooperative posture, although it was by no means certain that they would do so.[8] The Federal Reserve Board, having acknowledged the need for home equity loan regulation and having begun its own rule making, needed to ensure congruence between congressional action and its own. And industry groups recognized that the price of noncooperation might be a more punitive and less workable bill. This led to a rather grudging decision by the American Bankers Association not to oppose the bill actively, as well as to more positive collaboration by other industry groups. Some of the consumer lobbyists were inclined to push for "their bill or none," to test the limits of the developing consensus. But others, most notably the American Association of Retired Persons (AARP), needed to deliver a bill to their constituents, and committee allies of the consumer groups, like Annunzio and Schumer, let them know that they would not back an absolutist stance.

These conditions facilitated a successful initiative but did not ensure it. Successful entrepreneurship requires members and their aides to push continually and push hard. Furthermore, an initiative must be shaped to make the most of favorable conditions. In the home equity case, this approach meant taking full account of the Federal Reserve's preferences as the bill was drafted and refined. It meant consulting with and deferring to the committee leadership. It meant drafting the bill to attract bipartisan support, seeking that support, and insisting that all the major players be brought along at each successive stage. And it meant working hard to keep the intergroup negotiations on track.

Policy entrepreneurship is irreducibly personal. It does not lend itself to easy predictions or determinate explanations. One can identify the conditions that encourage or facilitate entrepreneurial ventures, but the shape and the success of such initiatives still depend on the motivation, style, and skill of members and their aides—the kind of job they wish to do and the strategic choices they make in pursuing that goal.

Amending the Housing Bill

The Banking Committee and the House had done little on housing in the 100th Congress, but the 101st promised more action. Senators Alan Cranston (D-California) and Alfonse D'Amato (R-New York), chairman and ranking Republican on the Senate Housing Subcommittee, were nearing the culmination of an ambitious, two-year effort to draft an overhaul of federal housing policy. Henry Gonzalez (D-Texas), longtime chairman of the House Committee's Subcommittee on Housing, had remained aloof from this effort because of what some termed "a combination of ego, institutional rivalry, pent-up frustration from the beating liberal housing advocates in the House took when Republicans controlled the Senate in 1981–1986, and a lack of desire to revamp existing programs."[9] But Gonzalez was drafting his own bill, and he was in a stronger position to push it after the 1988 election, which saw St. Germain defeated and Gonzalez inheriting the chairmanship of the full committee as well as that of the Housing Subcommittee. In addition, the George H.W. Bush administration, with an energetic new Housing and Urban Development (HUD) secretary in Jack Kemp and a legacy of HUD scandals to overcome, seemed more amenable than its predecessor to housing initiatives.

During 1989, however, housing, like everything else on the Banking Committee agenda, took a backseat to the legislation to recapitalize the savings and loan insurance fund and revamp regulation of the industry—the Financial Institutions Reform, Recovery, and Enforcement Act (FIRREA). The three amendments I added to this bill as it made its way through the Financial Institutions Subcommittee set the pattern for more extensive attempts to modify and augment the housing bill a year later. My first term on the committee (and the experience it provided with the issues and "interested outsiders" in the agencies, academia, and financial institutions) made such a role more feasible and comfortable for me and my staff than it would have been two years earlier.[10]

These additions to FIRREA and the six comparable additions I made to the housing bill are typical of the policy entrepreneurship a variety of members undertake as a major bill is considered in committee. FIRREA and the housing bill contrasted sharply in the degree of congressional responsibility for their initiation and their content. FIRREA was mainly a presidential initiative, which the Banking committees and the Congress amended at the margins. The housing bill also contained presidentially initiated elements, most notably a program pushed by Secretary Kemp to help public housing tenants and other low-income people buy housing units. But the fact that the administration put forward this proposal when it did was partially a result of congressional pressure, and the great majority of the provisions in both the House and Senate bills were congressional in origin. The heart of the Cranston-D'Amato bill, for example, was what later became the HOME program, designed to encourage partnerships among local governments, nonprofit organizations, and private industry through federal matching grants. This provision was based on a major recommendation of the well-regarded National Housing Task Force.[11] I strongly backed it as a way to introduce innovation and flexibility into the federal housing effort, and we subsequently made extensive use of it in North Carolina.

My active involvement in shaping the housing bill and my public identification with the issue were facilitated when Gonzalez agreed to schedule a field hearing of the Housing Subcommittee in Raleigh in early 1990. The full day of testimony we heard reinforced several ideas for amendments that I had been working on. It also helped provide a basis for later cooperation with the colleagues who made the trip—Steve Bartlett (R-Texas), Liz Patterson (D-South Carolina), and Peter Hoagland (D-Nebraska).

The first amendment set up a $20 million demonstration program for "soft second" mortgages. We used the Raleigh hearing to highlight the success of this financing technique in several local affordable-housing developments. In this financing arrangement, a bank loaned a borrower approximately 70 percent of the home's value. A local government or nonprofit organization made a second loan—the soft second—to the borrower for the remaining percentage of the home's value. Principal and interest payments on the second mortgage were deferred for several years or until the house was sold again. Such schemes, several witnesses testified, were bringing monthly mortgage payments within reach for home buyers of modest income. However, the resources for such financing were limited; "the problem," said one mayor, "is now that we know this works, we don't have the resources to replicate it."[12]

Providing second-mortgage resources seemed to be a feasible federal role, a way of stimulating substantial public and private investments in affordable housing with a relatively modest federal contribution. (In fact, it later became a familiar feature of HOME projects.) I proposed that we set up a demonstration program at HUD that would allow local governments and nonprofits to apply for funds for soft second mortgage financing. After a good deal of discussion, mainly at the staff level, Chairman Gonzalez agreed to include a modest authorization as part of his home ownership title in the "chairman's mark," the revised draft of the bill offered to the subcommittee for markup.

My second amendment loosened the so-called federal preference eligibility rules for public housing and rental assistance projects. By law, 90 percent of such units had to go to families in the preference categories— families who were paying more than 50 percent of their income in rent, had been involuntarily displaced, or were living in substandard housing. The administration defended such targeting as a way of giving priority to the most needy, but the people who actually had to administer these developments told a different story. "The concept of dealing only with the neediest of the poor . . . was well intended," the director of the Raleigh Housing Authority told our subcommittee, but as a result, "we have driven the low-income working families out of our public housing and we have driven the role models out, we have driven the two-parent households out and [have helped create] much of the negative environment that we are now being criticized for in public housing."[13] Rigid preference rules meant that public housing was not working as a community, for the neediest or for anyone else.

I was predisposed to attend to such arguments by consulting I had done in 1978–1979, helping HUD evaluate community development programs, and by my academic work in ethics and public policy (see Chapter 12). I did enough checking to assure myself that there was hardly a public housing director in the country who did not believe the preference rules should be relaxed. I then proposed that up to 30 percent of the slots in public and assisted housing could go to persons who met the income eligibility requirements but fell outside the federal preference criteria. The amendment drew skeptical responses from liberal Democratic members like Gonzalez and Joe Kennedy (D-Massachusetts), as well as administration partisans on the Republican side. But members like Schumer and Bartlett who knew a great deal about how housing programs actually worked came to the amendment's defense, and in the end the subcommittee adopted it by voice vote.

The third amendment raised the maximum value of a home eligible for Federal Housing Administration (FHA) mortgage insurance to $124,875 (or 95 percent of the median sale price in a given area, if that were a lower figure). Although I had proposed a similar increase the year before as part of a bill to make FHA mortgage insurance more accessible to first-time home buyers, I was by no means the only member interested in raising the FHA ceiling. In many cities across the country—like Raleigh, Cary, and Chapel Hill in my district—the median price of a home had risen far above the existing FHA limit. Realtors, home builders, and housing officials and advocates were united in seeking a more flexible limit; the private mortgage insurers were the only major group opposed.

In late 1989, the Appropriations Subcommittee on VA, HUD, and Independent Agencies included a one-year increase to $124,875 in its fiscal 1990 appropriations bill. Gonzalez angrily opposed the increase, without success, on the House floor as an encroachment on the Banking Committee's prerogatives. Nonetheless, he recognized members' growing impatience with such arguments and knew that several others and I were ready to propose farther-reaching changes in FHA mortgage insurance criteria as amendments to the housing bill. Gonzalez therefore elected to include a permanent increase to $124,875 in the chairman's mark, assuming correctly that we would be willing to accept that and declare victory.

My fourth amendment expanded an FHA demonstration program to insure "reverse mortgages" for elderly homeowners. The AARP and other housing advocacy groups put great stock in the concept, which allowed cash-poor homeowners to draw down a portion of their equity to meet monthly expenses and still remain in their homes. But these groups were dissatisfied with the scale and the scope of the existing demonstration, which involved only 2,500 participants, and they began talking with several members' staffs about expanding the program. Schumer and I decided to offer an amendment to the housing bill to increase the demonstration to 25,000 participants and to clarify and expand the options available to borrowers. We consulted with administration representatives and Republican members to head off opposition and got the amendment adopted in subcommittee by voice vote.

My fifth amendment required that consumers be clearly informed of what they must do when paying off FHA-insured mortgages to avoid additional interest charges beyond the date of payoff. This problem was brought to my attention by a couple of letters from constituents who had been charged interest for an entire month even when they had paid off their mortgage early in the month. My first inclination was simply to forbid such charges, but Feldman's conversations with regulators and industry representatives convinced us that a flat prohibition would have costs and complexities beyond what we had anticipated. As a result, we settled for a disclosure and notification requirement, and this we were able to get added to the bill without dissent.

The sixth amendment, which I offered in collaboration with Tom Carper (D-Delaware), Patterson, and Hoagland, was by far the most complex and controversial of the lot. We developed our own compromise solution to the vexed question of whether and under what conditions landlords who were eligible to prepay federally subsidized mortgages and convert their properties to uses other than low-income housing should be allowed to do so. I felt that the owners clearly had a right to prepay because their contracts so stipulated. For the government to renege on this promise would discourage future private participation in low-income housing ventures. At the same time, it was clearly desirable that prepayment and conversion not occur on a large scale, for hundreds of thousands of lower-income tenants would then risk eviction.

The chairman's mark, reflecting the views of low-income housing advocacy groups and members like Gonzalez, Kennedy, and Barney Frank (D-Massachusetts), essentially forbade prepayment. An amendment, sponsored by Bartlett and Doug Barnard (D-Georgia) and backed by the realtors and other supporters of the owners, upheld the right to prepay while providing certain incentives for owners to remain in the program and protections for tenants who might be displaced. My collaborators and I were not entirely happy with either proposal, and we realized that we might well be the swing votes determining which approach the committee approved. We therefore decided to work with Bartlett on devising modifications that would let us support his proposal with more enthusiasm. We chose this course because we were in fundamental agreement with him on the right to prepay and because he and Barnard had already gone some distance to develop a balanced solution and seemed willing to go further. Our proposal strengthened owner incentives and tenant protections—requiring direct relocation assistance from owners, for example, and facilitating the transfer of properties to nonprofit organizations—and was accepted by Bartlett as a friendly amendment. Thus augmented, the Bartlett-Barnard amendment passed the full committee by a 29–19 vote. In the meantime, our group announced that we would continue to work on the prepayment issue and would bring further refinements to the House floor.

We used the seven weeks between the committee vote and floor consideration on August 1 to devise a more comprehensive amendment that gave nonprofits and others who intended to use the property for low-income housing a clear right of first refusal when an owner elected to prepay his or her mortgage and sell the property. It also extended the low-income use restrictions for those who elected to stay in the program and provided incentives for owners to improve services for the elderly living in their units. The latter provision, as well as the first refusal requirement, helped attract AARP support. Some low-income housing advocates worked with us in devising the floor amendment, although others kept their distance. We continued to consult with Bartlett and the groups working with him as well. In the end, our amendment passed by a vote of 400–12. Among the opponents, however, were Gonzalez and Kennedy, who were still unreconciled to their defeat in committee.

All six of my amendments survived in conference with minor modifications, although I was not there to defend them in person. Because of my relatively junior status, I had not expected to be appointed to the conference committee. But when a senior member like Carper was also omitted and when I saw members at my seniority level and below being named, it became clear that Gonzalez was not taking our disagreement lightly. (The Speaker, who was formally responsible for naming conferees, only rarely deviated from the chair's recommendations.) Consequently I had to request help from several conferees in protecting my interests, and most were happy to oblige. Bartlett, for example, helped persuade HUD officials not to press for the deletion of the federal preferences amendment. On October 25, 1990, the conference report cleared the House—a more significant bill than many had believed possible when Congress had begun working on it in earnest less than five months before.

These housing amendments demonstrate the range of sources from which legislative initiatives may flow—agencies, advocacy groups, constituency complaints, one's own ideas and experiences, discomfort with the existing alternatives—and the alliances and compromises that are essential to their success. Like the home equity bill, they demonstrate the centrality of creative and persistent staff work to successful entrepreneurship and the importance of agency and group support. They also show that the Banking Committee was more amenable to policy entrepreneurship than was at first apparent. Though the committee had a reputation for arbitrary leadership and persistent conflict, it remained quite permeable in terms of members' ability to shape its legislative product. Its patterns of conflict, moreover, were sufficiently fluid to permit the assemblage, from issue to issue, of all sorts of coalitions, often across party lines.

This is not to say that policy entrepreneurship comes easily: One has to work at it. But despite the obstacles, difficulties, and political and budgetary constraints, my Banking Committee experience is fairly typical. The incentives for an activist legislative role remain strong, and such efforts are often rewarded with success.

Education and Training Initiatives

The issue that comes to me most naturally by virtue of my background and experience is education. My mother was a high school English teacher; I have early memories of former students coming up to her on the street, recounting what she had done for them, and sometimes, to my amazement, thanking her for demanding so much. My father taught biology and served as high school principal until the needs of our growing family forced him to take a job with more adequate pay. Education opened up the wider world to me, and it probably surprised no one that I chose teaching as a career. When I ran for Congress, both my personal credentials and the preoccupations of my district dictated that the need to support and improve education would be a central campaign theme.

From my earliest months in the House, I was looking for a fit between my education interests and my committee assignments. This helped attract me to the Science Committee and to Science, Research, and Technology

(SRT) as the subcommittee most attuned to education policy. This in turn led my staff and me to focus on workplace literacy as a concept that tied education to the demands of workplaces that were becoming more and more technologically sophisticated. North Carolina leaders in industry and research continually told me of their need for a trained workforce; the two years beyond high school, provided most often by community colleges, was the level of training increasingly required by most new, good jobs. Yet neither the Department of Education nor the National Science Foundation (NSF), an agency under the Science Committee's jurisdiction, had done much to encourage educational improvements at that level.

Doug Walgren (D-Pennsylvania), chairman of the SRT Subcommittee, was a generous, accommodating colleague who had pushed for years to get NSF to use methods successfully employed at other educational levels to improve curricula and teaching methods in advanced technology at community colleges. He welcomed my interest and scheduled a subcommittee hearing in RTP for November 9, 1987, ten months into my first term. This allowed me to assemble a stellar cast of North Carolinians, including the president of the community college system, the general manager of IBM, and other business, education, and civic leaders, for a full day of hearings. I staked out training for the workplace and strengthening community colleges as education issues I intended to pursue. We defined workplace literacy broadly, hearing from organizers of various sorts of literacy programs, but the hearings helped define a focus on the particular challenges of the high-tech workplace that we maintained for the ensuing five years.[14]

One option was to make a renewed push for Walgren's community college proposal. But the bill had encountered resistance from NSF and even his subcommittee's own staff, and a strong community of advocacy had never developed around it. It seemed advisable to open up another arena for considering the issue, exploring alternative approaches and mobilizing additional interest and support. This I was able to do through the Sunbelt Caucus: Rep. Hal Rogers (R-Kentucky) and I cochaired a task force on workplace literacy and commissioned a Sunbelt Institute study that identified functional literacy as "the South's number one competitiveness issue."[15] I then organized a Sunbelt Caucus literacy summit in RTP early in the 101st Congress, which carried forward some of the interest and enthusiasm generated in our 1987 hearing.

By mid-1989, I was ready to introduce my own bill, the Science and Technological Literacy Act. I retained the basic thrust of Walgren's earlier proposal: individual project grants from NSF to community colleges to support meritorious training programs and the creation of ten "centers of excellence" among these colleges to serve as national clearinghouses for best practices in technical training and/or science and mathematics education. I added sections authorizing a focus, in this and other NSF programs, on curricular revision and the development of innovative instruction technologies. Before introducing the bill on August 3, I carefully assembled a bipartisan group of cosponsors, including Rogers and Sherwood Boehlert (R-New York), ranking Republican on the SRT Subcommittee, as well as Walgren and Robert Roe (D-New Jersey), chair of the full Science Committee.[16]

The SRT hearing on October 31 was an upbeat affair, with a number of members participating and former (and future) North Carolina governor Jim Hunt serving as leadoff witness. But NSF continued to drag its feet. Out of a budget approaching $3 billion, NSF acknowledged spending only $4 million annually on two-year institutions, with most of that going for instrumentation and laboratory equipment. The foundation insisted that it needed no new statutory authority to do what the bill envisioned and that these kinds of training programs would be best handled by the Education and Labor Departments.[17] This attitude changed somewhat in the ensuing months. When NSF Director Erich Bloch made a rare joint appearance with Secretary of Education Lauro Cavazos before our subcommittee on February 28, 1990, he identified "adult science and technical training" as an area that was "falling through the cracks" between the two agencies—an admission I immediately seized on as a demonstration "that strengthening NSF's . . . support for the development of exemplary technical training programs . . . might not be quite as distant from NSF's mission as some have suggested in the past."[18] We were not able to move the bill in the 101st Congress, a disappointment to me as I prepared to leave the Science Committee for Appropriations. But we had made some headway, not only in softening NSF and Bush administration opposition but also in mobilizing the national community college associations and institutions in the districts of key members. I was determined to press ahead in the 102nd Congress.

Election night 1990 brought unwelcome news of Walgren's defeat and necessitated a fine-tuning of our strategy. His successor as subcommittee chair, Rick Boucher (D-Virginia), was a friend and a sponsor in past years of the Walgren bill. But with the accession of my North Carolina colleague Tim Valentine to the chair of the Subcommittee on Technology and Competitiveness, Valentine and I and our staffs saw an opportunity to give the bill an added boost. On reintroducing the bill (H.R. 2936) on July 17, 1991, I sought and received a joint referral to both subcommittees. I had refined the earlier bill considerably and added provisions authorizing grants to community colleges for partnerships with four-year colleges aimed at helping students pursue degree programs in mathematics, science, engineering, or technology. I reenlisted most of my 1989 cosponsors, including George Brown (D-California), the new chair of the full committee; the list eventually grew to sixty-four. Valentine's subcommittee held a hearing and then forwarded the bill to the full committee on October 31. The momentum this created and the continuing efforts of Valentine, ranking Republican Sherwood Boehlert, and their staffs were critically important in pressing Boucher's Science Subcommittee and the full committee to act.

Committee and subcommittee staffs worked on the bill prior to a March 18, 1992, markup, addressing the concerns of NSF and its defenders in various ways.[19] The full committee reported the bill to the House on April 30, but floor consideration was delayed while the staff of the Education and Labor Committee, to whom H.R. 2936 had been jointly referred, scrutinized its provisions. They eventually agreed, after minor changes, to release the bill; the House passed it without dissent on August 10 and sent it to the Senate. This would have been impossibly late in the session had the Senate been required to consider the House bill de novo. Fortunately, however, Senator Barbara Mikulski (D-Maryland) and her staff had been working with community college leaders and my staff on a companion bill (S. 1146) that tracked H.R. 2936 in most respects. House passage of my bill enabled Mikulski to put S. 1146 on a fast track. Senate Labor and Human Resources Committee members, many of them hearing from community college leaders in their own states, agreed to bring the bill more closely into line with the final version of H.R. 2936 and expedite its consideration on the Senate floor. The Senate passed the Mikulski bill by voice vote on October 2, and the next day the House gave its final approval. On October 23, President Bush signed what was now called the Scientific and Advanced-Technology Act of 1992 into law.

The bill as finally approved was more tightly focused than the earlier proposals we fashioned around workplace literacy and fully addressed any lingering concerns about diverting the NSF. Agency reluctance and the multiplicity of committee and subcommittee checkpoints had made for a long and torturous road to passage. By the same token, responsibility for the final product was widely shared—with Doug Walgren, who initially pushed for NSF–community college engagement and provided support for my early efforts; with Valentine, Boehlert, Boucher, and other committee leaders and staff members who persevered after Walgren and I left the Science Committee; with Mikulski, who did a skillful end run around Senate procedures; and with community college leaders who brought home to many members what otherwise might have been an obscure Science Committee initiative. As always, I was indebted to my staff for creative strategizing and repeated reformulations that enabled us to respond to critics while retaining the basic thrust of my bill.

My second major education initiative was less complex but took even longer to achieve: the Education Affordability Act of 1997. Here too I had the benefit of an early collaboration that I carried forward in subsequent Congresses under changed circumstances. The initial idea came from Martin Lancaster, a friend and fellow member of the class of 1986 who represented eastern North Carolina's Third District. Lancaster suggested that we jointly offer a bill to restore income tax deductibility for interest on student loans, which had been removed by the Tax Reform Act of 1986, and to make scholarships and fellowships tax-exempt. We introduced our bill, sought cosponsors, and promoted it to anyone who would listen in each of the succeeding Congresses from 1987 until we were both defeated in 1994.

Because our bill dealt with the tax treatment of loans and scholarships, it was referred not to the Education and Labor Committee but to Ways and Means. This was not a committee with which Lancaster and I, as relatively junior members, had a great deal of leverage. Because of the constraints of the budget process (and after the budget agreement of 1990, explicit rules that required tax reductions to be offset with equivalent tax increases or entitlement reductions), Ways and Means rarely reported freestanding bills like ours. Tax measures were typically wrapped into omnibus bills, often in the context of budget "reconciliation" or a broader budget agreement (see Chapter 7). We thus concluded that our best prospect was to build support for our proposal and push for its inclusion in whatever omnibus vehicles became available. We came closest in 1990, when the Bush administration expressed support for tax credits or deductions for student loan interest in the course of bipartisan budget negotiations. But Lancaster and I had many reminders of the difficulty of influencing such negotiations, particularly when we were pushing a proposal that would lose revenue, in competition with many other such proposals in tight budgetary circumstances.

I received a great deal of reinforcement over the years, however, for what we were trying to do. Heads invariably nodded in community meetings when I expressed the view that if you could deduct the interest on the mortgage on your home (or even on your second home at the beach!), you surely ought to get a break on something as basic as an educational loan. Financial aid and other higher education administrators, locally and nationally, endorsed the idea strongly and began including it in their policy agendas. When I returned to Congress in 1997, I had every reason to reintroduce the bill. I added to the Lancaster-Price proposal a section permitting the drawdown without penalty of individual retirement account (IRA) savings for educational purposes. I invited my newly elected colleague from the neighboring Second District, Bob Etheridge, who had served as North Carolina's Superintendent of Public Instruction, to join me in introducing the bill. We did so on February 4, 1997 (H.R. 553), and eventually enlisted fifty-six additional cosponsors, including minority leader Dick Gephardt.[20]

Our best opportunity, once again, was not to pass a free-standing bill but to incorporate the essence of the Education Affordability Act in omnibus legislation—which in this case meant the Taxpayer Relief Act, companion to the Balanced Budget Act, under negotiation between the president and the leadership of Congress through much of 1997 (see Chapter 7). I realized early in the process that our prospects for success were better than in earlier years. The budget situation was less desperate and a generous list of tax breaks was certain to be included in the overall package. The president made clear that HOPE Scholarships (tax credits for tuition expenses) and other initiatives for higher education were at the top of his priority list. And although I and most of the sponsors of H.R. 553 were minority Democrats, our ideas were also being pushed by Republicans such as Nancy Johnson (R-Connecticut), a senior Ways and Means member, and Charles Grassley (R-Iowa), a senior member of the Senate Finance Committee. If this meant that responsibility (and credit) for the final outcome would be more widely shared, it also increased the chances that that outcome would be favorable.

Throughout the budget discussions, I maintained communication with congressional and administration leaders who were in a position to shape the final product and helped higher education representatives do the same. I particularly wanted to make certain that the support of Democratic leaders for such measures as HOPE Scholarships and expanded Pell Grants (which I shared) did not displace support for my proposal. The five-year cost of the student loan and IRA components ($690 million and $812 million, respectively) was low relative to many other proposals under discussion. This made it easier to include them, but it also raised the possibility that congressional or administration negotiators might be tempted to drop them when the time came to balance out the numbers and fine-tune the package. I wanted to give our proposals sufficient visibility and evidence of support to make certain that did not happen.

There was never much doubt that the IRA drawdown provision would make it. The president included it in his proposed budget, and it was included in both the Senate and House versions of the Taxpayer Relief Act. But we had a harder time with the interest deductibility proposal. Nancy

Johnson failed to get it included in the Republican bill, passed by the House on June 26, 1997, and I failed to get it included in the Democratic alternative. We knew its prospects were better in the Senate and were promised sympathetic attention in conference by our respective leaders. The president included the IRA drawdown but not student loans in his June 30 revised set of tax cut proposals. But as I lobbied administration officials and House conferees, I was assured by Treasury Secretary Robert Rubin that interest deductibility was a personal favorite of the president and he was pushing for its inclusion. In any event, both the IRA drawdown and a modified version of our interest deductibility proposal (available for five years per student, for joint filers with incomes up to $60,000) were included in the conference agreement, passed overwhelmingly by both houses on July 31. These Education Affordability Act provisions were hardly noticed amid the hoopla surrounding the conclusion of the budget deal, but I was not inclined to complain: I knew that their significance would later become evident and that they hardly could have been passed any other way.

My third major education initiative, the Teaching Fellows Act, has made some headway but is still a work in progress. The bill aims to secure federal support for state fellowship programs for prospective teachers similar to the Teaching Fellows program established by the North Carolina General Assembly in 1986.

I first introduced the bill in 2000, alarmed at predictions of a national teacher shortage and impressed by the arguments of a friend who was close to the North Carolina program and was convinced that it could be expanded and replicated nationwide. I conferred extensively with Secretary Richard Riley and other Department of Education officials as the Clinton administration wound down, hopeful that if a Gore administration materialized, teacher recruitment could be high on the education agenda. But I was well aware of the obstacles I would face in Congress as a member of the minority party not on the committee of jurisdiction. From the beginning I assumed that my best hope might be to pass the Teaching Fellows Act not as a freestanding bill but as a component of major education legislation, such as the reauthorization of the Elementary and Secondary Education Act (ESEA). I worked closely with Dale Kildee (D-Michigan), ranking Democrat on the Committee on Education and the Workforce's Subcommittee on Early Childhood, Youth, and Families, who persuaded Chairman Michael Castle (R-Delaware) to hold a field hearing in Raleigh on ESEA renewal on September 8, 1999. We used the hearing to familiarize the subcommittee with the workings of the North Carolina program and to plant the idea that teacher recruitment might suggest a "new area of policy direction" for an expanded ESEA.[21]

My staff and I conferred widely as we put the initial 2000 proposal together and refined it for reintroduction in the 107th Congress. At the urging of my former House colleague Martin Lancaster, who was now president of North Carolina's community college system, I proposed not only a traditional college scholarship program but also a Partnership Fellows program to encourage collaboration between community colleges and four-year schools; these fellowships would enable teaching assistants and others in two-year programs to go on to full certification. In seeking bipartisan cosponsors and pitching the bill to Bush Administration officials, I stressed that it transcended past partisan approaches: It would be administered at the state level within broad federal guidelines and could be run through nonprofit organizations separate from state departments of education—an arrangement that had fostered innovation and flexibility in North Carolina.

My press secretary earned his pay on February 27, 2001, the day we unveiled H.R. 839, the new and improved Teaching Fellows Act (see Figure 6.1). We staged the announcement in North Carolina State University's empty football stadium, pointing out that we would have to fill every seat, in addition to every seat in the basketball arena next door, and would still fall short by 6,000 of the 80,000 new teachers North Carolina needed to recruit in the next decade! The bill attracted twenty-one cosponsors and found a place on the legislative agendas of a number of educational associations. ESEA reauthorization, which had faltered in the 106th Congress, became a legislative centerpiece for the Bush administration, repackaged as the No Child Left Behind initiative. But the bill focused on standards and accountability, and the Education Committee was inclined to consolidate and block-grant "teacher quality" programs rather than add a new categorical program of the sort I had proposed.

I thus began to look for another legislative vehicle; the obvious candidate was the Higher Education Act (HEA), up for renewal in 2003–2004. I reintroduced the Teaching Fellows Act as H.R. 1805 and reenlisted cosponsors, one of whom turned out to be particularly important—Rep. Cass Ballenger, a North Carolina Republican, a senior member of the Education Committee who had cosponsored my bill at the urging of a mutual friend who was on the board of the North Carolina Teaching Fellows program. The Education Committee elected to reauthorize the Higher Education Act in six segments, starting with the Ready to Teach Act (H.R. 2211) introduced by Rep. Phil Gingrey (R-Georgia), which sought to renew and expand the HEA title pertaining to teacher preparation. As the Subcommittee on Twenty-First Century Competitiveness considered the Gingrey bill, Ballenger suggested that it would be enhanced by inclusion

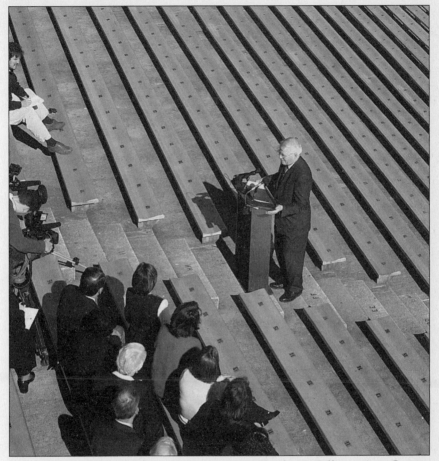

FIGURE 6.1   Press conference announcing Teaching Fellows Act, Carter-Finley Stadium, February 27, 2001. Photo by *Raleigh News and Observer.*

of programmatic elements from our Teaching Fellows bill. Subcommittee chairman Howard McKeon (D-California) was receptive, and ranking Democrat Dale Kildee again offered support. My staff thus worked with committee staff between subcommittee and full committee markups to incorporate key features of H.R. 1805 into the bill—scholarships for high school seniors and/or college sophomores; scholarships and institutional support for community colleges; extracurricular enrichment and professional development activities; and an obligation for recipients to teach in a public school for the term of their scholarship plus one year.

This legislative opportunity came up quickly, and we were able to respond to it by virtue of the groundwork we had laid and the determination of committee leaders to handle this portion of the HEA in a bipartisan fashion. The full committee adopted H.R. 2211 as amended without dissent on June 10, 2003, and the House passed the bill on July 8. I was careful, with a detailed statement on the floor, to provide some legislative history—an account of how the elements we had added to the bill would cohere in a functioning program.[22] It would have been preferable to pass my bill as originally formulated, and my chances of doing that would have been better had either the House or the White House been under Democratic control. Under the circumstances, however, I was pleased to have enacted, albeit in fragments, a bill whose prospects had looked bleak a few weeks before. I was also well aware of the challenges that lay ahead: securing Senate agreement, pushing for adequate appropriations (my bill had envisioned annual expenditures of $200 million for the college scholarship program and $100 million for the Partnership program), and overseeing executive branch implementation. But the need is urgent—the nation must recruit 2.5 million new teachers over the next decade, and none of the education reforms we envision will work without a first-rate teaching force. I am confident that my proposal will have increasing appeal as a way to enhance the federal contribution to teacher recruitment and retention.

Appropriations Initiatives

I will describe, finally, the kinds of policy initiatives I have undertaken on the Appropriations Committee. Work on Appropriations is often seen as a matter of district service instead of policy entrepreneurship, and I will discuss it in that context (Chapter 10). But Appropriations matters range across a continuum from local projects to programs of broad national scope, and many initiatives that may be local in origin draw members into larger policy issues.

In his landmark 1973 study of congressional committee operations, Richard Fenno identified two "strategic premises" that governed the work of the House Appropriations Committee. The first was to "reduce executive budget requests," the second "to provide adequate funding for executive programs."[23] The latter premise obviously was in some tension with the first, reflecting the ambivalence of House members as to how they wanted this powerful committee to perform. In the ensuing years, the second premise increasingly came to predominate, as the House vested fiscal control in the budget process instituted by the Congressional

Budget and Impoundment Control Act of 1974 and as the policies of the Reagan administration cast the Democratic Congress in the role of defender of governmental programs.

Nowadays the Appropriations Committee frequently finds itself chafing under budget constraints variously administered by the Budget Committee, the party leadership, and/or the Office of Management and Budget. The severity of the conflict at a given time may depend on which party is in control where. For a time after the 1995 Republican takeover, it appeared that the role of appropriators as budget guardians might be restored with a vengeance. At the committee's organizational meeting on January 10, the new chairman, Bob Livingston (R-Louisiana), who had been handpicked by Speaker Gingrich over four more senior members, brandished an alligator-skinning knife, then a foot-long bowie knife, and finally a machete to dramatize his determination to cut spending. But before long, Republican as well as Democratic appropriators found themselves at odds with House Republican leaders who demanded that legislative riders be attached to appropriations bills and that draconian budget caps be imposed. Such conflict was easily predictable given the expectations members place on Appropriations as the protector of specific programs and projects. But even when tight budget allocations are accepted and agreed on, it is left to Appropriations to determine specific funding priorities within these allocations. That is why an Appropriations seat is so valuable: It enables one to influence such decisions directly and broker requests from colleagues.

In shifting from Banking and Science to Appropriations, I encountered marked differences in committee organization and procedures, which influenced the way policy entrepreneurship worked. Most authorizing committees, including Science and Banking, have devolved significant decisionmaking power to subcommittees, but none more than Appropriations. The most opportune time to get an item into an appropriations bill is when the subcommittee is preparing it for the full committee, and the most important players are the subcommittee chairman and his or her staff. On the Banking and Science Committees and their subcommittees, the "chairman's mark" is a document of considerable importance, but it is often only a starting point for a protracted and public process of revision and amendment. Not so on most Appropriations subcommittees. The chairman, ranking minority member, and their staffs assemble and evaluate myriad member requests and incorporate many of them, in some fashion, in the chairman's mark. That draft is generally altered only at the margins. Under both Democratic and Republican regimes, there has been variation among subcommittees as to the bipartisanship of this process,

FIGURE 6.2   Full committee markup session in the House Appropriations
Committee, May 25, 2000.

ranging from full collaboration to giving the ranking minority member a
quick look before bringing the mark to the subcommittee. But in general,
the decision process on Appropriations is far less partisan than on most
authorizing committees, and the chances for minority members to have
significant input are much greater.

The starting point for the chairman's mark is the administration's budget request, which has been presented and defended by agency heads in
subcommittee hearings. Members are furnished documents showing how
the chairman's draft differs from the administration's request on each
item. The differences are often substantial, and there is usually little question that the bill has been reviewed item by item and given the subcommittee's own imprint.

I have served on seven Appropriations subcommittees; on each, the requests of subcommittee members have been given special consideration
and members have been informed, usually through staff channels, of how
their items fared shortly before the chairman's mark is unveiled. It is difficult to alter these decisions in any way that requires a major reallocation
of funding among items, but marginal changes are sometimes accepted
by the chair before or during subcommittee markup. There is also great

resistance to "opening up the bill" in full committee markup, where even the layout of the room suggests a certain collegiality (see Figure 6.2). But since 1995 some of the bipartisan deference shown subcommittees has weakened. This is especially evident in efforts to alter bills such as Labor–Health and Human Services–Education that deal with conflicting partisan priorities and in the proposal of legislative "riders" to appropriations bills by various members, not only dissenting Democrats but also conservative Republicans. Still, Appropriations markups are more abbreviated and less substantive than markups on most authorizing committees, and policy entrepreneurship is more of an inside game.

I have undertaken many of my Appropriations efforts, on matters both within and beyond the jurisdictions of my subcommittees, as part of a broad coalition of members pushing for enhanced funding. Examples include the biomedical research programs of the National Institutes of Health (NIH), the Women, Infants, and Children (WIC) nutrition program, HOME housing partnerships, and housing for the elderly and disabled. These efforts have generally been rooted in my knowledge of what these programs have meant at home as well as my convictions about competing national priorities.

In other cases, generally involving programs of more limited scope, I have been the primary or sole advocate on my subcommittee for a given item. This requires a more concerted effort to communicate with committee leaders and staff, enlist colleagues, and work with interested groups and agencies. One example is the NSF Advanced Technical Education (ATE) program, established to implement my Scientific and Advanced Technology Act of 1992. Fortunately it fell under the jurisdiction of the VA-HUD appropriations subcommittee to which I gained membership after returning to the House in 1997. I helped push the Bush administration's anemic funding requests into the $23 million range in the program's first years. By 1997 I found that NSF had overcome much of its reluctance and was administering the program with some vigor, but that current funding ($27.9 million) and President Clinton's request for fiscal 1998 ($29.2 million) were still hovering below authorized levels and were holding the program back. Community college leaders and NSF administrators testified as to the impact of the program and their ability to use more resources well. As a result, I again took up the cause of advanced technical training: I was able to get the 1998 appropriation up to $31.2 million, 12 percent above the 1997 number, and have continued my efforts since then. I have not done equally well each year, but by 2004 the ATE appropriation was $45.2 million, the result of annual increases averaging more than 8 percent since I joined the VA-HUD Subcommittee.

A second example is Department of Veterans Affairs (VA) medical and prosthesis research. Veterans health care has strong advocates among veterans organizations and many House members on and off the VA-HUD Subcommittee, which has resulted in increases to the veterans budgets of Republican and Democratic presidents alike. VA medical research has not enjoyed the same level of visibility and support, and by 1997 the department's career development program for young researchers was in decline and the portion of meritorious research proposals being funded was stuck below 30 percent. I was aware of the value of this research, not likely to be replicated elsewhere, from conversations with national and state veterans leaders, particularly from the Disabled American Veterans (DAV). My staff and I also had extensive discussions with administrators of the Durham (North Carolina) VA Medical Center, one of the department's major research operations, about the program's needs.

In 1997 I concentrated on reversing President Clinton's proposed reduction (from $262 to $234 million) in the VA research budget for fiscal 1998 and considered it a victory when we agreed on a final number of $272 million. This helped the department secure a more adequate request of $300 million from the president for fiscal 1999, which I was able to raise in our subcommittee bill to $316 million. Veterans Affairs secretary Togo West testified in 1999 as to the effects of this funding: an increase from 88 (1997) to 168 (1999) in the number of young clinician-investigators being supported in the career development program and an increase to 40 percent in the portion of meritorious proposals funded.[24]

The appropriations process reveals program failures and abuses as well as successes and additional needs. It also provides a forum for reviewing agency decisions. Sometimes this results in corrective action, although appropriations are not always a precise instrument for achieving this purpose. I will cite three examples, one involving a funding cut, the second the reversal of agency abuses revealed in a hearing, and the third a congressional attempt to counter a regulatory decision.

During my first term on Appropriations, when I was on the Agriculture Subcommittee, I was reluctantly approached by a friend who was a longtime civil servant in the Department of Agriculture. Hardly the stereotypical whistle-blower, he was nonetheless deeply troubled by what he perceived as abuses and extravagances in the administration of the department. He had a long list, but one item struck me as particularly outrageous and relevant to the subcommittee's upcoming hearings on fiscal 1993 budget requests: a lavish awards ceremony put on by the Agricultural Stabilization and Conservation Service (ASCS) to honor 900 employees, most of them flown to Washington from state and county offices. This amounted to almost one-fourth of the total ASCS workforce, and the cost was $674,226—compared to costs well under $15,000 for awards ceremonies at other Agriculture Department agencies.

I expected Agriculture Secretary Edward Madigan to come to our hearing prepared to defend the ASCS, for my aide had been gathering information from the department for several weeks. But apparently none of Madigan's subordinates told him about the inquiry: "I have previously not been acquainted with these numbers by anyone," he acknowledged. Embarrassed by the publicity, the department made last-minute efforts to cut back the already planned June 8–9, 1992, ceremony (which ended up costing $492,000, cut to "the absolute minimum," the ASCS administrator said). Our subcommittee's response was to look far more critically at ASCS salaries and expense accounts. We cited "excessive" awards ceremony expenses as partial justification for reducing the account $5.2 million below its 1992 level.[25]

An abuse of a different sort was revealed to me by a small businessman in my district who was working with the National Emergency Equipment Dealers Association (NEEDA). Their complaint was that a program designed to give state and local law enforcement officials access to drug interdiction equipment from central suppliers at discounted prices had been taken far beyond its original intent by the General Services Administration (GSA), to the disadvantage of small local suppliers. The State and Local Law Enforcement Equipment Procurement Program, commonly known as the "1122 program" after the relevant section of the 1994 defense authorization bill, had initially involved the federal supply schedules relevant to drug interdiction. But in 1998 and 1999, GSA, seeking to expand its reach, collect increased fees, and please its state and local patrons, added numerous supply schedules, including such items as lighting fixtures, food service equipment, musical instruments, and others seemingly unrelated to the program's mission.

The complaints from NEEDA and my constituent came just as GSA was preparing to testify before my Treasury–Postal Service Appropriations Subcommittee. When several other members of the subcommittee and I questioned the GSA director on March 17, 1999, concerning these program expansions, he was caught off guard and had no convincing explanation. He acknowledged the appearance of overstepping and promised to respond to our questions. I began to prepare language for our subcommittee report to direct GSA to scale back the 1122 program to its intended purposes. But this proved unnecessary after GSA indicated, in a letter to the Defense Department, its intention to "revert to the ten schedules that were originally decided upon" in response to the concerns raised in our hearing. Our report thus commended GSA for this action and expressed the expectation that consultation "with the appropriate committees of the Congress" would precede any future program expansions.[26]

My third example came in the wake of a controversial decision by the Federal Communications Commission (FCC) to loosen the rules limiting concentration in media ownership. In the early weeks of 2003 it became clear that FCC chairman Michael Powell was prepared to push for an early and far-reaching ruling. But he had a formidable opponent in Democratic commissioner Michael Copps, who was opposed to further deregulation and offended that Powell had scheduled only one public hearing on the matter. Copps convened unofficial hearings around the country during the spring, the first of which I helped him stage at Duke University on March 31. We were astounded at the enthusiastic response. Media concentration clearly resonated across the political spectrum, from family values advocates disturbed that "reality" television shows that demeaned marriage were being foisted by networks on their local affiliates, to Dixie Chicks fans appalled that the group was being removed from a radio conglomerate's playlist because of their outspoken opposition to President Bush.

I had earlier seen the negative local effects of the consolidation of radio ownership that came in the wake of the Telecommunications Act of 1996 and had talked at some length with a prominent local media executive, James Goodmon of Capitol Broadcasting in Raleigh, about the undesirability of taking television down the same path. Goodmon devoted considerable time and resources to the issue in early 2003 and helped bring Rep. Richard Burr (R-North Carolina) into the fray. Burr was an important recruit—a prominent member of the Energy and Commerce Committee (which had jurisdiction over the FCC) who was willing, up to a point, to oppose the FCC's Republican majority and the White House. I also established contact with several Democrats interested in the issue. As it became clear that Powell and the Commission majority intended to move ahead without deliberation or delay, we and our staffs began to consider congressional options to thwart the ruling. These came into play almost immediately after the FCC handed down the 3–2 decision on June 2.

The most straightforward approach, which faced almost insuperable obstacles in the opposition of the House Republican leadership and Energy and Commerce Committee chairman Billy Tauzin (R-Louisiana), was simply to legislate a reversal of all or part of the FCC ruling. I helped organize support for a bill (H.R. 2050) introduced by Burr and Energy and Commerce's ranking Democrat, John Dingell (D-Michigan), to leave in place the existing cap of 35 percent on the share of the national audience television stations owned by any one company would be allowed to reach (the FCC ruling raised the cap to 45 percent). I also cosponsored a bill (H.R. 2462) authored by Rep. Bernard Sanders (I-Vermont) to nullify the entire FCC rule, including the lifting of the ban on one company owning newspapers and television stations in the same market and the loosening of the limits on the number of stations any one company could own in a single market. Another possibility was to introduce a "resolution of disapproval," a procedure that the Republican Congress had devised in 1996 to facilitate overturning federal regulations but had been used successfully only once. Senator Byron Dorgan (D-North Dakota) eventually (September 16) got such a resolution through the Senate, 55–40, but it never had a chance to reach the House floor.

An appropriations amendment would be of more limited scope and duration; in order to escape an adverse parliamentary ruling, it could only forbid the expenditure of funds appropriated by the bill for the next fiscal year to implement one or more of the FCC rules. House Republican leaders were certain to object to waiving House rules, which a farther-reaching amendment would require. But an appropriations strategy had major advantages: the Commerce-Justice-State (C-J-S) bill, which included FCC funding, was must-pass legislation, and the Appropriations Committee markup offered us an opportunity to offer a provision free of parliamentary obstacles. As the July 16 markup approached, Rep. Dave Obey (D-Wisconsin), the full committee's ranking Democrat, prepared an amendment to withhold funding for the new 45 percent rule, calculating that it was the element of the FCC decision we had the best chance of blocking. My staff and I conferred with several other members and their aides, settling on a common strategy and contacting prospective supporters on the committee. When the vote came, all Democratic members were in their seats voting aye, and we were joined by eleven Republicans. The 40–25 vote was a stunning rebuke to the FCC, the White House, and the House GOP leadership.

When the bill reached the House floor on July 22, we came close to an even larger victory. Representative Maurice Hinchey (D-New York) and I prepared an amendment to block funding for the remaining FCC rules involving cross-media ownership and local ownership concentration. While we had agreed with Obey's strategy in committee to focus on blocking the 45 percent rule in order to maximize our favorable vote, we regarded the other components of the ruling as equally important and sensed a groundswell of support. We anticipated Republican leadership opposition but were unpleasantly surprised when, after mixed signals and minimal consultation, Dingell and Obey announced that they opposed our amendment. Both claimed to agree with us on the merits but professed concern that adding our provisions might provoke a presidential veto. The White House, however, had already threatened a veto because of the Obey amendment alone, and it was unclear why we should hesitate to challenge the administration on an issue that was fast becoming a major embarrassment. My only concern in going forward was that opposition from Dingell and Obey might cause us to receive a small enough vote to slow progress toward a broader resolution of disapproval in the Senate.

I need not have worried. Our amendment attracted 174 votes, including 34 Republicans—giving a boost to our Senate collaborators and once again demonstrating the wide resonance of the issue.[27] MoveOn.org, joined by groups across the spectrum from Consumers Union to the National Rifle Association, generated thousands of calls and e-mails to members' offices in a remarkably short period of time. I talked at length with our Democratic leaders to ensure that they would not work against the Hinchey-Price amendment. In the end, most of them voted for it, and the outcome prompted speculation that we might have won had they been willing to challenge Dingell and Obey more directly.

The C-J-S bill passed the House overwhelmingly with Obey's committee amendment intact, and on September 4 the Senate Appropriations Committee reported their C-J-S bill with a similar provision. Senate Commerce Committee chairman John McCain (R-Arizona) put a "hold" on the bill, opposing the FCC amendment as an infringement on the authorizing panel's jurisdiction. As the October 1 beginning of the fiscal year came and went, Congress passed a series of continuing resolutions to keep the agencies running whose appropriations bills had not been passed. The C-J-S measure became caught up in the end-of-session effort to combine the remaining bills into an "omnibus" measure. This situation enhanced the leverage of the Republican leadership in both houses, and there was considerable speculation that the ownership cap provision might be dropped despite its inclusion in both C-J-S bills. The resistance of Senate Appropriations chairman Ted Stevens (R-Alaska) and other senior appropriators sufficed to avoid that result, but at the last minute the administration still got much of what it wanted: the existing 35 percent cap was raised to 39 percent, high enough to accommodate CBS and Fox, the networks that had already exceeded the 35 percent ownership limit. "The Republicans went into a closet, met with themselves and announced a 'compromise,'" explained Sen. Ernest Hollings, ranking Democrat on both Commerce and the C-J-S Appropriations Subcommittee. "We weren't a part of it whatsoever."[28]

The media concentration amendment to the C-J-S bill obviously fell short of a total victory. It reached only one of the FCC rules, and that only in part. Still, it serves as an example of how an appropriations provision can reduce agency discretion or block implementation of an agency ruling, offering a way around the conventional legislative process.

Appropriations also offers opportunities to launch innovative programs, usually through the funding of a specific project but sometimes through the creation of new funding categories. An example of the first type is the launching of research in the management and utilization of animal waste by constructing and sustaining North Carolina State University's (NCSU) Animal and Poultry Waste Management Center. During my term on the Agriculture Subcommittee, I began discussing the project with NCSU administrators and scientists, who understood the challenge of controlling poultry and swine waste and the potential of converting it to value-added products long before waste became a headline issue in North Carolina and the nation. I obtained $888,000 for facility construction in fiscal 1993 and $414,000 and $373,000 for research operations in 1994 and 1995, respectively. Funding lapsed with my departure, although Fred Heineman managed to secure an appropriation of $150,000 (increased to $215,000 in conference) for fiscal 1997. On returning to the House, I put the center at the top of my request list to the Agriculture Subcommittee, bolstered by the urgency of the waste issue and the center's national and international renown. I got the appropriation back to $300,000 for fiscal 1998 and, with the help of sympathetic members and staff, secured a nonincremental increase to $500,000 for fiscal years 1999 and beyond.

My second example of program innovation did not involve a specific project, although I had an organization in mind that I believed could successfully apply for the funds. The proposal was comparable to my soft second mortgage amendment to the 1990 Housing Bill, although I developed and proposed it from the Appropriations Committee. The idea was to encourage home ownership among low-income borrowers by making credit from private institutions more available to them; the device was HUD grants to nonprofits, usable for capital reserves, to help them create a secondary market for these mortgages.

I had been impressed by the success of the Center for Community Self-Help, a community development financial institution (CDFI) in Durham, in pioneering a secondary-market demonstration that encouraged lenders to serve persons who had hitherto been considered high risk and, with counseling and good management, kept default rates low. I was therefore attentive when Self-Help shopped its idea of HUD secondary-market demonstration to me in anticipation of the fiscal 1998 appropriations cycle, and I was pleased to find that their prior reputation, in addition to the persuasive case they were prepared to make, gained them a respectful hearing among Republican as well as Democratic staff as we tested the political feasibility of their idea.

Still, this was a much more ambitious venture than beefing up appropriations for existing programs like ATE or VA research. HUD administrators did not oppose my proposal, but they were distinctly unenthused. And because we were creating authority for a new housing program (however small and experimental) on an appropriations bill, we faced possible parliamentary objections from Banking, the authorizing committee. But VA-HUD chairman Jerry Lewis (R-California) and ranking Democrat Louis Stokes (D-Ohio) and their staffs were receptive to my idea and accommodating in finding a place for it in the bill. We settled on a $10 million earmark in the HOME account, which was already being increased by $191 million over the administration's request.

The secondary market provision was still vulnerable to a point of order on the House floor. To try to head that off, I enlisted the help of Mel Watt (D-North Carolina), a Banking Committee member who at that time represented Durham, knew Self-Help well, and had considered offering its proposal on his own committee. We spoke selectively with members and staff, not wishing to call more attention to this rather obscure provision than it had already attracted. But we did not know until the moment of floor consideration whether any Banking member would appear to object. As the bill title containing HOME was considered, Watt stood at one door to the chamber and I at the other. The member we most feared would offer objections finally appeared, but only after the title was closed and objections were not in order. We are not certain to this day whether he was late inadvertently or was deferring to our request.

In any event, the bill was passed on July 16, 1997, with the secondary market demonstration intact, and the provision survived in conference. HUD did not implement the new program with great dispatch. It took considerable goading, including my sharp exchanges with Secretary Andrew Cuomo in subcommittee hearings, before the department finally issued a notice of funding availability on March 10, 1999. The program then got underway, and Self-Help received one of two $5 million grants awarded in 1999. It leveraged the grant at a 20 to 1 ratio in just one year, financing $100 million in loans that allowed 1,800 families who fell outside the traditional underwriting criteria to buy their first homes. As a demonstration, the program has shown major players in the secondary market the feasibility of making capital available to lenders to enable hundreds of thousands of hardworking low-income families to become homeowners.

The EPA Building Saga

My final example of appropriations entrepreneurship is the construction of a new research facility for the Environmental Protection Agency in Research Triangle Park (RTP). It shows how appropriations efforts—normally local in orientation, muted in partisanship, and of limited complexity—can break out of that mold. This fight drew in authorizers as well as appropriators, opened up deep partisan and political divisions, and carried broader implications for not only the location but also the scale of the nation's environmental research.

The founders of RTP regarded federal labs as potential tenants from the beginning. A series of North Carolina governors, congressional representatives, and business leaders set out to lure EPA's predecessor agency and the National Institute of Environmental Health Sciences (NIEHS; founded in 1966 and the only NIH institute located outside of Washington, D.C.) to North Carolina. In 1968 the Research Triangle Foundation set aside 509 acres for eventual occupation by federal environmental labs. In 1971, shortly after its reorganization as an independent agency, EPA opened a research center in rented space in RTP. NIEHS moved to its permanent RTP site in the early 1980s, but by 1991 EPA had not even designed its permanent facility. In the meantime, its operations had spread to twelve locations, with rental and associated costs of about $15 million annually.

I got to know administrators at EPA and NIEHS during my first term. They proved responsive to my concerns about procurement opportunities for small and/or local businesses and provided me a quick education on their needs for modernized and expanded lab space. Before I was appointed to the Appropriations Committee, I was able to obtain a $1.7 million planning grant, which led to construction on the University of North Carolina campus of a human studies laboratory to be leased and operated by EPA. Appointment to the committee put me in an improved position to promote NIEHS requests for lab expansion ($42 million from 1992–1995) and to get planning and design work underway on the long-deferred EPA project in RTP.

I worked with Tim Valentine (D-North Carolina), a member of EPA's authorizing committee (the main research facilities were then located in Valentine's district), successive VA-HUD Subcommittee chairmen Bob Traxler (D-Michigan) and Louis Stokes (D-Ohio), and EPA officials in North Carolina and Washington to secure planning funds in fiscal 1992 and succeeding VA-HUD appropriations bills. We made some headway, but with $5 million in 1992 and $5.5 million in 1993, we seemed destined to spend five years piecing together the planning budget for a project already long overdue. I was not on the VA-HUD Subcommittee, and both the administration and the subcommittee seemed unlikely to propose larger amounts. But we knew that the GSA would eventually be involved with the project, and we had a supportive colleague in Steny Hoyer (D-Maryland), chair of the Treasury–Postal Service Subcommittee that appropriated for GSA. We therefore devised a scheme. For fiscal 1994, $8.8 million for the design of the EPA building would be included in the GSA budget, along with another $3 million in the EPA budget. This brought the planning and design total to $22.3 million and enabled us to complete the funding in three years rather than five. It also speeded up the interagency "value engineering" process, which in early 1994 produced a revised cost estimate for the project, $231.9 million, down 12 percent from earlier projections.

In the meantime, Lauch Faircloth replaced Terry Sanford as North Carolina's junior senator. Sanford, who as governor had helped recruit EPA in the 1960s, had been a valuable partner in our funding efforts. But the project had enjoyed bipartisan support, and I expected Faircloth to help push the project in the Senate. During his earlier years as a Democrat he had been state commerce secretary and energetically promoted economic development. It soon became clear that I was totally mistaken. Faircloth lost little time in expressing his disdain for the EPA and his view that reducing federal spending should start with this project (despite demonstrations of $166 million in savings [1994 dollars] over thirty years when compared to rental costs). Faircloth brought along Senator Helms, who had hitherto been a supporter but now told the press that he would rather see EPA housed in Quonset huts than increase the national debt.

Faircloth sat on the Public Works Committee, which authorized for the EPA. He used a hearing on May 12, 1993, at which the new EPA administrator, Carol Browner, was testifying, to announce his opposition to the RTP project. He and Helms subsequently got the 1994 planning funds deleted from both the GSA and EPA bills in the Senate. But aided by strong support from House appropriators—and by the fact that Senate committees were still under Democratic control—we managed to get the full $11.8 million restored in conference.

Numerous perils remained, however, most immediately a requirement that the GSA planning be authorized before it could be fully executed. This placed the project back before the Senate Public Works Committee, where Faircloth resolved to defeat it. Valentine and I enlisted the help of Bill Hefner, a North Carolina colleague and senior appropriator, and Governor Jim Hunt, an energetic promoter of RTP. We worked for several days, coordinating carefully with Administrator Browner, lobbying the Public Works senators one by one before their scheduled January 27, 1994, meeting. Even among Democrats, we were concerned about the senatorial custom of deference to a colleague about a project in his or her state, to say nothing of those who coveted EPA funds and facilities for their own states. Harry Reid (D-Nevada) voted with Faircloth, no doubt mindful of likely future votes on the placement of a repository for high-level nuclear waste in his state. But the other Democratic senators held firm, enabling us to defeat Faircloth on his own committee by a single vote (8–9).

Then came the 1994 election, which put Faircloth in the Senate majority and replaced Valentine (who retired) and me with two declared opponents of the EPA building. But the project survived. The election seemed to call the Republicans' bluff: Faced with the potential to kill the project, they chose not to do so. Fred Heineman had opposed the project during the campaign, but in an offhand way. EPA officials brought him around to a position of support within a few months, and he in turn helped persuade Faircloth. On May 20, 1995, the two jointly announced their change of position, justifying it by reference to reductions in project costs realized at their insistence. That explanation did not bear scrutiny, for the cost reductions they touted had come as the result of the value engineering study, announced on January 20, 1994, before Faircloth tried to kill the project in the Public Works Committee and before Heineman was even nominated. But EPA received the support gratefully as it sought to secure the $50 million in first-year construction funding proposed by President Clinton for fiscal 1996.

The VA-HUD Subcommittee omitted the building from the bill it brought to the House floor in July 1995. Heineman supported the bill anyway, along with the deep cuts in EPA research and enforcement budgets and the seventeen antienvironmental riders that made the bill a symbol of the excesses of the Gingrich "revolution" (see Chapter 3). As the appropriations deliberations continued long after the beginning of the 1996 fiscal year, Heineman and Faircloth lobbied for inclusion of the $50 million in the omnibus measure into which the overdue appropriations bills were rolled. The bill finally passed in April 1996, with the EPA appropriation included but contingent on the approval of the entire project by the House and Senate authorizing committees. By then the president's 1997 request had also been submitted; at the urging of Governor Hunt and EPA leaders, Clinton asked for the full $182 million to complete construction. The House VA-HUD Subcommittee reduced the amount to $82 million; the Senate Subcommittee, citing authorization problems, appropriated nothing, but the conferees settled on $60 million, bringing the two-year total to $110 million.

I made calls and wrote letters of support to the ranking Democrats on the House authorizing committee, now called Transportation and Infrastructure, and on Appropriations, noting that the project once again had bipartisan backing. But by now the 1996 campaign was heating up, and Heineman and his aides were publicly claiming that he had succeeded where I had failed and even that my Democratic allies and I were attempting to sabotage the project. To the extent that the competition between us motivated Heineman to pursue funding and Republican leaders to respond favorably, I suppose the cause was helped.[29] But in denigrating my longest-running and most difficult appropriations undertaking and accusing me of bad faith, the attacks hit close to home and provoked some of the sharpest exchanges of the 1996 campaign.

On returning to the House and the Appropriations Committee in 1997, I expected to seek the $122 million in construction funding not yet appropriated. This was one reason I was so pleased when I unexpectedly gained a seat on the VA-HUD Subcommittee. But it turned out that I needed that seat more than I had thought, for the bids on the project came in $40 million to $80 million higher than anticipated. EPA was faced with the unattractive alternatives of breaching the authorization figure that Heineman and Faircloth had made sacrosanct or cutting back on elements integral to the building's design. My staff and I examined the situation carefully, including the economies earlier achieved through the value engineering process, the reasons for the high bids, and what components should not be sacrificed. I concluded that a $40 million increase in the authorization to $272.7 million was fully justified and that we should seek to implement it through the appropriations process if possible, avoiding another visit to the authorizing committees.

Faircloth was now on the Senate Appropriations Committee, and I had no idea how he would react. I proceeded carefully, working closely with EPA, securing the support of VA-HUD chairman Jerry Lewis (R-California) and ranking Democrat Louis Stokes, making certain that VA-HUD chief clerk Frank Cushing, who knew the project well, was fully briefed on the situation we faced, and attempting to give the authorizers due notice without encouraging their intervention. I was also pursuing a sizable increment of funding. Chairman Lewis put the full $162.7 million needed to complete the project, $40 million above the president's request, in the House bill, and the conferees agreed on $90 million. But I placed even greater importance on getting the total $272.7 million authorization written into law. This we were able to do, passing the VA-HUD bill in the House on July 16, 1997, and, with Cushing's help, persuading Senate staff to retain the authorization provision in conference.[30] Faircloth did not object, and when the president signed the bill on October 27, I felt that the project had cleared its last major hurdle. All that remained was to appropriate the remaining $72.7 million, which we did in the fiscal 1999 and 2000 bills.

FIGURE 6.3   Installing the flagpole and raising the flag at the EPA construction site in Research Triangle Park, with chief administrator William Laxton, April 7, 2000.

In the meantime, construction on the building proceeded (see Figure 6.3). On September 11, 2000, Administrator Browner came to RTP to dedicate the cornerstone, and on May 29, 2002, the completed facility was dedicated with President Bush's EPA administrator, Christine Todd Whitman, in attendance.

The twists and turns of the EPA story, I said to a reporter after one particularly narrow escape, were reminiscent of the silent movie saga *The Perils of Pauline*. There was never much doubt that the project was important to North Carolina. EPA employs 1,300 in the state and contracts with 900 more, injecting $220 million directly into the state economy each year. Constructing the lab made sense in terms of ultimate savings and EPA operating efficiency. But the nine-year appropriations effort was shaped and almost overcome by partisan politics within and beyond Congress and by broader conflicts over environmental funding. The complexity of the process, with its requirements for authorizer-appropriator as well as House-Senate concurrence, often gave opponents an opening, but it also sometimes gave proponents a chance to recoup.

The new EPA lab will help ensure, as I often put it in community meeting presentations, that environmental regulation will be based on sound science and that North Carolina will remain the center of the nation's environmental research—a simple formulation that captures the lab's national and local significance. But keeping the project on track year to year was anything but simple. If the EPA building saga illustrates the potential for policy entrepreneurship from the Appropriations Committee, it also reveals a process that offers few shortcuts and many strategic challenges.

Notes

1. Robert A. Dahl, *Pluralist Democracy in the United States: Conflict and Consent* (Chicago: Rand McNally, 1967), p. 136. Dahl qualified this view considerably in later editions. See, for example, *Democracy in the United States: Promise and Performance*, 4th ed. (Boston: Houghton Mifflin, 1981), pp. 135–138.

2. See Richard Fenno, *The Power of the Purse: Appropriations Politics in Congress* (Boston: Little, Brown, 1966) and Ralph Huitt and Robert L. Peabody, eds., *Congress: Two Decades of Analysis* (New York: Harper & Row, 1969).

3. David E. Price, *Who Makes the Laws?* (Cambridge, Mass.: Schenkman, 1972).

4. For a summary and update of these findings, see David E. Price, "Congressional Committees in the Policy Process," in Lawrence C. Dodd and Bruce I. Oppenheimer, eds., *Congress Reconsidered*, 3d ed. (Washington, D.C.: Congressional Quarterly Press, 1985), chap. 7.

5. See David E. Price, "Professionals and 'Entrepreneurs': Staff Orientations and Policy Making on Three Senate Committees," *Journal of Politics*, May 1971, pp. 316–336.

6. Roger H. Davidson and Carol Hardy, "Indicators of House of Representatives Workload and Activity," *Congressional Research Service Report* 87–4925, June 8, 1987, pp. 13, 32, 63; and Ilona B. Nickels, "The Legislative Workload of the Congress: Numbers are Misleading," *CRS Review*, July–August 1988, pp. 23–24. These articles also point up a number of difficulties in using such data as a precise indicator of the falloff in legislative initiative. Data on numbers of bills introduced are especially problematic because of changes in the rules of cosponsorship in the House. The increasing tendency to bundle complex budget and other measures together resulted in fewer—but longer—bills; at the same time, the popularity of commemorative bills and resolutions kept the overall number of enactments deceptively high. For a survey that discerns overall "a sudden and striking contraction" in congressional workload indicators during the 1980s, see Roger H. Davidson, "The New Centralization on Capitol Hill," *Review of Politics*, Summer 1988, pp. 352–355.

7. On the incentives to policy entrepreneurship provided by "environmental factors," especially perceived levels of public salience and conflict, see David E.

Price, *Policymaking in Congressional Committees: The Impact of "Environmental" Factors* (Tucson: University of Arizona Press, 1979).

8. On the place of "interested outsiders" in committee affairs, see Richard Fenno, *Congressmen in Committees* (Boston: Little, Brown, 1973), p. 15 and passim.

9. *Congressional Quarterly Almanac* 45 (1989): 655.

10. For an account of the FIRREA amendments, see Price, *Congressional Experience*, 1st ed., pp. 65–66.

11. National Housing Task Force, *A Decent Place to Live* (Washington, D.C.: National Housing Task Force, 1988), pp. 18–25.

12. Testimony of Chapel Hill Mayor Jonathan B. Howes, *Affordable Housing*, field hearing before the Subcommittee on Housing and Community Development, Committee on Banking, Finance and Urban Affairs, U.S. House of Representatives, 101st Congress, January 26, 1990 (serial no. 101–75), pp. 14, 153. Also see the exchanges on pp. 33–40.

13. Testimony of Floyd T. Carter, *Affordable Housing*, p. 124.

14. *Scientific and Technical Literacy in the Workforce*, field hearing before the Subcommittee on Science, Research, and Technology of the Committee on Science, Space, and Technology, U.S. House of Representatives, 100th Congress, November 9, 1987.

15. Portraying functional literacy as a moving target, the author went on to suggest that "literacy must be seen as a continuum of basic and applied skills measured against the increasingly complex demands of society and the workplace." Richard A. Mendel, *Workforce Literacy in the South* (Chapel Hill, N.C.: MDC, 1988), pp. 3, 10.

16. Also on the list was Tom Sawyer (D-Ohio), sponsor of the Adult Literacy and Employability Act, a bill dealing mainly with the Adult Education Act and the Job Training Partnership Act, both under the jurisdiction of the Education and Labor Committee. To stress the continuity of our efforts, we cosponsored one another's bills and numbered them sequentially (H.R. 3122 for mine, H.R. 3123 for his). We then testified at each other's hearings.

17. When pressed, NSF witness Bassam Shakhashiri, assistant director of science and engineering education, acknowledged that the distinction between science education and technical training had narrowed considerably, falling back on a plea that NSF not be "overloaded." See *Scientific, Technical, and Literacy Education and Training*, hearing before the Subcommittee on Science, Research, and Technology of the Committee on Science, Space, and Technology, U.S. House of Representatives, 101st Congress, October 31, 1989, pp. 65–66, 159–160.

18. *Precollege Science and Mathematics Education*, hearing before the Subcommittee on Science, Research, and Technology of the Committee on Science, Space, and Technology, U.S. House of Representatives, 101st Congress, February 28, 1990, pp. 66, 84.

19. Committee on Science, Space and Technology, U.S. House of Representatives, 102nd Congress, *Report to accompany H.R. 2936*, April 30, 1992, pp. 6–7.

20. The totals were fifty-three Democratic sponsors, four Republican sponsors, and one Independent sponsor. Representative Nancy Johnson (R-Connecticut) also introduced a bill, H.R. 1627, providing deductibility for educational loan interest and penalty-free drawdowns from retirement plans (5 cosponsors, all Republicans). Other bills proposing deductibility for loan interest included H.R. 82 (Rep. Charles Schumer, D-New York, no cosponsors); H.R. 319 (Rep. Gerald Solomon, R-New York, no cosponsors); H.R. 724 (Rep. Patrick Kennedy, D-Rhode Island, 3 cosponsors); and H.R. 1465 (Rep. Jim Bunning, R-Kentucky, no cosponsors).

21. *Challenges and Innovations in Elementary and Secondary Education*, field hearing before the Subcommittee on Early Childhood, Youth and Families, Committee on Education and the Workforce, U.S. House of Representatives, 106th Congress, September 8, 1999 (serial no. 106–73), pp. 4–5, 36–37, 51–54.

22. *Congressional Record*, daily ed., July 8, 2003, pp. H6366–67.

23. Richard Fenno, *Congressmen in Committees* (Boston: Little, Brown, 1973), pp. 48–49.

24. *Departments of Veterans Affairs and Housing and Urban Development, and Independent Agencies Appropriations for 2000*, hearings before the Subcommittee on VA, HUD, and Independent Agencies, Committee on Appropriations, U.S. House of Representatives, 106th Congress, April 20, 1999, p. 95.

25. *Agriculture, Rural Development, FDA, and Related Agencies Appropriations for 1993*, hearings before the Subcommittee on Agriculture, Committee on Appropriations, U.S. House of Representatives, 102nd Congress, April 29, 1992, p. 899; and Committee on Appropriations, *Report to accompany H.R. 5487*, 102nd Congress, June 25, 1992, p. 59.

26. Letter from GSA Assistant Commissioner Gary Feit to William Croom, assistant secretary of the army for acquisition, logistics, and technology, April 29, 1999; and Committee on Appropriations, *Report to accompany H.R. 2490*, 106th Congress, July 13, 1999, pp. 50–51.

27. John Nichols, "The Online Beat: Media Giants Get Slapped," *The Nation*, July 23, 2003, online ed.; see also Gal Beckerman, "Tripping Up Big Media," *Columbia Journalism Review*, November–December 2003, pp. 15–20.

28. Frank Ahrens, "Democrats Decry 'Compromise' on FCC Rule," *Washington Post*, November 26, 2003, p. E1.

29. See David Rogers, "House Republicans Offer Concessions on Domestic Spending as Elections Near," *Wall Street Journal*, May 31, 1996, p. A12. Rogers cited the EPA building as one of several examples. Democrats, he noted, "seemed torn between declaring victory and crying foul."

30. See the justification provided in the House report on the bill: Committee on Appropriations, *Report to accompany H.R. 2158*, 105th Congress, July 11, 1997, p. 64.

7

Budget Politics

I received a memorable lesson in budget politics early in 1987, my first year in Congress. Four competing versions of the budget resolution—the framework within which all subsequent spending and revenue measures must fit, adopted early in each congressional session—were before the House. President Reagan's proposed budget received a grand total of twenty-seven votes, having been rejected by Republicans and Democrats alike. A proposal put forward by Rep. William Dannemeyer (R-California) that anticipated a return to the gold standard attracted forty-seven hardy souls. And the Black Caucus alternative budget received fifty-six votes. What the House finally passed by a 230–192 vote (and what I voted for as the best of the available alternatives) was a budget resolution reported by the Democratic majority on the Budget Committee in collaboration with the House Democratic leadership.

In the course of these sequential votes, it occurred to me that 140 of my colleagues were voting for no budget whatsoever.[1] The easiest vote politically was no. I would wager that not one of those members paid any serious political price for ducking the issue. For those of us who felt it was our responsibility to put a budgetary framework in place, however, the political costs were all too evident. In my case, the reward was thirty-second ads in the 1988 campaign alleging my eagerness to raise everyone's taxes.

The budget battles of 1987 were child's play compared to those that followed. The 101st Congress stayed in session until nine days before the 1990 election, locked in a struggle to finalize spending and revenue measures for fiscal 1991 and conclude a five-year budget agreement between Congress and the White House. A relatively ambitious deficit-reduction plan was finally approved, along with new budget rules that greatly strengthened controls over spending. But the difficulty of the decisions and the messiness of the process by which they were made denied political credit to all involved. The episode had a great deal to do with congressional incumbents' slipping margins of victory in 1990 (see Chapter 2) and President Bush's 1992 defeat.

The next multiyear budget plan, passed during President Clinton's first year in office, was similar to the 1990 agreement in scope and was no easier to pass, despite unified Democratic control of Congress and the White House. The plan eventually cleared both the House and the Senate without a vote to spare. I was by now on the House Budget Committee and got extensively involved in the struggle to pass the plan, which Democrats had to do without a single Republican vote. This 1993 plan eventually proved the most successful of all, helping produce steadily declining deficits and a sustainable economic recovery and making Republican predictions of economic catastrophe look foolish. But this was not sufficiently clear before November 1994 to avert electoral disaster, which many saw as the Democrats' reward for taking on the deficit. Once again, the most advantageous vote politically on budgetary pain was no.

This seemed to change in 1997, when the Balanced Budget Act was passed by large bipartisan majorities. The combined effects of the 1990 and 1993 plans and the fruits of a good economy had brought a balanced budget within reach. It was politically appealing to vote to "finish the job," particularly when a substantial tax cut sweetened the package and the required deficit reduction measures were far less ambitious than those of 1990 or 1993. But if anyone supposed that budget politics had suddenly become bipartisan or the politics of budgetary surpluses would be markedly easier than dealing with deficits, the balance of the Clinton administration provided ample evidence to the contrary.

Then came fiscal collapse. During the first three years of the George W. Bush administration, the ten-year projection of a unified budget surplus of $5.6 trillion was transformed into an addition of more than $3 trillion to the national debt. A reversal of this magnitude was unprecedented in our country's history—the product of President Bush's massive upper-bracket tax cuts, recession and a sluggish economic recovery, and increased defense and security expenditures. At the same time, the 1990 budget rules that had capped spending and required that tax cuts be paid for were allowed to lapse, leaving the budget process in a weakened state and a budgetary consensus more elusive than ever.

In this chapter, I will highlight these episodes and the budgetary politics that loom so large in the policymaking environment in Congress, not only for members of the Appropriations or Budget Committees like myself but for anyone seeking to move policy in new directions. Whether the budgetary mechanisms and processes serve their intended function is another question. They facilitated movement toward a balanced budget in the 1990s, and they also facilitated budgetary irresponsibility on a grand scale in the early 1980s and 2000s, helping create the problems that the measures of 1990, 1993, and 1997 sought to remedy. Allen Schick's 1980 observation that "for every confrontation there have been dozens of legislative decisions routinely made with fidelity to the budget process" still holds.[2] But during my years in the House, which cover roughly half of the thirty-year history of the budget process, it is the confrontations that have stood out. The process has been subject to evasion and manipulation and has required strong leadership to make it work.

From Reaganomics to "Read My Lips"

The Congressional Budget and Impoundment Control Act of 1974 was an immediate response to President Richard Nixon's extensive impoundments of appropriated funds and his accusations that Congress was fiscally irresponsible. But it also reflected longer-term congressional concerns about failures of budgetary coordination and control and the president's domination of the budget process. New House and Senate Budget Committees were authorized to bring to the floor, early in each congressional session, a budget resolution that would set overall spending limits and guide other committees as they passed individual authorization, appropriations, and tax bills. The idea was to empower Congress without creating major new power centers within Congress. In the House especially, with term limits for members and the chairman and required representation from the Appropriations and Ways and Means Committees, the Budget Committee's independence and continuity of membership were limited.

During the first year of Ronald Reagan's presidency, the concentration of budgetary power reached new heights, albeit under conditions that enhanced presidential, rather than congressional, control and with results that mocked the ideal of fiscal responsibility. In late 1980, Congress had experimented for the first time with implementation of the budget act's "reconciliation" provisions, originally designed to bring final congressional spending decisions on individual bills into line with the comprehensive fiscal blueprint adopted in the budget resolution. This procedure was moved to the beginning of the congressional budget cycle in 1981 under a plan promoted by David Stockman, Reagan's budget director, and Sen. Pete Domenici (R-New Mexico), new chairman of the Senate Budget Committee. The first budget resolution that year included a set of authoritative instructions to Congress as it went about its work, greatly increasing the constraints the budget process placed on the authorizing committees and entitlement programs.

The Reagan administration exploited the reconciliation process (and political momentum from the 1980 elections) to push through a series of omnibus bills that reduced tax revenues over the next five years by nearly

$700 billion, reduced domestic spending by more than $100 billion over three years, and paved the way for substantial increases in defense spending, from $133 billion in 1980 to $266 billion in 1986. The numbers added up to massive annual deficits and eventually to a tripling of the national debt. As a repentant Stockman observed after the president's successful 1984 reelection campaign, "The White House proclaimed a roaring economic success . . . when, in fact, [its policies] had produced fiscal excesses that had never before been imagined."[3]

That feat was not matched by the administration in subsequent years. Shifts in the political climate induced by the recession of 1982–1983 soon weakened the president's hand, and Congress found his budget proposals less and less palatable. But consensus within the Congress was difficult to achieve as well. The Budget Committees in the Senate, under Republican control from 1981 to 1986, and in the Democratic House often produced widely disparate resolutions, and both were challenged by restive appropriations and legislative committees. Just how badly the process had deteriorated—and how difficult it was going to be to secure the cooperation between the parties and between the branches of government to make the machinery work—became evident as my first term in Congress began.

President Reagan proposed his fiscal 1988 budget in early 1987. He acknowledged that it would be $108 billion in deficit, while some analysts predicted a $135 billion shortfall. But the Reagan budget was not accepted, even by members of his own party. It received eleven votes in the Senate and, as already noted, twenty-seven votes in the House. Republicans were skittish about many of the particulars—the total elimination of vocational education funding, almost $2 billion in student aid cuts, and deep cuts in Medicare and veterans health care. But few expressed a desire to formulate a GOP alternative; their preference was simply to vote no. Many heeded the counsel of Republican whip Trent Lott (R-Mississippi): "You do not ever get into trouble for those budgets which you vote against." To which majority leader Tom Foley retorted, "'Don't vote and you won't get into trouble.' What a motto for statesmanship!"[4]

For most of the twentieth century, the budget process was presidentially driven and relied heavily on executive–congressional cooperation. Despite its jealous guardianship of the power of the purse, Congress depends on the executive to propose a viable budget and generally alters it only marginally.[5] Instituted in the 1920s, the process assumed that Congress was ill suited to undertake budgeting on its own and executive leadership was required. The budget reforms of the 1970s did not alter that fundamental reality, although they left Congress somewhat better equipped to develop its own budget in the event of severe intragovern-mental conflict or executive default. That is basically the test that the 100th Congress faced, with results falling considerably short of the ideal.

Democratic Budget Committee members worked with party leaders to formulate an alternative budget resolution, which passed the House on April 9, 1987, with Democratic votes alone. The Democratic proposal im-proved on Reagan's projected deficit reduction by $1 billion, directing House committees to match $18 billion in new revenues with equivalent reductions in projected spending, equally divided between military and nonmilitary accounts.[6] The House proceeded to pass most of its appropri-ations bills, but the Senate had more difficulty and the prospect of presi-dential vetoes and deadlock loomed. This led a number of members to propose a revival of the 1985 Gramm-Rudman-Hollings (G-R-H) law, mi-nus the constitutionally questionable provisions that had led the Supreme Court to reject it. Although some Democratic leaders had initially op-posed G-R-H, they came to see its reinstatement as a way to force all par-ties to the table and put multiyear deficit reduction on track.

The basic concept of G-R-H was to impose increasingly stringent deficit targets on the budget process over five years, so that at the end of this period, the budget would be in balance. If the target was not met in a given year, percentage cuts would be imposed across all accounts (except Social Security and some other mandatory programs) to bring the budget into line. Presumably the threat of such an indiscriminate "sequestration" would give all parties the incentive to reach a settlement. The administra-tion, which had paid lip service to G-R-H originally, was notably unen-thusiastic about its revival, rightly perceiving that it might force President Reagan to modify his rigid stance on new revenues and/or defense spending, which was making substantial deficit reduction impossible. Proponents therefore chose the one legislative vehicle for the G-R-H pro-posal that they knew the administration had to request: an increase in the debt ceiling. The debt ceiling increase with G-R-H attached was cleared in September after protracted negotiations, during which the administration was able to get the deficit reduction target for 1988 reduced to $23 billion from the $36 billion contained in the congressional budget resolution.

It was not certain that even the threat of sequestration would bring the administration to the table. Congressional leaders speculated that the president might be willing to see the indiscriminate cuts occur, assuming that Congress would receive the blame for the ensuing damage. But the stock market crash of October 19 changed everything. It made the adverse impact of the budget crisis on the national interest plain for all to see and created political perils for anyone who appeared to be stalling the process.

By this time the fiscal year had ended, and Congress was forced to re-sort to a series of "continuing resolutions" (omnibus short-term appropri-ations measures) to keep the government running. The Congressional and administration leaders finally agreed on a package that included domes-tic spending cuts of about $8 billion for 1988, defense cuts of $5 billion, and another $5 billion in federal asset sales. Additional revenues would total $9 billion in 1988, produced through tightening some loopholes and continuing some taxes that were to expire; neither excise tax increases nor changes in personal or corporate income tax rates were included. This package produced $30 billion in deficit reduction for 1988, and its second-year provisions were to net a reduction of $46 billion for 1989. These fig-ures more than met the G-R-H targets, although they fell considerably short of what many had hoped for when negotiations began.

This agreement resulted in reduced budget conflict during the second session of the 100th Congress, with both the House and Senate producing most of their fiscal 1989 appropriations bills on schedule. The lull, how-ever, was deceptive. The budget crisis had not gone away, and the G-R-H targets for 1990 and succeeding years were going to be far more difficult to meet than those for 1988 and 1989. The demands for spending were in-tensifying to sustain the Reagan defense buildup; cover rising Social Se-curity, Medicare, agriculture, and other entitlement costs; fund major projects in science and space; and deal with the backlog of need from the Reagan years in areas such as housing, education, and infrastructure. The collapse of the federal savings and loan insurance fund required a mas-sive infusion of public funds, and an ominous slowdown in the economy threatened to exacerbate all of these problems. The confluence of these factors made the budget the most serious and difficult problem facing the 101st Congress, and it compelled a budget agreement going beyond any-thing attempted or achieved in the Reagan years.

George Bush, who had derided Ronald Reagan's supply-side dogmas as "voodoo economics" when he was a presidential candidate in 1980, was widely expected to take a more flexible and cooperative approach to budget matters than had his predecessor. But such hopes were dashed as he assumed a rigid campaign stance on taxes. "Read my lips: no new taxes," he declared in his acceptance speech at the 1988 Republican Na-tional Convention, and he essentially threw the budget problem in the lap of the 101st Congress.

The Bush budget submitted in February 1989 was not a conventional budget but a set of recommendations for marginal adjustments in the fis-cal 1990 budget prepared by the outgoing Reagan administration. Bush sought to establish an activist image for the incoming administration by asking for increases in antidrug, science and technology, and environmental cleanup funding, but he declined to specify where the funds would come from. He managed to reach the G-R-H deficit target by relying on extremely optimistic economic assumptions and proposing reduced overall outlays in Medicare, agriculture, defense, and a large cluster of nonpriority domestic programs. It would be left to Congress, however, to identify the specific reductions. This suggested to most Democrats that Bush was no more willing than his predecessor to face budget reality and that he expected us to take the fall for the painful cuts that would have to be made. "He's saying, 'I'll take care of the increases, and you can be in charge of the cuts,'" one member quipped.

The administration's approach gave the Democratic leadership a strong incentive to seek a bipartisan budget agreement (one that would spread the blame), and the budget resolution passed by both houses in early May resulted from nine weeks of negotiations between congressional leaders and the White House. The budget resolution hit the G-R-H target, but only because it retained many of the White House's optimistic economic assumptions. A good number of Bush's proposed cuts in Medicare and other domestic programs were rejected, and limited initiatives in maternal and child health, child care, education, and drug control were incorporated. The resolution anticipated $5.3 billion in revenues from tax law changes, the same amount proposed by the administration (which claimed that such changes need not violate Bush's "no new taxes" pledge), but left the specifics to the Ways and Means Committee. "This is not an heroic agreement," said Speaker Jim Wright, although he also praised the deal as a "very good start in the direction of better cooperation and better performance."[7]

Disappointment ran deep among members who had hoped for a fresh start on budget policy. Office of Management and Budget (OMB) director Richard Darman ostensibly shared that disappointment, although he was the main architect of the Bush strategy. "Collectively we are engaged in a massive Backward Robin Hood transaction," he said in a widely publicized speech in mid-1989, "robbing the future to give to the present." He went on to hold out the hope that the admittedly "modest" fiscal 1990 agreement could, with "good will and responsible leadership," be followed by a more substantial multiyear package.[8]

What the ensuing weeks brought, instead, was a bruising battle over the capital gains tax. President Bush had included a reduction in the capital gains tax rate as part of his original budget proposal, counting on the reduction to prompt a short-term turnover of assets and thus increase revenues by $4.8 billion in fiscal 1990. Congressional Budget Office (CBO) estimates were considerably less optimistic for the first year, however, and they projected revenue losses over a five-year period of $25 billion.

The Democratic leadership (Wright had by now resigned and Tom Foley had been elected Speaker) regarded the proposal as fiscally irresponsible and antithetical to tax reform. (The tax reform legislation of 1986 had predicated its reduction in the top marginal rate to 28 percent on the repeal of tax breaks such as that accorded capital gains.) But the proposal had majority support on the Ways and Means Committee—all the Republicans, plus six Democrats—and when capital gains was brought to the House floor, the new leadership team, in its first major test, suffered a 190–239 defeat.

The administration continued to press its advantage on capital gains, and in so doing jeopardized the long-term prospects for deficit reduction. Foley left no doubt about this in a somber appearance before our Democratic Budget Group on September 13. The prospects for a multiyear, bipartisan budget agreement were "rapidly collapsing," he said. For Democrats to agree to a "giveaway" on capital gains, the Republicans' top priority, he argued, would make it harder to get the administration back to the table later and would remove one of the key elements that might facilitate a broader agreement. "They have put all their chips on winning capital gains, and it has little to do with deficit reduction," observed House Budget Committee chairman Leon Panetta (D-California). "That poisons the well for the relations you need if you're going to tackle this seriously."[9]

Senate Finance Committee chairman Lloyd Bentsen (D-Texas) and majority leader George Mitchell (D-Maine) managed to keep the capital gains provision out of the Senate reconciliation bill, but the administration and House Republicans demanded that it be retained in conference. Meanwhile, the new fiscal year began. Because most appropriations bills had not yet passed, a continuing resolution was approved to keep the government running, and on October 15 the first stages of G-R-H sequestration were imposed. This increased the pressure on the negotiations considerably, and finally the logjam began to break. On November 2, Bush announced that he was willing to drop his demand that a capital gains tax reduction be included, but he simultaneously demanded $14 billion in "real" deficit reduction as defined by OMB. This prompted angry Democratic charges that Darman was "moving the goal posts" as the game neared its end. Finally conferees agreed on a package that picked up $4.6 billion, one-third of the savings it achieved, by reducing all accounts to what they would have been had sequestration remained in effect through January. The final result fell considerably short of the already modest spring budget agreement. It left exhausted members wondering how they would ever find and agree on the $40 billion in additional savings that G-R-H would require in the next budget cycle.

Budget Summitry, 1990

Despite lingering animosities from the 1989 budget battle, both congressional and administration leaders had strong incentives to seek some sort of major bipartisan deal as the fiscal 1991 cycle loomed ahead. It could not be a Band-Aid agreement of the 1987 or 1989 variety. The new G-R-H target required more than that and made across-the-board sequestration to meet the target an unthinkable alternative for both Congress and the White House. The constant budget wrangling was bringing both branches into disrepute, yet we had remarkably little to show for our efforts. The White House was locked into a rigid position on taxes and displayed only minimal flexibility on defense; neither party felt it could afford to tamper with Social Security; and congressional Democrats were unwilling to sacrifice domestic programs, which already had borne the brunt of Reagan-era cutbacks. No one, therefore, could imagine where savings of the magnitude required were going to come from, unless a new kind of agreement (Darman liked to speak of the "deal of the century") could be reached. When talk turned to an unprecedented five-year plan aimed at $500 billion in deficit reduction, those of us who had long advocated a major effort to break the budget impasse imagined that our day finally had come. But several months of posturing and positioning would pass before a serious agreement began to emerge.

The budget submitted by the president on January 29, 1990, anticipated a fiscal 1991 deficit of $64.7 billion, falling beneath the $74 billion G-R-H ceiling. But it reached the target only by leaving the exploding costs of recapitalizing the savings and loan insurance fund off budget, making impossibly optimistic economic assumptions, and engaging in a good deal of smoke-and-mirrors accounting. The CBO estimated that Bush's budget would in fact produce a deficit of $131 billion. Democratic congressional leaders were ambivalent about highlighting this discrepancy, however, because it made their task of putting together and passing a budget resolution that hit the G-R-H target all the more daunting. "For us to play a 'real' game while they're playing an 'unreal' game," majority leader Dick Gephardt told the Democratic Budget Group in February, "simply creates political pain for us." The Democratic budget resolution therefore retained many of the president's economic assumptions and dubious revenue projections, while requiring greater savings in defense, reducing Bush's proposed Medicare cuts, and adding $6.2 billion for new activity in education, health, and other domestic areas.

The House passed the budget resolution on May 1 with Democratic votes alone. The Republicans had no desire to vote for the president's budget; their ranking Budget Committee member, Bill Frenzel (R-Minnesota), who had been authorized by the Rules Committee to offer the Bush budget on the floor, declined to do so. This prompted as angry a whips meeting as I have ever witnessed: Democratic members were sick of casting tough budget votes while Republicans ducked the issue. Foley, who thought he had a commitment from Frenzel to call for a vote on the Bush budget, vowed that it would never happen again.[10]

It had become clearer than ever that the normal budget process was not up to the task before us. The economic indicators and deficit projections had worsened to the point that even OMB could no longer paper over them. The House had produced its budget resolution tardily and with great difficulty, and in the Senate, where the Democratic margin was slimmer and disagreements about spending priorities deeper, the prospects were far worse. Both Congress and the White House needed a budget deal that went considerably beyond what the regular process was likely to produce, if, indeed, it could produce agreement at all. Thus the budget summit of 1990 got underway. Bush invited congressional leaders to the White House for a preliminary discussion on May 6, after which full-scale talks involving seventeen congressional and three White House negotiators began.

Our Democratic Budget Group brought Panetta and Frenzel in for a progress report on May 23. Clearly not much was happening; "so far it's been like a bunch of strange dogs sniffing at each other," Frenzel said. Noting that negotiators would need to find $50 to $60 billion in first-year savings, he warned that "if you are a defense hawk, or welfare bleeding heart, or antitax zealot, there's no comfort in this for you." Panetta reported a lack of a real sense of urgency despite the magnitude of the problem, and he reminded us that it had taken a stock market crash to produce the modest 1987 agreement. Most of us agreed that the threat of sequestration was unreal for our constituents, while antitax sentiment was high. This meant that the pressures the negotiators felt to push toward agreement were matched by a desire to avoid blame for unpopular moves on taxes or entitlements.

White House adviser John Sununu, addressing Republican fears that Bush's agreement to talks with "no preconditions" indicated a weakened antitax position, put the administration's gloss on the agreement: "It is [the Democrats'] prerogative to put [taxes] on the table, and it's our prerogative to say no. And I emphasize the 'no.'"[11]

This led Foley and other Democrats to wonder out loud whether the Republicans were negotiating in good faith and whether the talks should continue. But House Democrats were hardly in a position to go it alone. We could and did pass appropriations bills within the terms of our own budget resolution, but we knew they were unlikely to clear the Senate, to say nothing of the White House. Nor were we in a position to unilaterally unveil our own long-term budget plan; the political liabilities would have far exceeded the benefits, with the president retaining the antitax high ground. Consequently it was in our interest to keep everyone at the table but also to insist on a serious offer from the president before revealing our own hand.

This finally came on June 26 when Bush, after a protracted meeting with the bipartisan congressional leadership and his own negotiators, issued a statement acknowledging that "tax revenue increases" would have to be part of any realistic deficit-reduction plan.[12] But if the president expected this declaration to jump-start the negotiations or win him praise for his political courage, he was to be sorely disappointed. A howl of protest went up from the right, and the House Republican Conference soon passed a resolution opposing any new taxes as a means of reducing the deficit. Democrats felt some satisfaction that Bush at last had uttered what all involved knew to be true and some relief that he finally seemed willing to invest political capital to reach an agreement. But few of us saw much reason to praise him for rescinding a demagogic promise he should never have made in the first place. Rather, we sought to use Bush's reversal to shift the focus of the budget debate.

For ten years, Presidents Reagan and Bush had framed the debate as taxes versus no taxes. Despite the popular support for such a proposition, it was in truth a contrived issue. People continued to pay taxes, and middle-class people, despite the antitax rhetoric, bore an increasing share of the overall tax burden through the 1980s. But Reagan and Bush never asked how the tax burden was distributed, what share of the load different income groups were bearing. We all knew that the tax fairness issue was Democratic turf. President Bush's reversal offered us the opportunity to shift to this more advantageous political ground and, we hoped, influence the shape of the final agreement.

I therefore joined with 133 other House Democrats in sending a letter to Speaker Foley suggesting that any new taxes should target the upper-income persons who had benefited most from the Reagan policies. I also joined with several other members affiliated with the Democratic Leadership Council (DLC), sometimes called "New Democrats," in publicly insisting that any acceptable agreement would have to make the tax system more progressive. A key negotiator, Senate majority leader Mitchell, made it clear that any consideration of a capital gains tax cut, still a key administration goal, would require an adjustment in the top marginal rate for the wealthiest taxpayers as a likely quid pro quo.

The deep partisan divisions prompted by the tax issue, as well as disarray in GOP ranks, made it very difficult to move toward a broad agreement. But an agreement had to be reached, as deficit projections soared and the amount of the projected sequester reached $100 billion. After a flurry of activity in late July came to naught, negotiators resolved to return to the table immediately after the August recess and try to finalize an agreement in a matter of days, in time for the new fiscal year.

The September talks, held in semiseclusion at the Andrews Air Force Base, specified what the White House and the Democratic congressional leadership were willing to support and produced a developing consensus on the magnitude of the spending cuts to be sought in various areas. But each side remained immovable on the tax issue. The White House insisted on a capital gains tax reduction but refused to combine it with any adjustment in the top rates, while the Democrats insisted that capital gains cuts were acceptable only if combined with other changes that made the tax code more progressive.

Finally, on September 30, the last day of the fiscal year, President Bush appeared with the summit participants to announce that a five-year agreement had been reached. The negotiators had dropped both capital gains reductions and top-rate increases from the package and had backed away from any alterations in Social Security. But the plan still projected $500 billion in savings from the current-services baseline (i.e., from the levels required to maintain current activity, adjusted for inflation and, in the case of entitlements, also for the size and circumstances of eligible populations) over the next five years, with $134 billion of this coming from tax increases, $65 billion from debt-service savings, and $301 billion from spending cuts. Almost two-thirds of these cuts would come from defense and the rest mainly from entitlement programs like Medicare, agricultural price supports, and civil service retirement. Domestic and international discretionary spending would increase only for inflation.

Substantial budget process and enforcement reforms were also proposed. The G-R-H deficit targets, susceptible to evasion and manipulation through overly optimistic economic forecasts and revenue projections (the infamous "rosy scenarios"), would be replaced by statutory caps on discretionary spending to be enforced by sequestration. For the first three years there would be separate caps for domestic, international, and defense spending, with "firewalls" between them. Reductions in one category could not raise the caps for another, nor could excesses in one area trigger sequesters in another. For nondiscretionary spending and revenues, new pay-as-you-go (PAYGO) rules would require tax reductions or entitlement increases to be accompanied by whatever revenue increases or entitlement cuts were required to offset their budget impact.

We passed a continuing resolution to head off sequestration and keep the government running through October 5 and prepared anxiously for a close vote on the summit agreement. Minority whip Newt Gingrich pointedly skipped the White House announcement and began to organize Republican opposition to the plan in defiance of President Bush and his own minority leader. Gingrich's point of departure was not any alternative plan for reducing the deficit—he had none—but rather a dogmatic insistence that taxes not be raised and a conviction that the GOP politically could not afford to abandon that position. As the *Washington Post* editorialized:

> The balking Republicans say they are against all tax increases. But they are of course against the deficit as well—and no more willing or able than Ronald Reagan or George Bush has been to name the spending cuts that by themselves might bring the deficit out of the red zone. Instead they continue to parrot that what the country needs is more tax cuts to grow its way out of the deficit. You last heard that sort of happy talk about $2 trillion in debt ago.[13]

Speaker Foley and other House Democratic leaders, although acknowledging the agreement's deficiencies, nonetheless strongly urged a "yea" vote. They presented the package as the best that could be attained after five months of negotiations and warned that we would reject it at our political peril. The shakiness of our Senate majority put us in a poor position to push a budget measure through on our own. "We're only as strong as our weakest senator," Gephardt lamented at one point. Moreover, time had run out. We faced an imminent government shutdown, for which the Democratic Congress was likely to take the fall. "We're about to hand the president a pardon and a machine gun," Foley told a Democratic Caucus meeting as the negative whip counts came in. Democratic rejection would take the spotlight off GOP disarray and Gingrich's rebellion and would give the president an excuse to "do anything he wants," perhaps to assume extraordinary powers to avert governmental breakdown.

Such pleas were to no avail. Democrats mainly objected to the agreement's regressive character. The tax package had some progressive elements (e.g., luxury taxes and cuts in allowable deductions for those earning over $100,000) and nonentitlement domestic programs had been spared further cuts, but the wealthy nevertheless got off lightly. The problem with the package, commented Charles Schumer (D-New York), was that "Democrats think it's a Republican budget and Republicans think it's a Democratic budget."[14] As it became clear that the package was in trouble and after meeting with the president, Foley issued a statement stressing that Ways and Means and other committees, in writing the legislation to implement the agreement, would be free to alter its distributive impact: "The President and the Bipartisan Leadership always understood that many of the policies set forth in the budget agreement are for illustrative purposes only and that the committees of jurisdiction retain the right to achieve the savings required through alternative policies."

But despite the scrambling and importuning, including a national television address by the president, the budget agreement was rejected on October 5 by a vote of 179–254, with a majority voting no among both Democrats (108–149) and Republicans (71–105).

One reason for the skittishness in both parties was the chorus of protest that came from affected constituencies, prompted in large part by the tendency of the media, especially television, to cover the budget agreement by focusing on its supposed victims. I knew we were in trouble when I saw the network news coverage immediately after the agreement was announced: motorists at the gas pump, frail nursing home residents (who probably would not have been affected by the proposed Medicare premium increases), and others bewailing their victimization. Not much was made, however, of the potential victims of sequestration (including 113,000 children dropped from Head Start, 1.4 million students losing their Pell grants, and 83,000 inpatients and 1.7 million outpatients losing their Veterans Administration medical care), who would suffer if we did not act, not to mention the effects of the economic downturn to which the deficit was contributing. The media, as far as I could tell, provided almost no context for understanding the agreement—why it was necessary, why it was difficult to conclude, why it could not be painless. They instead focused on victimization and governmental ineptitude, which greatly reinforced the tendency of members of Congress, especially in an election year, to distance themselves as far as possible from budgetary unpleasantness, to simply vote no.

I voted for the agreement, although I had strong substantive objections and could only imagine what my Republican opponent would make of my vote in his campaign ads. I did not see how I, after having advocated extraordinary efforts to put our fiscal house in order for years, could credibly or in good conscience vote against a plan that, despite its flaws, represented the largest deficit-reduction package in our nation's history. I felt that we Democrats would be in a stronger position to shape the final implementing legislation to our liking if we produced our quota of votes for the agreement. This reasoning was reflected in notes I made the day after the vote:

What a different situation it would be today if the budget agreement had gone down for a lack of Republican votes alone, with some 130 [instead of

108] Democrats recorded "yes." The news stories would be of Republican division and default, and we would have the upper hand in rewriting a budget that more faithfully reflects Democratic priorities. As it is, we share in the public blame for the failure to act, and we seek partisan accommodation with a weaker hand. . . . If, on the other hand, the agreement had gone down for a lack of Democratic votes alone, there would be hell to pay. The fact that both parties defaulted forces the president to moderate the blame game and in fact helps turn the spotlight back on him and his failure to lead.

The budget vote produced the spectacle of a weekend government shutdown, with hundreds of tourists who had been denied entrance to national museums packing the House and Senate galleries. This was because the president chose to veto the continuing resolution that we passed to keep the government running until October 12. He did this, no doubt, to heighten public awareness of congressional failure, but the result was to highlight his own failure as well. A subsequent *New York Times*–CBS News poll showed that only 27 percent of the American public approved of the way Congress was handling its job, down from 42 percent in January. But only 24 percent registered the view that President Bush was likely to do a better job than Congress on the deficit.[15]

Meanwhile, House and Senate leaders (minus the divided House Republicans) frantically sought to get a new budget resolution approved to replace the failed agreement. This was accomplished just before the holiday weekend ended by a 250–164 vote (including only 32 Republican yeas) in the House and a bipartisan 66–33 vote in the Senate. This time Bush signed the accompanying continuing resolution. Government employees came to work as usual, and our committees proceeded to tackle the final budget reconciliation and appropriations bills for the balance of the fiscal year.

The new budget resolution differed from the rejected agreement mainly in its omission of specific reconciliation proposals, such as the increased Medicare premium. The spending limits and budget process reforms remained largely intact. Having registered a no vote on the first resolution and having (arguably) given the committees added flexibility to write a more equitable reconciliation bill (and recognizing that public outrage at our gridlock was fast surpassing the discontent of specific groups on specific items), more than one hundred Democrats switched to a yes vote on the second resolution. This left only twenty-eight negative Democratic votes, an impressive change from the earlier picture of disarray and a hopeful sign that the majority party might be able to seize control of the process.

House Democrats, buoyed by indications that our tax fairness message was finally hitting home, regrouped nicely over the next week as the

Ways and Means Committee went about its work. On October 16, we passed a reconciliation bill that dropped most of the budget agreement's regressive tax proposals (e.g., on gasoline and home heating oil) and substituted (1) an increase in the top marginal rate to 33 percent,[16] (2) a surtax on millionaires (which, as Elizabeth Drew noted, gave us "small revenue and a big symbol"),[17] and (3) an expansion of the earned income tax credit for the working poor. Republicans were reduced to carping at the Democratic plan, for Foley quite rightly refused to make any alternative proposal in order on the House floor unless it hit the overall $500 billion deficit-reduction target. This the Republicans were unable to produce, given their commitment to no new taxes and their inability to agree on spending cuts sufficient to make up the difference (see Figure 7.1).

Senate approval still depended on maintaining bipartisan support. The Senate consequently passed a reconciliation bill that was much closer to the original budget agreement, setting the stage for a difficult House-Senate conference. During the next few days, the White House considered pulling out of the discussions, and House Democrats considered rejecting the conference agreement they saw shaping up. But both sides feared the political consequences of failure, and in the end the conference bill—which contained a 31 percent top rate (with a 28 percent maximum rate for capital gains),[18] no surtax, and a complex scheme for reducing deductions and phasing out personal exemptions for upper-income taxpayers—was passed with the president's approval. The 228–200 vote finally came on October 27, 1990, with the Democratic margin slipping to 181–74 and House Republicans still unreconciled (47–126). After the subsequent passage of the last of the thirteen appropriations bills, our work was done, and the 101st Congress wearily adjourned.

Many Democratic House members complained bitterly that the summit process coopted party leaders and preempted the role of the majority. They claimed vindication when, after the initial rejection of the summit agreement, Ways and Means Democrats reported and the House passed a reconciliation bill more consistent with Democratic values. But the normal budget process, without summitry, could not have produced anything approximating the final 1990 outcome, given the shakiness of the Democratic majority in the Senate and the realities of divided government. The president's resources included not only a veto pen but also the rhetorical high ground. Unless he could be brought into the fray and compelled to offer genuine solutions, Democrats faced the prospect of becoming the party of sacrifice and pain and inviting their own political demise. The summit process, although it blurred the lines of institutional and party responsibility, forced a measure of seriousness and realism on the leaders of both branches (with the notable exception of House Republi-

cans) and heightened their incentives to formulate a constructive solution to an intractable national problem.

Might the process have worked better under unified party control of Congress and the White House? Those who raised that question soon had a chance to answer it, as deficits and pressures for renewed action continued to mount. Whoever won the 1992 election was certain to face the necessity of negotiating another multiyear agreement. That turned out to be a Democratic president paired with a Democratic congressional majority, a situation that had not existed since the early, tentative years of the budget process. This set up a political dynamic for 1993 that contrasted sharply with that of 1990 while producing a remarkably similar substantive outcome.

The 1993 Budget Battle

Congress adhered to the 1990 budget agreement for the remaining two years of the Bush presidency. The discretionary spending caps and pay-as-you-go rules proved less susceptible to gamesmanship than the former G-R-H procedures. But deficit-reduction hopes were frustrated as the economy slid into a recession and health care inflation produced higher than anticipated entitlement costs. In early 1991, when the Congressional Budget Office predicted that the deficit for the current fiscal year would exceed $300 billion, Budget chairman Leon Panetta spoke for many of us in exclaiming, "We went through an awful lot of hell to get to $300 billion deficits. I never see the light at the end of the tunnel. Everybody predicts it, but we never get there."[19] Although the CBO explained that without the 1990 agreement the projected deficits would have been far worse, it soon concluded "that the main accomplishment of [the agreement] was not to reduce the size of the structural deficit, but rather to prevent it from becoming substantially larger."[20]

To these long-term fiscal problems were added growing restlessness with the 1990 agreement itself. Appropriations bills were passed in 1991 without major controversy, but by 1992 there was considerable sentiment among Democrats to adjust the caps on discretionary spending, which were holding many programs below inflation levels. The agreement provided separate caps for domestic, defense, and international spending through year three (fiscal 1993), making it likely that the specific caps and the advisability of maintaining firewalls between them would be reconsidered at that time. In the meantime, the Soviet Union had collapsed and Cold War defense spending levels had come under question. President Bush's budget for 1993 proposed to reduce defense spending $7 billion below the caps while protecting defense in future years by extending the firewalls to 1997. The House Democratic leadership, by contrast, wished to dismantle the firewalls a year early so that defense savings could relieve the pressure on domestic spending. In the end, enough Democratic members joined with Republicans in both the House and Senate to leave the firewalls in place for 1993 and in effect dedicate the savings in defense ($11 billion below the caps) to deficit reduction.

As Bill Clinton prepared to take office, there was little question that budget issues would be his first major test. The deficit had reached a record high of $290 billion in 1992 and showed no signs of abating. Interest payments on the national debt had topped $200 billion, more than any other budget items except defense and Social Security. Medicare and Medicaid costs were growing at double-digit rates, nullifying the effects of discretionary spending restraint. The 1990 firewalls were coming down, and the agenda of both congressional Democrats and the new president required securing a better deal for their domestic priorities. The president announced his goals in an address to a joint session of Congress on February 17, 1993: "jump-starting the economy in the short term and investing in our people, their jobs, and their incomes over the long run" while "substantially reducing the federal deficit, honestly and credibly."

The budget plan he unveiled would dominate the first session of the 104th Congress.[21]

Clinton proposed savings of $704 billion from projected five-year spending and revenue levels: $375 billion from spending cuts and $328 billion from tax increases. A third of the savings would be applied to a "stimulus package" to get the economy moving and to longer-term domestic "investments" in areas such as infrastructure, education, health care, tax incentives for business, and an expanded earned income tax credit (EITC) for the working poor, leaving $473 billion for net deficit reduction. His tax increases were primarily aimed at upper-income taxpayers, proposing a new top rate of 36 percent for joint filers making more than $140,000 and a surtax that would give those making more than $250,000 a marginal rate of 39.6 percent. He also proposed a more broadly based "BTU" excise tax based on the heat output of various energy sources.

Although public reaction to the president's proposal was initially very favorable, Republicans attacked it relentlessly. The president's stimulus package had been hastily assembled and contained elements that made it vulnerable to caricature as pork-barrel spending; it passed the House on a party-line vote and was killed by a Republican filibuster in the Senate. But it was the tax issue that dominated partisan debate throughout the year, as most Republicans adopted the no-new-taxes stance Newt Gingrich had enunciated in walking away from the 1990 bipartisan agreement. Many thought George Bush had erred fatally in abandoning his "read my lips" pledge and regarded reinstating it as the key to Republican electoral success. Although the major impact of the president's proposals fell on upper-income taxpayers (only 1.2 percent of filers, for example, were affected by the top-rate increases and 17 percent stood to benefit from the expanded EITC), Republicans promoted expectations of a broad middle-class impact. My calls, letters, and community meeting encounters provided daily confirmation of their success.

I admired the president's willingness to take on the deficit issue and was pleased to be appointed to the Budget Committee as it prepared a fiscal 1994 budget resolution to implement his proposal. Martin Sabo (D-Minnesota) was elected Budget Committee chair, succeeding Leon Panetta, who had been appointed director of OMB. Sabo proved responsive to the political concerns of moderate and conservative Democrats and united the committee majority around a plan that cut spending $63 billion more than the president had proposed, increased prospective deficit reduction to $510 billion over five years, and maintained the 1990 agreement's overall caps on discretionary spending for 1994 and 1995. The Budget Committee's new ranking Republican, John Kasich (R-Ohio), to his credit, insisted that the GOP offer an alternative plan rather than simply vote no. His plan omitted any tax increases but also fell short (with net savings of $429 billion over five years) of the Democratic deficit reduction figure. Although the Republican Conference declined to endorse Kasich's proposal, passing only a resolution rejecting all tax increases, he attracted 135 votes (132 Republicans, 3 Democrats) on the House floor.

The House passed the Democratic budget resolution on March 18, 1993, by a 243–183 margin, with no Republican support and eleven Democratic defections. But there were already indications, particularly in the Senate, that the votes would be harder to come by when particular tax increases and entitlement cuts were specified in a reconciliation bill. Indeed, the politicking that went into initial House passage of the reconciliation bill on May 27 (219–213) and final approval of the conference report on August 5 with one vote to spare (218–216) was the most intense I have experienced during my time in the House.

The energy tax caused particular discomfort and was the focus of intense negotiations in the House Ways and Means and Senate Finance Committees, as well as in conference. House leaders pressed ahead with a floor vote on the BTU tax, which helped explain our shrinkage to a six-vote margin by May 27. This led to intense resentment when the Senate later dropped the BTU provision with the administration's acquiescence. Many House members concluded that they had taken a tough vote for naught. We subsequently spoke of being "BTU'd" when asked to walk the plank for something likely to be rejected by the Senate or abandoned by the Clinton White House. By the time the conference completed its work, the only remnant of the BTU tax was a 4.3 cents per gallon increase in the fuels tax, which picked up only a fraction of the revenue but still led some members to vote against the entire bill. I was torn between defending the proposal against the exaggerations and distortions of its detractors and wishing the president had not given his opponents any pretext for portraying the middle class as the victim of his tax increases.

I was part of the whip's task force on both reconciliation votes, checking and rechecking likely votes, uncertain until the end that a majority would coalesce. Most of the members in question were conservatives or moderates, including many who had argued strongly for deficit reduction in the past. The president, they knew, had rebuffed liberal critics in giving the priority he did to deficit reduction, and his plan in most respects mirrored New Democratic priorities—fiscal discipline, investments in human capital and economic development, an expanded EITC, incentives for business investment, a more progressive tax code. But the wavering members frequently came from marginal districts where they felt vulnerable to the drumbeat of Republican criticism, picked up on the talk shows and in the media, that this was a tax-and-spend plan that would hurt ordinary Americans. The waverers included New Jersey members traumatized by the power of the tax issue in that state's gubernatorial politics, many members from oil-producing areas, some insecure new members, and some who had always displayed a cautious, self-protective style. For them, as well as others, the most advantageous vote politically was no.[22] But for the president and for Democrats collectively, a defeat would have been absolutely devastating, conclusively demonstrating our inability to govern. The mission of our task force was to prompt enough members to act on this collective interest to pass the bill.

The individualism of the U.S. Senate was on particularly extravagant display. From the Finance Committee to the floor to conference, senators constantly announced that their support was in peril and demanded concessions from their leaders or the White House on this item or that. Given their six-vote margin of control and the complete absence of Republican support, Democratic leaders had little choice but to heed. House Democrats sensed the corrosive effect these machinations had on public regard for both Congress and the budget plan, and we knew how unsettling the grandstanding of several senators was to their wavering home-state House colleagues. Some of this was vented when Senator David Boren (D-Oklahoma) appeared before a tense session of our Democratic Budget Group the day before the first reconciliation vote. Boren made his usual objections to the energy tax and to the alleged predominance of tax increases over spending cuts in the president's plan. This struck many of us as perpetuating Republican distortions and public misperceptions of what was in the plan, and we welcomed the chance to tell him so. In the end, Senate Democratic defections were held to six on both reconciliation votes. Under Senate rules such votes required only a majority and were thus not subject to filibuster; therefore, Vice President Gore's tie-breaking votes sufficed to provide the margin of victory.

As the final August 5 vote in the House approached, the bill was in serious trouble. The president and his cabinet secretaries talked with numerous members, often promising cooperation on specific projects. To the various accommodations made in conference were added White House and leadership promises to conservatives of future efforts to reduce spending. These maneuvers no doubt persuaded some and eased the way to a yes vote for others. But for most of those switching from no on May 27 to yes on August 5 (8) or for the larger number (11) switching the other way, the more powerful explanation was either awareness of the country's and the party's stake in passing the plan or the imperative of individual political survival—powerful conflicting forces. To understand is not necessarily to excuse: I have an indelible memory of Democrats from safe districts, some of them committee or subcommittee chairs, voting no and standing by to let vulnerable freshmen provide the margin of victory. But the showdown also produced numerous profiles in courage, some of whom paid dearly in the next election.

Republican opposition remained at fever pitch, with no Republican ever voting for the plan in either chamber. Many made apocalyptic statements that read strangely a few months later as the markets responded favorably to the plan and it began to have its desired effects. Dick Armey spoke scornfully of "the hollow promises of deficit reduction and magical theories of lower interest rates" and predicted that the plan would "grow the government and shrink the economy," precisely the reverse of what occurred. Republican whip Newt Gingrich said the plan would "lead to a recession and . . . actually increase the deficit."[23] "Right, guys," the *Raleigh News and Observer* declared six months later in an editorial that delighted me but provided only limited political benefit. "That must be why all of us got up this morning to endure still another day of low interest rates, booming housing markets, rising business investment, job creation roaring along faster than the Bush years ever saw, and—in the Triangle—a business climate rated second to none in the land."[24]

Some persisted in the view that a bipartisan approach to the budget might have been crafted, had the president extended his hand.[25] But that was never a realistic possibility. The Republican attitude after 1992 was, You won the election; be our guest. GOP members had no interest in putting their fingerprints on any budget deal, and many even argued against Kasich's plan to formulate a Republican alternative. Even if a bipartisan approach had been possible, the result would have been less deficit reduction. Republicans were bound to accept no new taxes. Although they talked bravely of Medicare cuts beyond the $56 billion agreed to among Democrats, no package they would have accepted would have reached even the $429 billion in savings that Kasich, assuming large, unspecified spending reductions, claimed for his plan.

The monolithic Republican opposition required no organizational effort, given the ease of voting no and the party's history of rejecting the budgets of its own presidents. But it clearly served a partisan purpose—creating maximum pressure on Democrats, setting off a scramble to win the votes of wavering members, and exposing the limits of party discipline. I will argue in the next chapter that the final outcome—getting 84 percent of the Democratic votes in the House and all but six Democratic votes in the Senate—represented a (narrow) victory for party responsibility. But press coverage and public perceptions, which focused on the struggle for marginal votes under unrelenting opposition attack, suggested desperation and disarray. The president and the Democratic Party in Congress won a fight that was unthinkable to lose, but the battle exposed dangerous weaknesses and left us largely unfortified for the escalating struggles of 1994.

The 1997 Agreement and Beyond

Although partisan conflict increased on most fronts in 1994, the fiscal 1995 budget resolution and subsequent appropriations bills were adopted without a major fight. Much of the economic and budget news was good, for which Federal Reserve chairman Alan Greenspan gave due credit to the president's economic plan: "The actions taken last year to reduce the federal budget deficit have been instrumental in creating the basis for declining inflation expectations and easing pressures on long-term interest rates."[26]

None of this prevented Republicans from continuing to make political hay from what they (inaccurately) called the "greatest tax increase in history." Fights over proposed budget process changes and the balanced budget amendment to the Constitution stoked partisan fires, although some Democrats were among the proponents, and perpetuated the impression that the 1993 plan had accomplished nothing. The Democratic leadership barely averted House debate of a bizarre "A to Z" proposal for a fifty-six-hour spending-cut derby on the House floor that Rush Limbaugh and other talk show hosts were promoting.[27] Accusations and perceptions about taxing and spending were central to the 1994 campaign; the GOP Contract with America included the balanced budget amendment, a package of "family-friendly" tax cuts, repeal of the Clinton plan's tax on the benefits of upper-income Social Security beneficiaries, a 50 percent capital gains tax cut, and authority for the president to veto individual line items in appropriations bills. (Interestingly, the Republicans did not propose to repeal the upper-bracket rate increases, the biggest revenue raisers from the 1993 plan.) There was little doubt as the Republicans took control of the House in 1995 that budget changes would head their agenda and budget politics would be as sharply partisan as ever.

Many of the Contract items, plus a bill rescinding $17 billion in 1995 appropriations, passed in the frantic first one hundred days of the 104th Congress. On May 18, 1995, the House passed a budget resolution that laid out a bold seven-year master plan: to balance the budget by 2002, to provide a huge tax cut (a net revenue loss of $287 billion over seven years), and to place more than half of the federal budget (Social Security, defense, and interest on the debt) off-limits for spending cuts. As columnist E. J. Dionne noted, this required hard choices by members and leaders who in earlier budget battles had elected not to face them:

> As long as Democrats controlled one or both houses of Congress, a large group of conservative Republicans could stand at the sidelines, clamor for more tax cuts, attack a vague entity called "big government," and vote "no" on every budget. . . . What will be on the table now is not "big government" as an abstraction but Medicare . . . and a long list of smaller programs. . . . The choice facing the country is not, as the Speaker often argues, between giving money to "bureaucrats" and letting citizens put more money in their own pockets. . . . The choices are over how much we want to spend on such things [as defense, medical care, and Social Security] and how to pay for them.[28]

House Republicans, led by Speaker Gingrich and Budget chairman John Kasich, turned to the only places left to turn, proposing unprecedented cuts in nondefense appropriations bills and entitlements, with seven-year reductions of $288 billion and $187 billion from the current-services baselines for Medicare and Medicaid, respectively. The bills achieving these savings generally passed the House with solid partisan majorities; Republicans showed far more discipline than Democrats had in 1993. But they later ran into firm resistance from President Clinton, provoking repeated vetoes and two government shutdowns.

At the end of the fiscal year, having cleared only two of the thirteen appropriations bills for 1996, Congress passed the first of a series of continuing resolutions (CRs) to keep the government running. Confident that they held the upper hand politically, Republican leaders used the threat of a government shutdown to compel Clinton to come to agreement on the appropriations measures and their massive reconciliation bill, which included entitlement cuts in Medicare, Medicaid, welfare, and agriculture and restrictions on eligibility for veterans benefits and for the EITC, as well as a large tax cut.

Clinton moved some distance in their direction, agreeing to the seven-year timetable for balancing the budget and deeper cuts in domestic programs than he had earlier accepted, thus shifting the parameters of future budget debate. But the president held out against the Republicans' farthest-reaching demands and vetoed the second CR (to which the Republicans had attached a Medicare premium increase), the reconciliation bill, and four individual appropriations bills (which would have eliminated his national service and community policing initiatives and cut deeply into housing, environmental protection, legal services, and U.N. peacekeeping). The president was fortified in his resistance when the public blamed the ensuing government shutdowns mainly on the Republicans. Congressional Democrats had successfully conveyed a message of GOP extremism, noting especially the comparability of the figures for Medicare reductions and tax cuts mainly benefiting the wealthy ($270 billion and $245 billion, respectively, in the final budget resolution) and the trade-off between them. House Republicans then reinforced their extremist image by rejecting the budget deal Gingrich and Senate majority leader Robert Dole were considering to end the second government shutdown.[29]

By January 1996, it was clear that the shutdown strategy had failed and there would be no comprehensive budget agreement. Six appropriations bills remained either unpassed or unsigned; by late April, when the remaining five of these were rolled into an omnibus appropriations measure, Congress had passed fourteen CRs covering over half of the fiscal year. At this point, budget preparations for fiscal year 1997 were also underway, and the disposition of many congressional Republicans was shifting as they contemplated the negative political fallout from 1995 and the challenge of the 1996 elections. Popular programs and individual projects such as the EPA building in North Carolina (see Chapter 6) thus received relatively generous treatment in the omnibus 1996 bill and the 1997 appropriations bills, all of which were passed by the beginning of the new fiscal year. Six of the 1997 bills were unfinished as October 1 approached, but Republican leaders, mainly motivated by a desire to conclude negotiations and adjourn, rolled them into an omnibus bill and "virtually surrendered" to the president on most money and policy items.[30]

Republicans nonetheless could, and did, claim to have cut projected domestic discretionary spending significantly during the 104th Congress, with reductions from the $246 billion annual level set by the initial 1995 appropriations bills totaling some $50 billion for fiscal years 1995 through 1997. Outlays for 1996 and 1997 fell below the president's requests for nondefense discretionary accounts by $22 billion but above his requests for defense by $14 billion. As a result, overall discretionary spending fell only slightly under the caps established by the 1993 budget plan, $19 billion below the cap for 1996 and $5 billion for 1997.

With the failure of their reconciliation bill, Republicans learned in the 104th Congress what Democrats had learned in 1993: It is extremely difficult and often politically damaging to attempt major budgetary change from one side of the aisle. By 1997 it was clear that another five-year budget plan was due. But neither party was disposed to go it alone; the 1996 election results both necessitated and offered positive incentives for cooperation.

Because that election produced a mixed verdict—reducing the margin of Republican control in the House but not by enough to put Democrats in charge and maintaining divided control of the executive and legislative branches—many commentators treated it as inconclusive, lacking a mandate. That was not my conclusion, however, based on what I heard on the doorsteps and in the shopping centers of the Fourth District. What was unmistakable in my district was a disgust with political posturing and excessive partisanship and a desire to see the country's problems, including the budget deficit, addressed. As the 105th Congress convened, many members had come to a similar conclusion: Neither party was going to be totally in control, and both would look better if they found a basis for cooperation.

Therefore, the president, looking for a positive start for his second term, and congressional Republicans, seeking to shed the image of revolutionary excess and government shutdowns, found a common interest in negotiating a new five-year budget deal. Fortunately the economic conditions also were auspicious, posing win-win possibilities that contrasted with the zero-sum conflicts of years past. The deficit had come down more rapidly than anticipated, and the strong economy made it feasible to balance the budget in five years while providing a sizable tax cut and increased spending for domestic needs in the bargain. That is precisely the deal administration and congressional negotiators put together over a two-month period, announcing on May 2, 1997, what Clinton called "a balanced budget with balanced values."[31]

The agreement was translated into a budget resolution that called for five-year reductions from the current-services baseline of $139 billion in discretionary spending ($77 billion in defense, $62 billion in nondefense) and $170 billion in entitlements, tax cuts netting $85 billion, and new spending of $38 billion, mainly to extend health insurance to 5 million uninsured children and restore some benefits to legal immigrants denied them by the 1996 welfare reform law. The result was $204 billion in deficit reduction and a balanced budget projected by 2002. The pay-as-you-go rules and caps on discretionary spending instituted in 1990 would be extended through 2002, with firewalls between defense and nondefense spending reinstated for 1998 and 1999. In response to White House fears that the revenue provisions might be taken in unacceptable directions by Republican tax writers and could threaten the entire package, the resolution provided for two separate reconciliation bills, one making net entitlement reductions (Balanced Budget Act) and the other net tax reductions (Taxpayer Relief Act).

The budget resolution passed both houses by large bipartisan margins, but severe partisan disagreements later threatened the reconciliation bills, especially in the House. Most Democratic members, including me, voted against both when they first cleared the House in late June. The main problems with the Balanced Budget Act, later fixed in conference, were the flawed design of the children's health insurance initiative and provisions that would have weakened state regulation of health insurance and would have denied minimum-wage protection to welfare-to-work participants. The problems with the Taxpayer Relief Act were more severe. Chairman Bill Archer (R-Texas) and the Ways and Means Committee proceeded on a highly partisan basis to mark up a bill that was criticized for its upscale bias even by many within the GOP; it received only twenty-seven Democratic votes when it first passed the House.

After a month of hard bargaining, however, the final version of the Taxpayer Relief Act passed both houses with large bipartisan majorities. The bill reduced the top individual tax rate on capital gains from 28 to 20 percent and eliminated the tax entirely on the sale of most homes, reflecting the Republicans' top priority over many years as well as the willingness of Democrats like myself to support capital gains tax reduction within a balanced and fiscally responsible total package. Year-by-year increases were provided in the amount of inheritance exempt from taxation, and the estate tax exemption for family-owned farms and businesses was more than doubled (to $1.3 million). Conferees also provided a new $500-per-child tax credit and acceded to the president's demand that it be available to low-income working families that paid only payroll taxes, not income taxes. And Clinton secured $35 billion of the package for education-related tax breaks, including HOPE scholarship and lifetime learning tax credits as well as the student loan interest deductibility and IRA drawdown provisions described in Chapter 6.

With both reconciliation bills signed, Congress proceeded, for the first time since the Republicans had taken control, to pass its thirteen appropriations bills without resorting to an omnibus bill, although final action on four of them was pushed into November because of disputes over controversial riders.

Despite the 1997 agreement and steadily improving economic projections that promised a balanced budget ahead of schedule, serious budgetary conflict resumed in 1998. For the first time in the history of the budget process, Congress failed to adopt a budget resolution. Budget Committee chairman John Kasich reported and House Republicans passed a resolution that provided five-year cuts of $56 billion in mandatory spending and $45 billion in nondefense discretionary outlays below 1997 budget agreement levels to make room for $101 billion in new tax cuts. The resolution was generally regarded as a political statement tied to Kasich's presidential ambitions rather than a serious budgetary blueprint. It provoked considerable resistance among GOP moderates, including most senior appropriators, and was passed only with a strong leadership push on June 5, almost two months behind schedule. Kasich's proposal was also unacceptable to most Senate Republicans, whose budget resolution had adhered closely to the 1997 agreement, and the two chambers never reconciled their differences. This left the appropriations committees in both houses to mark up their bills without definitive budget allocations, thus complicating a situation where partisan divisions, House-Senate differences, and conflicts within the Republican majority already made agreement difficult.

Ironically, resistance by Republican hard-liners to accommodation strengthened the president's hand and led to more spending in the end. Eight of the appropriations bills had not been cleared by the beginning of the 1999 fiscal year and had to be combined in an omnibus measure. Despite the looming impeachment proceedings, the president had some major advantages in the negotiations that ensued. The 1999 budget was now forecast to be $70 billion in surplus, creating some flexibility for spending beyond the 1997 caps. At the same time, Clinton had successfully deflected Republican calls for major tax cuts, insisting that the surplus should not be tapped for such purposes until a long-term plan to ensure the future of Social Security was in place. And the 1998 elections were only a month away: The Republicans were skittish about being charged with obstruction and eager to go home to campaign.

The result was a 4,000-page, 40-pound, $520 billion omnibus appropriations bill, passed by the House on October 20, that gave the president much of what he wanted, including a $1.2 billion down payment on his plan to reduce class size by hiring 100,000 new teachers. The bill pushed defense spending $7 billion and nondefense discretionary outlays $9.1 billion over the levels set by the 1997 budget bill's caps for 1999, mainly through the device of designating $13.2 billion in outlays as "emergency" spending not subject to the caps.[32] The designation included traditional emergency items such as disaster and farm relief and peacekeeping in Bosnia. But it also included longer-term items such as military readiness, embassy security, year 2000 computer problems, and antidrug programs that stretched the definition of emergency and set a troubling precedent.

Budget politics became even more fractious in 1999. With more good news on the surplus and the 2000 elections almost two years away, some of us hoped for a period of cooperation similar to 1997, during which Congress could extend and refine the budget agreement and address the long-term challenges facing Social Security and Medicare. But it was not to be: The postimpeachment partisan atmosphere was more rancorous; Republican control of the House was narrower and shakier, allowing budget hard-liners to hold the party hostage to their preferences; and electoral calculations loomed larger and earlier, with both parties seeing some advantages to a standoff that left them with a clear message and someone to blame.

Budget projections for 2000 and subsequent years showed for the first time surpluses in the non–Social Security portion of the budget as well as in trust fund receipts, but the disposition of the surplus proved almost as contentious an issue as reducing the deficit had been earlier. The politics of 1998 had produced more agreement than either party acknowledged on the Social Security portion of the surplus (estimated at $2 trillion for 2000–2009). Since the Social Security reforms of 1983, the trust fund had been running an annual surplus by design, building up assets in anticipation of the claims of baby boomer retirees after 2010. The surplus funds were required by law to be invested in Treasury bonds at market rates of interest. This reduced the need for the Treasury to borrow from the public and helped finance general government expenditures. But as the deficit in the unified budget disappeared, it became obvious that the vaunted surplus was an artifact of the surplus in Social Security receipts and was in fact masking a continuing general fund deficit. It thus seemed disingenuous and risky to use the presence of this overall surplus as a warrant for cutting taxes or raising spending, either of which would increase the general fund deficit. President Clinton and congressional Democrats used this argument effectively against proposed Republican tax cuts in 1998. As a result, by 1999 both parties were pledged to keep "hands-off" the Social Security surplus. It would still be invested in Treasury bonds, but the proceeds would be used only to buy down publicly held debt, thus reducing the annual burden of debt service (which stood at $229 billion in 1999) and putting the Treasury in a stronger position to meet its eventual obligation to the trust fund.

The 1999 debate focused at first on the non–Social Security portion of the surplus, which official midyear forecasts (assuming unrealistically that the 1997 caps would be adhered to) estimated at $1 trillion for the period 2000–2009. In fact, simply increasing discretionary spending for inflation would have absorbed three-fourths of that amount while failing to address pressing demands in areas such as military pay and readiness, transportation, and medical research. Nevertheless, House Republicans forged ahead with a massive tax cut that would have cost $932 billion in revenue losses and interest savings forgone in the first ten years and would have ballooned to losses of $2.8 trillion in the second ten years. President Clinton proposed a package better balanced among debt reduction, extending Medicare solvency, sustaining existing programs, and a smaller tax cut. With the president's veto of the Republican tax bill, both sides resolved to forgo extensive negotiations and take their case to the voters.

In the meantime, the appropriations process was in disarray. I began telling constituents in 1999 that the only thing worse than not having a budget resolution (as in 1998) was having one (as in 1999, when the resolution imposed limitations on domestic discretionary spending that made the appropriations bills virtually impossible to pass). In both cases, the Budget Committee defaulted on its obligation to the House. The difficulty stemmed in part from the low caps the architects of the 1997 budget agreement had set for 2000 and beyond, seeking to maximize the savings they could claim and assuming that the matter could later be reconsidered. But the Republican leaders, pressed by their right wing, refused to adjust the caps and then exacerbated the problem, taking advantage of the firewalls coming down to allocate $8.4 billion above the president's request for defense. This required a 9.9 percent average reduction below nominal 1999 levels in nondefense discretionary accounts. Appropriations leaders sought to stretch these limits in order to pass some of the less controversial funding bills, but GOP conservatives withheld their votes on the floor until their leadership forced reluctant appropriators to scale back the bills. This tactic forfeited Democratic support and seriously undermined the tradition of bipartisan accommodation on the Appropriations Committee.

Eventually the required cuts exceeded what most Republicans as well as Democrats were willing to support. In order to create the slack necessary to report passable bills, Republican appropriators in some instances gave subcommittees disproportionately large budget allocations (e.g., VA-HUD) and in others stretched the budget rules almost beyond recognition (e.g., designating the 2000 census, required by the Constitution, as an "emergency"). Despite these machinations, by November 1, one month into the new fiscal year, only eight of the thirteen appropriations bills had been passed and signed by the president. Once again Republican leaders were compelled to roll the remaining bills into an omnibus package and negotiate its terms with the White House. These weeks were particularly busy for my staff and me as we pushed, with partial success, for the inclusion of relief and recovery funds for victims of Hurricane Floyd—a real emergency—in the final package. The process was finally completed on November 17, after eight continuing resolutions, with the president bargaining successfully for such priorities as the payment of back dues to the United Nations, the acquisition of environmentally sensitive lands, and assistance to communities in hiring more teachers and police officers.

Republicans justified their unrealistic, unworkable budget resolution in terms of fealty to the 1997 caps. But as 1999 wore on, realizing that they were likely to end up breaching the caps and seeking to trump the Democratic position on Social Security, the Republicans adopted a new litmus test for budgetary responsibility: refusing to spend funds borrowed from Social Security. Often using rhetoric suggesting that Democrats wished to divert money from the trust fund itself, Republicans shifted civilian and military pay dates, NIH expenditures, and other outlays into fiscal 2001, all with the intent of leaving funds generated by fiscal 2000 Social Security revenues intact.[33] Even so, they were on track to spend $17 billion borrowed from Social Security until upwardly revised surplus estimates in early 2000 let them off the hook.[34]

The election-year budget politics of 2000 followed a familiar pattern. President Clinton's budget for fiscal 2001 took advantage of mounting surpluses to propose a Medicare prescription drug benefit, hefty increases in education funding, and a ten-year, $350 billion package of targeted tax cuts, while reserving the Social Security portion of the surplus entirely for debt reduction. Republicans again countered with a budget resolution featuring a major tax cut and domestic discretionary spending allocations that would make the appropriations bills difficult to pass.

Election-year spending pressures made the GOP strategy less tenable than ever. Appropriations subcommittees pressed for allocations more generous than the budget resolution allowed, and numerous members wrote their funding priorities and various controversial riders into the major bills. Only two appropriations bills were cleared in time for the new fiscal year, and after twenty-one continuing resolutions, four were rolled into an omnibus bill in a postelection lame-duck session. President Clinton's hand, particularly on the Labor-HHS-Education bill, was weakened by the outcome of the presidential race, but the final measure still raised education funding by a record 18 percent. By that time, total spending had reached $635 billion—$35 billion above the budget resolution and $10 billion above Clinton's original request—as a result of pressures in both parties.

Still, the Social Security surplus was reserved for buying down more debt; this resulted in a total reduction of $485 billion in the publicly held debt in fiscal years 1998 through 2001. The budgetary standoff, with neither party getting all it wanted in spending or tax cuts and both promising to keep Social Security funds sacrosanct, produced a reduction of debt commensurate with the unspent surplus. "The Social Security surplus is more of a restraint on spending than the budget caps ever were," one budget expert noted.[35] After a presidential campaign in which both candidates pledged to protect Social Security revenues in a "lock box" forever, many assumed that neither party would dare cross the line they had drawn in the sand. As it turned out, however, the sands were about to shift, and our four-year winning streak of balanced budgets was about to end.

The Great Reversal

With the advent of the George W. Bush administration in 2001, the political standoff and budgetary inhibitions that had protected the surplus in the late 1990s fell away. Large tax cuts trumped everything else, becoming the predominant factor in an unprecedented national fiscal reversal that was then exacerbated by the terrorist attacks of September 11.

The year began with the most optimistic surplus projections ever—$5.6 trillion over ten years—and a debate (quaint in retrospect) about how quickly and how completely the publicly held debt should be retired. The president proposed tax cuts that, when associated interest costs and the adjustments necessary to prevent millions from being brought under the alternative minimum tax (AMT) were factored in, would absorb almost all of the ten-year non–Social Security, non-Medicare surplus. While holding out the promise of a significant long-term defense buildup and the addition of a prescription drug benefit to Medicare, the president omitted estimates for the former and provided only $153 billion over ten years for the latter. This raised the prospect—which became a certainty as budget projections worsened—that the Bush budget would require spending the Social Security revenues that had been declared forever off-limits only months before.

The Democratic alternative was basically formulated by the time the Senate and House Budget Committee ranking Democrats, Kent Conrad and John Spratt, appeared before our Democratic Budget Group in early February. The Social Security and Medicare surpluses would be reserved entirely for debt reduction. The non–trust fund surplus would be divided in thirds: one-third for additional debt reduction and a contingency fund in the event of declining revenues; one-third for anticipated expenditures for a Medicare prescription drug benefit and investments ranging from education to infrastructure to defense; and one-third for a $750 billion tax cut and associated interest costs. Besides being far less expensive, the Democratic tax proposal differed from the president's in targeting relief to those in the middle and lower brackets and stopping short of full estate tax repeal. The president's proposal offered some lower-bracket relief but actually provided a lesser economic stimulus in the near term and directed 43 percent of its benefits to the wealthiest 1 percent of taxpayers.

As the economy crossed the threshold into recession, President Bush changed the rationale for his tax cuts, though not the proposals themselves. What had been justified as a return of excessive surpluses to taxpayers now became the elixir for a sagging economy. His long-term rate reductions were not well suited to that task, however, and they threatened lasting budgetary damage: a lose-lose proposition. The House nonetheless passed a budget resolution faithfully reflecting the president's wishes on March 28 on a 222–205 party line vote.

The 50–50 Senate, which was under Republican control only by virtue of Vice President Cheney's tie-breaking vote (Jim Jeffords had not yet defected), cut the ten-year tax reduction total by $400 billion and moved $85 billion of the tax cuts into fiscal 2001 for stimulative purposes. In the end this made little difference, for GOP leaders wrote a tax bill that stayed within the budget resolution's ten-year $1.35 trillion ceiling only with a complicated set of phase-ins and an unlikely provision that most of the cuts would "sunset," or expire, after nine years—outcomes they immediately pledged to avoid by pushing legislation to accelerate the cuts and make them permanent. The true cost of the measure, including interest savings forgone, was probably closer to $2.6 trillion (soaring to $7 trillion in its second decade).[36] The bill gave more emphasis than the president had to stimulating the economy by including a provision pushed by Senate Democrats for rebate checks of $300 and $600 respectively for individuals and couples filing returns in 2001.

All of this happened before the end of May. Utilizing reconciliation procedures as protection against a Senate filibuster, the president and the Republican congressional leadership made the tax cut their first order of business, far in advance of congressional spending decisions for fiscal 2002. In our Budget Committee hearings and elsewhere, Democrats pressed administration officials in vain for their spending projections. Budget estimates released by the CBO on August 27 confirmed that because of the tax cuts and the deteriorating economy, the Bush administration was on track to invade the Social Security surplus for each of the next six years and the Medicare surplus for the next eight. These "baseline" estimates, moreover, omitted any additional spending planned for defense and Medicare prescription drugs, as well as likely disaster relief, the pending farm bill, AMT adjustments, and the continuation of expiring tax provisions.[37]

Then came September 11, which dealt the economy a further blow and immediately necessitated another $40 billion in emergency spending. It also gave members incentives to minimize the partisan conflict that was holding up several 2002 appropriations bills. As a result, overall discretionary spending once again went well beyond the confines of the GOP budget resolution.

Although budget conflict was temporarily subdued, it did not end. With the Senate now under (narrow) Democratic control, there was considerable partisan byplay over how much discretion to give the president in spending the $40 billion appropriation for post–9/11 recovery and the antiterrorism offensive. Completion of the 2002 spending bills dragged into December and required eight continuing resolutions.

The parties continued to push sharply differing economic stimulus proposals, finally settling in early 2002 on a scaled-back package of unemployment benefits and business tax breaks. Most members agreed that both the state of the economy and the challenge of terrorism required a substantial commitment of budgetary resources. We disagreed strongly, however, on whether the president's repackaged tax cuts provided the optimal economic stimulus, on which spending categories should bear the brunt of the necessary fiscal constraints, and, above all, on whether we could have it all—particularly hundreds of billions of dollars in tax cuts disproportionately targeted to the wealthiest Americans, with limited stimulative impact—in disregard of deteriorating budget projections and mounting debt. These questions dominated our 2002 budget debates and continued to divide the parties and polarize the Congress through 2004.

The House and Senate failed to agree on a budget resolution in 2002, and eleven of the thirteen appropriations bills for 2003—excluding only defense and military construction—were not passed until the fiscal year was almost half over. The president requested $45 billion in increased defense spending, a 13 percent increase that received bipartisan support, but his budget fell short by $16 billion of what was needed to maintain current services in nonsecurity domestic programs. This set up a conflict with the Senate and with House appropriators in both parties. The House again passed a budget resolution that conformed to the president's request. The Senate Budget Committee's resolution was not pressed to a floor vote because of uncertain support in the closely divided chamber, but it nonetheless guided Senate Appropriations Committee decisions and was capacious enough to let the committee report all thirteen bills with bipartisan backing.

House Democrats failed, for the first time in the history of the budget process, to formulate a budget resolution. We were in a tight spot by virtue of our support for sizable increases in defense and security spending, the reluctance of our leaders to make rescinding any of the president's tax cuts a party position (as the economy continued to languish and the midterm elections approached), and our pledge to fence off Social Security and Medicare revenues. The Senate Committee used a "trigger" to escape this conundrum, conditioning implementation of future tax cuts on a demonstration that they would not necessitate borrowing from Social Security. Such devices were subject to legitimate criticisms. But it would not have been difficult to improve on the Republicans' offering, and I strongly backed John Spratt in his efforts to persuade our leadership to get behind a Democratic resolution. Our sense that our credibility in debate would be seriously weakened without an alternative was frequently borne out in the weeks that followed. While many members no doubt found it comfortable personally to vote no on all proffered options, this was not tenable as a party position.

In the meantime, the appropriations process in the House collapsed. Republican conservatives since 1998 had written stringent aggregate limits into House budget resolutions only to see them compromised as appropriations bills were bargained over at session's end. One of the last dealt with was often the Labor-HHS-Education bill, where the pressures and needs for additional spending were especially strong. In mid-2002 a group of conservative members resolved to break this pattern and extracted from Speaker Dennis Hastert a promise to move Labor-HHS-Education to the front of the line, to increase the chances of passing it under the limits prescribed in the budget resolution. At home during the August recess, I speculated with interested constituents about how the GOP leadership could pass a Labor-HHS bill and/or get beyond it to the rest of the appropriations agenda. It never occurred to me that they might simply bring the whole process to a crashing halt. But that is exactly what they did. When it became apparent that they did not have the votes to pass the Labor-HHS bill under the limits dictated by the budget resolution and the White House, House GOP leaders simply refused to bring any more bills to the floor.

Republicans suffered no apparent ill effects in the fall elections from this monumental failure to govern. In fact, the election outcome—giving Republicans control of the Senate and five additional seats in the House—prompted Speaker Hastert to rescind his promise to appropriations leaders to bring their bills forward in a lame-duck session. Instead, they would be taken up in the new Congress, where Republicans would be more firmly in control. The eleven-bill omnibus still proved difficult to pass, clearing on February 13, 2003, after weeks of wrangling that left falling back on a yearlong continuing resolution a distinct possibility. The final product adhered closely to the administration's aggregate numbers while directing limited increases to popular items such as basic education, NIH health research, and emergency drought relief.

Fiscal 2002 also saw the expiration of the budget rules—statutory caps for discretionary spending and pay-as-you-go for tax cuts or entitlement increases—which had been first enacted in 1990 and renewed for five years as part of the 1997 agreement. Both provisions had increasingly been waived under pressures for end-of-session spending increases or for tax cuts, prompting some to argue that the rules were ill suited to an era of surpluses. Ironically, just as that era came to an end and the need for such rules was again manifest, the White House and the Republican congressional leadership—despite last-ditch efforts by Domenici, Conrad, and majority leader Tom Daschle in the Senate and protests from Spratt and other House Budget Committee Democrats—acquiesced in their demise.

"Led by the Bush Administration," the *New York Times* editorialized in early 2003 as the nation was preoccupied with the invasion of Iraq, "the Republican Congress [is] about to march under the public's radar screen and lead the country into a decade of budgetary disaster."[38] The president had requested additional tax cuts with a ten-year cost, including interest expenses, of $1.9 trillion—accelerating the 2001 cuts and making them permanent, eliminating the tax on stock dividends, and various measures of lesser scope. Republican congressional leaders deferred his expensive ($601 billion) request to extend to 2013 the provisions due to expire in 2010, while accommodating his other major proposals in their budget resolution. The Senate and the House, both now under Republican control, did not easily come to agreement. Senate "moderates" successfully held out for a $350 billion cap on the ten-year cost of the reconciliation tax bill. But the conference deal came closer to the House bill, providing rate reductions to 15 percent for dividends and capital gains and a retroactive January 1, 2003, implementation date for the 2001 income tax rate reductions. Conferees also dropped the PAYGO-type revenue offsets the Senate had added to stay within the $350 billion limit; instead, the likely ten-year cost was masked, as in 2001, by putting early (and unlikely) expiration dates on most of the bill's provisions.

In a welcome contrast to 2002, House Democrats developed and promoted an alternative budget, rejecting Republican efforts to take domestic discretionary spending below the current-services baseline, making room for a more generous prescription drug benefit under Medicare, and adding $821 billion less to the national debt. The alternative resolution's tax cuts cost far less than those proposed by the president and were designed to encourage near-term consumer spending and business investment. Our message offensive, developed by the new minority leader, Nancy Pelosi, featured an alliterative formula touting the plan's stimulative virtues: *fast-acting* (tax cuts for 2003, mainly one-time rebates, exceeding those proposed by the Republicans; immediate aid to the states and unemployment insurance extensions);[39] *fair* (targeting *all* taxpayers); and *fiscally responsible* (mostly short-term measures with a minimal out-year budget impact). The three-way test resonated well in my district, where the economic rebound was slow in coming, and it was not difficult to demonstrate that the Bush plan fell short on all counts.

The majority again adopted a "dessert first" strategy of passing the tax cuts before appropriations requests were considered. Democratic objections had more force than in 2001, however, because the president's budget forecast record deficits of $304 billion for fiscal 2003 and $307 billion for 2004, *not* including costs of the war in Iraq, natural disasters, and other likely obligations. (Supplemental appropriations bills for $78.5 billion and $87.5 billion, mainly for military and reconstruction efforts in Iraq and Afghanistan, were passed before year's end.) We often found ourselves citing the first rule of holes: when you're in one, stop digging! To "stop digging" would have meant to hold off on most elements of the 2003 tax cuts, which had limited stimulative effects, and to freeze in place further top-bracket rate reductions.[40] But the president, in contrast to President Reagan in 1982 and President George H.W. Bush in 1990, refused to moderate his budgetary policy in the face of economic reality, and the institutional constraints variously imposed by the 1990 budget rules and divided party control of government had fallen away. The unified budget deficit for fiscal 2003 ended at $374 billion—$531 billion, or 4.9 percent of the gross domestic product, without the cushion of the Social Security surplus—with a plunge beyond $450 billion predicted for 2004.

Figure 7.2 shows the path of the unified budget deficit/surplus since the onset of the Reagan administration and in the wake of the 1990, 1993, and 1997 budget plans. Note particularly the deficit path that was predicted on the eve of the adoption of Clinton's 1993 economic plan, had no action been taken. Deficit projections beyond 2004 vary considerably according to policy assumptions. The CBO projection assumes that present policy remains unchanged, including the patchwork of tax cut "sunsets." The four organizations formulating the second projection, making the more realistic assumptions that the tax cuts will be extended and the AMT adjusted, anticipate annual deficits ranging from $340 billion to $640 billion, cumulating to $4.6 trillion over the decade 2005–2014.[41]

What explains the reversal of about $9 trillion from the surpluses predicted in early 2001 for 2002–2011 to the deficits now anticipated? Several factors are involved, not all of them equally amenable to correction or change. The economy has performed more poorly than anticipated, which accounts for 8 percent of the deterioration according to the Center for Budget and Policy Priorities. Another 31 percent is attributable to flaws in CBO economic models, which overestimated revenue flows, and other technical factors. Increased spending has also played a role: 21 percent of the deterioration comes from above-inflation increases in defense, international, and homeland security spending, while lesser amounts come from entitlement changes, including Medicare prescription drugs (8 percent). Domestic discretionary spending, which President Bush and Republican leaders often portray as the villain in the piece, in fact accounts for 1 percent. By contrast, 31 percent of the deterioration comes from tax cuts—$2.2 trillion from those already enacted and $600 billion more if they are made permanent and the AMT is adjusted.[42]

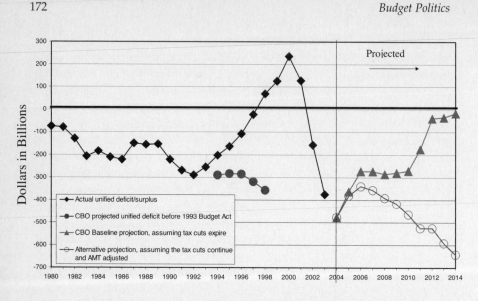

Sources: Congressional Budget Office; alternative 2005-2014 projections by the Committee for Economic Development, Concord Coalition, Committee for a Responsible Federal Budget, and the Center for Budget and Policy Priorities

FIGURE 7.2   Unified budget deficit/surplus, fiscal years 1980–2014.

In another attempt to put the fiscal impact of the tax cuts in perspective, the Center estimated in 2004 that the tax cuts already enacted, if extended as proposed by the Bush administration, would cost more than $11 trillion in 2003 dollars (depending on what adjustments were made in the AMT) over the next seventy-five years—*three times* what it would take to make Social Security whole.[43]

Budget politics and the budget process have shaped the political and policymaking environment in Congress in significant ways since 1974—augmenting the power of the party leadership, constraining the work of the appropriations and authorizing committees, placing a burden of proof on initiatives and investments, and often shifting policy debate away from substance and into primarily fiscal terms. Has the process lived up to its architects' hopes that it would improve the coordination and accountability of congressional policymaking, making certain the fiscal impact of disparate decisions was taken fully into account? At best, the verdict is mixed, representing as much a commentary on the quality of political leadership as on budgetary architecture. The budget debates of the 1980s often made a mockery of the analytic standards and fiscal soundness to which the framers of the process aspired. Budget leaders sometimes struggled valiantly, but the solutions to the problems they faced far exceeded what public opinion and any achievable political consensus would support. The result, all too often, was budget deliberations and decisions that became exercises in smoke-and-mirrors accounting and political evasion and only patched things up from year to year.

The 1990 and 1993 five-year plans broke with this pattern at considerable political cost to those supporting them but with eventual budgetary gain. This gain came not only through year-to-year cuts in spending and increases in revenue but through improved budget machinery, which replaced the easily manipulated G-R-H procedures. The results included lower interest rates and more confidence in the economy, which in turn led to increased investment, job creation, and productivity.[44] In the meantime, overly simplistic fixes like the balanced-budget amendment to the Constitution and the line-item veto (see Chapter 13) fell by the wayside.

While the budget process and its responsible use helped produce a brief era of balanced budgets, it has now fallen to the lowest point in its thirty-year history in terms of influence and effectiveness. To some extent the process was the victim of its own successful use. Budget caps seemed less useful in an age of surpluses, particularly when they were being set at levels that reflected ideology rather than the realities of the appropriations process. Pay-as-you-go was similarly allowed to lapse. But the most dramatic abandonment of budget discipline came precisely as economic and budgetary storm signals worsened in 2001. Far from offering a corrective, budgetary machinery was used in a way that hastened and worsened the fiscal reversal.

This recent experience, like most of the episodes recounted in this chapter, underscores the centrality of political leadership in determining the success or failure of the budget process. In charting a course beyond our present crisis, certain specific changes are essential—some procedural (reinstating rules that subject both spending increases and tax cuts to budgetary discipline), some substantive (recalibrating tax and eventually entitlement policy). More fundamental, however, is the need to recapture a sense of budgetary stewardship and responsibility. Budgeting will remain central to the management of both the executive and legislative branches of government, and regardless of the balance of party control, political competition and hard bargaining are inevitable. In both branches the success of the process requires that partisan positioning and posturing be tempered by respect for the basics of sound budgeting—reliable estimates and projections, honest accounting, fiscal prudence and a refusal to defer problems, contingency planning and preparation, and political realism. Above all, leaders in both branches must muster the political resolve and responsibility without which even the best-designed rules and procedures will fail.

Notes

1. The exact numbers were 122 Republicans and 20 Democrats. See votes 49–52, *Congressional Quarterly Almanac* 43 (1987): 18H–19H.

2. Allen Schick, *Congress and Money* (Washington, D.C.: Urban Institute, 1980), p. 361.

3. David A. Stockman, *The Triumph of Politics* (New York: Avon, 1987), p. 409.

4. *Congressional Quarterly Weekly Report,* April 11, 1987, p. 659.

5. On this point and for an excellent account of executive and congressional roles in the deficit making of the early 1980s, see Paul E. Peterson, "The New Politics of Deficits," in John E. Chubb and Paul E. Peterson, eds., *The New Direction in American Politics* (Washington, D.C.: Brookings Institution, 1985), chap. 13.

6. These guidelines proved difficult to sustain, particularly in the Senate, and at one point (House passage of the postappropriations reconciliation bill on October 29) I cast a negative vote to protest Democrats' departure from our announced determination to match revenue increases with spending cuts and earmark all revenue increases for deficit reduction. This was a positive vote for me politically, demonstrating my consistency and willingness to stand up to party pressure. But I cast it with difficulty, for the bill passed by one vote (206–205) after a highly visible vote switch by a freshman member and caused the leadership considerable embarrassment.

7. *Congressional Quarterly Almanac* 45 (1989): 85.

8. Richard G. Darman, "Beyond the Deficit Problem: 'Me-Now-ism' and 'The New Balance'" (address to the National Press Club, Washington, D.C., July 20, 1989), pp. 5, 7.

9. Alan Murray and John Young, "Lingering Animosity from Capital-Gains Fight Threatens Bipartisan Efforts on Cutting Deficit," *Wall Street Journal,* October 5, 1989, p. A30.

10. Bush's budgets were thereafter subjected to annual votes on the House floor. The results were invariably embarrassing to the administration: an 89–235 defeat on April 17, 1991, and a 42–370 defeat on March 4, 1992.

11. *Congressional Quarterly Almanac* 46 (1990): 130.

12. *Congressional Quarterly Almanac* 46 (1990): 131.

13. "Now for the House Republicans," *Washington Post,* October 3, 1990, p. A22.

14. Quoted in Helen Dewar and Tom Kenworthy, "Conservative Republicans Assail Budget Pact; Democrats Skeptical," *Washington Post,* October 1, 1990, p. A8.

15. Robin Toner, "Sour View of Congress Emerges from Survey," *New York Times,* October 12, 1990, p. A21.

16. This was viewed as not merely a rate increase but the correction of an apparent anomaly in the 1986 tax reform legislation, whereby the effective marginal rate was 33 percent for joint filers earning between $78,400 and $185,760 (the so-called bubble) but reverted to 28 percent for those earning more.

17. Elizabeth Drew, "Letter from Washington," *New Yorker,* November 12, 1990, p. 116.

18. This provision, had it stood alone, would have provided a modest reduction for those in the bubble, as well as an increase for those earning more than $185,760. The net revenue gain for this provision, along with an increase in the alternative minimum tax from 21 to 24 percent, was estimated to be $11.2 billion over five years.

19. Quoted in John Yang, "The One-for-You, Two-for-Me School of Budgeting," *Washington Post,* national weekly ed., February 11, 1991, p. 8.

20. Projections of the underlying standardized employment deficit, with the effects of the business cycle on federal revenues and outlays removed and with Desert Storm contributions and savings and loan insurance expenditures and receipts excluded, were relatively constant, in the range of $164 to $188 billion from 1991 to 1996. "In relation to the size of the economy, such deficits are no better than those of the late 1980s and considerably worse than the average of the 1960s and 1970s." Congressional Budget Office, *The Economic and Budget Outlook: An Update: A Report to the Senate and House Committees on the Budget,* August 1991, pp. xi, xiii, 16.

21. *Congressional Quarterly Almanac* 49 (1993): 7-D; on the 1993 episode generally, see pp. 81–145. Also see in Steven S. Smith, *The American Congress* (Boston: Houghton Mifflin, 1995), chap. 11; Barbara Sinclair, *Unorthodox Lawmaking: New Legislative Processes in the U.S. Congress* (Washington, D.C.: Congressional Quarterly Press, 1997), chap. 10; and Robert Rubin (with Jacob Weisberg), *In an Uncertain World* (New York: Random House, 2003), pp. 118–131.

22. "The easy vote on the budget was a 'no' once Clinton lost the public debate about its contents months ago to the opposition's false claims that it would tax average Americans significantly." Thomas Oliphant, "The Votes—For and Against—That Really Counted on Clinton's Budget," *Boston Globe,* August 11, 1993, p. 15.

23. *Congressional Record,* daily ed., August 5, 1993, pp. H6267–68.

24. "Disappearing Doom," *Raleigh News and Observer,* February 20, 1994, p. 26A.

25. See, for example, David Broder, "Some Victory," *Washington Post,* August 10, 1993, p. A15.

26. Quoted in Albert R. Hunt, "Last Year's Budget Deal was a Success," *Wall Street Journal,* August 4, 1994, p. A13.

27. See *Congressional Quarterly Almanac* 50 (1994): 88.

28. E.J. Dionne, "Then They Met Medicare," *Washington Post,* May 9, 1995, p. A19.

29. For accounts of the events culminating in the government shutdowns of late 1995, see David Maraniss and Michael Weisskopf, *"Tell Newt to Shut Up!"* (New York: Simon & Schuster, 1996), chaps. 11–12; Sherrod Brown, *Congress from the Inside* (Kent, Ohio: Kent State University Press, 1999), chaps. 13–14; and Sinclair, *Unorthodox Lawmaking,* chap. 11.

30. *Congressional Quarterly Almanac* 52 (1996): 10–13.

31. *Congressional Quarterly Almanac* 53 (1997): 2–18. For an account of the 1997 negotiations and agreement, see Daniel J. Palazzolo, *Done Deal? The Politics of the 1997 Budget Agreement* (New York: Chatham House, 1999).

32. Congressional Budget Office, *Final Sequestration Report for Fiscal Year 1999,* October 30, 1998.

33. "Paradoxically," noted Henry Aaron, "the one line in this seemingly endless [budget] drama that is comprehensible, 'We must not raid the Social Security trust fund,' is nonsense. . . . Trust fund bond holdings will increase [by the amount of the Social Security] surplus, whatever budget decisions Congress and the White House may make." "Great Pretenders," *Washington Post,* weekly ed., November 15, 1999, p. 26.

34. Congressional Budget Office, *The Budget for Fiscal Year 2000: An End-of-Session Summary,* December 2, 1999.

35. Former CBO Director Robert Reischauer, quoted in Charles Babington and Eric Pianin, "Clinton Plan Ignores '97 Budget Pact," *Washington Post,* January 14, 2000, p. A1. Debt reduction calculation by Richard Kogan of the Center on Budget and Policy Priorities.

36. Joel Friedman, Robert Greenstein, and Richard Kogan, "The Administration's Proposal to Make the Tax Cut Permanent," *Center on Budget and Policy Priorities,* April 16, 2002, p. 2. On this result and the complicity of "moderate" Democratic senators in producing it, see E. J. Dionne Jr., "Gutless Moderates," *Washington Post,* May 4, 2001, p. A25; Dionne, "Tax Cuts: The Fight Is Just Beginning," *Washington Post,* June 1, 2001, p. A31; Paul Krugman, "The Big Lie," *New York Times,* May 27, 2001, p. 4–9; and Krugman, "Bad Heir Day," *New York Times,* May 30, 2001, p. A23.

37. Democratic Caucus, House Budget Committee, *CBO Confirms Bush Budget Taps Social Security and Medicare Surpluses,* August 27, 2001.

38. "Budgetary Shock and Awe," *New York Times,* March 25, 2003, p. A16.

39. The final reconciliation bill included $20 billion in Medicaid and other assistance to the states as part of the deal struck with Senate "moderates" from both parties. It also included a partial rebate in 2003 of an expanded per-child tax credit. As the conference on the bill concluded, a Democratic proposal to make a "refundable" per-child credit available to lower-income families who did not pay enough income taxes to claim the full credit (but did pay payroll taxes) was dropped. An outcry ensued, but majority leader Tom DeLay and other House opponents prevented the provision's reinstatement.

40. A widely cited study found most of the president's proposals to provide a relatively low stimulative impact per dollar of revenue loss or spending increase: 0.59 for the acceleration of personal rate reductions and a mere 0.09 for dividend taxation reduction. Leading Democratic proposals fared much better: 1.73 for the extension of unemployment benefits, for example, and 1.24 for state assistance. "The Economic Impact of the Bush and Congressional Democratic Economic Stimulus Plans," Economy.com, February 2003.

41. Congressional Budget Office, *An Analysis of the President's Budgetary Proposals for Fiscal Year 2005*, March 8, 2004; Center on Budget and Policy Priorities (CBPP), Committee for Economic Development (CED), Concord Coalition and Committee for a Responsible Federal Budget, *The Current Course: Deficits "As Far As the Eye Can See,"* April 20, 2004, p. 2. The CBO official baseline omits the cost of extending the 2001 and 2003 tax cuts beyond their scheduled expiration dates and assumes that defense and homeland security expenditures will not exceed the rate of inflation. The alternative projection assumes extension of the tax cuts, AMT adjustments to keep the number of taxpayers affected at approximately 2004 levels, and spending increases in line with historic patterns and Pentagon plans.

42. Richard Kogan and David Kamin, *Deficit Picture Grimmer Than CBO's March Projections Suggest*, CBPP, June 4, 2004.

43. Robert Greenstein and Peter Orszag, *Understanding the Social Security and Medicare Projections*, CBPP, April 2, 2004, p. 2. On the motivations behind the Bush tax cuts, how they were sold, and their reception by the public, see Paul Krugman, "The Tax-Cut Con," *New York Times Magazine*, September 14, 2003, pp. 54–62; and two complementary articles prepared for delivery at the 2003 annual meeting of the American Political Science Association: Jacob S. Hacker and Paul Pierson, "Abandoning the Middle: The Revealing Case of the Bush Tax Cut of 2001"; and Larry M. Bartels, "Homer Gets a Tax Cut: Inequality and Public Policy in the American Mind."

44. "Policies matter," concluded Allen Schick. "Wrong decisions in the 1980s condemned the nation to a decade of high deficits; right ones in the 1990s have liberated it from past budgetary misdeeds." "'A Surplus If We Can Keep It': How the Federal Surplus Happened," *Brookings Review*, Winter 2000, p. 36. On the ripple effects through the economy of the 1993 plan and the market confidence it engendered, see Rubin, *Uncertain World*, pp. 122, 125.

8

Parties and Partisanship

Newly elected members of Congress quickly confront the realities of party leadership and control. This comes as a surprise to some, for conventional wisdom says that American parties are in decline. Many members seem to confirm that view by running their campaigns largely independently. But despite the tenuous hold of the major parties on much of the electorate, party solidarity in roll call voting has displayed a remarkable comeback from its low point in the 90th–92nd Congresses (1967–1972). Party discipline and control in the House of Representatives still fall short of what is found in most parliamentary systems, but under Republican leadership they have reached levels not seen since the early twentieth century. In fact, never in U.S. history have the parties had a more extensive congressional organization and infrastructure.

Members of Congress, individually and collectively, also must come to terms with presidential leadership. The legislative and executive branches often find themselves in competition and conflict. During six of my eight terms, that conflict was exacerbated by divided party control over Congress and the White House. Yet Congress depends on the president for budgetary and legislative agenda setting, the institutions share responsibility for passing legislation and overseeing its implementation, and individual members must seek the assistance of executive officials on countless matters large and small.

In this chapter, I will attempt to elucidate congressional party and presidential relations by describing my own interactions with the Democratic Party while running for office and serving in the House—in the majority and the minority, under Democratic and Republican presidents. Not every member's story would be the same. Party organizations outside the Congress vary in their hold on voter loyalties and their control of campaign resources. Candidates are often largely on their own and work with or depend on party organizations to varying degrees. Although parties perform crucial institutional functions and every representative must come to terms with them in some fashion, constituency-based incentives to party regularity in the House are limited. Members differ in their voting behavior and in how they relate to the broad range of party functions and activities.

Despite these variations, members of both parties have generally supported, or at least acquiesced in, strong leadership prerogatives. What are the limits of party leadership and control, and are they different for Democrats and Republicans? How does strong, disciplined leadership by the majority party compare with bipartisan accommodation and cooperation as a way of governing? I will explore, if not definitively answer, such questions by describing the leadership structures and practices developed by Democrats and then Republicans, and some of the incentives to participation and support experienced by members like myself. I will describe the difference it made for the Democratic majority to have a Democratic president and for the Democrats to lose that majority. Finally I will consider what might be learned from several recent exercises in partisanship: the "responsible party" triumph on the 1993 budget, the sharply polarized impeachment battle of 1998, and the Republicans' escalation of tactics in 2003.

Parties and Elections

As a candidate for Congress, I had unusually strong party credentials. I had paid my dues through local party service and as a foot soldier in other Democrats' campaigns, and my background as executive director and chairman of the North Carolina Democratic Party gave me major advantages as a congressional candidate. The party chairmanship has changed in this regard; I remember being told when I accepted the job that the infighting would inevitably leave me with more enemies than friends and finish me politically. But the chairmanship in many places has become a more visible public role. What gave me credibility as a potential candidate in 1986 was receiving media exposure and being identified as a spokesman on key issues during the Hunt-Helms Senate race and the other campaigns of 1984, much more than my behind-the-scenes organizational activity.[1]

I chose the county Democratic conventions in my district (held simultaneously on April 13, 1985) to announce my candidacy, believing (as I still do) that party activists were an essential core of my political base. After surviving the primary, I received substantial support from the Democratic Congressional Campaign Committee (DCCC) and integrated my grassroots campaign with that of county party organizations. My campaigns thus illustrate the role that party can play. They also demonstrate the limits of that role, even when a candidate has an inclination (which many candidates do not) to run as part of the party team.

As recounted in Chapter 2, neither my familiarity among party activists nor my wider exposure as a party spokesman made me the favorite or gave me substantial name recognition in a Democratic primary. That came only as we formulated a television message and scraped together enough money to put it on the air. Relatively little of that money came from party sources; Democratic Party activists are generally able to contribute only modestly. North Carolina party organizations (like others in states with a one-party past where nomination was once tantamount to election) have a tradition of remaining neutral, financially and otherwise, in primary contests. The same was true in my case for the DCCC. Nonetheless, I called on its leaders during the primary season. I knew that a direct contribution was out of the question but hoped to convince them that I would be the best candidate against the GOP incumbent, thinking that they might informally pass the word to potential contributors. This happened only to a very limited degree. It was not within the power of local, state, or national party organizations to deliver the Democratic nomination. My fledgling campaign team and I were largely on our own in pursuing that goal.

That changed somewhat but not entirely after the primary. I was one of four Democratic challengers from North Carolina whom the DCCC was targeting for assistance in 1986. The committee contributed $39,848 to my effort, which, when added to the state tax checkoff money funneled through the state Democratic Party, came close to the legal maximum. The state party, having lost the organizational resources of the governorship in 1984 and having nothing like the Hunt-Helms Senate race to attract contributions and participation in 1986, was not in a position to replicate the state-level voter-contact operations undertaken two years before. Several congressional campaigns were weakened as a result. I was fortunate, however, in having relatively active Democratic organizations in most of my counties and a tradition of extensive phone bank and get-out-the-vote (GOTV) activity in Raleigh and Chapel Hill. We therefore decided after the primary to run our voter-contact operations as part of a Democratic "unity campaign," and our Senate candidate, Terry Sanford, did the same.

Although my campaign thus evinced relatively strong participation by the national campaign committee and local party organizations, it could not, when compared to parliamentary elections in other Western democracies or earlier American practice, be judged a party-centered effort. We gained numerous foot soldiers and saved scarce campaign dollars by combining forces with other Democratic candidates in our canvassing and turnout operations, but even here we gave as much as we got. Party precinct structures were spotty at best, and the cadres of volunteers often needed shoring up. So activists from the Price campaign helped make the party efforts work, as well as the reverse.

In other facets of the campaign, the party role was far less prominent. The state party organized a rally in each congressional district for all the Democratic candidates, and most county parties did the same thing locally. But most of my campaign appearances and fund-raising events were organized by our campaign alone. We drew on the state party's research and press resources, but we were largely on our own in devising a press strategy, formulating a message, putting together an advertising campaign, and raising the money to pay for it.

In the campaigns I have waged since 1986, often against aggressive, well-financed opponents, the party role has slipped even further. This is not because of any changed strategy on my part; rather, it reflects changed priorities and capacities on the party side. Only in my comeback race of 1996 did the DCCC come close to matching its 1986 financial support; I have not generally been in the top tier of most vulnerable candidates or most financially strapped campaigns. We have often drawn on the expertise of the National Committee for an Effective Congress (NCEC), a political action committee that works closely with the DCCC, in targeting precincts for door-to-door walking and GOTV activity and in calculating the likely effects of various redistricting proposals. We have continued to cooperate with our state and county party organizations, particularly in implementing voter-contact operations, and to develop synergetic relationships with other Democratic campaigns.

Besides trying to make the most of the party potential in my own campaigns, I have attempted to keep my local party ties in good repair between elections—attending and speaking at meetings, helping organize and promote events, consulting with party leaders. I value these organizations and believe elected officials can do much to enhance their role. Politicians who complain of the party's weakness and irrelevance and treat the organization accordingly often are engaged in a self-fulfilling prophecy; we do have significant choices as to how we relate to party organizations, and the choices we make have a considerable potential to harm or help. I am not suggesting that candidates or officeholders should be expected to sacrifice their basic interests to those of the party. Rather, I am suggesting that normally a range of viable strategies of campaigning and governance are available, some of which reinforce and others undermine party strength. The same is true of public policies, and I believe we should pay more attention than we normally do to the implications of policy enactments at all levels for the parties' electoral and organizational strength.[2]

The parties, however, must also help themselves. The national committees, the House and Senate campaign committees, and some state parties have done more than is commonly recognized to remodel themselves—increasing their financial base and their capacity to recruit candidates and offer a range of supportive services—and these efforts have sometimes paid off handsomely, especially for Republicans. Much depends on the quality of party leadership at all levels. Local parties are not tidy organizations, and they would lose much of their vitality if they were. Gone forever is the patronage system that bound loyalists to "the organization" and assured tight leadership control. Today's party activists are motivated mainly by issue and candidate enthusiasms, and they often give organizational maintenance a decidedly lower priority. Candidates and officeholders who would work with the party must recognize this and adapt to it. At the same time, partisans and their leaders need to understand that if they allow the party to degenerate into contending factions—each pushing for its own "pure" policy position or preferred candidate, unable or unwilling to work together after the nomination and platform battles are over—candidates and officeholders will be tempted to distance themselves, seeing the party tie as more hassle than help.

The 1994 Republican campaign to take control of the House represented a high point of party effort and impact. Republican leaders recruited and coached candidates vigorously, and the Contract with America provided a focused and uniform party message. Newt Gingrich and his colleagues effectively directed resources to Republican challengers and open-seat contenders, not so much through the National Republican Congressional Committee (NRCC) as through generous giving by GOP incumbent members and political action committees (PACs) under their influence. Given the party role in their election, it is hardly surprising that the Republican class of 1994 demonstrated exceptional partisan solidarity once in office. As noted in Chapter 3, however, antigovernment, antitax, anti-Clinton, and anti-Congress themes and sentiments, with roots extending far beyond the partisan campaign, had more electoral impact than did the Contract. Traditional factors such as incumbency, candidate experience, and the political makeup of the district still shaped electoral outcomes, often determining the reception given the GOP national effort.[3] Postelection voter surveys prompted doubts, as Jonathan Krasno pointed out, "that the GOP ever had a mandate from its own voters to do all of the things that it tried to do, let alone from the rest of the electorate."[4] This helps explain some of the resistance House Republicans ran into as the 104th Congress progressed, as well as their gradual realization that Speaker O'Neill's maxim ("All politics is local") hadn't been totally repealed.

Even for the Republican class of 1994, then, the partisan campaign was only a partial determinant of electoral success. And for most House members, the role of national, state, and local party organizations in my successive campaigns is more typical than is the experience of the 1994 freshmen. Most members face electorates that are disinclined to vote for them on partisan grounds alone or monitor their service or fealty to their party once in office. Candidates are usually on their own in raising the bulk of their contributions and building their organization. They can seldom rely primarily on national partisan swings or a national partisan message to get elected. Moreover, members of Congress have numerous ways of relating to their districts directly, unmediated by their party (see Chapter 10). District service operations have grown, responding to and sometimes stimulating expanded expectations on the part of constituents as to the role and obligations of government. The growth of television as the dominant medium of political communication in campaign advertising and the daily news offers manifold opportunities for more frequent and more direct communications with voters than was ever afforded by traditional friends-and-neighbors or clubhouse channels. The same is true of e-mail and the Internet, increasingly a staple of congressional offices and campaigns. Incumbents know that their opponents can also use these techniques. In casting roll call votes, for example, members must contemplate the use an opponent might make of them in thirty-second television commercials or fire-breathing direct mail solicitations during the next campaign. Such prospects can make the blandishments of party leaders pale by comparison.

How is it, then, that by 1988 House Democrats had developed a leadership structure that could plausibly be compared to "the days of Joseph Cannon"?[5] And how did Republicans manage to take their discipline and control beyond what even Gingrich achieved? Part of the answer lies in political and electoral trends, many of them reinforced by redistricting, which reduced the political cross-pressures on many members and gave them more homogeneous districts; increasingly consistent and polarized liberal and conservative views among Democratic and Republican activists respectively; a stronger correlation among party identification, ideology, and voting decisions in House elections; and fewer districts producing split-ticket results.[6] But the electoral constraints were hardly airtight. They left lots of slack to be filled by members' own policy preferences and their individual and collective desire for influence. An examination of the organizational development of the House over the past thirty years will leave little doubt as to where such considerations have led.

Organizing the House

Modern efforts to strengthen party operations in the Democratic-led House began in the 1970s, as more and more members came to believe that enhanced leadership powers would serve their political interests.[7] The elections of 1958, 1964, and 1974 had brought large numbers of liberal activist Democrats into the House. In the meantime, black enfranchisement and party realignment in the South had gradually produced a new breed of Democratic House member from that region, much closer to the party's mainstream. These crosscurrents produced significant shifts in ideology and policy preference within the House's majority party. Members came to see significant advantages in strengthening party organs, not by virtue of district-based party ties or pressures, but as a means to their personal and policy goals within the chamber.

Strengthening the party was not the dominant goal of congressional reform. Its initial and main thrust was decentralization—the dispersal of authority, resources, and visibility throughout the chamber. From 1965 to 1978 this produced what Roger Davidson termed the "rise of subcommittee government."[8] Reform, however, had a centralizing component from the first. The reformers' main targets were the senior committee chairmen, many of them conservative southerners, who stood in the way of the progressive policies and greater visibility and power that junior members desired. Revitalizing the House Democratic Caucus proved necessary in order to rewrite the rules, depose recalcitrant chairmen, and otherwise effect the desired transfer of power.

The leadership, moreover, was the only available counterweight to conservative bastions like the House Rules and Ways and Means Committees. Therefore, two key early reforms removed the committee-assignment function from Ways and Means Democrats and placed it in a leadership-dominated Steering and Policy Committee and gave the Speaker the power to nominate the chair and the Democratic members of the Rules Committee. For some reformers, such as Rep. Richard Bolling (D-Missouri), the strengthening of party organs was quite deliberate, aimed at giving a true "majority of House Democrats . . . effective control of the House" and enabling them to enact their legislative program.[9] For others, it was mainly a means to the end of breaking up the oligarchic power of the committee barons. The effect was to strengthen the party involvement of younger members and enhance the role of the leadership, even as the actual decisions of the caucus were helping atomize congressional power.

This atomization, as it proceeded through the 1970s, gave more and more members a stake in the new order. But it also created new problems for the institution that only strengthened parties could solve. The proliferating bases from which issues could be publicized and initiatives generated could also encourage conflict and obstruction when the time came to mobilize the chamber. Consequently there was widespread support for leadership efforts to overcome organizational fragmentation, including the use of intercommittee task forces, enhanced bill referral powers for the Speaker, the development of leadership agendas, and the strengthening of whip operations.

The decline in the deference paid to committees, the desire of members for visibility, and various rules changes resulted in increased amending activity on the House floor. In time, many members came to see this as more of a threat than an opportunity, as measures they favored were damaged or delayed and as members of the opposition party used the amendment process to force politically charged record votes. Thus the leadership began, with widespread member support, to pass more bills under "suspension of the rules" procedures that forbade amendments, to employ more special rules that restricted amending activity, and to otherwise rein in floor activity.

The budget process instituted in 1974 and the politics surrounding it also strengthened the role of the congressional leadership. Party leaders assumed control over appointments to the new budget committees and, of necessity, brokered negotiations among committees and between Congress and the White House. Even more determinative was the budget crisis that lasted into the 1990s. "Looming deficits and the need to reach painful decisions about priorities . . . pushed legislative structures and practices toward greater centralization."[10] Budget measures became more complicated, comprehensive, and conflicted, spilling over established timetables and processes and committee jurisdictions. Working out budget deals year to year with Republican administrations increasingly became a critical function of the Democratic leadership.

Many Democratic members of the House therefore became willing to support an enhanced party role. As the party organization developed, it reinforced these tendencies with a reward structure of its own. Meanwhile, the costs of cooperation were decreasing for many members as well. I have indicated how the political and budgetary climate of the 1980s made for less freewheeling policy entrepreneurship. Members had less to lose by being reined in and more to gain as the leadership sought to overcome some of the adverse conditions making legislative action difficult. Nor did House Democrats have as much trouble uniting under the party banner as they had in the recent past. Plenty of diversity remained, but the north–south gap that had bedeviled the party and had fueled much of the early reform effort continued to narrow. Thus the potential costs of assertive Democratic leadership in terms of disaffection and division were greatly reduced.[11]

These trends toward strengthened leadership reached a high point during my first term in the House, the 100th Congress of 1987–1988. As Roger Davidson observed:

Part of the equation was the advent of a new Speaker: Jim Wright (D-Texas), who had few inhibitions about exploiting the powers of the office. Even more important, however, were contextual factors that at last made vigorous party leadership feasible. First, after dominating the Washington scene for six years, President Reagan was irrevocably damaged by the 1986 elections and the Iran-Contra scandal that broke shortly afterward. With both houses of Congress in Democratic hands, the legislative initiative traveled down Pennsylvania Avenue to Capitol Hill. Democrats and their allies at last saw a chance to push their long-deferred legislative agendas. Moreover, Democratic officeholders again found reason to identify themselves with a partisan agenda: Not only was the party label worth more than in Reagan's heyday, but Democrats were anxious to compile a record of achievement to carry them into the 1988 elections. Finally, in order to pass a partisan agenda, both committee leaders and the rank and file understood that leadership coordination would be essential.[12]

Speaker Wright saw to it that the first five bills introduced, numbered H.R. 1 through H.R. 5, were those he regarded as lead items on the Democratic agenda. Two of these, the Clean Water Act and an ambitious highway bill, were passed shortly after Congress convened in January 1987; by April 2, both had again been whipped through over President Reagan's vetoes. The remaining three bills, an omnibus trade measure and reauthorizations of elementary and secondary education and housing programs, were all passed in the next two years, as were significant welfare reform, Medicare expansion, fair housing, farm credit reform, plant closing notification, and homeless assistance measures. The 100th Congress could fairly be regarded as the most productive since the Great Society congresses of the mid-1960s, and strong leadership in the House was a critical part of the equation. Observing this as he plotted his rise to power was a Republican backbencher named Newt Gingrich, whose Contract with America eight years later owed more to Wright's precedent than he ever cared to acknowledge.

The 101st and 102nd congresses found it difficult to maintain the same level of productivity, although the falloff was not as great as many commentators suggested. The leading agenda items were neither as obvious nor as easy to pass as the clean water and highway bills had been in 1987. The ethics troubles experienced by Speaker Wright and majority whip Tony Coelho deepened as the 101st Congress began, and both men departed by mid-1989. The 1988 presidential elections left Democrats on the defensive without a clear programmatic thrust; the White House vacuum they had moved to fill in 1987 and 1988 no longer existed. And the long-term constraints imposed by enormous budget deficits and divided party control of government remained.

Still, there was no major reversal of the trend toward extensive and active leadership operations. The new Speaker, Tom Foley, was not as aggressively partisan as Wright and resisted proposals to enhance leadership powers (see Chapter 13). Nonetheless, he became increasingly assertive in using the leadership tools at his disposal, while majority leader Dick Gephardt emerged as a forceful party spokesman. President George Bush sometimes proved a strong adversary, stymieing congressional action in areas ranging from civil rights to the minimum wage, campaign finance reform, family and medical leave, and the protection of Chinese nationals seeking to delay a return home after the Tiananmen Square massacre. But in other areas, he proved far more flexible than President Reagan, cooperating with the Congress to produce major clean air, handicapped rights, energy deregulation, and housing legislation, as well as the 1990 budget agreement. Under conditions of either confrontation or cooperation, the need for strong party leadership was generally supported by most Democratic members.[13]

The election of Bill Clinton in 1992, ending twelve years of divided party control of the executive and legislative branches, both empowered the House Democratic leadership and reduced its autonomy in defining the party's agenda. Congress passed and the president signed a number of bills that had been vetoed or otherwise held up during the Bush administration, including a National Institutes of Health reauthorization that permitted research utilizing fetal tissue, the Family and Medical Leave Act, the Motor Voter law linking voter registration to the driver's license process, and the Brady Law requiring background checks before handgun purchases. Also approved were the bill instituting National Service, the Goals 2000 education reform initiative, legislation implementing the North American Free Trade Agreement (NAFTA) and the General Agreement on Tariffs and Trade (GATT), the 1994 Crime Bill, and the five-year budget plan of 1993. With the exception of the trade agreements, these were partisan measures that the House Democratic organization was largely responsible for passing. Yet the budget and crime victories came after long struggles that revealed deep divisions among Democrats, and the president's initiatives in health care and welfare reform died conspicuous deaths. The House Democratic leadership ended the 103rd Congress looking ineffectual and beleaguered—an impression that did not do justice to its substantial accomplishments but nonetheless contributed to the party's negative image going into the 1994 elections.

Those elections produced a new majority, a new Speaker, and a major consolidation of leadership power.[14] Republicans in earlier years had tracked Democratic rule changes that shifted power from committee to party leaders, but Gingrich took this process considerably further. Party rules were changed to give the leadership a stronger hand on the Steering Committee and thus in making committee assignments, and Gingrich saw to it that numerous freshmen indebted to him were given coveted slots on the Appropriations, Ways and Means, Rules, and Commerce Committees. Gingrich ignored seniority in engineering the selection of several key committee chairs, including fifth-ranking Bob Livingston (R-Louisiana) on Appropriations, second-ranking Tom Bliley (R-Virginia) on Commerce, and second-ranking Henry Hyde (R-Illinois) on Judiciary. Committee chairs were weakened by the imposition of six-year term limits, staff reductions, and the abolition of proxy voting. In turn, committee chairs were given the power to appoint subcommittee chairs and hire all staff, reversing Democratic practice. But here too Gingrich did not hesitate to intervene. For example, he directed that two freshmen be given Government Reform subcommittee chairmanships, dismissing the claims of more senior members.

Gingrich also took control of the House agenda to an extraordinary degree, forcing consideration of the Contract with America in the first one hundred days of the 104th Congress and imposing a master schedule on committees and subcommittees. He made extensive use of intercommittee legislative task forces and did not hesitate to bypass committees, issue directives to their chairmen, or alter their handiwork in order to accomplish the party's objectives. As noted in previous chapters, the Republican leadership further consolidated power by commandeering the appropriations process and defunding legislative service organizations (LSOs).

Most Republican members willingly acquiesced in and adapted to these changes. The 1992 and 1994 elections heightened GOP intraparty homogeneity and a sense of solidarity in opposition to Democrats. Gingrich had a special relationship with the enormous freshman class, and initially he took pains to maintain active involvement from all elements of the party. This greatly facilitated his consolidation of power, aimed at achieving Republican policy goals and maintaining majority control.

Member support came under increasing strains as the 104th Congress wore on and Gingrich and the Republican revolution lost popular approval. GOP leaders shifted tactics as they looked toward the 1996 elections, striking bipartisan deals on legislative matters such as health insurance portability, welfare reform, drinking water protection, and the minimum wage, and in the process delegating more responsibility to committees. Gingrich was further weakened by an ethics investigation that culminated in his admission of serious lapses on December 21, 1996, and House approval of a reprimand and a $300,000 penalty on January 21.

Gingrich was narrowly reelected as Speaker for the 105th Congress, and GOP leaders agreed to several organizational changes designed to shift authority and resources back to committee chairs. But Republicans had no desire to give committee leaders the kind of power that chairmen like John Dingell (Commerce), Dan Rostenkowski (Ways and Means), and Jack Brooks (Judiciary) had asserted under Foley's speakership. GOP conservatives were among those most distrustful of committee prerogatives, which they associated with past practices of bipartisan accommodation. As the 105th Congress began, they unsuccessfully attempted to subject even subcommittee chairmanships to conference approval.

Gingrich's troubles subsequently deepened. He barely survived a coup attempt that several of his colleagues in the leadership had encouraged, and Republican leadership performance displayed an erratic quality for much of 1997 and 1998. The Speaker's resignation was finally forced when the GOP nearly lost the House majority in the 1998 elections. Ironically the solidarity the GOP then displayed in impeaching President Clinton and blocking any path to compromise was less an indication of strong leadership than of weakness at the top that allowed Republican whip Tom DeLay (R-Texas) and other impeachment hard-liners to seize control of the process.

Part of the appeal of Bob Livingston (R-Louisiana) as Gingrich's prospective successor was that, as a generally respected Appropriations chairman, he balanced an assertive leadership style with an appreciation of the strengths of the committee system. But Livingston withdrew his name when news of his marital infidelities became public, and Republicans settled on Dennis Hastert (R-Illinois), a colleague of mine from the class of 1986. Hastert was a behind-the-scenes operator who displayed little of Gingrich's bombast and charisma. He was often beholden to the conservative activists in the Republican Conference, organized as the Conservative Action Team (called the Republican Study Committee after 2001). The conservatives held the party hostage by virtue of its narrow margin of control, and they had in whip Tom DeLay, who was elected majority leader in 2003 after Dick Armey retired, a leader who was willing and able to press their advantage.

Hastert's speakership began with another round of assurances that leaders would consult widely and work cooperatively with committee and subcommittee chairs, and indeed there was a return to the "regular order" whereby most legislation proceeded through committee channels. But leadership and the capacity for deliberation had atrophied on a number of committees, and incentives and member support remained strong for party leaders' continued control over committee appointment, leadership, and policy decisions.[15] The approach of the six-year expiration date

(2000) for the terms of most of the committee chairs who had taken office after the 1994 election created headaches for Republican leaders but also numerous opportunities for leverage and control. For example, a contest between Billy Tauzin (R-Louisiana) and Michael Oxley (R-Ohio) for the chairmanship of the Commerce Committee was resolved by Hastert in Tauzin's favor. At the same time, he determined that the jurisdiction of the Banking Committee (over securities regulation) should be augmented at the expense of Commerce and awarded the Banking chairmanship to Oxley, rejecting the claim of their apparent among longtime Banking members, Marge Roukema (R-New Jersey).

When a Republican president was elected in 2000, the House GOP leadership further consolidated its power. When Clinton was in the White House, Hastert was at pains to avoid a replay of the 1995–1996 government shutdown that had been so damaging to Republicans. This encouraged a degree of accommodation, especially on funding issues, and gave leverage to moderates and appropriators in the Republican Conference. Some predicted that the advent of George W. Bush, who had campaigned as a "compassionate conservative" and touted his ability to work with Democrats, would have a similar effect. But this turned out to be a misreading of Bush and of the role the House would assume relative to the more moderate and less regimented Senate. In most instances, Bush chose to govern from the "right in" rather than the "center out," and House Republican leaders put together their winning majorities in the same way. The 2001 reauthorization of the Elementary and Secondary Education Act (a.k.a. No Child Left Behind) was a significant exception, but the pattern held on budget resolutions, tax cuts, energy, Medicare prescription drugs, family planning and abortion, trade, and most other major bills.[16] Democrats, even centrist Democrats, were left out of the equation and Republican moderates were pressured to acquiesce in positions formulated by the conservative "majority of the majority."[17] The White House encouraged the strategy, not only because the conservative positions were close to its own but also because it wanted to start as far to the right as possible in negotiations with the Senate.

The right-in approach exacted a high price in partisan alienation and conflict. Power-concentrating leadership tactics also had to be ratcheted up to keep the narrow Republican majority in line and safeguard against deviant outcomes. Most obvious was the tactic of going to the floor with a narrow whip count and holding the vote open, if necessary, to cajole the last few members to vote yes. Republican leaders also brought bills to the floor under increasingly restrictive rules, excluded Democrats from participation in key House–Senate conferences, and intervened in committee work in ways that damaged and devalued long-standing processes of deliberation and bipartisan accommodation. I will revisit these tactics when discussing the limits of partisanship, for I believe that many of them represent dangerous excesses that threaten long-term institutional damage.

The powers and prerogatives exercised by the party leadership ultimately rest on the perceived self-interest of diverse individual members—shaped by partisan polarization in the electorate but related more directly to the conviction that strong party control secures policy goals and personal influence.[18] Leadership strength has a less secure foundation than it does in most parliamentary systems, and there is ample historical evidence that it can change as members' calculations of their personal and collective advantage change. But the leaders of both parties, especially the Republican Party, have created extraordinarily powerful self-reinforcing mechanisms. For the foreseeable future, the party role will loom large in the House, and most members will find it advantageous to keep their ties to party leaders in good repair and find a means of participating and exerting influence within the party organization.

The Party Network

Newly elected members of Congress, when they come to Washington for the week of organizational meetings before the session begins, confront the fact that the House is a party-led chamber. Representatives attend orientation sessions organized by the majority and minority leadership, vote to choose party leaders and adopt caucus rules, and jockey for committee assignments in a process that is controlled by the parties and necessitates get-acquainted visits with party leaders (see Chapter 5). Members also learn of opportunities to become active participants in the party network, at least at its outer reaches. Party participation is a way of placing oneself in the crosscurrents of information and influence and, for some but not all, it is a pathway to power within the institution. The leadership ladder is crowded, with numerous members competing for every appointive and elective leadership post. But all members can become involved in the work of their caucus or whip organization. This is a legacy of the 1970s, when these organizations were revitalized and expanded. It represents a deliberate strategy of inclusion by leaders of both parties, who recognize that members are more likely to be cooperative and helpful when they feel they are being informed and consulted and have a role to play in party affairs.

During the years of Democratic control, my party involvement was centered in the Organization, Study, and Review (OSR) Committee; the issues task forces of the caucus, which I coordinated in the 101st and 102nd

Congresses; and the whip organization. OSR is the caucus housekeeping committee, highly responsive to the Speaker (or minority leader), which screens proposed changes in caucus or House rules and renders judgment on requests from members or committees for waivers of the rules or adjudication of rules disputes. The committee emerged from obscurity briefly in 1974, when the highly controversial recommendations on committee reorganization of the Select Committee on Committees were sent to OSR for a thorough reworking. We were relatively busy in 1992, working on a reform plan in anticipation of the 103rd Congress. But most of the time OSR operated behind the scenes—a good place for a member to learn the organizational ropes and work with party leaders on internal House matters. With Democrats in the minority, it became even less visible and had less work to do, although discussions picked up in 2000 in anticipation of a possible Democratic return to majority status.

The task force projects I coordinated in 1990 and 1992 were the latest in a series of election-year efforts begun when Democratic Caucus chairman Gillis Long formed the Committee on Party Effectiveness (CPE) in 1981–1982. The CPE was an ambitious effort to fill the agenda-formation gap that had come with the loss of the White House. It was intended to develop issues and formulate positions that could inspire agreement among Democrats; involve caucus members, many of them quite junior and from outside the relevant committees, in broad policy discussions; and nudge reluctant committee leaders along.[19] By the time I came to the House, the CPE was not a committee at all but a series of caucus-sponsored "party effectiveness" luncheons on important national issues, often featuring outside experts. I found these sessions valuable but saw a need for more focused discussions, aimed at producing a preelection document trumpeting Democratic achievements and aspirations. I was therefore pleased when caucus chairman Steny Hoyer (D-Maryland) asked me to coordinate the task force projects. The presence of two able political scientists, Paul Herrnson and Kelly Patterson, on my staff as Congressional Fellows in 1990 and 1992, respectively, made me more confident in taking on the assignments.[20]

Our efforts were not as far-reaching as Long's party effectiveness projects. In 1990 we appointed nine task forces containing members from the relevant committees and interested members from outside. Unlike the intercommittee task forces occasionally appointed by Democratic speakers and extensively utilized by Speaker Gingrich, our task forces had no legislative function. Still, some committee chairmen were conspicuously indifferent or even hostile to our efforts, although others cooperated fully. We kicked off the process at the annual caucus retreat in February. Several task forces met repeatedly in the following months and hammered out consensus positions, while some leaders did little more than order staff-produced drafts. After much cajoling and editing, we produced an issues handbook, *Investing in America's Future*, stressing that it represented neither an official party position nor a short-term legislative program but rather "a set of goals and aspirations that Democrats seek to accomplish."

The 1992 project was similarly organized and resulted in a two-volume handbook, *Taking Charge of America's Future*, and a separate report, *The Challenge of Sound Management*, produced by a tenth working group we had added, the Task Force on Government Waste. These handbooks were useful resources for the 1990 and 1992 campaigns and laid groundwork for the 1992 national platform. The usefulness of the task forces as outlets for their members varied greatly. When a Democratic president was elected in 1992, most agenda formation shifted back to the White House. Consequently the caucus task force project was not continued in the 103rd Congress.

My third area of party involvement has been with the whip organization. I learned quickly that the most informative meeting of the week in the House was the Thursday morning whips meeting, where plans for the coming week were discussed and strategy was debated in a wide-open fashion. I began to attend these meetings regularly, although I was not yet formally part of the organization. From time to time I volunteered for the ad hoc task forces put together by the whip's office to count votes and mobilize support on specific bills. By 1991 I had been designated one of forty-eight at-large whips and was helping with whip operations on most major bills.

I found this involvement useful in at least three ways. First, it let me help mobilize support for measures that I thought were important, such as the 1990 housing bill, on which I had worked extensively, and the 1993 budget legislation. Second, it made me a partner, albeit a junior one, in leadership undertakings. This is intrinsically satisfying and can bring other rewards. Throughout 1990 those of us who were trying to position ourselves to gain the next Appropriations Committee seats joked about what a coincidence it was that we so often found ourselves on the whip's task forces. Finally, it brought me into discussions of floor strategy and the last-minute alterations needed to maximize votes on various bills. Certain committees, most notably Judiciary and Education and Labor, tended to bring bills to the floor that were acceptable to the liberal majorities on those committees but needed further work to gain the full assent of a healthy majority of Democratic members. This happened too often, and whip task forces were hardly the ideal place to work out accommodations. But on bills like child care in 1990 and striker replacement in 1991, the vote counts and feedback garnered by the whip organization served as a reality check for committee leaders and gave members like me a means of pushing for needed refinements in advance of floor consideration.

On returning to the Congress as a minority member in 1997, I again worked with the whip organization. David Bonior (D-Michigan) was still Democratic whip, task forces were still organized to whip specific bills (with participation essentially open to all comers), and the Thursday morning whips meeting was still a fixture on the weekly schedule. Nowhere, however, was it more evident what a difference it made to be in the minority. Those Thursday meetings were powerful reminders that Democrats were not in charge. We often faced uncertainty about the week's schedule and frustration that our amendments or alternatives were being denied floor consideration or were being placed at a disadvantage by virtue of the rules governing floor debate. We were more often trying to defeat rather than pass major bills, as well as to mobilize votes for Democratic amendments or alternatives and against the majority's restrictive rules.

Leadership changes came in 2002, as Bonior left the whip position to run for the Michigan governorship, and in 2003, as Gephardt left the leadership to run for president. I worked closely with Hoyer in the hotly contested race to succeed Bonior. He lost the race to Nancy Pelosi (D-California) but was the unanimous choice of the caucus when she assumed the minority leadership a year later. Hoyer expanded the whip organization, relying less on ad hoc task forces and more on appointed groups of twenty-eight senior whips and thirty-eight assistant whips to follow up with members after the initial contact made by the regional whips (24 members, still elected by the 12 regional caucuses). As an assistant whip, I had a list of five members with whom it was my responsibility to check on every major bill.

The whip's vote-gathering operation, in the minority as in the majority, remains an essential component of the strengthened party operations I have described. This machinery has developed in both parties in response to the growing divergence between and convergence within the congressional parties since the 1970s and has helped strengthen and solidify an increase in partisan voting. As Figure 8.1 shows, members have become more and more inclined to stick with their party on divided votes. Party voting now exceeds the levels established during Harry Truman's presidency, a time when party divisions were sharp and party loyalties well defined in the electorate.

Post-1970s trends in party voting reflect another period of national polarization. Ronald Reagan's presidency was a highly ideological one, and both the content of his proposals and his uncompromising style prompted sharp partisan divisions on Capitol Hill. Democrats, by virtue of the political threat Reagan posed and the impact of his policies on their constituencies, were constrained to develop and promote distinct alternatives and to unify against a common adversary. They were aided in this by the narrowing of the gap between the northern and southern wings of the congressional party.

Figure 8.1 also reflects growing Republican solidarity under more militant leadership. This began in the 102nd Congress, was reinforced by the galvanizing effects of Bill Clinton's presidency, and reached a new high under George W. Bush. The crossing of the Democratic and Republican trend lines after the Republicans gained control suggests some of the advantages that come to the majority party from the control it wields over the agenda and the rules governing floor debate. This is something moderates from swing districts (such as myself) feel very acutely. Majority party and committee leaders can frame legislation and floor amendments to attract votes from the other side and/or make a no vote politically difficult. By the same token, they can refuse to permit the consideration of amendments or alternatives that might divide the majority vote.

Under Democratic control, I sometimes thought a rule should have been granted for an amendment, often proposed by a moderate Democrat, that had merit and deserved an up-or-down vote, regardless of whether it had the potential to divide our party or was opposed by the floor manager or the interest groups backing the bill. Under Republican control, I often face a decision to vote for or against a major bill that, though important, has been written with a partisan slant, with opportunities to amend either denied or defeated. Or I may face an array of hot-button amendments designed to make life difficult for Democrats.[21] Sometimes these tactics backfire, but most of the time the party setting the agenda and the terms of debate has an obvious advantage, and party unity voting statistics reflect this fact.

Vote gathering in both parties frequently runs up against the electoral and constituency pressures experienced by individual members, and leaders frequently have to decide how vigorously to use the carrots and sticks at their disposal. During the early 1980s, for example, the Democratic leadership fluctuated in its treatment of the so-called boll weevils—conservative Democrats who were prone to vote with the Reagan administration—sometimes attempting to win their loyalty through generous treatment and choice committee assignments, but other times passing over them in favor of their loyalist rivals.[22] The approach taken was dictated by the political situation the Democrats faced. They were more accommodating to the conservatives when their House majority was shaky and Reagan was riding high, less accommodating when they had regained the initiative.

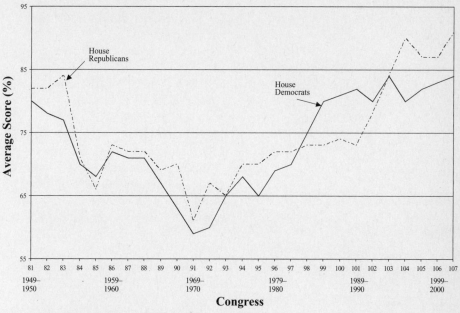

Source: Data in Congressional Quarterly Almanacs

FIGURE 8.1 "Party unity" voting for House Democrats and Republicans (average individual support for party on votes dividing party majorities), 81st–107th Congresses (1949–2002).

I noted in Chapter 5 how Speakers Wright and Foley differed in utilizing their influence over committee assignments. Wright once floated the unheard-of idea of putting members on probation for their first term in a new assignment.[23] After Wright resigned, two midsession committee appointments raised questions about the new leadership's intent. A choice Energy and Commerce slot was awarded in early 1990 to a member who had voted against the leadership on the highest-profile party test of the previous fall, a capital gains tax reduction. And the Appropriations slot that opened up in the spring of 1990 was awarded to the only one of the five major contenders who had defected on the most visible leadership vote of that session (in this case, the leadership of both parties), the pay raise/ethics package. As one of those five contenders, I took special note of the discussions that followed these episodes and concluded that the pattern was unlikely to continue. The leadership's hand was far more evident in the committee assignments made by Steering and Policy at the beginning of the 102nd Congress, and I was elected at that point to Appropriations as part of a slate endorsed by the Speaker.

House Republicans have generally surpassed Democrats, at least in the post-1991 years of conservative ascendancy, in their voting discipline and in their ability and willingness to use the tools at their disposal to encourage partisan solidarity. This applies to the recruitment, coaching, and funding of candidates; the use of committee assignments, leadership positions, and other perquisites to cement and reward loyalty to the Speaker and the party; and whip operations that display a harder edge than their Democratic counterpart. A 1995 episode involving freshman Rep. Mark Neumann (R-Wisconsin) illustrates the tactics the leadership was willing to use as well as the limits of such leverage, even in year one of the Gingrich revolution. Neumann, one of the freshmen Gingrich had appointed to the Appropriations Committee, refused to support the Defense Subcommittee's fiscal year 1996 conference report. Chairman Bob Livingston, consulting with Gingrich, then removed him from the subcommittee. But Neumann's freshmen colleagues regarded this as a dangerous precedent and rallied behind him, threatening to force a vote on the matter in the Republican Conference. Gingrich then instructed Livingston to work out an accommodation—giving Neumann a seat he wanted on the Budget Committee.[24]

My own party voting scores were 84 percent for my first term in the House, 91 percent for my second, and an average of 88 percent since returning to the 105th Congress in the minority—somewhat above the average scores indicated in Figure 8.1 and relatively high for a Southern Democratic member. These scores have come naturally in that they reflect a congruence among Democratic Party positions, my own values and beliefs, and what I take to be the interests of my district. They also reflect the leadership practices and powers I have described: setting agendas, scheduling and structuring decisions, informing and persuading, modifying and accommodating—all designed to facilitate party support among members. My record contains some defections, mostly on minor matters but occasionally on important ones. I once found myself at odds both strategically and substantively with Speaker Wright on some key budget votes in late 1987 (see Chapter 7). I had a few uncomfortable moments with Wright and Coelho, particularly during my first term when I had little opportunity to help shape decisions and they were sending some signals to me. But most often I have been treated as a member of the team and reinforced in my basic inclination toward party loyalty.

As I stressed at the beginning of this chapter, no two representatives have the same mix of personal predilections, electoral constraints, and district interests, and we work in a system that gives individual differences considerable leeway. But the party structure remains the most important mechanism we have to impose a measure of collective responsibility on ourselves. The fact that the tools of control can be abused—and I will turn next to the limitations of partisanship—should not obscure the basic fact: It is the party connection that enables a House of disparate parts to function. Ultimately that lets the individual member move beyond good intentions to what Edmund Burke called "doing his duty with effect."[25]

The Limits of Partisanship

I welcomed the unified party control of Congress and the presidency that followed the 1992 elections, not only as a committed Democrat but also as a political scientist reared in the tradition of responsible party government.[26] This despite the friendly warning of a Republican colleague: "You're going to find it's no picnic serving with a president from your own party." He spoke more presciently than he knew. It was indeed no picnic.

There were many advantages, not only in the legislative realm but also in simply getting things done that I needed to do. Some of these matters involved the White House directly, such as awarding American Airlines a route to London from Raleigh-Durham Airport in 1993, securing a recess appointment for a U.S. marshall in 1999 after Senator Helms had blocked his confirmation, and getting critical items included in Hurricane Floyd relief and recovery packages in 1999 and 2000. In other instances, it helped to have receptive departments and agencies as I pushed for the implementation of programs such as advanced technical education at NSF or my secondary market housing initiative at HUD (see Chapter 6) or made certain that North Carolina funding applications were given full consideration.

Having a Democratic administration did not always open doors, however. The appointments process, for example, was highly competitive, complicated, and slow. Additional barriers were erected by the Republican Senate and individual senators. Nor could agency receptivity always be counted on. The Army Corps of Engineers and Department of Veterans Affairs stiff-armed me on two matters of considerable local urgency during the Bush administration, but early signals from Clinton appointees gave me little assurance of greater responsiveness. I therefore wrote directives to the two agencies into fiscal year 1995 appropriations bills (see Chapter 10).

As for policy, most Democrats in the House felt we were doing what we were elected to do in 1993 as we whipped and passed long-stalled measures such as Family and Medical Leave, Motor Voter, and the NIH reauthorization (minus fetal tissue research bans) and prepared to take on the year's greatest challenge, the five-year budget plan. It was an exhilarating but anxious time, for the 1992 elections provided an uncertain mandate, and Republicans had little compunction against opposing Clinton and little inclination to help Democrats succeed. We were on our own, feeling more and more pressure to demonstrate that we could govern. On the critical budget votes, as shown in Chapter 7, we were fighting not only the Republicans and conservative detractors in the media but also the bad habits bred by years of divided government. We were being asked to assume responsibility rather than shift blame—to make our institution work and to undertake the hard choices of governance, as opposed to distancing ourselves from both.

The Democratic whip organization was energetically deployed around the budget votes and helped produce a series of critical, though increasingly narrow, victories. Unified party control worked as it was supposed to work, but the pattern did not hold as the 103rd Congress progressed. NAFTA, though a major victory for Clinton, was passed by a cross-party coalition over the opposition of the House Democratic leadership, and in 1994 the president and congressional Democrats conspicuously failed to deliver either health care or welfare reform. Overall, the output of the 103rd Congress did not measure up to either the ambitions of Democratic leaders or the expectations of responsible party government proponents. David Mayhew saw in this performance confirmation of his argument that the volume—and to a significant degree the content—of important laws enacted by Congress does not vary greatly between conditions of divided and unified party control.[27]

The point about content is debatable. Clearly a sizable list of Democratically initiated measures that could not be enacted under Bush were enacted under Clinton. Although the 1993 budget plan resembled the 1990 plan in its overall dimensions, a bipartisan plan would have neither raised marginal rates for the wealthiest taxpayers nor achieved nearly as much deficit reduction as did the Democratic plan.[28] But Mayhew places the 1993–1994 experience in a historical context that goes beyond arguments about Clinton's or congressional Democrats' specific failings. He demonstrates that unified party control, in and of itself, does not lead to legislative productivity. It can help, but the mere presence of a congressional majority may not suffice for legislative initiatives to overcome intraparty divisions, the multiplicity of decisionmaking checkpoints, or the Senate filibuster. Above all, partisan control is unlikely to bear fruit without strong, reliable public support.[29]

It was the budget battle, our most significant victory, more than our legislative disappointments and defeats that prompted second thoughts on my part as to the potential and limitations of partisanship. This was not simply because the struggle was so difficult and politically costly, but because of what it portended for related areas of policymaking, where the need for difficult decisions often exceeds the political incentives to undertake them.

In his study of the 1983 Social Security rescue, Paul Light coined the term "dedistributive" to denote policies that neither distributed nor redistributed desirable goods but instead, under pressure of necessity, cut back by raising taxes and/or reducing benefits, imposing costs, and lowering expectations.[30] The 1983 plan certainly fit the description, raising payroll taxes and cutting back benefits as the Social Security trust fund was about to run dry. It required the strong support of President Reagan and the Democratic congressional leadership, not merely because partisan control of government was divided. For either party to have taken up the cause unilaterally would have meant political suicide. Even with both parties knowing they must act, success came only with moving the decision from Congress to a bipartisan commission that operated outside the glare of daily publicity and permitted a sharing and blurring of the lines of personal and partisan responsibility.

The resemblance of the Social Security rescue to the 1990 bipartisan budget agreement—both the dedistributive character of the decisions and some of the expedients used to achieve resolution—is striking. It renders all the more remarkable what was done in 1993 with Democratic "heavy lifting" alone, without recourse to summitry or to extra-congressional mechanisms. But it is an open question as to which episode provides a more promising model for dedistributive decisions of the future, the formalities of unified or divided party control notwithstanding. In 1997, after the Republicans had gotten burned pursuing unilateral budget reform, Congress again concluded a bipartisan budget agreement (see Chapter 7). Single-party plans might have balanced the budget sooner: Democrats acting alone would have included fewer upper-bracket tax cuts, while Republicans would have been willing to cut Medicare and domestic discretionary spending more deeply. But if the cross-partisan accommodations rendered the agreement less heroic, they also mitigated its dedistributive character and increased both its legitimacy in the eyes of the public and its political viability.

I thus concluded, as I told a National Academy of Public Administration gathering in 1997, that

> when it comes to putting [and keeping] our fiscal house in order—and, I hope in the not too distant future, ensuring the long-term solvency of Social Security and Medicare—we've got to find, and institutionalize, ways of

reaching common ground, not only sharing partisan credit but defusing partisan blame. There will still be plenty of legitimate partisan fights, and we should take them on with relish. But we should protect the bipartisan comity reflected in the 1997 budget agreement, because [on the most difficult dedistributive issues] we will need it to get the job done.

The parties will, and should, continue to formulate distinctive positions on budget and entitlement issues. Under conditions of unified partisan control, parties may find it necessary to seek enactment unilaterally and, with a supportive public consensus, may succeed. But even then, action will not come easily or without considerable political risk. And when divided partisan control returns, the parties will invariably find they need one another. In some policy areas, where the parties are competing to do popular things, one may effectively compel the other to act; recall the Republicans' pressing of welfare reform and the Democrats' of the minimum wage, even amid the sharp divisions of the 104th Congress. But when the short-term incentives to obstruction and blame shifting predominate, as they often do in the dedistributive arena, the parties must keep the mechanisms of bipartisan communication and cooperation, as well as those of partisan mobilization, in working order if they are to govern successfully.[31]

If budget and entitlement conflicts showed the practical and political limits of partisanship, the politics of impeachment in 1998 went far over the line. Impeachment is a congressional prerogative that extends to the balance of powers under the Constitution. Its exercise should be undergirded by a strong and widely shared sense of legitimacy. In carrying out this function, partisan arguments and pressures are singularly inappropriate. Yet House Republicans, in marked contrast to the 1973–1974 impeachment proceedings against President Nixon, impeached President Clinton with votes drawn almost exclusively from the Republican side of the aisle and with manipulations of process and procedure that provoked a deep sense of unfairness and doomed any hope for recapturing the comity of 1997 in the 106th Congress or beyond.

It was not until August 17, 1998, when Clinton was compelled to testify before Independent Counsel Kenneth Starr's grand jury, that he publicly acknowledged a relationship with Monica Lewinsky that was "not appropriate" and "wrong" and about which he had "misled people, including even my wife."[32] Within a month, Starr had delivered his report, specifying eleven possible grounds for impeachment, and the House had voted 363–63 to release its contents. Subsequently every major decision displayed a sharp partisan cleavage. Gingrich sometimes paid lip service to the need for deliberation and objectivity, but his words and actions betrayed an assumption of the president's guilt and a determination to exploit the situation politically.[33] Judiciary Committee chairman Henry Hyde initially recognized that impeachment procedures needed to be bipartisan if they were to be seen as legitimate and fair and announced his intention to follow the "Watergate model." But the Judiciary Committee was among the most ideologically polarized in the House. From the beginning, its members voted overwhelmingly along party lines, and Hyde did very little to challenge or change that pattern.

The partisan divide was starkly evident in the House vote of October 8 to move forward with the impeachment inquiry. Unlike the actual impeachment votes to follow, this was not a matter of high principle. But it nonetheless became a partisan showdown. Republicans proposed an open-ended inquiry in terms of subject matter and duration; Democrats proposed to limit the inquiry to the Starr referral and set a termination date of December 31. As I recounted in Chapter 3, this vote caused me great anxiety, for I seemed bound to alienate voters no matter how I voted. Democratic leaders in the House helpfully modified the resolution formulated by Judiciary Committee Democrats to make it less restrictive, and some of them urged the White House to accept the Republican resolution once the Democratic resolution failed, thus sparing marginal Democrats a politically perilous vote. I argued that "defusing" the vote in this way would not only help members like myself but would also let the president (who was not going to win the vote in any case) appear confident and cooperative and would put the onus on the Republicans to proceed with fairness and restraint. But the president and his hard-line advisers did not see it that way, and the plight of imperiled congressional Democrats seemed low on their list of concerns.

As it turned out, Gingrich and the Republicans would have had more to gain than Clinton and the Democrats from defusing the vote. The GOP inquiry ended up adhering, for the most part, to the terms of the Democratic resolution. Had they simply accepted these terms at the outset, they would have given the process a bipartisan cast and could have put eighty or ninety Democrats, who were skeptical of any inquiry and had united behind the Democratic resolution only in the sure knowledge it would fail, in a tight spot. But Gingrich, like Clinton, conceived of his advantage narrowly and was loath to give it up. So both sides charged ahead: Republicans voted 1–226 against the limited inquiry and 227–0 for the open-ended inquiry. All but ten Democrats (5 of whom voted against both resolutions) voted for the limited inquiry, and when that resolution failed, only thirty-one then voted for the GOP resolution. I joined the 175 who did not—a decision I soon came to see as not only right on the merits but also politically advantageous. I continued to believe that the partisan showdown was unnecessary; had the vote been defused by one or both sides, the subsequent course of impeachment might have been quite different.

The kind of ads Tom Roberg had run against me in September became more common across the country in October as Gingrich and other Republican strategists urged candidates to exploit the scandal and staged a national media blitz toward the end of the campaign. The election results discredited the strategy and prompted Gingrich to resign. Members and pundits alike predicted that at least two dozen Republicans would vote against impeachment. But as it turned out, they underestimated both the intensity of Republican base voters on the issue and the determination of GOP leaders to see the process through. Hyde and Judiciary Republicans pressed on inexorably. On November 19 they called Starr before the committee to give a lawyer's brief for impeachment and gave him a standing ovation at the end of his testimony. On December 8–9 they heard from Clinton's lawyers but drafted articles of impeachment and released them to the public before the lawyers had finished testifying.[34] In the meantime, Republican whip Tom DeLay, a longtime impeachment advocate, filled the vacuum left by Gingrich's resignation and by prospective Speaker Bob Livingston's aversion to controversy, devising a strategy to impeach the president with Republican votes alone.

That strategy had two major elements: denying members an opportunity to vote on censure as an alternative to impeachment and "defining down" impeachment itself, portraying it as the equivalent of an indictment (with definitive judgment to be rendered by the Senate) and/or a rebuke that the House could administer without further consequences (since the Senate was unlikely to convict). Impeachment proponents downplayed the historical and constitutional gravity of the step they were advocating and in the process misrepresented the threshold question facing the House. Most Democratic members, Republican rhetoric to the contrary notwithstanding, were appalled at the president's behavior and were prepared to hold him accountable. The threshold question was not whether the president had engaged in the behavior of which he was accused (which turned only partially on the legalistic definitions on which he and his lawyers insisted) or whether that behavior deserved condemnation. Rather, the question was whether impeachment, reserved by the framers of the Constitution for "treason, bribery, or other high crimes and misdemeanors [against the state]," was the appropriate remedy.[35] That decision was for the House to face, hardly a matter to be blithely bucked to the Senate.

The appropriate sanction, I and many others thought, was a resolution of censure. But even allowing for disagreement on the merits, there were no legitimate grounds for denying members the ability to offer and vote on this alternative. If there is any instance where this kind of high-handed manipulation of the rules is out of line, it is in carrying out the solemn constitutional duty of impeachment. As one editorial noted after the DeLay strategy became clear:

> Mr. DeLay and the Republican hard-liners on impeachment know that both the public and a majority of House members favor a condemnation of Mr. Clinton instead of impeachment, unless new evidence emerges. But Mr. DeLay calculates that if he can prevent a censure vote, the House may vote to impeach rather than to let Mr. Clinton go unpunished. But it is an insult to duty for any Congressional leader to ram through an impeachment vote by using parliamentary trickery of the kind more suitable to votes on highway bills.[36]

The closing off of the censure alternative, along with the intense pressures Republican members felt from their leaders and their core electorate, had the desired effect on December 19. All but five Republicans voted for the first article of impeachment (perjury before the grand jury) and all but twelve voted for the third (obstruction of justice). These were the two articles that passed, each with only five Democratic votes. I remember sitting in the chamber as debate began, wondering if anyone found the pleas to pull back from the brink persuasive and then rebuking my own naïveté. Republican leaders had proclaimed this a "vote of conscience" to the end, but party lines in the House had never been more harshly drawn, nor partisan power exercised with a harder edge.[37]

I wrote a lengthy statement to insert in the *Congressional Record* and circulate among my constituents citing the constitutional arguments and historical precedents for censure as opposed to impeachment. I particularly noted Alexander Hamilton's prescient observation that in cases of impeachment "there will always be the greatest danger that the decision will be regulated more by the comparative strength of parties, than by the real demonstrations of innocence or guilt."[38] But time for floor statements was severely limited, as is generally the case in major debates. In the one minute I was given to distill my argument, I linked the House's failure to live up to its historic responsibility to the abuse of partisan leadership:

> Mr. Speaker, this institution is failing to live up to its responsibilities, just as surely as the president has failed to live up to his, and the House's failure may well do the more lasting damage to our Constitution.

Where there should be an extraordinary effort to work across party lines and find a consensual basis for action, I see a hard-charging majority bringing articles of impeachment to the floor on a strictly partisan basis. Where there should be scrupulous attention to the constitutional and historical basis for impeachment, I see a cavalier willingness to "define impeachment down" to get a favorable vote, in disregard of what the framers [of the Constitution] intended.

And where there should be assurances that this is a vote of conscience, I see a cynical and unfair manipulation of the rules [in order] to deny members the right to vote on a motion of censure and to tilt the outcome in favor of impeachment.

This shuts off consideration of the most appropriate sanction under the Constitution for the behavior we are considering. It denies many of us the right to vote our consciences on the most serious question we are ever likely to face as members of this body. It is manipulative, it is cynical, it is unfair. It is as though the Republican leaders of this House have set out to confirm all of the worst suspicions Americans have about politics and politicians.

Mr. Speaker, this House is on the brink of an historic and tragic failure. I beg my colleagues to take heed.[39]

We cannot yet assess the full impact of the Clinton impeachment. The future may show that the 1998 exercise dangerously lowered the barriers to politically motivated impeachment, although the lesson—considering the adverse public and political reactions to the House's action and the subsequent acquittal verdict in the Senate—may well be the opposite. In the House, the experience had few of the cathartic or sobering effects some had hoped for. On the contrary: in terms of procedural high-handedness and political polarization, impeachment shaped the atmosphere and the tactics of partisanship in the House for years to come. Not even the September 11, 2001, terrorist attacks could induce more than a temporary and partial deescalation.[40] House Republicans under the second Bush presidency—with a presidential agenda anchored on the right, a narrow Republican House majority and conservative-dominated Republican Conference, and an assumed role of counterweight to the Senate, even after Republicans regained the majority—took the tactics of partisan control to a level unprecedented in the modern history of the institution.

Republican restrictions on floor debate surpassed those they had bitterly condemned when Democrats were in control. Structured rules were often extremely restrictive. In 2003, for example, twenty-one amendments were proposed by Democrats to welfare reform legislation (H.R. 4) and only two made in order; ten were proposed to Bush's Healthy Forests bill (H.R. 1904) and one made in order; seven proposed and one allowed for the bill reforming management of employee retirement accounts (H.R. 1000); twenty-five proposed and two allowed for Head Start reauthorization (H.R. 2210); and fifteen proposed and one allowed for the bill authorizing pooled health plans for small businesses (H.R. 660).[41] Democrats objected most strongly to completely closed rules, which permitted no amendments whatsoever, including the traditional minority substitute. Examples in the 2000–2003 period included rules on bills extending unemployment insurance, cutting taxes on dividends, "reforming" medical malpractice, adding a prescription drug benefit to Medicare, banning "partial-birth" abortions, and authorizing fast track consideration of trade agreements. Overall, the incidence of such rules went from 9 percent in the 103rd Congress, when the Democrats were last in control, to 22 percent of rules approved in both the 106th and 107th Congresses.[42]

The exclusion of Democrats from conference committees reached a new high in 2003, facilitated by unified Republican control of the House, Senate, and presidency. Few explicit rules govern conference procedures, and majority party leaders have often taken advantage of this flexibility to shape conference outcomes. There has been considerable variability regarding how much conference business is worked out in formal meetings with debates and votes among all participants and how much is "preconferenced" in informal discussions among leaders.[43] Appropriations conferences have tended toward the informal model, with substantial but varying levels of minority inclusion by House and Senate subcommittee chairmen. Conferences on major authorization bills have generally been more structured and more public.

That pattern was dramatically altered by Republican leaders in 2003; their handling of three major conferences proved especially controversial. House Commerce chairman Tauzin and Senate Energy chairman Domenici largely wrote the conference version of the administration's energy bill (H.R. 6). They conferred with Republican leaders and the White House but included Democrats only in a few ceremonial sessions. Representative Bill Thomas, chairman of the conference on the Medicare prescription drug bill (H.R. 1), excluded all Democratic conferees from the House and most of the Senate delegation, which included minority leader Tom Daschle, from conference sessions. He admitted two Democratic senators he perceived as ready to deal, but told the others that sessions would be canceled if they showed up.[44] Finally a revised version of a conference report on the authorization of the Federal Aviation Administration (FAA), which Democrats had succeeded in sending back to the conference over the issue of privatizing air traffic control, was brought to the floor with language that would allow privatization to continue (H.R. 2115). This ignored provisions in both House and Senate FAA bills and was produced by a "conference" that never even met.

The extraordinary lengths to which Republicans went to win roll call votes further shut out Democrats, the idea being to win with as little bipartisan accommodation as possible. It also required Republican leaders frequently to coerce their own members. "Is anyone from the office of the attending physician present?" Dave Obey quipped as a roll call was being held open to turn around enough votes to win. "I understand someone's arm is being broken."[45]

Here too Republican leaders went far beyond the Democratic leadership practices they had decried when they were in the minority. When Speaker Wright kept a budget vote open an extra fifteen minutes in 1987, Dick Cheney, then the House Republican whip, described the move as "the most arrogant, heavy-handed abuse of power I've ever seen in the ten years that I've been here."[46] But Wright's tactic did not come close to what Hastert and DeLay did on November 22, 2003, holding open the vote on the Medicare prescription drug conference report for almost three hours until three errant members could be turned around. This was a feat unmatched in the history of the House, but the pattern had been established months before, when the initial House Medicare bill, Head Start reauthorization, and a D.C. Appropriations bill that included school vouchers had all been passed by one vote after protracted roll calls.

Frequent leadership intervention in the work of the committees has also marginalized Democrats; many of those committees (e.g., Transportation and Infrastructure and Armed Services) have a history of strong bipartisan cooperation. I have most closely witnessed the effects on Appropriations, where since the late 1990s the Republican leadership—joined by the Bush administration since 2000—has precipitated end-of-year battles over spending measures, compromising not only the content of appropriations bills but also the bipartisan process by which those bills were assembled. This has weakened both the Appropriations Committee and the legitimacy of the appropriations process. Some members have been drawn, for example, to arguments for a two-year budget cycle as an escape from endless budget conflict—although such a "cure" would fail to address fundamental budget abuses and would further weaken the best instrument Congress has for calling the executive branch to account and exercising full partnership in the setting of national priorities.[47]

The influence of the Republican leadership over appropriations decisions is now well advanced. Much of what happens when the normal process breaks down (multiple continuing resolutions, omnibus bills, negotiations with the White House, severe time pressures) maximizes leadership leverage. Here too 2003 saw an escalation in tactics. Republicans once again passed a restrictive budget resolution at the insistence of conservative members, resulting in a Labor-HHS-Education Appropriations bill that fell short of authorized funding for the No Child Left Behind initiative, education for the disabled, NIH research, and other programs. For this reason, Democrats unanimously voted against the House bill. Democratic appropriators normally would have a hand in improving the bill in conference and allocating the district-specific earmarks (a prominent component of the Labor-HHS bill since Republicans took over the leadership) to be added in conference. Instead, subcommittee chairman Ralph Regula (R-Ohio) announced that projects from all 205 districts represented by Democrats would be omitted from the omnibus bill in retaliation for the earlier vote. The fact that the blow was delivered by Regula, who had generally exemplified the norms of the committee, underscored the toughness demanded by Republican leaders (who soon would be considering Regula and others for the Appropriations chairmanship) and the way the partisan "patterns of the whole House [were] bleeding over into Appropriations."[48]

"The Republicans had better hope that the Democrats never regain the majority," Sen. John McCain warned in late 2003.[49] Some journalists tended to write off House Republican tactics as the normal partisan tit for tat. But their commandeering of the legislative process (which DeLay augmented with such moves as pressing the Texas legislature, newly unified under Republican control, to reopen a court-ordered redistricting plan from two years before in order to produce seven new Republican seats) went far beyond past Democratic practice. "It's worse," said Thomas Mann of the Brookings Institution. "It's been carried to a new extreme." Most congressional scholars seemed to share Mann's assessment.[50]

Do these tactics transgress the appropriate limits of partisanship? I believe the answer is yes, even granting the need for strong party leadership and discipline in the House. There is a legitimate question of fairness, regarding not only the participation of Democratic members but also the ability of the House to address the interests of the districts—almost half of the country—they represent. Beyond that, there are questions of effectiveness and ability to govern. The administration's energy bill, which faltered in the 108th Congress, would have been more balanced and less politically vulnerable had it been finalized by a more inclusive conference. Certainly it is hard to imagine the major dedistributive issues that lie just over the horizon being successfully addressed under the partisan conditions and with the partisan tactics of 2003.

I expressed some of this to President Bush on one of the rare occasions when he chose to confer with Democrats like me: the push for "fast track" trade authority in late 2001. I told him that it was unnecessary and undesirable to make this vote a "cliff-hanger," which would signal division and uncertainty as we set out to negotiate and approve ambitious trade deals. It would be much better to have resounding bipartisan approval. Moreover, the votes of pro-trade Democrats like myself were within reach if we had had firmer assurance that the reduction of disparities in labor and environmental standards that put our country at a disadvantage would be a central negotiating objective. Bush chose not to heed this counsel; Republican leaders passed the fast track bill by a one-vote margin with minimal Democratic support. But I believe my advice was sound, and the costs of the president's partisan strategy are now evident as the administration looks for support on controversial trade agreements.

Although I close this chapter with a catalog of partisan excesses, I do not wish to reinforce the negative attitudes Americans often express about parties and partisanship. In fact, one of the dangers of these excesses is that they threaten to give partisanship in its legitimate manifestations a bad name. It is basically a good thing that both parties have gained strength and solidarity in the modern House, opening up productive, cooperative rules for individual members, overcoming fragmentation, and enabling the majority to rule. But those who would lead the parties successfully must make accommodations—with the needs of individual members, with committees and caucuses, with the opposing party and the executive branch. There are practical, political, and moral limits to what purely partisan exertion can accomplish, as illustrated during the last decade by budget standoffs, government shutdowns, a partisan impeachment, and the polarization produced by exclusionary tactics. Pondering those experiences carefully, we need to understand the possibilities and limitations of partisan leadership in securing effective and legitimate governance and temper the practice of partisanship so that its abuses and failures do not displace or discredit its legitimate exercise.

Notes

1. Four of the Democratic state chairs with whom I served—Nancy Pelosi of California, Bart Gordon of Tennessee, Dave Nagle of Iowa, and Chester Atkins of Massachusetts—later became House colleagues.

2. For an inventory of possible impacts ranging from state laws to court decisions, presidential nomination rules, and campaign finance reforms, see David E. Price, *Bringing Back the Parties* (Washington, D.C.: Congressional Quarterly Press, 1984), chaps. 5–8.

3. Gary C. Jacobson, "The 1994 House Elections in Perspective," in Philip A. Klinker, ed., *Midterm: The Elections of 1994 in Context* (Boulder: Westview, 1996), chap. 1.

4. Krasno, "Interpreting the 1994 Elections," in John G. Geer, ed., *Politicians and Party Politics* (Baltimore, Md.: Johns Hopkins University Press, 1998), p. 233.

5. Lawrence C. Dodd and Bruce I. Oppenheimer, "Consolidating Power in the House: The Rise of a New Oligarchy," in *Congress Reconsidered,* 4th ed. (Washington, D.C.: Congressional Quarterly Press, 1989), p. 60; Dodd and Oppenheimer, "Revolution in the House: Testing the Limits of Party Government," in *Congress Reconsidered,* 6th ed. (Washington, D.C.: Congressional Quarterly Press, 1997), pp. 38–45.

6. On these trends and their influence on support for strong party leadership among reelection-minded members, see John H. Aldrich and David W. Rohde, "The Logic of Conditional Party Government: Revisiting the Electoral Connection," in Dodd and Oppenheimer, eds., *Congress Reconsidered,* 7th ed. (Washington, D.C.: Congressional Quarterly Press, 2001), chap. 12, and the studies there cited.

7. For useful accounts that base strengthened party operations in the profit-and-loss calculations of individual members, see Barbara Sinclair, *Legislators, Leaders, and Lawmaking: The U.S. House of Representatives in the Postreform Era* (Baltimore, Md.: Johns Hopkins University Press, 1995), chaps. 1–2, 4–5; and David W. Rohde, *Parties and Leaders in the Postreform House* (Chicago: University of Chicago Press, 1991).

8. Roger Davidson, "The New Centralization on Capitol Hill," *Review of Politics,* Summer 1988, pp. 350–351.

9. "Three important goals for the Democrats are to enhance the authority of the Speaker; make sure that Democratic membership on legislative committees is representative; and to increase the individual responsibility of each Democrat toward his leaders." Richard Bolling, *House Out of Order* (New York: Dutton, 1965), pp. 236–238.

10. Davidson, "New Centralization," p. 355.

11. For a survey of postreform Democratic factions and an account of the "considerable increase in Democratic unity and cohesion," see Rohde, *Parties and Leaders,* pp. 45–58.

12. Davidson, "New Centralization," p. 358.

13. Foley continued to experience and express some discomfort with demands for tightened discipline in the Democratic Caucus. Revealingly, after he and House Democrats were defeated in 1994, he acknowledged the attraction of the parliamentary model of the "honorific and politically impotent" speaker. But he then emphasized, as if correcting himself, "that there is need for a centralizing, organizing principle in the House of Representatives that is best expressed by the Speakership." See Jeffrey R. Biggs and Thomas S. Foley, *Honor in the House: Speaker Tom Foley* (Pullman: Washington State University Press, 1999), pp. 135–137, 272.

14. The account that follows draws on John H. Aldrich and David W. Rohde, "The Transition to Republican Rule in the House: Implications for Theories of Congressional Politics," *Political Science Quarterly*, Winter 1997–1998, pp. 541–567; Barbara Sinclair, "Leading the Revolution: Innovation and Continuity in Congressional Party Leadership," in Dean McSweeney and John E. Owens, eds., *The Republican Takeover of Congress* (New York: St. Martin's, 1998), chap. 4; C. Lawrence Evans and Walter J. Oleszek, *Congress Under Fire: Reform Politics and the Republican Majority* (New York: Houghton Mifflin, 1997), chaps. 4–6; Lawrence C. Dodd and Bruce Oppenheimer, "A House Divided: The Struggle for Partisan Control, 1994–2000," in Dodd and Oppenheimer, *Congress Reconsidered*, 7th ed., chap. 2; and Jonathan Allen, "Effective House Leadership Makes the Most of Majority," *Congressional Quarterly Weekly*, March 29, 2003, pp. 746–751.

15. For contrasting contemporary assessments of the potential for committee restoration, see Richard E. Cohen, "Crackup of the Committees," *National Journal*, July 31, 1999, pp. 2210–2217; and Gary J. Andres, "Observations on a Post-Gingrich House," *P.S.: Political Science and Politics*, September 1999, pp. 571–574. On the decline and partial restoration of committee power in the 104th and 105th Congresses, see Roger H. Davidson, "Building the Republican Regime: Leaders and Committees," in Nicol C. Rae and Colton C. Campbell, eds., *New Majority or Old Minority? The Impact of Republicans on Congress* (Lanham, Md.: Rowman & Littlefield, 1999), chap. 4.

16. Passage of the Medicare prescription drug bill in 2003 was a mixed case in terms of "right-in" vote gathering. Democrats (with the exception of two senators) were excluded from the conference, which adhered to the House's preference for subsidizing private drug-only plans rather than strengthening basic Medicare. Only eleven of the thirty-five Democrats who had voted for the Senate bill voted for the conference report. But in the House, most of the twenty-five Republicans who voted against the conference bill came from the conservative wing of the party.

17. Hastert listed as one of the principles guiding his speakership "to please the majority of your majority." Remarks at a conference on "The Changing Nature of the House Speakership," sponsored by the Congressional Research Service and the Carl Albert Center, November 12, 2003, p. 4. "Time and again," Juliet Eilperin observed, "Hastert and his lieutenants have calibrated the likely yeas and nays to the thinnest margin possible, enabling them to push legislation as much to their liking as they can in a narrowly divided and bitterly partisan House. More often than not, that direction is to the political right, and generally in line with President Bush's priorities." "Practicing the Art of One-Vote Victories," *Washington Post*, weekly ed., October 20–26, 2003, p. 13.

18. Aldrich and Rohde aptly termed this system "conditional party government," less encompassing than party government in parliamentary systems but

strong and coherent by historic American standards. Party "responsibility" can vary from issue to issue, but where the necessary conditions of high intraparty agreement and high interparty difference are present, members will be willing to give extensive powers to party leaders, who will "be expected to use the tools at their disposal to advance the cause." The concept, Aldrich and Rohde concluded, was even better suited to the 104th Congress "than to the earlier Democratic Congresses for which it was originally devised." Rohde, *Parties and Leaders*, p. 31; Aldrich and Rohde, "Transition to Republican Rule," p. 565. Also see the discussion by Lawrence C. Dodd and Bruce T. Oppenheimer of the circumstances that might undermine conditional party government or require its modification: "Congress and the Emerging Order: Assessing the 2000 Elections," in Dodd and Oppenheimer, *Congress Reconsidered*, 7th ed., chap. 16.

19. See Price, *Bringing Back the Parties*, pp. 280–282; and Paul S. Herrnson and Kelly D. Patterson, "Toward a More Programmatic Democratic Party? Agenda-Setting and Coalition-Building in the House of Representatives," *Polity*, Summer 1995, pp. 607–628.

20. Herrnson and Patterson have produced a useful analysis of the projects: "Crafting a Partisan Agenda in the House," in Colton C. Campbell and Paul S. Herrnson, eds., *War Stories from Capitol Hill* (Upper Saddle River, N.J.: Prentice-Hall, 2004), pp. 51–65.

21. The first situation was exemplified by the House's initial handling of the accounting industry reform bill (H.R. 3763) in 2002, after the collapse of the Enron Corporation. A good example of the second type is the array of amendments, ranging from the required posting of the Ten Commandments to the imposition of expulsion requirements for drug offenses on local schools, made in order for the juvenile justice bill, H.R. 1501, in 1999.

22. See Rohde, *Parties and Leaders*, pp. 47, 78–81. On the particularly instructive case of Rep. (later Sen.) Phil Gramm, who convinced his constituents that his richly deserved discipline by Democrats was a badge of honor and used it to gain reelection as a Republican, see Price, *Bringing Back the Parties*, p. 67.

23. See the episodes recounted in John M. Barry, *The Ambition and the Power* (New York: Viking, 1989), pp. 393, 542–543.

24. See *Congressional Quarterly Almanac* 51 (1995): 1–16; and Evans and Oleszek, *Congress Under Fire*, p. 126.

25. Edmund Burke, "Thoughts on the Cause of the Present Discontents," in *Works*, 3d ed. (Boston: Little, Brown, 1871), 1:526.

26. See Price, *Bringing Back the Parties*, chap. 4.

27. David Mayhew, "Clinton, the 103rd Congress, and Unified Party Control: What Are the Lessons?" in Geer, ed., *Politicians and Party Politics*, chap. 10; and Mayhew, *Divided We Govern: Party Control, Lawmaking, and Investigations, 1946–1990* (New Haven: Yale University Press, 1991).

28. Mayhew partially acknowledged the point: see "Clinton, the 103d Congress, and Unified Party Control," pp. 269–271. On the question of whether 1993–1994 was a fair test, given Democrats' lack of a filibuster-proof majority in the Senate, see pp. 273–274. Compare Gary Jacobson: "Divided partisan control of policymaking persists as long as the minority party holds at least forty seats in the Senate and can therefore kill any bill it wants to kill. [In 1993–1994] the illusion of unified government put the onus of failure on the Democrats; the reality of divided government let Senate Republicans make sure the administration would fail." "Divided Government and the 1994 Elections," in Peter F. Galderisi, ed., *Divided Government: Change, Uncertainty, and the Constitutional Order* (Lanham, Md.: Rowman & Littlefield, 1996), p. 70.

29. See Morris P. Fiorina, "The Causes and Consequences of Divided Government: Lessons of 1992–94," and Leroy N. Rieselbach, "It's the Constitution, Stupid! Congress, the President, Divided Government, and Policymaking," in Galderisi, *Divided Government*, chaps. 2, 5. For a review of the voluminous literature spawned by Mayhew's thesis and an argument that, subject to a range of facilitating conditions, "unified government produces greater quantities of significant enactments and is more responsive to the public mood than is divided government," see John J. Coleman, "Unified Government, Divided Government, and Party Responsiveness," *American Political Science Review,* December 1999, pp. 821–835.

30. Paul Light, *Still Artful Work: The Continuing Politics of Social Security Reform* (New York: McGraw-Hill, 1995), pp. 2, 13, and passim.

31. Joseph Cooper and Garry Young, surveying the patterns of partisanship manifested in Congress since the New Deal, stressed the importance of finding "some common ground as a basis for cooperation and action" during periods when divided government is combined with heightened partisanship. Otherwise, "a politics marked by halting and limited responses to critical national needs and intense competition to assign blame is likely. Such a politics cannot fail to be damaging both to the preservation of the current two-party system and to the power of Congress." "Partisanship, Bipartisanship, and Crosspartisanship in Congress Since the New Deal," in Dodd and Oppenheimer, *Congress Reconsidered,* 6th ed., p. 269. See also Dodd's and Oppenheimer's brief for "constructive partisanship," marked by the construction of "shifting coalitions within and across the majority and minority parties," bridging governmental and political divisions, as a more promising model than "conditional party government" (n. 18 above) for the majority party that wishes to govern effectively and legitimately and to be returned to power by the electorate. "Congress and the Emerging Order," pp. 385–387. My argument differs from these mainly in distinguishing the type of issue (dedistributive) that is most likely to prove resistant to the workings of conditional party government and to require crosspartisan or bipartisan approaches.

32. *Congressional Quarterly Almanac* 54 (1998): D13.

33. See Elizabeth Drew, "Why Clinton Will Be Impeached," *Washington Post,* September 23, 1998, p. A25; and Albert R. Hunt, "Unfit to Preside," *Wall Street Journal,* October 1, 1998, p. A23. Gingrich in April had basically declared the president guilty of obstruction of justice and had promised "never again, as long as I am speaker, [to] make a speech without commenting on this topic." Jackie Koszczuk, "Gingrich, Leading Attack on Clinton, Takes off Gloves, Goes Out on a Limb," *CQ Weekly,* May 2, 1998, pp. 1127–1131.

34. On the committee's handling of the impeachment hearings, see Steven S. Smith and Sarah Binder, "Deliberation: Where, Oh Where Has It Gone?" *Washington Post,* weekly ed., December 21–28, 1998, p. 23.

35. See the discussions recorded by James Madison, *Notes of Debates in the Federal Convention of 1787* (New York: Norton, 1966) on July 20 and September 8, 1787. The words "against the State" were dropped by the Committee of Style, but with no intent to broaden the application of the terms.

36. "The Impeachment Bully," *New York Times,* December 6, 1998, pp. 4–18. For an analysis linking Republican tactics to their long years out of power, "uninvolved in managing the governmental process and free to lob grenades at the institutions that make it work," see Alan Ehrenhalt, "Hijacking the Rulebook," *New York Times,* December 20, 1998, pp. 4–13. "Having been lifted by the American electorate into a position of genuine power, they have continued to behave more like a party of insurgents, probing for cracks in the constitutional structure rather than taking its rules seriously and looking for ways to make them work."

37. The Republicans, the *Washington Post* editorialized, were "exercising power to prevent the very conscience vote they claim to be holding." "Censure and the Constitution," December 16, 1998, p. A30. Just before the House debate, Henry Hyde engaged in some mysterious backstairs maneuvers that were apparently intended to reopen the possibility of censure but came to naught. See Bob Woodward's account in *Shadow: Five Presidents and the Legacy of Watergate* (New York: Simon & Schuster, 1999), pp. 483–489.

38. Hamilton, "The Federalist," no. 65, in Clinton Rossiter, ed., *The Federalist Papers* (New York: Mentor, 1961), pp. 396–397.

39. For both the complete and the abbreviated statements, see *Congressional Record,* daily ed., December 18, 1998, pp. H11914–15.

40. On the asymmetry of the post–9/11 partisan truce, exemplified by House Republicans' handling of the airport security and economic stimulus issues, see Jacob Weisberg, "Republicans Behaving Badly," *Slate* (www.slate.com), November 9, 2001; and Michael Kinsley, "Bipartisan Etiquette," and E. J. Dionne Jr., "Back to Usual," *Washington Post,* October 26, 2001, p. A35.

41. Data furnished by Democratic staff, House Rules Committee. On Republicans' use of the rules process, see Michael Crowley, "Oppressed Minority: The Misery of Being a House Democrat," *The New Republic,* June 23, 2003, pp. 18–23.

42. Tabulated by Donald R. Wolfensberger, "The House Rules Committee Under Republican Majorities: Continuity and Change" (paper prepared for delivery at the annual meeting of the Northeastern Political Science Association, 2002, revised), table 3. Under closed rules, Democrats had recourse only to a "motion to recommit" (with or without instructions), a parliamentary move that is less straightforward and more difficult for the public to understand than a substantive amendment or alternate bill. Democrats, particularly under Wright's speakership, had earlier limited or denied instructions on minority recommital motions. The practice tailed off under insistent Republican criticism. When the Republicans took control, they wrote into House rules as a minority prerogative the ability to offer a motion to recommit with instructions. However, as Donald Wolfensberger notes, Republicans subsequently used the existence of this prerogative as a pretext for imposing increasingly restrictive rules on the minority. "A rule of fairness [was] converted into an excuse for unfairness." "The Motion to Recommit in the House: The Creation, Evisceration, and Restoration of a Minority Right" (paper prepared for delivery at the conference on the History of Congress, University of California, San Diego, 2003), p. 2 and passim.

The use of self-executing rules also increased under Republican leadership, from an average of 19 percent of all rules in the 101st–103rd Democratic Congresses to 29 percent for the 104th–107th. Wolfensberger, "House Rules Committee," table 4. These rules are used to alter the bill as it comes to the floor, sometimes to make technical corrections but also to accommodate member and leadership interests. This avoids a separate debate and vote on the amendments being folded into the bill, and House Republicans objected to the tactic mightily when they were in the minority.

43. For useful historical perspective, see Jonathan Allen and John Cochran, "The Might of the Right," *Congressional Quarterly Weekly*, November 8, 2003, pp. 2761–2762. The 1993 budget plan was conferenced as well as passed by Democratic members alone, but Republicans expressed no desire or willingness to participate.

44. See Helen Dewar, "A Seat at the Table," *Washington Post*, weekly ed., October 27–November 2, 2003, p. 12. A pertinent question is why the two senators who were included, Max Baucus (D-Montana) and John Breaux (D-Louisiana), agreed to the arrangement. No doubt they saw possibilities for compromise and wished to influence the outcome. But they could have held out for the inclusion of their duly appointed Democratic colleagues as the condition of their participation. In failing to press the issue, Breaux and Baucus enabled the Republicans to put a "bipartisan" gloss on an exclusionary and unfair process.

45. Eilperin, "One-Vote Victories," p. 13.

46. Quoted in "Government by Juggernaut," *Washington Post*, November 26, 2003, p. A24.

47. See David E. Price, "Biennial Budgeting Not the Answer," *Roll Call*, March 6, 2000, p. 38. In 2000 I worked successfully with a bipartisan group to defeat (201–217) a biennial budgeting plan backed by the House Republican leadership. *Congressional Record*, daily ed., May 16, 2000, pp. H3108–28.

48. Norman Ornstein, "Don't Take Civility Out of the House Appropriations Panel," *Roll Call*, November 5, 2003, p. 6.

49. Quoted in Charles Babington, "Scorched Earth Politics," *Washington Post*, weekly ed., January 5–11, 2004, p. 23.

50. Crowley, "Oppressed Minority," p. 22; see also Jim VandeHei and Juliet Eilperin, "The Majority Rules the Way It Wants To," *Washington Post*, weekly ed., August 4–10, 2003, p. 15 (quoting Norman Ornstein); and Babington, "Scorched Earth Politics," p. 23 (quoting Ross Baker and James Thurber).

9

Foreign Policy and Defense

In dealing with foreign affairs, wrote former House International Relations Committee chairman Lee Hamilton (D-Indiana), Congress tends "either to defer to the president or to engage in foreign policy haphazardly."[1] Most members have far stronger incentives in terms of constituency pressures and electoral gain to involve themselves in domestic affairs. Even when strong constituency interests exist, they may encourage sporadic and/or symbolic gestures (e.g., demonstrations of support for Taiwan, Israel, Greece, or India in their ongoing conflicts or opposition to trade liberalization) more than sustained, serious involvement.

Both my personal background and the nature of my district, with increasing ethnic diversity and relatively high levels of education and international exposure, predisposed me to take an interest in foreign affairs. This involvement has intensified during my time in office, partly because of the press of external events but also because of the interests and the channels for pursuing them that I have developed. I gave priority to domestic policy in seeking committee and subcommittee assignments, but found a number of other affiliations, both within and outside of Congress, helpful in pursuing foreign policy interests. In this chapter, I will focus on a number of interparliamentary endeavors, efforts to promote the Middle East peace process, and involvement in House debates over terrorism and the Iraq War.

My work on the Appropriations Committee has also had foreign affairs and defense components, requiring me to work with subcommittees of which I was not a member—Foreign Operations, Defense, and Military Construction—from my full committee position. For example, I secured Foreign Operations support for the MBA Enterprise Corps—a program to send young business school graduates to assist new enterprises in Eastern Europe, initiated at the University of North Carolina and including fifteen other business schools—and for directives to the U.S. Agency for International Development (AID) relevant to the business development work of the UNC Kenan Institute in Thailand. I helped obtain funding for facilities requested by the North Carolina National Guard and defense research projects in which Triangle area universities were involved. Full committee deliberations sometimes offer an opportunity for engagement on substantive issues, particularly in the area of foreign assistance, which has been operating since 1985 without comprehensive authorizing legislation. I took particular interest, for example, in recurring battles over international family planning assistance, usually fighting restrictions proposed by abortion opponents, and over the payment of overdue assessments to the United Nations.

Among the educational opportunities available to members of Congress, nothing matches the work of the Aspen Institute, led by former Sen. Dick Clark (D-Iowa). Supported by a number of major foundations, Aspen has developed a highly successful formula: transport twenty senators and House members and their spouses to a desirable North American or overseas location and expect, in return, four days of their undivided attention to the topic under discussion. Annual conferences are now held on China, Russia and the former Soviet Union, Latin America, Islam and politics, and educational and environmental policy. I have attended conferences on China, Russia, Mexico, and Islam, as well as a number of the breakfast discussions on all these topics that Aspen organizes during the weeks Congress is in session.

The conferences and breakfast sessions normally feature presentations by academic and other experts, followed by extensive discussion. We normally do not meet with government representatives, although we did take advantage of our in-country presence to talk with Premier Zhu Rongji in Beijing in 2002 and with a number of Russian leaders in Moscow in 2003. Regular participants include Senate Foreign Relations chairman Richard Lugar (R-Indiana) and a number of other active and influential members from both parties. I have found the sessions extremely useful, not only educating me on critical issues but also providing a basis for consultation and collaboration among colleagues back in Washington.

Parliament to Parliament

I was invited during my first term to visit West Germany as part of a parliamentary exchange sponsored by the German Marshall Fund of the United States. With the fund's support, seven other "founding members" and I then established the Congressional Study Group on Germany, with Lee Hamilton as our first chairman. My turn to lead the group came at a particularly opportune time in 1990, when excitement about German reunification was at its peak. Along with Sen. Bill Roth (R-Delaware), chairman of the Senate study group, I led a congressional delegation visit to Bonn, Berlin, and Budapest. Chancellor Helmut Kohl, grateful for American support of reunification, welcomed us warmly, and we had extensive discussions with our counterparts in the Bundestag and the East German Volkskammer.

The German Study Group is one of the more active organizations of its kind on Capitol Hill, enabling nonspecialist members like me to sustain discussion and contacts between and beyond exchange visits. We hold luncheons for visiting parliamentarians and political leaders and periodic sessions with the German ambassador. We have provided a model for other international caucuses, including the Congressional Caucus on India and Indian Americans (see Chapter 5). Here too the establishment of ongoing ties has facilitated communications when difficulties or crises have arisen. For example, on May 27, 1999, after Pakistan shot down an Indian plane over disputed territory in Kashmir, six of us from the India Caucus met with the Indian ambassador, not only to hear his version of the incident but also to communicate our concerns about escalation of the conflict.

I was one of four India Caucus members who went to New Delhi and Bombay in 1999 to meet with various government, opposition, and business leaders and to launch an Interparliamentary Working Group for members of the Indian Lok Sabha and the U.S. House. We have subsequently welcomed several groups of Indian parliamentarians to Washington. While such exchanges vary in their format and organizational backing, they offer a number of members an opportunity for international involvement, far more freewheeling and participatory than serving as a member of the U.S. delegation to an interparliamentary gathering. During my time in the House, I have participated in exchanges with parliamentarians from the United Kingdom, Norway/Sweden, and Japan, as well as Germany and India.

The interparliamentary endeavor that I found most rewarding (and hope to see renewed) was the extension of support to the emerging parliaments of Central and Eastern Europe after the fall of communism. Proposed and then chaired by Rep. Martin Frost (D-Texas), the Task Force on the Development of Parliamentary Institutions in Central and Eastern Europe was formed in 1990 and over the next six years worked with ten emerging democracies. The idea was to offer encouragement, technical support, and equipment to parliamentary leaders and members as they established modern, democratically functioning institutions.[2]

House members traveled to the participating countries mainly to launch the projects or to celebrate their successful conclusion. I went to Poland,

Estonia, Latvia, and Lithuania in 1992 and to Hungary, Slovakia, and Albania in 1993. Staff members from the Library of Congress and the House Information Systems office went over for weeks at a time, delivering the
equipment, assistance, and training necessary to establish modern library
facilities and computer capabilities. The assistance we rendered depended
in part on what equipment and personnel were already in place. Poland,
Hungary, and the Czech Republic were ready for a fairly rapid takeoff,
while in Albania our delegation delivered typewriters and a wall clock;
the other countries were somewhere in between. The assignment was a
political scientist's dream and a moving human experience as well, as we
met with courageous democratic leaders—at a reception in the ambassador's residence in Tirana, we realized that the parliamentary leaders in
the room had spent on average over twenty years in Albanian prisons—
and saw what an inspiration the U.S. Congress, despite its flaws, was
to them.

I returned to Bratislava as a former member after the 1994 election, joining with several European parliamentarians in an orientation program for
new Slovakian legislators. Unfortunately, between the program's planning
and execution, the "wrong" party—the authoritarian Movement for a
Democratic Slovakia, led by Vladimir Meciar—staged a political comeback,
producing as unreceptive an audience as I have ever tried to address! (Fortunately Slovakia turned the corner politically in 1998 and in 2004 attained
membership in NATO.) In the meantime, the new Republican House leadership allowed the parliamentary assistance project to lapse—prematurely,
in my view. In 2004, Rep. Doug Bereuter (R-Nebraska), chairman of the
International Relations Subcommittee on Europe, and I introduced a resolution (H.Res. 642) to authorize the renewal of the program. Likely participants would include most of the former Yugoslav republics, Georgia, and
other former Soviet and Middle Eastern states if and when they developed
freely functioning parliaments.

A third opportunity for interparliamentary work has come from the
NATO Parliamentary Assembly, an organization of parliamentary representatives from the NATO countries that has been quick to extend observer status to the former communist states of Central and Eastern
Europe and Central Asia. I was initially drawn into participation in the
early 1990s through my work with the German Study Group and because a member of my state delegation, Rep. Charlie Rose (D-North Carolina), was working his way up to the presidency of the assembly. These
meetings generally offered fewer opportunities for serious participation,
especially for less senior members, than smaller and less formal parliamentary exchanges. But I renewed my involvement in the NATO Assembly in 2002 as Doug Bereuter prepared to assume the presidency, this

time participating at a more senior level and assuming a subcommittee vice chairmanship.

The NATO Assembly has no formal authority with respect to its constituent parliaments, but its work is taken seriously by most of them, and it has provided a valuable forum at a time when major changes and difficult issues have faced the Western alliance. The discussions undertaken and resolutions approved in the past fifteen years have focused on the post–Cold War character of NATO, the role of the alliance in conflicts in the Balkans and beyond Europe, and the collective response to terrorism. The assembly has also played an important role in the eastward expansion of NATO, both in debating the terms of the expansion and in establishing ties with parliamentarians from the new member states.

My wife, Lisa, and I were especially eager to attend the Parliamentary Assembly meetings in Prague, the capital of one of the new member countries, in May 2003. We had visited Czechoslovakia on our honeymoon in 1968 during the height of the Prague Spring, the ill-fated attempt by President Alexander Dubcek to liberalize communist rule and break free of Soviet domination. Through friends of Lisa's family we looked up a young Czech plastic surgeon and artist, Jara Moserova, and her husband, who showed us around Prague while expressing the apprehension that "all of this is too good to be true." Indeed, Soviet tanks rolled into Prague a few days after we left, and Czechoslovakia's experiment with "socialism with a human face" was extinguished for a generation.

But here we were in Prague thirty-five years later, in a free and democratic Czech Republic, preparing to claim full NATO membership! As I rose to address the assembly, seated in the front row as a member of the Czech delegation was *Senator* Moserova, our hostess from that memorable 1968 visit.

The topic of that plenary session, which Bereuter had wisely decided should be aired and could not be avoided, was the conduct of the war in Iraq and its increasingly challenging aftermath. As the only Democratic U.S. spokesman, I acknowledged continuing questions about alternative means that might have been chosen to address the threat posed by Saddam Hussein, while urging a concerted mutual effort to repair the diplomatic breaches that had accompanied the war, undertake the stabilization and reconstruction of Iraq, and revive the Middle East peace process. In the few minutes allotted to me, I felt compelled also to recall our 1968 visit and mark the significance of the NATO Assembly meeting in Prague at this historic juncture:

> Such memories remind us of how far we have come and what we have been through together. Remembering where we are and the momentous occurrences

that have brought us to this point should put our present challenges in perspective and reinforce our commitment to the values and alliances and institutions that have made this day possible.

Promoting Middle East Peace

I first visited Israel in early 1990, midway in my second term, in a bipartisan group of four members hosted by the Anti-Defamation League of B'nai B'rith (ADL). A national unity government was in power, headed by the Likud Party's Yitzhak Shamir and including Yitzhak Rabin and Shimon Peres of the Labor Party as ministers of defense and finance respectively. The ADL made certain that we met with a wide range of government leaders, and at our request they made time for us to meet with several Palestinian leaders and visit a refugee camp as well. It was a tense time in Israel, with the uprising, or intifada, continuing in the occupied West Bank and Gaza and serious friction developing between the Israeli government and the first Bush administration over steps that might resolve the conflict.

Lisa and I had never visited Israel, and the trip left a powerful impression. I also gained some political insights. One had to do with the diversity of Israeli political opinion, picked up from government leaders, Knesset members, and Israeli academics I had known at Yale and Duke. The range was far wider than one would have assumed from the litmustest positions (e.g., refusing to recognize or negotiate with the Palestine Liberation Organization [PLO]) urged on congressional candidates by the American Israel Public Affairs Committee (AIPAC) and allied groups. Another insight had to do with the potential quality of Palestinian leadership beyond the familiar figure of Yasser Arafat and the extent of the contacts our government had cultivated with moderate elements, mainly through our consulate in Jerusalem. I was struck by the widespread desire for a fair settlement on both sides as well as the formidable obstacles to getting there, and I resolved to be more attentive to the issue and seek avenues for positive engagement.

Such opportunities greatly increased in the wake of the 1991 Madrid Conference, convened by the United States and the Soviet Union and attended by Israeli, Palestinian, Syrian, Lebanese, and Jordanian leaders, and the signing of the Declaration of Principles (the Oslo Accord) by then–Prime Minister Rabin and PLO chairman Yasser Arafat at the White House in 1993. Clearly a continuing mix of American encouragement and pressure was essential if the successive steps envisioned in the Oslo Accord were to be taken. On returning to the House in 1997, I was drawn to the work of the Center for Middle East Peace and Economic Cooperation, an organization cofounded by Slim-Fast Foods chairman Daniel Abraham and former Rep. Wayne Owens (D-Utah), a friend from his days in the House. The center had actively promoted the peace process behind the scenes since the run-up to the Madrid Conference. Owens was convinced that visits by members of Congress to the region were useful, not only in engaging and educating them but also in demonstrating American support for the process, nudging the participants along, and encouraging positive moves by political and business leaders in the region.

In late 1997 I set out with Abraham, Owens, and two House colleagues, Gary Ackerman (D-New York) and Jim Moran (D-Virginia), to Israel, the Palestinian territories, Jordan, Syria, Lebanon, Egypt, and Qatar. The experience convinced me that a small, independent, and creative organization could do significant work in this difficult environment and might have some advantages over formal delegations. We were not freelancing, however; we conferred with State Department officials before leaving and with our ambassadors in each country we visited. Our conversations ranged more widely and were more candid than those I had experienced in official settings. We benefited from the credibility and respectful relations Abraham and Owens had developed across the political spectrum in Israel, in the Palestinian community, and in most Arab states. We were almost always received by the head of state, and our conversations ranged from exchanging information to airing bilateral issues to exploring specific steps to improve the prospects for discussions, such as those Secretary of State Madeleine Albright was to hold with Yasser Arafat and Israeli prime minister Benjamin Netanyahu preparatory to their January 1998 talks in Washington.

The visit to Qatar, which was not then on most Middle East itineraries, was indicative of Owens's distinctive approach. He stressed the importance of regional backing for the peace process, particularly in the Gulf States and North Africa, and understood the role trade and investment prospects could have in stimulating such support. He also was impressed with the large-scale water desalination underway in the Gulf States and made water policy and planning a major focus of center activity, addressing what is perhaps the region's most threatening long-term conflict of national interests.

Owens, Rep. Robert Wexler (D-Florida), and I returned to the Middle East in early 2000. Israeli–Syrian talks were then underway and Israeli–Palestinian negotiations in prospect; we focused on broadening regional support for those efforts. We visited Morocco, Tunisia, Kuwait, the United

FIGURE 9.1   Oman: At the sultan's encampment in Nakhl, January 17, 2000. From my left: Sultan Qaboos bin Said; Rep. Robert Wexler; former Rep. Wayne Owens, president of the Center for Middle East Peace and Economic Cooperation.

Arab Emirates (UAE), and Oman (see Figure 9.1). We noted that King Mohamed VI had hosted Israeli foreign minister David Levy in Rabat, the UAE had financed needed housing in Gaza, and Oman had opened a trade office in Tel Aviv. We explored what further moves of this sort might be possible. Wexler and I also found ways to follow up after we returned—passing a resolution of support for Kuwait's efforts to compel Iraq to account for prisoners taken during the Gulf War, for example, and helping persuade President Clinton to include a visit with Sultan Qaboos in Oman on the itinerary of his March trip to India.[3]

It was a hopeful time. Although the peace process had never recovered from the blow dealt by Rabin's assassination in late 1995, Israel had a new prime minister, Ehud Barak, who seemed determined to move ahead with negotiations. The timing also seemed right for Syria's ailing President Hafiz Asad, if not for Palestinian Authority president Arafat; Asad knew that time was running out on any hope he had that the Golan

Heights, occupied by Israel since the 1967 war, would be returned to Syrian rule.[4] But the process ran aground within a year, as first the Syrian and then the Palestinian talks narrowly failed, Israeli–Palestinian violence reached levels not seen in a decade, and a new American administration came to power determined to disengage from assertive Middle East peacemaking.

My Middle East involvement was rooted in a dual commitment to the security and integrity of Israel and to justice and self-determination for the Palestinians—two goals that not only were consistent but were essential to each other. I was convinced that the conflict was unlikely to be resolved without active American engagement. The quest for a lasting peace was compelling in its own right, but it was given a powerful additional rationale and new urgency by the terrorist attacks of September 11, 2001, and the need to mobilize internationally against al Qaeda and related groups. Osama bin Laden displayed little interest in the plight of the Palestinians until he used it in a postattack bid for support, a fact well understood by most Arab leaders. Still, the continuing Israeli–Palestinian violence, given the widespread perception that the United States had not only disengaged from peacemaking but had taken a hands-off attitude toward the policies of Israeli prime minister Ariel Sharon's government, fed anti-American sentiment in the Arab world. The festering conflict, featured as never before on satellite news outlets, made it more difficult and dangerous for friendly governments to ally themselves fully with our antiterrorism offensive.

The collapse of the peace process, together with the urgency of the war on terrorism, made for an altered mood and message as I returned to the region, again under the center's auspices, in 2002. In January, Sen. Dick Durbin (D-Illinois), Rep. Jim Davis (D-Florida), and Rep. Adam Schiff (D-California), and I went to Egypt, Syria, Lebanon, Jordan, Kuwait, Saudi Arabia, Israel, and the Palestinian territories. Owens and I took a shorter trip in May focusing on Israel, Syria, and Lebanon; in December Owens, Abraham, Davis, and I returned to the countries we had visited in January plus Oman and Qatar (and minus Kuwait). We stressed that terrorism was no longer an abstraction for the American people and that our country was united in its determination to remove this threat. We expressed appreciation, where warranted, for cooperating with our military, sharing intelligence, and closing financial conduits to al Qaeda, and we expressed concern over failures to crack down on the terrorist groups wreaking havoc in Israel. We heard, in return, many complaints about sporadic, ineffectual efforts by the Bush administration to rein in Israeli–Palestinian violence and get the parties back to negotiations.[5]

Our January trip came at a time when the Israeli government was setting out to "delegitimate" (the word Sharon used in our meeting, which
he would hardly have chosen casually) Yasser Arafat as a purveyor of violence with whom Israel no longer could deal. Our government, while
frustrated with Arafat, still recognized him as the elected president of the
Palestinian Authority, and our delegation had scheduled meetings with
him as well as other Palestinian leaders.

As we were driving into Jerusalem from Amman, we received word
from our embassy that another group of House members would soon be
holding a press conference to announce their refusal to meet with Arafat.
While this was a tempting political course for some (AIPAC had asked
members to boycott Arafat), it created concern among consular officials
who had requested the meetings. Had our group also canceled, it would
have been impossible for the other Palestinian officials on our agenda
(including a future prime minister, Ahmed Qureia) to see us. After extensive discussion, we determined that Jim Davis and I would keep our appointment with Arafat; this allowed Consul-General Ron Schlicher to
deliver personally our government's demand for a response to reports
linking Palestinian leaders to a major arms shipment Israelis had just in-
tercepted at sea. Davis and I reinforced that message and preserved our
group's schedule with other Palestinian leaders, some of whom offered a
promising counterweight to Arafat. I had to contend with a Raleigh
press report of the critical comments of a local AIPAC representative, but
the responses I received to the story were far more favorable that not.[6]

President Bush signaled a change in U.S. policy in a speech on June 24,
conditioning further American support for an independent Palestinian
state on the election of new Palestinian leaders "not compromised by terror." This cemented the administration's "special closeness" with the
Sharon government and, in tying American policy to the replacement of
Arafat, erected a barrier (deliberately, some suspected) to flexible engagement.[7] The president's position pressured Arafat and other Palestinian
leaders in 2003 to choose reputable men as prime minister—first Mahmoud Abbas (Abu Mazen) and then Ahmed Qureia (Abu Ala), both of
whom we had met during our 2002 visits—and develop a more accountable structure of governance. It also complicated the task of those prime
ministers, however, by prompting a defiant support of Arafat among
Palestinians and a determination by Arafat himself not to be marginalized.

Our 2002 visits underscored the altered context of Middle East peacemaking. The Oslo process had collapsed and diplomats were again
searching for openings, converging interests, and glimmers of hope that
could be built on. We met as before with heads of state and foreign minis-

ters, but this time many of our visits were narrowly targeted to learn about and encourage promising initiatives. For example, we met in Cairo with intelligence chief Gen. Omar Seuliman regarding the next round of cease-fire talks to be brokered by Egypt among Hamas, Fatah, and possibly other groups. We met with Palestinian Authority finance minister Salam Fayyad regarding financial and budget reform, where there had been enough progress to allow the United States to broker the release of a portion of the Palestinian revenues impounded by Israel. And we talked with Sari Nusseibeh, head of Jerusalem Affairs for the PLO, and former Israeli justice minister Yossi Beilin about back-channel peace initiatives that they and others had underway.[8]

Our December trip ended with a terrible personal blow, the death of Wayne Owens. After seven intense days of travel, Owens saw Jim Davis and me off at the Tel Aviv Airport. By the time we arrived at home, word was waiting that he had suffered a fatal heart attack. Our shock and sorrow were acute, and the passing of this gifted, determined peacemaker left a tremendous gap for the center and those of us who collaborated with him to fill.[9]

The invasion of Iraq launched by President Bush in March 2003 did not receive the same consensual congressional and public support given to the war on terrorism. But many with differing views on Iraq shared the hope that the altered Middle East landscape would prove conducive to a fresh start for the peace process. I stressed this in my speech to the NATO Assembly in Prague, as did many other parliamentarians. The main vehicle for these hopes was the Middle East Road Map, a plan for reciprocal Israeli and Palestinian steps to end terror and violence, normalize Palestinian life and reform Palestinian institutions, freeze Israeli settlement building, and eventually undertake negotiations to produce an independent Palestinian state. The State Department formulated the Road Map in 2002 as part of the Quartet, which included the United Nations, the European Union, and Russia. But there was never any doubt that American leadership was the key ingredient. Bush delayed the release of the plan, first to get past Israeli elections and then to get past the Iraq war. This frustrated the Quartet partners, particularly British prime minister Tony Blair. As an ally in the Iraq invasion, Blair had urged the president to show that he was serious about Israeli–Palestinian peacemaking. The delay also made it more difficult for Mahmoud Abbas to show progress as he struggled to establish himself as Palestinian prime minister.[10] Finally, on April 30, the plan was released. In the weeks that followed, Bush secured expressions of support from both Sharon and Abbas, leading many to hope that a page had been turned.

Congress was largely unhelpful. Few members were as outspoken as majority leader Tom DeLay, who spoke scornfully of the "Quartet of Appeasement" and later muddled the president's message in a hard-line August address to the Israeli Knesset.[11] Efforts by DeLay and other Republican strategists to woo Jewish voters from their Democratic allegiance and forge an alliance between conservative Jews and fundamentalist Christians set up a dynamic whereby party leaders competed to demonstrate their support for the Israeli government, with a focus on near-term advantage. For many members, encouraged by AIPAC, this translated into an insistence that the Road Map be read in light of the president's Rose Garden speech of June 24, 2002, which suggested that no Israeli moves would be required before Palestinian governance had been reformed and terrorist attacks had ceased. This viewpoint was expressed in a letter to the president circulated in the House by Chairman Henry Hyde (R-Illinois) and ranking member Tom Lantos (D-California) of the International Relations (IR) Committee and signed by a vast majority of House and Senate members, as well as in language included by the IR Committee in its State Department authorization bill (H.R. 1950).

In an effort to show that such efforts did not fully express House attitudes toward the Road Map initiative, I joined with Darrell Issa (R-California) and Lois Capps (D-California) in organizing a supportive letter. Within three days we obtained forty-four names, including many who had also signed the Hyde-Lantos letter. Headed by Edgar Bronfman of the World Jewish Congress, a group of prominent Jewish leaders sent an open letter to House and Senate leaders expressing confidence that the Road Map would help Israel "escape the bloody status quo" and decrying the attempts of others to "sidetrack implementation."[12] Despite such efforts, as well as broad international support for the initiative, the Road Map proved fragile, and the administration's persistence did not outlast the predictable attempts at sabotage by terrorist groups and the resumption of the cycle of violence.

Congress did little to strengthen the president's resolve. The three weeks following his June 4 summit in Aqaba with Sharon and Abbas were marred by escalating violence: suicide bombings and other attacks killing twenty-nine Israelis, retaliatory raids and other actions killing fifty-nine Palestinians. The House passed a resolution on June 25 (H.Res. 294) that managed in its ten "resolved" clauses to avoid any mention of the Road Map effort! The resolution condemned "the recent terrorist actions" and expressed "solidarity with the Israeli people." I voted for it, along with 398 other members, for I felt those sentiments as strongly as anyone; it had been barely a year since my visit to the site of a terrible

Passover bomb attack in Netanya. But I found it baffling and regrettable that the resolution expressed no support for our country's major peace-making initiative, and I said so on the House floor: "We must condemn terrorism without qualification, and that is consistent with promoting the simultaneous accommodations by both sides which the Road Map envisions. We must affirm Israel's right to defend itself, but that is consistent with urging on Israel tactics and timing that do not undermine the Road Map initiative, as our President and our Secretary of State have recently articulated."[13]

By early 2004, terrorist bombings were continuing, Israel was unilaterally building a security fence incorporating large segments of West Bank territory, neither side was fulfilling the Road Map prescriptions, and Bush's promises to "ride herd" on the parties to pursue peace were a fading memory. Against that backdrop Thomas Friedman gave a desperate prognosis: Israelis and Palestinians, he wrote, "are locked in an utterly self-destructive vicious cycle that threatens Israel's long-term viability, poisons America's image in the Middle East, undermines any hope for a Palestinian state, and weakens pro-American Arab moderates."[14] The Israeli government, reluctant to challenge the settlers in any case, was doubly so when the likely reward was another horrific bombing by Hamas or another group that the Palestinian Authority was unable or unwilling to control. As for the Palestinians, they felt they were being asked to risk a civil war by taking on militant groups by force without assurances that settlements would actually be removed from Palestinian territory or statehood achieved.

Neither side was likely to move without American pressure and assurances, but the Bush administration settled back into its pre–9/11 passivity. The disengagement was not complete: Bush, like Clinton, had a competent, dedicated Middle East team at the State Department that worked quietly and persistently on such issues as Palestinian financial and governmental reform and the route of Israel's security fence. I also found them, along with our diplomatic personnel in Tel Aviv and Jerusalem, effective in specific interventions with the Israeli government. We were able, for example, to halt demolitions in 2002 and 2004 involving a struggling Bethlehem school I had first learned about through my church: first of the principal's home (he was accused of harboring terrorists and later cleared), and then of a school building near one proposed security fence route. Such efforts were important in avoiding disasters and keeping lines of communication open. But they did not add up to the kind of determined effort at the top required to prompt Road Map compliance and push toward longer-term solutions.

Some concluded—and I was tempted by this view—that the Road Map's model of reciprocal accommodations was too vulnerable to conflicting interpretations, stalling, and sabotage to succeed: The United States, perhaps leading some international partners, again needed to put a peace plan on the table proactively, along with the security commitments to make it work. What was certain was that neither the Road Map nor any other plan would work without the political will to make it work. Thus far, such will has been in short supply in the Oval Office.

Members of Congress would do well to seek out more opportunities to engage with Middle Eastern leaders, in their home countries and Washington. True friendship, internationally as well as interpersonally, requires us to tell our friends the truth, as opposed to offering uncritical support or simply saying what they want to hear. Friends of Palestinian aspirations need to tell the truth about terrorism—it is unacceptable morally and counterproductive politically, and it drives away the elements of the Israeli center and left on which any peace initiative will ultimately depend. Friends of Israel must also tell the truth—that land seizures and settlement activity cede the moral high ground, and giving the Palestinian people hope and inducing a majority to support the difficult steps toward peace will require more than demands, sanctions, and retaliation.

We should not underestimate the progress represented by support for a two-state solution among most Arab governments and across the political spectrum in Israel. The outlines of an eventual viable settlement are widely known (the proposal President Clinton put on the table at Taba came close) and are unlikely to change. But the situation on the ground is deeply discouraging, and leadership on neither side seems able or inclined to make the sort of bold moves that led to earlier breakthroughs in the region. The United States, as the country that combines a huge stake in a fair and durable settlement with a unique ability to broker a settlement, must lead. As members of Congress, we should not sell ourselves or our country's interests short by disengaging or reflexively signing letters or voting for resolutions when asked to do so. There is no substitute for presidential leadership in this kind of diplomatic endeavor, but members of Congress variously situated have considerable ability to advise, prod, encourage, and support (or undermine and discourage) administration efforts. There is a pressing need for us, individually and collectively, to bring more focus, discernment, and persistence to this task.

The "Use of Force"

The president's "ears have been burning," surmised the *Washington Post* in reporting on the January 20, 2004, State of the Union message. "Bush has heard what the Democrats have been saying about him . . . that the war on terrorism is lagging, that he has squandered international goodwill with his actions in Iraq, that he misled the public into war."[15] The list went on to include familiar economic and fiscal issues. But the content and the tone of the president's message (which was indeed "reactive," listing seventeen countries with at least a few troops in Iraq and insisting that inspectors had identified "weapons of mass destruction–related program activities") was noteworthy for the prominence given foreign policy conflicts and for the indications that they had become a political battleground, highly relevant to the next election.

The main reason for the heightened prominence of foreign policy and defense on the national agenda was the al Qaeda attacks of September 11, 2001, and the continuing threat of international terrorism. But that did not alone explain where the country found itself in 2004. The administration's immediate response to 9/11, the pursuit of al Qaeda and the removal of the Taliban from power in Afghanistan, had broad, consensual support in Congress and among the American public, and in most of the international community as well. It was what followed—the announced doctrine of preemptory and/or preventive war, the marked penchant for unilateral action, the willingness to use American power to topple hostile governments in the absence of a direct attack on the United States or its allies, all exemplified in the invasion of Iraq—that made the Bush administration's approach to the world so controversial and divisive, at home and abroad. Ivo Daalder and James Lindsay argued persuasively that the "hegemonist" views of Bush and his most influential advisers antedated the 9/11 attacks and represented a decisive break from the "basic foreign policy consensus," with its strong reliance on military alliances and international organizations, embraced by both parties since World War II. But one can only speculate how fully the hegemonist agenda would have been acted on, absent the terrorist attacks: "What September 11 provided was the rationale and the opportunity to carry out [the Bush] revolution."[16]

Within three days of 9/11 both the House (420–1) and the Senate (98–0) passed a joint resolution (S.J.Res. 23) authorizing the president to "use all necessary and appropriate force against those nations, organizations or persons he determines planned, authorized, committed or aided the terrorist attacks . . . or harbored such organizations or persons." Both houses also passed a $40 billion emergency supplemental appropriations bill (H.R. 2888) on September 14 without dissent. These actions were not totally without controversy; the administration at first requested resolution language limited neither to retaliation for 9/11 nor to terrorism and authority to disburse the entire appropriation as it wished. But congressional leaders resolved such questions cooperatively, and most members gave the administration full support as it mounted the offensive against the Taliban and al Qaeda. The concerns and criticisms that I and other members later developed reflected the view that the antiterrorism offensive and the postwar stabilization of Afghanistan were receiving too little rather than too much emphasis, particularly as the war in Iraq trumped other military and diplomatic priorities.

Like most members, I assumed Iraq had retained a biological and chemical weapons capability that was potentially a threat to our country. I regarded Saddam Hussein as a brutal tyrant and thought the world would be a safer place were he gone. But as it became clear that many in the Bush administration wished to use 9/11 as a pretext for invading Iraq, I developed misgivings and began to share them with colleagues and constituents. Did the threat from Iraq warrant the priority the administration was giving it among the range of dangers and threats that we faced? And even if it did, might not a complex of policies either already in place or proposed (e.g., a renewed and strengthened regime of coercive inspections, U.N.-supervised weapons destruction, no-fly zones, intense surveillance, a tight embargo on strategic and dual-use materials, announced readiness for a devastating response to any aggressive Iraqi military action) serve to contain, deter, and ultimately disarm Iraq, rendering a military invasion unnecessary?

I wanted better answers to these questions before giving the president the authority to undertake an invasion—an extreme option with heavy costs and risks. Without acknowledging that an authorization was constitutionally or legally required, Bush announced on September 4, 2002, that he would seek a resolution of approval from Congress to "do whatever is necessary to deal with the threat posed by Saddam Hussein's regime." The resolution's language was negotiated among party and committee leaders and the White House over the next few weeks. Senate majority leader Tom Daschle's efforts to place additional conditions on unilateral action were undercut when Dick Gephardt, House minority leader and a prospective presidential candidate, independently came to agreement with the administration. The result was a resolution (H.J.Res. 114) giving the president the open-ended authority for the "use of military force" that he wanted, subject only to the reporting requirements of the War Powers Act and to presidential certifications regarding the failure of diplomacy and consistency with antiterrorism efforts.

One reason for Gephardt's ready agreement was reportedly his conviction that he had been mistaken in his opposition to the resolution authorizing the first war against Iraq. I did not draw the same conclusion. Like such Democratic leaders as Lee Hamilton and Senator Sam Nunn

(D-Georgia), my concerns in 1991 had mainly been about timing and tactics.[17] I had no doubt that Iraq's occupation of Kuwait could not be tolerated and that force was a legitimate option. I found my own vote against invasion, both originally and in retrospect, a difficult call. But I had no trouble distinguishing it from the decision we faced in 2003, when the international coalition the first President Bush had skillfully assembled was nowhere in sight, the aftermath of war posed far greater dangers, and there was a likelihood of diversion from critical military and diplomatic priorities.

Gephardt did not attempt to impose his view on the Democratic Caucus, and he helped ensure that Democratic alternatives received fair consideration on the House floor. I thought it was important to have an alternative addressing the Iraq challenge but without granting the president open-ended authority to take the nation to war, and I worked with John Spratt (D-South Carolina), second-ranking Democrat on the Armed Services Committee, and nine other like-minded members to develop one. The Spratt substitute amendment authorized the president to use military force for enforcement actions pursuant to a new U.N. resolution to eliminate Iraq's weapons program. If the president wished to act in the absence of such a resolution, he would be required to come back to Congress to seek a separate vote on the use of force. Congress would take this vote on an expedited up-or-down basis on certification by the president that further U.N. action was not likely to compel Iraq to disarm, force was the only remaining option, the United States was building as wide a coalition as possible, and action against Iraq would not adversely affect the broader war on terrorism.

The Spratt substitute received 155 votes (147 Democrats, 7 Republicans, 1 Independent) on October 10, considerably more than we had anticipated when we began. We lost some votes to the "left" as well as to the Hastert-Gephardt resolution; a resolution simply urging the president to work through the United Nations and seek the return of weapons inspectors to Iraq garnered seventy-seven votes. Some who voted for the Spratt substitute voted for the Hastert-Gephardt resolution after the substitute failed, helping produce a final vote of 296–133. I did not, for I was not ready to authorize a unilateral invasion months in advance of circumstances I could not anticipate. The Senate equivalent of our substitute, offered by Carl Levin (D-Michigan), was rejected 24–75, a weaker showing than we had managed in the House; final Senate passage came on October 11 by a vote of 77–23. The president now had the authority he wanted, and the ensuing weeks erased any remaining doubts that he was determined to use it, with or without a U.N. resolution.

In supporting the Spratt substitute, I focused on the abdication of congressional responsibility. Constitutionally and historically, the executive branch is dominant in the conduct of foreign and military policy. An up-or-down congressional vote on a resolution authorizing force is at best a blunt instrument. Why, I asked, would we wish to make it blunter still, by giving the president open-ended authority to mount an invasion under circumstances about which we could only speculate? Such an abdication, I thought, was especially problematic in light of the president's announced intention of going beyond the generally accepted right of anticipatory self-defense to what former secretary of state Henry Kissinger termed "an unfettered right of preemption against [the nation's] own definition of threats to its security." But my larger institutional quarrel was with those who seemed to regard a congressional resolution as essentially an arrow in the president's quiver. Many members justified their vote in terms of the credibility it would give the president as he went to the U.N. Security Council and sought to apply maximum pressure on Iraq. Some even argued that the best way to prevent war was to authorize war. This argument had some force, but in the end it did not do justice to our duty as a coordinate branch of government. Passing a resolution was more than a tactic for applying "pressure." The test should rather be its merits as the nation's policy should measures short of war either fail or not be fully attempted.[18]

"What accounting do we have of the costs and risks of a military invasion? How are we to secure and maintain the support and engagement of our allies? Can Iraq be disarmed by means that do not divert us from, or otherwise compromise, equally or more urgent antiterrorist or diplomatic objectives? Do we have a credible plan for rebuilding and governing postwar Iraq, and have we secured the necessary international cooperation to ensure that this does not become a perceived U.S. occupation?" I raised these questions—to which the Bush administration provided no satisfactory answers—in a floor speech on the eve of the war, and I repeated them six months later as Congress debated Bush's $87 billion supplemental appropriations request (on top of $79 billion earlier appropriated) to finance the war and Iraq's postwar reconstruction.[19]

Despite the size of the request and the sticker shock it prompted, the administration failed to give a credible plan, complete with cost and deployment estimates, going forward. Clearly a midcourse correction was needed to secure international cooperation and reengage the United Nations, avoid further diversion from the antiterrorism offensive in Afghanistan and elsewhere, bring our personnel mix into line with the security and reconstruction functions being performed, and maintain a steady course on the Road Map initiative. It was also critically important, I argued, to get to the bottom of the persistent questions that weapons expert Joseph Wilson and others had raised concerning the quality of prewar intelligence on Iraq's alleged weapons of mass destruction and the way the administration had used it in making the case for war.[20] This was not merely a matter of "clearing the air" but of clarifying the level of performance and standard of truthfulness Congress and the public must demand of the Bush administration, or any administration, in the future.

The House Appropriations Committee "scrubbed" and improved the president's request in several respects, shifting another $400 million to Afghan reconstruction, cutting several questionable spending items, and directing funds toward enhanced body armor and other items related to the safety and well-being of our troops. We passed amendments during markup to require more extensive reporting to Congress by the president and to require competitive bidding on reconstruction contracts, while failing in an attempt to utilize reconstruction funding more effectively to leverage international participation. In the end, I joined eighty-two other House Democrats in voting for the supplemental appropriation, including twenty of us who had voted against the Hastert-Gephardt war resolution. I was not entirely satisfied with the steps our bill took toward the needed midcourse correction. Yet we had troops in the field with pressing needs, and it was unthinkable to let Iraq or Afghanistan revert to either tyranny or chaos. Questions would linger for years about how we went into Iraq, and I intended to help press those questions, but we could not walk away from the task of reconstructing Iraq and facilitating an orderly transition to self-rule.[21]

One month after the vote I went to Iraq with an Appropriations delegation headed by Foreign Operations Subcommittee chairman Jim Kolbe (R-Arizona). We based ourselves in Amman, Jordan, and flew into Baghdad one day and Kirkuk the next.[22] There was no mistaking the tight security. We were largely kept out of helicopters and were taken to the Baghdad airport by a circuitous route because roadside explosives had been discovered on the two more direct routes. We saw the steel hulk that used to be Baghdad's main power plant and other examples of the magnitude of the rebuilding task, as well as a reopened school, a multiethnic city council, and other hopeful developments in Kirkuk.

In talking to soldiers in Iraq and the military hospital at Ramstein Air Base in Germany, we gained a graphic sense of how well planned and precisely executed the Iraq invasion had been (as contrasted to the unplanned and chaotic aftermath) and of the difficulties and dangers our troops faced daily in securing the country. I gained enormous respect for the competence and dedication of the military and civilian personnel, many of them from North Carolina, carrying out the stabilization and reconstruction effort. But I wondered how much fortitude and perseverance administration leaders and legislators in Washington, who had been so eager to go war, would show in seeing the endeavor through.

The reelection–minded Bush administration subsequently set a June 30, 2004, deadline for turning over the reins of government to Iraqis. The feasibility of this goal was complicated by the continuing lack of security, maneuvering for advantage among major ethnic factions, and insistence by the majority Shiites on early national elections. The administration, finally realizing that "guiding Iraq from tyranny to tranquillity [was] not something a Pentagon-directed American occupation could accomplish on its own," enlisted U.N. Secretary-General Kofi Annan to legitimate its view that hastily scheduled direct elections were not feasible.[23] International cooperation would be essential in designing a legitimate interim government that would make certain no major element of Iraq's population was disenfranchised. American force was an essential part of the equation, and our troops seemed destined for a lengthy stay. But the Iraq experience leveled a telling blow to the unilateralist pretensions of the "Bush revolution," forcing the administration to return to allies and institutions it had disdained and prompting the widespread realization that "the most important foreign policy challenges America faced . . . required the active cooperation of others."[24]

Notes

1. Lee H. Hamilton, *A Creative Tension: The Foreign Policy Roles of the President and Congress* (Washington: Woodrow Wilson Center Press, 2002), p. 7.

2. See the final report of the task force: *Parliamentary Assistance Programs*, Congressional Research Service, Library of Congress, March 18, 1998.

3. Our Kuwait resolution, H.Con.Res. 275, passed the House on June 23, 2000.

4. Obviously the clock was also running out for the Clinton administration, which had made Middle East peace negotiations its top foreign policy priority. See Secretary Albright's account: *Madam Secretary* (New York: Miramax Books, 2003), chap. 28.

5. See the article I wrote after the January trip: "The Truth About Peace," *Middle East Insight*, March–April 2002, pp. 53–54.

6. See John Wagner, "Price Has Stern Words for Arafat; Meeting Questioned," *Raleigh News and Observer*, January 11, 2002, p. 15A.

7. The quote is from Sharon: Robert Kaiser, "A Special Closeness," *Washington Post*, weekly ed., February 17–23, 2003, p. 14.

8. On the plans produced by these efforts, which resembled the solution proposed to Israeli and Palestinian negotiators by President Clinton at Taba at the end of his presidency, see Jackson Diehl, "A Better Road Map," *Washington Post*, October 27, 2003, p. A19; and Thomas L. Friedman, "Wanted: Fanatical Moderates," *New York Times*, November 16, 2003, p. 4–13.

9. David E. Price, "Owens' Commitment to Mideast Peace Should Inspire Others," *Roll Call*, January 29, 2003, p. 8.

10. I focused on the Road Map delay as part of an extended floor speech dealing with the prospect for war: *Congressional Record*, daily ed., March 11, 2003, p. H1740.

11. Quoted in Jonathan Riehl, "Israel Supporters Warn Bush Against Mideast Policy Shift," *Congressional Quarterly Weekly*, April 5, 2003, p. 832.

12. Letter from Edgar Bronfman, Larry Zicklin et al., dated April 29, 2003. On support and opposition among Jewish leadership, see M. J. Rosenberg, "A Firm 'Road Map,'" *Los Angeles Times*, April 6, 2003, p. M1; and Philip Weiss, "Big Jewish Leaders Tear the Road Map into Little Pieces," *New York Observer*, May 14, 2003, p. 1.

13. *Congressional Record*, daily ed., June 25, 2003, p. H5858. Casualty figures for June 4–25 taken from Israeli Ministry of Foreign Affairs and Palestine Red Crescent Society Web sites.

14. Friedman, "War of Ideas, Part 4," *New York Times*, January 18, 2004, p. 4–11. "Yet the Bush team," Friedman continued, "backed up by certain conservative Jewish and Christian activist groups, believes that the correct policy is to do nothing. Well, that is my definition of insane." On the president's disengagement from the Road Map endeavor, "slipping back into a pattern that has prevailed from the beginning of the Bush Administration," see Glenn Kessler, "'Road Map' Setbacks Highlight U.S. Pattern," *Washington Post*, October 6, 2003, p. A1. On the negative implications for Israel's long-term interests, see Gershom Gorenberg, "Road Nap," *American Prospect*, April 2004, pp. 12–14.

15. David Von Drehle, "Ears Burning, the President Takes a Reactive Tone," *Washington Post*, weekly ed., January 26–February 1, 2004, p. 7.

16. Ivo H. Daalder and James M. Lindsay, *America Unbound: The Bush Revolution in Foreign Policy* (Washington, D.C.: Brookings Institution Press, 2003), pp. 11, 13, 40–47. The "Bush revolution" also represented a break with the approach taken by the first Bush administration, as exemplified by the positioning of key players. "In the first Bush Administration, Cheney had been the outlier. He was the assertive nationalist who frequently found himself butting heads with pragmatic internationalists such as [Brent] Scowcroft, [Colin] Powell, James Baker, and the president himself. In the second Bush Administration, Powell was the outlier. Cheney, [Donald] Rumsfeld, [Condoleezza] Rice, and Bush were all to his right—with Cheney and Rumsfeld considerably so" (p. 57).

17. As Lee Hamilton later pointed out, the fact that the war was won quickly with relatively few casualties did not mean that alternative approaches could not

have worked as well. Hamilton, "Who Voted 'Wrong'?" *Washington Post*, March 10, 1991, p. D7.

18. *Congressional Record,* daily ed., October 9, 2002, pp. H7336–37. The Kissinger quote was taken from "Consult and Control: Bywords for Battling the New Enemy," *Washington Post*, September 16, 2002, p. A19.

19. *Congressional Record,* daily ed., March 11, 2003, pp. H1739–41; and September 25, 2003, pp. H8944–47. Some $12 billion of the $87 billion request was earmarked for military operations and reconstruction in Afghanistan.

20. Wilson was dispatched to Niger in early 2002 to investigate reported sales of uranium ore to Iraq. "Based on my experience with the Administration in the months leading up to the war," he wrote, "I have little choice but to conclude that some of the intelligence related to Iraq's nuclear weapons program was twisted to exaggerate the Iraqi threat." "What I Didn't Find in Africa," *New York Times*, July 6, 2003, p. 4–9.

21. See my statement during House debate: *Congressional Record,* daily ed., October 15, 2003, p. H9458.

22. We also took two days for discussions of bilateral issues with Prime Minister Faisal al-Fayez of Jordan and President Bashir Asad and Foreign Minister Farouq Sharaa of Syria. Leaders in both countries were critical of the Road Map effort, but for significantly different reasons. The Jordanians were frustrated by Bush's lack of persistence, the Syrians by the exclusive focus on the Palestinian issue as opposed to the "comprehensive" peace pursued after the Madrid Conference. Relations between the United States and Syria were at a difficult point. The Syrians had cooperated in pursuing al Qaeda and keeping the Israeli–Lebanese border quiet, but they had not cooperated satisfactorily in shutting down terrorist organizations that had bases in Syria and were doing great damage in Israel, and the United States was still pushing for a tighter sealing of the Syrian–Iraqi border. Congress's dubious contribution to the situation was the Syria Accountability Act (H.R. 1828), resisted by the State Department for two years but finally passed with the administration's acquiescence three weeks before our trip. Pushed by AIPAC, the bill required the administration to choose among several sanctions to be imposed on Syria, with limited waiver authority. The problem was not that such measures should be ruled out, but that the bill envisioned no diplomacy beyond them. "We must solidify a network of nations to confront terrorism, not stake ourselves out as an isolated combatant," I argued on the House floor. "This struggle could be far more successful with Syria as a full-fledged partner. But if that is to happen, our diplomacy will have to be far more skilled and flexible than the formula prescribed in the Syria Accountability Act." *Congressional Record,* daily ed., October 15, 2003, p. H9427.

23. "A Growing U.N. Role in Iraq," *New York Times*, February 22, 2004, p. 4–10.

24. Daalder and Lindsay, *America Unbound*, p. 195.

10

Serving the District

This book has mainly focused on the aspects of my job that I share with 434 other members of the House of Representatives in Washington, D.C. I am only one of these strong-willed people trying to shape national policy outcomes. But as I often remind constituents in my community meetings, I am the *only* one of the 435 who is responsible for assisting individuals, organizations, and local governments in the Fourth District in their dealings with the federal government. The district-based aspects of the job are as important and demanding as the three or four days per week that I normally spend in Washington. Like roughly half of my colleagues, I keep my main residence in the district and return there every weekend and every recess. I spend almost as many workdays there as in Washington, in and around the three district offices where almost half of my staff is based. And even in Washington, much of what my staff and I do is district centered. That is especially true of my work on Appropriations, as I will demonstrate in this chapter. Much of the work of my legislative aides also deals with the policy concerns of local groups and correspondents.

Keeping in Touch

Much of my time in North Carolina is spent traveling the district and maintaining an extensive schedule of public appearances. During my first four years in office, I addressed forty-four local civic club or chamber of commerce meetings; spoke at fifty-one school classes or assemblies and at nine high school, college, or professional school commencements; held ninety community meetings across the five counties; visited churches and synagogues on fifty-two occasions; and toured forty-seven district plants and research facilities. In subsequent years I continued this level of activity, with some changes in approach and emphasis.[1] Visits to schools, churches, and civic groups continued unabated. But we diversified the community meetings, often making them a component of workplace visits or holding them in retirement communities or under sponsorship of

local organizations. We added neighborhood office hours to our reper-
toire, setting up a card table in a large store or other prominent location
and talking with anyone who came by (see Figure 10.1). I also began doing "neighborhood walks" on Saturday mornings, going door to door to
seek out constituents' views and to leave information about how to contact our offices.

My community-wide meetings are still come one, come all affairs. We
announce the sessions in the press and often through postcards or newsletters sent to every box holder in a given area. I then hold an open meeting on the date announced, giving a brief report on congressional activities
and taking any and all questions from the floor. The meetings are normally
scheduled in the late afternoon or early evening in a school, town hall, or
county courthouse, and they generally draw 50 to 150 people. Most of my
presentation is about policy matters, but I always have staff members
along to assist constituents with individual problems. The openness of the
meetings lets diverse groups of constituents attend and express themselves freely. The format also can be abused by those who wish to disrupt
or by political opponents who wish to stage confrontations with their tape
recorders or video cameras running.

As the incidence of such disruptions increased in 1993–1994 (see Chapter 3), we began to vary the format—organizing meetings around specific
topics, for example, and utilizing meeting sponsors who invited their
own members or employees. After losing the 1994 election and before
deciding to run again, I felt the need to hold open discussions involving
people of varying political persuasions. These grew into the "neighborhood gatherings" held in the homes of friends, who were specifically requested to seek a diversity of participants. Such meetings are of obvious
utility during a campaign, but we continued them year-round as a means
of communication and outreach, especially in suburban neighborhoods.

Post-1996 innovations include a greater number of workplace visits,
with community meeting–type discussions with employees almost always included in the schedule, and forays into the shopping centers via
neighborhood office hours. I have found that people who would never
venture to a community meeting will come by neighborhood office hours
on seeing an announcement or spotting me there. Various supermarkets
and other large stores cooperate in making well-traveled space available,
although some hold the view that anything involving a member of Congress is "political" and therefore to be avoided. In fact, neighborhood office hours are neither advertised nor conducted as political events, and
we discontinue them during the campaign season. A two-hour session
will normally involve a steady flow of constituents talking with staff

FIGURE 10.1   Neighborhood office hours.

members and me about a wide array of issues and their needs for personal assistance.

We have also continued a number of annual events aimed at particular groups of constituents. The Farm Breakfast became a Fourth District tradition under my predecessor, Rep. Ike Andrews, and I now cohost it with my Second and Thirteenth District colleagues, Bob Etheridge and Brad Miller. Agriculture Secretary Dan Glickman was once our guest speaker, and various congressional and administration leaders have joined us. We generally attract 150 to 200 farmers and others involved in agribusiness or agricultural research. The annual Veterans Breakfast, which we organize in conjunction with major veterans organizations, has a similar format and generally attracts about 120 to 150 on or around Veterans Day. We also sponsor a multidistrict small business procurement workshop, Marketplace, with the cooperation of our Small Business and Technology Development Center and the procurement offices at the Environmental Protection Agency (EPA) and National Institute of Environmental Health Sciences (NIEHS). The last time this workshop was held, we had booths for some 50 federal agencies, military bases, and prime contractors and some 450 business participants.

Much of my local scheduling involves responding to invitations, but we often work with friends in creating our own opportunities and events. For example, we regularly schedule town meetings with senior citizens organizations and in the numerous retirement communities that have sprung up across the district. We make a special effort to reach business-people, sometimes through town meetings or breakfast briefings organized by the chamber of commerce or other business organizations, sometimes with sessions involving start-up entrepreneurs, trade-oriented firms, or other groups that we organize ourselves.

The advent of e-mail, faxes, and low-cost long distance calls has made it easier for constituents to communicate with me and for interest groups and advocacy organizations to generate a large volume of incoming messages. Before the September 11, 2001, terrorist attacks and the discovery of anthrax powder in letters addressed to congressional offices, one-third of the written communications I received from constituents came via e-mail. Now less than a third comes by regular mail, which is often delayed and rendered brittle by the irradiation to which it is subjected. The total volume of letters, e-mails, and calls from the Fourth District averages about 600 contacts per week. My policy is to respond in writing to every communication from a constituent, and our greatest ongoing management challenge is to ensure that these letters and e-mails are on point and on time. There is a trade-off between speed and substance. Some offices achieve fast turnaround by sending responses that are little more than acknowledgments; we tend to take more time to make appropriate individual modifications to standardized letters and to include more information. My district is relatively demanding in terms of the volume, diversity, and sophistication of constituent contacts, and my staff and I devote a large part of our time to producing effective responses.

We initiate a great deal of communication ourselves. Like most members, I maintain a home page on the Internet, which contains recent speeches and press releases as well as basic information about me and my offices and how we can be of help. I communicate with the district through one or two newsletters per year, which are mailed to every box holder and mainly focus on legislative matters. I also make extensive use of specialized "targeted" mailings that provide legislative updates for people I know are interested in education, health care, the environment, or other issues, and I have begun to send periodic briefings on congressional activity to my e-mail subscribers.

At least once each Congress, I include a mail-back questionnaire in a newsletter and also post it online, giving constituents an opportunity to register their views on a number of major issues. Having been skeptical of the way some members asked loaded questions designed to elicit preferred responses, I have tried to word my questions straightforwardly. We usually get a good rate of response—5,000 to 6,000 questionnaires completed, many with elaborations on answers written in the margins or in accompanying letters. We spend a great deal of time tabulating and disseminating the results and sending out specific responses when needed. It is well worth the effort, for this enables us to establish a direct communications link with thousands of new people and develop lists of constituents interested in particular issues for future reference.

During most of my years in office, I have appeared on a monthly call-in show on cable television's local access channel. Because Time Warner Cable now owns all the systems in my district, we can reach the entire area with a single broadcast. Thanks to the efforts of producer Bill Bagley, *Keeping in Touch* has steadily improved in production quality and has won a couple of Telly Awards from the communications industry's Center for Creativity (Figure 10.2). We sometimes include clips from a recent speech on the House floor or a brief presentation on a pressing issue, but the show focuses on the callers and gives me a chance to respond with more than sound bites. Because local systems rerun the shows frequently, channel surfers sometimes get the impression that I am omnipresent.

My staff and I also try to maintain effective contact with the news media in the district. Members of the media, especially television, are often attracted to campaign fireworks, but it takes considerably more effort to interest them in the day-to-day work of Congress. We send television feeds by satellite to local stations from Washington, offer radio commentary about matters of current interest, and arrange interviews on these topics when I am home. We provide a steady stream of press releases to newspaper, radio, and television outlets; most either offer news about my initiatives or interpret major items of congressional business, often relating them to North Carolina. We also furnish copies of my statements and speeches and let stations know when they can pick up my floor appearances on C-SPAN.

A different strategy is required to meet the needs of smaller radio stations and weekly newspapers, which will generally cover a member of Congress only when he or she visits the community or announces something that pertains to that locality. We let these outlets know when and why I will be in town, and I often arrange to drop by the radio station or newspaper office while there. The smaller papers are also concerned with human-interest items, such as pictures of local school groups that recently visited Washington or summer interns in my office from that community.

Considerable ingenuity is required to relate the work of the Congress to local concerns in an informative and interesting way and to provide the "visuals" that television requires. In announcing a homeland security

FIGURE 10.2   On the set of my call-in cable show, *Keeping in Touch*, with host
Clay Johnson. Photo by Bill Bagley.

research grant to North Carolina State University, for example, we
treated the local media to a "pyro-man" demonstration, showing how
protective clothing being developed enabled a mannequin to withstand
intense flames. Announcing the introduction of my Teaching Fellows Act
in the empty NCSU football stadium dramatized the number of teaching
positions North Carolina needed to fill (see Chapter 6), just as announcing a school construction initiative in the midst of trailers serving as
temporary classrooms furnished a striking visual image and reminded
viewers of the local importance of the issue. Staging a ride-along with
the local police dramatized the importance of funding I had helped secure for data retrieval systems for patrol cars, and inviting the press to a
campus-based child care center at North Carolina Central University
highlighted a provision I was pushing for inclusion in the Higher Education Act.

　As congressional districts become more populous and spill over existing community boundaries and as constituents become more reliant on
the media and less on personal and party channels for their political in-

formation, members must develop extensive mail and media operations if they are to communicate effectively. There is no substitute for moving around the district personally; people like to see their representatives. But such forays miss thousands of people, while television and computerized mail offer manifold new possibilities for reaching them. Even those of us who regard ourselves stylistically as "workhorses" still have to pay attention to media and public relations, far more than our predecessors ever did. The political landscape is littered with fallen members who assumed that their work in Washington would speak for itself and did not fully understand what effective communication under modern conditions requires. At its best, such communication conveys a sense of partnership, bringing constituents in on what is happening in Congress and what their representative is thinking and doing; it is a process of explaining and interpreting but also inviting reciprocal communications.

Media and mail operations have the potential to improve a member's political standing, and some criticize them as giving an unfair advantage to incumbents. These privileges unquestionably can be abused; I have seen members' newsletters that I thought went over the line, looking more like campaign brochures. Indeed, the line is hard to draw with precision. It is one thing to limit the quantity of mailings (House mail allowances effectively limit members to no more than two districtwide newsletter mailings per year), but it is considerably more difficult to regulate their content (one rule limits the number of times one can use "I" or "my" in a newsletter). Nevertheless, House members invite public cynicism if we do not enforce the rules seriously and, more importantly, honor the spirit of the rules personally.

Critics have a credibility problem of their own, however, when they interpret efforts to communicate as nothing more than a crass attempt to gain political advantage. My standard way of handling such charges is to invite the critics to examine the newsletter or targeted constituent letter, to see whether it communicates useful information or self-promoting puffery. The fact is that such mailings often contain information about the congressional agenda and specific issues that does not make the evening news or the daily press and is difficult to obtain otherwise. Fortunately, for every critic I have hundreds more who find these efforts to communicate informative and valuable.

Casework and Grants

The staff members in my three district offices spend much of their time on casework, assisting individuals and sometimes firms or organizations in their dealings with the federal government. The most common areas of concern are Social Security, Medicare, veterans benefits, tax problems, immigration and naturalization, and passports. Some of these services are routine, as when we expedite the issuance of passports; others involve convoluted disputes over benefits or entitlements that have been years in the making. We cannot tell an agency what to do; our role most often is to inform an agency of our interest in a case, seeking to ensure that it is given timely and fair consideration and that the constituent understands the reasons for the agency's decision and what, if anything, he or she can do about it.

It is impossible to please everyone. I remember an amusing demonstration of this from my days on Senator Bartlett's staff. One day the senator received a plaintive letter from a young woman fearing that her boyfriend, who was stationed at a military base in Alaska, was about to be transferred out of the state. Could the senator do anything to help? While my friend who handled military cases was still pondering how to respond, a second letter came from the serviceman himself. Dear Senator Bartlett, he asked, could you please help me get transferred out of Alaska as soon as possible?!

Our interventions often result in the correction of an agency error or the rectification of an injustice. In one such case, a family petitioning for asylum to the Immigration and Naturalization Service (INS) had traveled to Arlington, Virginia, for an interview as instructed by the agency, only to be told that no interview had been scheduled. After waiting for nine months for the interview to be rescheduled, family members contacted our office. We found that their case had been mistakenly closed and their file sent to storage. The INS then reopened the case, and asylum was granted just in time for their daughter, about to turn twenty-one, to be included in the petition. In another instance, the widow of a veteran had applied numerous times for Veterans Administration survivor benefits for her daughter, but because of various bureaucratic snafus, the claim was never processed. Four days after my staff contacted the VA regional office, the benefits were started, and retroactive payments totaling $2,632 were sent. A third case involved a small business with considerable experience in specialized electronics work for the military. The firm was unable to bid on a particular job because military procurement officials had decided not to open the project to competitive bidding. Our inquiries revealed that the military had no defensible reason for this decision; subsequently, the bidding process was opened, and the local firm was able to pursue the contract.

The collapse of communism in the Soviet Union and Eastern Europe and the economic hardships that followed spawned numerous emigration cases involving my office—family reunification, the adoption of orphaned and abandoned children, and so forth. It opened up a remarkable family saga for a constituent of mine who had fled from Poland in the 1930s as Nazism swept across Europe. He had heard secondhand that his brother and father had been killed early in the war and had presumed them dead for fifty years. Then in 1992, totally out of the blue, he received a letter from someone purporting to be his brother from the capital of one of the former Soviet states. He was excited but wary, fearing that someone was using his brother's name in an effort to get money or to leave the country. The constituent came to my office, asking for help in determining whether the correspondent was really his long-lost brother. My aide worked with the State Department on a plan whereby my constituent would write several questions to which only his brother would know the answers (What was our father's nickname? What color was his hair?—a trick question, for he had lost his hair early in life—and so forth). The brother was then called to the U.S. embassy, was asked the questions by an official, and answered them perfectly. The brothers were overjoyed to find each other, and my constituent brought his brother by my office for a memorable visit when he came to the United States a few weeks later.

Congressional casework often provides a kind of appeals process for bureaucratic decisions, a function that has sometimes been likened to that of the ombudsman in Scandinavian countries. It is not an ideal mechanism, and constituents vary considerably in their ability and inclination to use it. Nonetheless, House members have a strong incentive not only to help constituents who present themselves but also to advertise the availability of their services and handle the cases in ways that inspire favorable comment. A reputation for good constituent service is an important political asset; party and ideological differences often mean nothing to a constituent who has been helped, just as they mean nothing to us as we perform the service.[2] Helping people in these ways is inherently satisfying, and the results are frequently more immediate and tangible than in legislative work.

Casework experiences sometimes lead members to fixes that go beyond individual cases. I have already described (Chapter 6) how complaints from constituents who had paid off their FHA-insured mortgages led to one of my amendments to the 1990 Housing Bill. Our experiences with several constituents with disabilities, whose medical benefits were denied once their condition improved enough to let them leave the house or take a job, led me to seek more rational eligibility rules. I petitioned the Health Care Financing Administration (HCFA) and supported corrective legislation, which passed in 1999. Since my appointment to the

Veterans Affairs–Housing and Urban Development (VA-HUD) Appropriations Subcommittee, I have used hearings and committee reports to call the VA to account for long delays in veterans eligibility determinations in the North Carolina regional office and to push the department toward needed changes. Our experience has been even worse with the INS, with long waiting lists and interminable delays in processing applications for visas and naturalization. In 1999 I sat with the Commerce, Justice, and State Appropriations Subcommittee when the INS commissioner testified, in order to seek specific assurances on backlog reduction in the Southeast region. Now, as a member of the new Homeland Security Appropriations Subcommittee with jurisdiction over successor agencies to the INS, I am able to act on such concerns more directly.

Members are also often asked for assistance with another sort of bureaucratic decision: funding projects and proposals submitted by local agencies and organizations. Many of these organizations are already well versed in the funding process, and they simply ask me to register support for their applications. But sometimes we need to help at ground level. A staff member in my district office works with groups to identify possible funding sources and demystify the application process, and we periodically hold meetings and workshops to share information about funding opportunities, especially in the housing area. Occasionally I need to work with an organization to ensure that its proposal is suitable for my support and/or agency approval. For example, I initially declined to endorse Raleigh's application to HUD for a HOPE VI grant to demolish and replace dilapidated public housing because of the number of people it would displace and the lack of local consensus around the project. The city responded to feedback from my office and HUD, consulted more widely, revised its application, and eventually received a $36 million grant.

The ground rules for expressing support or advocating for a project to be funded at the discretion of a federal agency, generally after a process of professional review, are not always clear. Precedents and practices vary from program to program. In some cases, when asked by an applicant in whom I have confidence, I have simply dropped a note to the agency, flagging the application as one I hope will be given careful consideration. On other occasions, my staff and I have gotten more directly involved, for example, helping nudge applications for wastewater treatment grants from small towns in my district through the Farmers Home Administration (now the Rural Utilities Service) approval process, arguing strenuously for a Raleigh-Durham Airport/American Airlines London route application at the White House, and bringing U.S. Postal Service officials into high-growth communities to witness and assess the need for new facilities.

In one instance, I feared that unorthodox features of a funding application for a county's magnet schools might lead to a routine rejection. Consequently I took pains to ensure that Department of Education officials understood the rationale for the unorthodox features and gave the proposal individual attention. Occasionally I have intervened when trouble developed in what should have been a routine review and award process—as when a local university's grant for an engineering research center from the National Science Foundation got held up in an interagency dispute. Such applications from local groups, institutions, and governments are more numerous than requests for direct appropriations, and the procedures for handling them are far more routinized, located in another branch of government. Yet a member of Congress does well to follow them closely and can sometimes intervene with good effect.

Appropriations

Local organizations, agencies, and individuals seeking federal funding approach the appropriations process in various ways. For programs where localities are entitled to a share, determined by objective criteria, of the funds available (e.g., HUD community development block grants), local governments lobby for the largest overall appropriation possible. For programs where traditions of peer review and merit selection are strong, such as National Institutes of Health (NIH) and National Science Foundation (NSF) research grants, scientists and institutional applicants in my district urge generous overall funding. Earmarking specific projects and bypassing the merit-selection process are resisted. In areas like agriculture and transportation, where earmarking is a well-established tradition and those who eschew such tactics are likely to be left at the gate, I am often asked to write specific projects into bills. But in all of these instances it is clear that appropriations is a lifeline to the district and the Appropriations Committee is an important place to be.

I have already described a number of my appropriations initiatives and the decentralized and bipartisan character of the committee's operations (see Chapter 6). Some of what I was able to do under Democratic control (e.g., securing funding for a nutritional educational center in Raleigh and for construction of the North Carolina State University Animal and Poultry Waste Management Center, both from unconventional sources in the agriculture appropriations bill) would have been more difficult from a minority position. On the other hand, my success in authorizing full construction costs for the EPA lab and establishing the secondary market pilot project at HUD left me saying after the 105th

Congress that I had done as well under Republican leadership as when my own party was in control.

I was able to secure favorable action on a number of items as a petitioner from outside the committee during my first two terms, often with the help of Bill Hefner, an Appropriations member from my state who had the distinct advantage of being a subcommittee chairman, one of the so-called college of cardinals. But in 1991, as a new Appropriations member, I was able to lift my sights considerably. Drawing on my augmented staff resources, I consulted widely in the district and statewide, gathering the information I needed to defend an expanded list of projects but also winnowing through the growing number of requests my new position attracted. Sometimes I had to ask for help (e.g., from the state Department of Transportation and the NCSU central research office) in coordinating the flow of requests and setting priorities among them. I tried to ensure that every proposal I submitted had a solid justification and could demonstrate complementary funding from nonfederal sources, and I avoided pie-in-the-sky requests. Following these rules helped me attain a batting average well over .500, though I also experienced many disappointments.

I concentrated initially on my two subcommittee assignments: transportation and agriculture. In both cases, I developed a list of funding priorities, which my staff reviewed in detail with the subcommittee staff and I then discussed with the subcommittee chairman. I asked three witnesses from the district to come to Washington for the transportation hearings—the Raleigh transportation director, the head of the regional transit authority, and the director of the Raleigh-Durham Airport—to engage them in the process and make our case publicly. In the end, all had reason to be pleased, for our committee's bill contained $750,000 for the federal share of a $1 million study of long-range transportation needs and possible mass-transit alternatives in the Research Triangle area, a grant to the city of Raleigh to purchase ten vans for an experimental suburban feeder service for the city's bus system, an earmarking of Amtrak funds to support an additional intrastate train for North Carolina, $2.5 million to upgrade the instrument landing system at Raleigh-Durham Airport, and a directive to the FAA to permanently install the airport's experimental radar system on schedule. The agriculture bill included several similar funding items and a programmatic initiative: $2.5 million in program preparation assistance for nonprofit organizations to put together rural housing proposals in an attempt to remedy the sporadic utilization of Farmers Home Administration programs we had found in North Carolina.[3]

Committee membership also placed me in an improved position to request assistance from other subcommittees for the NIEHS and EPA con-

struction projects discussed in Chapter 6; multi-university research con-
sortia (including NCSU) on textiles, severe storms, and air quality; various
land acquisition and preservation projects; and such foreign operations
and defense items as the MBA Enterprise Corps and others mentioned in
Chapter 9.

In two areas of particular local importance, I wrote directives into appropriations bills after years of cajoling federal agencies to do right by my
constituents. In the fiscal year 1995 energy and water bill we ordered the
Army Corps of Engineers to raise the height of the dam at Falls Lake,
which contained most of Raleigh's future water supply, thus correcting a
major shortfall from the lake's original intended capacity. And in the 1995
VA-HUD bill we earmarked funding for a long-sought Veterans Center in
Raleigh. The veterans population in Raleigh was among the largest of any
city in the country without one of these centers, which offered counseling,
group therapy, and other mental health services, particularly to Vietnam
veterans.

I recounted in Chapter 5 how, on returning to the House in 1997, I lost
my Transportation Subcommittee seat only to pick up VA-HUD. My new
assignment gave me the opportunity to pursue matters of national and
local interest involving HUD, VA, NSF, EPA, the National Aeronautics
and Space Administration (NASA), and other agencies as well as to provide direct support for urban corridor development and community center construction in Durham; wastewater and water reuse projects in
Pittsboro, Efland, Hillsborough, Holly Springs, and Cary; an EPA-NCCU
partnership to research environmental hazards in minority communities;
NCSU research on the biological effects of weightlessness and the outfit-
ting of a Mobile Science bus by the UNC Morehead Planetarium; and
other projects. Fortunately there was no equivalent loss in dropping
Transportation. Successive leaders of that subcommittee proved responsive to my annual requests for funding for buses and bus facilities and for
regional rail as the Triangle Transit Authority's plans for service from
Raleigh to Cary, RTP, and Durham advanced.

Although the mix of local and national concerns is especially evident in
the work of the Appropriations Committee, it is built into every member's
job description. Most of us are constantly attentive to our districts, proposing legislation and securing funding, interpreting and explaining what
Congress is doing and how we are representing our constituents, deploy-
ing staff and budgeting our own time and attention. Life in Congress is, by
definition, a divided existence: living in Washington and in the home district, overseeing staff in both locations, constantly traveling between the
two, serving at once as national legislators and local representatives, both

shaping the rules and assisting individuals in coping with them. These multiple roles create strains and tensions with which members must learn to deal. But the mix can be enormously challenging and stimulating. At least, that is the way I have experienced it. I know of no other job like the one I have, and I feel extraordinarily fortunate to be where I am.

Notes

1. These changes do not, for the most part, reflect the movement from "expansionist" to "protectionist" stages in relating to the constituency that Richard Fenno found characterized most members' careers. See Fenno, *Home Style: House Members in Their Districts* (Boston: Little, Brown, 1978), p. 172. The nature of my district—rapidly growing, politically volatile—has required constant and expansive outreach, as has the addition of new territory through redistricting.

2. For a sophisticated analysis of the relation of constituency services to electoral success, see Douglas Rivers and Morris P. Fiorina, "Constituency Service, Reputation, and the Incumbency Advantage," in Morris P. Fiorina and David W. Rohde, eds., *Home Style and Washington Work* (Ann Arbor: University of Michigan Press, 1989), pp. 17–45.

3. See *Affordable Housing,* field hearing before the Subcommittee on Housing and Community Development, Committee on Banking, Finance, and Urban Affairs, U.S. House of Representatives, 101st Congress, January 26, 1990 (serial no. 101–75), pp. 60–61, 65–67.

11

Religion and Politics

I had the good fortune to come of age politically in the early years of the modern civil rights movement—the years between the Montgomery, Alabama, bus boycott that brought Martin Luther King Jr. to prominence (1955–1956) and the passage of the landmark Civil Rights Act of 1964. I say good fortune because of the particularly challenging and positive kind of political experience this movement gave me and thousands like me in my student generation. Had we come along a few years earlier, I often thought, we would have faded into the blandness of the Eisenhower years. And the generation following ours had a far different political experience as the civil rights movement splintered into reformist and radical wings and the Vietnam War brought forth disillusionment, protest, and fierce political conflict. Many lost faith in politics as an instrument of positive change.

This contrasted markedly with the climactic moment of my own early political experience, which occurred on June 19, 1964, during my second summer as a junior staff member in a U.S. Senate office. On that day, I crowded into the Senate gallery to witness the final passage of the Civil Rights Act. It could scarcely have been a more dramatic moment, as the dying Sen. Clair Engle (D-California) was wheeled into the chamber to cast this momentous vote. It was a moment capable of convincing a young person that the system worked, that enough dedicated people, working together, could right ancient wrongs—a fitting climax to the formative political years that many in my generation experienced.

An important element in this experience for many of us was religion. Our religious backgrounds shaped our response to the civil rights struggle, and our religious outlook was challenged and broadened in turn. Religion had been central to my own upbringing; the Price family had been pillars of the First Christian Church of Erwin, Tennessee, ever since my grandfather's family had moved there in 1901. We were present whenever the church doors were open, including Sunday evening services and Wednesday night prayer meetings. Henry Webb, the minister there during

my teenage years who also taught at nearby Milligan College, particularly
influenced me. I went off to Mars Hill College intending to be an engineer,
as befitted a member of the Sputnik generation, but with Webb's urging
that I consider the ministry in the back of my mind.

Mars Hill was identified with a Baptist regimen considerably stricter
than my own upbringing. However, Robert Seymour, the community's
young pastor who had trained at Yale Divinity School, helped me and
many others move from a primarily individualistic understanding of our
faith to appreciate its social and prophetic dimensions. Just before I transferred to the University of North Carolina, Seymour came to Chapel Hill
to help found the Binkley Memorial Baptist Church, a progressive, racially
inclusive congregation affiliated with the American as well as the Southern Baptist Convention.[1] This became my church home in Chapel Hill, as
it still is today. And despite my lack of Baptist credentials, I was elected
president of the Baptist Student Union at the University of North Carolina.

On campus the religious organizations took the lead in protesting discrimination and pressing for change. Many took to heart Martin Luther
King's indictment of the church as a "thermometer that records the ideas
and principles of popular opinion," rather than a "thermostat that trans-
forms the mores of society."[2] And many of us saw in civil rights a challenge
to translate the personal ethic of "love thy neighbor" into social terms.

One who has lived through such an experience is unlikely to make the
mistake of assuming that the separation of church and state can or should
mean a neat compartmentalizing of religion and politics. Indeed, the ensuing years have seen an increase in religiously oriented political movements.
A number of those churches that King criticized for their "completely
other-worldly religion [making] a strange, un-Biblical distinction between
body and soul, between the sacred and the secular"[3] have been politically
mobilized, though frequently in the service of an agenda considerably different from what King had in mind. As a result, the debate over the place of
religion in politics has intensified. In the present chapter, I will reflect on
how that debate has looked from Capitol Hill and how its terms might be
clarified.

Religious Agendas

If I had not already been sensitive to the problematic relationship between religion and politics by virtue of my own religious background
and divinity school training, my first campaign, against an incumbent
identified with the religious right, certainly would have made me so. I
have already described his "Dear Christian Friend" letter to prospective
supporters, warning that he might be replaced by "someone who is not

willing to take a strong stand for the principles outlined in the Word of God" (i.e., me). But that experience paled in comparison to what I encountered in 1994, with the Christian Coalition at the peak of its influence nationally and locally. People involved with or influenced by the coalition and like-minded organizations flooded our offices with calls and provoked confrontations in community meetings. Churchgoers across the district found Christian Coalition scorecards giving me a zero rating on their windshields the Sunday before the election. A woman who snarled in my face at a North Raleigh polling place epitomized the onslaught for me: "You're a counterfeit Christian!"

As someone who thought, by virtue of my own religious background and involvement, that I would have something in common with almost anyone approaching politics from a perspective of faith, these negative experiences came as a rude awakening. The civil rights movement had taught me a powerful lesson in interfaith cooperation and had convinced me of religion's power to heal and unify, as people from diverse traditions found common ground in attacking injustice. What I have since confronted is religion's capacity to exclude and divide. Fortunately I have had enough positive experiences to convince me that communication and even collaboration across religious boundaries are still possible. For example, our coalition in attempting to reverse the FCC media concentration rules in 2003 (see Chapter 6) included the Family Research Council and the Traditional Values Coalition.

It is important not to overgeneralize about the political attitudes of conservative or evangelical Christians. Our early polls, when the Rev. Jerry Falwell was the religious right's most prominent spokesman, showed that, of the 20 percent of white voters of the Fourth District who regarded themselves as fundamentalists, only 36 percent expressed a favorable view of Falwell. Later polls showed 34 percent of the white voters in the district identifying themselves as fundamentalists or evangelicals but only 43 percent of this group evaluating the Christian Coalition positively. Many, perhaps most, of the others resisted the efforts of self-styled leaders to mobilize them on behalf of their political agenda.

The second half of the present chapter had its origin as a talk prepared for a 1986 meeting with local ministers that I had scheduled before the "Dear Christian Friend" letter. It took on added significance after the letter appeared. In subsequent campaigns (and, even more, between campaigns) I have continued to meet with ministers and religious leaders, visit congregations, and speak to Sunday school classes and other religious forums. I have worshiped with dozens of African American congregations, which I have found especially welcoming (although many look askance at candidates who do not remain for the entire service or drop in only during

campaign season). I began working with congregations and religious organizations on housing and social service initiatives (e.g., the construction
of housing for the elderly under the HUD section 202 program) long before "faith-based initiatives" became a buzzword. Extra-congregational
groups such as Bread for the World and Witness for Peace have been active
in my district. Much of this demonstrates how the awakening of social
concern and activism that I witnessed in the 1960s has continued to characterize American religious life.

Still, in my district and across the country, the religious right is a force
to be reckoned with. During my early years in office, the issue that inspired the most communication and advocacy from religious communities was the Civil Rights Restoration Act of 1988—*against* the bill. I found
this especially ironic and sad in light of my memories of the passage of
the 1964 Civil Rights Act (which the 1988 proposal sought to protect from
adverse judicial interpretations). To be sure, the mainline Protestant,
Catholic, and Jewish bodies lined up in favor of the bill. But their efforts
at grassroots mobilization were anemic compared to the thousands of letters and calls from the other side that kept the phones in all of my offices
tied up for two weeks. "Grove City" (the bill's shorthand designation,
taken from the Supreme Court decision it sought to reverse) was talked
about among my staff for years, becoming the high-water mark against
which all future floods of calls about flag burning, gun control, congressional pay raises, and the like, were measured.

Many of the calls were inspired by a widely circulated memorandum
from Jerry Falwell, head of the Moral Majority, that described this rather
modest bill as "the greatest threat to religious freedom and traditional
moral values ever passed." The Civil Rights Restoration Act, he warned,
could force churches "to hire a practicing active homosexual drug addict
with AIDS to be a teacher or youth pastor."[4] My incredulity that people
could ever believe such an absurd statement was overwhelmed by the
mass of calls that we received, many from well-meaning, genuinely concerned people. In the end, however, Falwell and his allies did not succeed, and the White House operatives who had hoped the religious right
could help them sustain President Reagan's veto of the bill had reason to
doubt the utility of the alliance. It was a textbook case of a lobby overreaching—using such outrageous tactics and such absurd misinformation
that it became a point of honor with members not to be swayed. As Bill
Hefner said on the House floor,

> I find reprehensible not those thousands of people who have made the
> phone calls, but . . . the people that have instigated this misinformation. . . .
> If it means that I lose my position in the U.S. House of Representatives [if I

do not] cave in . . . and base my vote on what people believe to be true but what I know not to be true, I say to my colleagues this job is not worth that to me.[5]

In the end, the House voted to override the veto by 292–133, displaying remarkably little slippage from the original vote in favor of the bill (315–98).

A new offensive by religious right organizations was evident in 1990, nowhere more so than in North Carolina, with Sen. Jesse Helms on the ballot, organized mainly around three issues: abortion, pornography, and child care. Abortion, of course, is the touchstone issue for most of these groups. Pornography was revived as an issue by controversies over the funding of some allegedly obscene and sacrilegious works of art by the National Endowment for the Arts (NEA). Congress sent the NEA an unmistakable message in 1988, cutting its appropriation by the amount of the offending works, and set up additional procedures for the review of grants. This was not enough, however, for politicians like Senator Helms and many of the protesting organizations that had their own reasons for keeping the pornography issue alive.

The most anomalous of this triumvirate of issues—and certainly the strangest protest effort for organizations professing concern for family values—was child care. I gained a greater understanding of some of the angry calls and letters we had been getting on this subject when I happened to tune in to James Dobson's national radio program, *Focus on the Family*. Ironically, his preoccupation that day was with distortion—the way the media had deliberately (and conspiratorially, he thought) underestimated the size and enthusiasm of the antiabortion demonstrations recently held in Washington. Dobson then turned to the child care bill just passed by the House and proceeded to give the most distorted account of it imaginable.

This was something I knew a good deal about for I had been active in the discussions and compromises undertaken prior to the consideration of the child care issue on the House floor. It was an important bill that expanded the remarkably successful Head Start program in early childhood education, authorized school-based latchkey programs for young children who otherwise would go home to empty houses each day, and expanded social services block grants to the states for child care assistance. The critics argued that the bill encouraged mothers not to stay at home with their children, showing remarkable insensitivity to single-parent households or to the economic factors often forcing both parents to work. Mothers who stayed home often did so at some financial sacrifice, and we agreed to an expansion of the earned income tax credit for families with young children that could be claimed both by families that purchased child care and those with stay-at-home mothers. We also responded to the critics' claim that the bill discriminated against church-based day care; we agreed that the model of church–state separation applicable to public education was not appropriate here and devised a program of certificates and vouchers that could be utilized at church-run centers.

These compromises, which addressed what the critics had said were their major concerns, had no effect on leaders like James Dobson or on many of their followers, like the angry "stay-at-home moms" who packed my community meetings. They seemed determined to maintain the sense of a great cultural and religious divide between themselves and politicians like me, the sense that their "traditional values" were being conspired against. I finally concluded, admittedly with some difficulty, that I was wasting my breath to discuss what the child care bill actually contained.

By the time President Clinton took office in 1993, the Christian Coalition had replaced the Moral Majority as the vanguard of the religious right and wielded sufficient influence within the Republican Party to give issues like abortion and the status of gays and lesbians a prominent place on the opposition agenda. Clinton's proposal to lift the ban on gays in the military and the modification of several long-standing anti-abortion policies deepened the antagonism of religious conservatives toward the administration and Democrats in Congress. By early 1994, the pattern was well established: Every few weeks a flood of calls and letters would materialize on the current issue of choice. At one point, the focus was on the right to protest at abortion clinics, at another on (unfounded) accusations that the Equal Employment Opportunity Commission intended to forbid Bibles or religious objects in workplaces, or on alleged threats to home schooling from educational authorities.

The reauthorization of the Elementary and Secondary Education Act provided a cornucopia of opportunities for attack by religious conservatives and their allies. Consideration of the legislation continued intermittently for four weeks in February and March; during that time, the House passed amendments eliminating any requirement that parents involved in home schooling be certified (a requirement the bill had never contained) and withholding federal money from school districts that prohibited voluntary prayer in school. Additional amendments, to make eligibility for federal funding dependent on the teaching of abstinence in sex education programs and to prohibit any programs "encouraging or supporting" homosexuality as a lifestyle (thus putting much counseling in jeopardy) were averted by the proposal and passage of Democratic alternatives.[6] If I had any doubt that such themes were likely to figure prominently in the 1994 campaign, they were dispelled by this debate, most of which I witnessed directly by virtue of having been chosen by the Speaker to preside, and by the rising volume of calls and letters from my district.

As the 1994 elections approached and congressional Republicans attempted to bring down most of the remaining Democratic agenda, Newt Gingrich secured an alliance with the Christian Coalition to defeat the Lobbying Disclosure Act, a reform measure that had earlier passed the House and on which members from both parties had been working for eighteen months. With Rush Limbaugh fanning the flames daily on his radio show, Gingrich and the religious right network suddenly raised the specter of grassroots Christian lobbyists being "gagged," despite language in the bill that specifically excluded religious organizations from registration or reporting requirements. Gingrich, as minority whip, led the effort to defeat the conference report on lobbying reform on procedural motions. He took the floor to warn of "grassroots gag rules" and to suggest that "an administration that appoints Roberta Achtenberg" (an acknowledged lesbian whom Clinton had appointed HUD assistant secretary for Fair Housing and Equal Opportunity) should not be allowed to interpret freedom of religious communication. I vividly remember sitting in the chamber during the debate and thinking that I had never witnessed a more cynical performance. Gingrich's effort narrowly failed but left the conference report "easy pickings" for a Republican end-of-session filibuster in the Senate.[7]

The relationship between the religious right and the Clinton administration remained adversarial, culminating in the prominent role conservative religious leaders took in seeking the president's impeachment. Most of them warmly welcomed the advent of George W. Bush, who made it clear during the 2000 campaign that he was "one of them" personally and promised action on their major issues. One of his first moves after taking office was to reinstate the "Mexico City policy" that prohibited aid to any international family planning organizations that performed or provided information about abortions, even if they used their own funds to do so. He also withheld family planning appropriations from the U.N. Fund for Population Activities, accepting the allegations of antiabortion groups that such funds could indirectly aid forced abortions in China.

In 2003, with a Republican majority in both houses, an eight-year crusade by social and religious conservatives culminated in the enactment of the so-called partial birth abortion ban. Twice vetoed by President Clinton, the measure placed federal restrictions on abortion procedures for the first time since the Supreme Court's 1973 *Roe v. Wade* decision. The

Fetal Protection Act followed in 2004. By establishing separate legal status for the fetus in cases of assaults against pregnant women, some contended that the bill could provide the foundation for a legal challenge to *Roe v. Wade.*

In the meantime, President Bush established an Office of Faith-Based and Community Initiatives in the White House and pushed for a vast expansion of the "charitable choice" provisions Congress had added to scattered welfare and antipoverty programs during the Clinton administration. The idea was to enable religious organizations to receive federal funding to deliver social services without altering their religious practices or character. But the initiative foundered in the Senate on contentious issues such as the federal funding of sectarian activity and religious discrimination in hiring, and the president instead implemented its major provisions by executive order (no. 13279) in late 2002.

This recent history helps explain why many have come to see the "religious" agenda in Washington as virtually synonymous with the program of religious conservatives. Some have come to regard religion as a dangerous and imperious presence in politics. But that is not a satisfactory conclusion or, indeed, a realistic one, given the inseparability of religious faith and belief from the wellsprings of motivation across the political spectrum. The fact that the political applications of religious convictions may be misguided or wrong does not justify dismissing or condemning all such expressions. But it does underscore the importance of thinking carefully about what the relation between religious life and the political order ought to be in a democracy.

The Two Realms

The relation of the sacred and the secular has inspired theological discussion for thousands of years. The Jewish and Christian faiths are distinctive in setting up a problematic relationship, a tension, between the kingdom of God and earthly kingdoms. In some of the earliest writings in the Hebrew scriptures, the book of Samuel, a great ambivalence is expressed about the very idea of an earthly king in Israel, so that it "may be like all the nations."[8] That ambivalence about the political realm reappears in various forms throughout the Bible.

Theologians have related the sacred and the secular, the religious and the political, in a variety of ways. This variety was best analyzed in H. Richard Niebuhr's masterful *Christ and Culture,* where a "series of typical answers" to this "perennial Christian perplexity" were elaborated.[9] Some theologians have seen worldly kingdoms as a vehicle for divine law. Others have seen this world as virtually abandoned by God. Most theologians, however, have tried to keep those two views in tension. God's word has been interpreted as both a call and a guide to social involvement. Yet God's word remains transcendent, always imperfectly embodied in our institutions, always standing in judgment over them. Other religious traditions have been much more single-minded, either in renouncing the world or in identifying earthly and Godly rule. Judaism and Christianity, over most of their histories, have maintained the tension and thus have witnessed recurring debates about what the relationship should be. I do not aim to contribute to that debate so much as to reflect on it and its implications for our contemporary American situation. My thoughts fall into six related propositions, the first being that religious faith powerfully and positively shapes our political advocacy and practice.

Our capacity to compartmentalize our lives is often quite remarkable. This was particularly evident as the civil rights movement challenged the southern church in the 1960s; people who were loving and generous in their personal relationships often saw no contradiction in their support of social practices and laws that denied others their humanity. But such compartmentalization is ultimately untenable. Many in my generation found guidance in the writings of Reinhold Niebuhr, whose interpretation of the relation of the religious ethic of love to politics is still helpful today.[10] A love ethic can never be perfectly embodied in politics, he taught, but it nonetheless compels its adherents to seek justice as a proximate public expression of love. To fail to pursue justice in our common life is just as surely a betrayal of the ethic of love as it would be to reject a neighbor's need face-to-face.

William Lee Miller brought the point home in a gloss on Jesus' familiar parable of the Good Samaritan. The Samaritan came upon a man who had been robbed and wounded. He bandaged his wounds and took him to an inn for care and safekeeping, thus proving himself a true neighbor, in contrast to the priest and Levite who "passed by on the other side." What if the Samaritan had come by the same spot next day and found another man robbed and wounded? And then suppose he met wounded and victimized travelers again and again. How long would it take him to conclude that his individual acts of kindness were not enough, that the road needed to be patrolled? "Would there not be something deficient," Miller asked, "in the faith that never [sought] to prevent the attacks on travelers? What if the servant of God would give his last bread to a starving stranger in a bread line, yet never think to ask questions about the economic conditions that cause the bread line to exist?"[11]

The civil rights movement led many people of faith to rediscover the Hebrew prophets and their call for justice that "rolled down like waters."[12] Rabbi Abraham Joshua Heschel, who worked closely with Martin Luther King, tellingly placed the call to social justice in the context of prayer, the most personal and "inward" of religious acts:

> Religion as an establishment must remain separated from the government. Yet prayer as a voice of mercy, as a cry for justice, as a plea for gentleness, must not be kept apart. Let the spirit of prayer dominate the world. Let the spirit of prayer interfere in the affairs of man. Prayer is private, a service of the heart; but let concern and compassion born of prayer dominate public life.[13]

This explains what Heschel said upon returning from the voting rights march in Selma in 1963: "I felt my legs were praying."[14]

Translating religious convictions into social action is not always simple or straightforward. In the years prior to World War II, for example, Niebuhr challenged those who interpreted the love ethic to counsel nonresistance and pacifism. Such a view, he said, owed more to Enlightenment notions of human perfectibility than to a "Christian realism" that, in taking full account of human sin and the will to power, recognized "that justice [could] be achieved only by a certain degree of coercion on the one hand, and by resistance to coercion and tyranny on the other hand."

While such realism warns against oversimplifying the task of "achieving justice in a sinful world," it also recognizes that world for what it is and thus preserves a tension between religious ideas and their historical manifestations. Our basic American political values have readily identifiable religious roots. But our religious traditions also prompt an ongoing critique of our faltering efforts to realize liberty and justice, just as they offer a corrective to the excesses of individualism and materialism in American life.

My second proposition is that in a pluralistic democracy we must seek common ground with people of diverse traditions and those whose values do not have conventional religious roots. I remember discussions in the 1960s among people whose involvement in the civil rights movement stemmed from religious convictions as to whether persons from radically different backgrounds and traditions could work together effectively for the cause. Of course, the answer to that was yes. We bring our deepest convictions and insights to our political advocacy, but at the same time, we recognize the validity of other traditions and the common ethical ground we share. In politics, we debate the issues, not the doctrines. We debate with people whose theological and philosophical perspectives differ, and we can often find a basis for concerted action. This is the happy experience of American democracy.

My third point is that if we cannot find common ground, there may be good reason for stopping short of embodying our religious and moral precepts in civil law. In the absence of a broader supportive consensus, it is often preferable to leave the individual and communal expression of conscience free.

Theologians have long debated the question put by Thomas Aquinas: "Whether an effect of law is to make men good?"[15] Our religious traditions contain lawlike moral codes that continue to shape civil law. There are also reciprocal effects, despite protestations that "you can't legislate morality." The legal order inculcates rudimentary moral standards, and obedience to the law may habituate one to at least the external forms of goodness. But morality is prior to the law, and its imperatives are never exhausted by religious or civil codes. Nor can the legal order compel behavior that is, in the deepest sense, moral. This is partly because of inevitable flaws in human law and partly because law, in its generality, falls short of the individual's moral potential. Most fundamentally, however, it is because the instrumentalities of law and government cannot compel the good will and "clean heart" from which morality springs.

Our religiously inspired judgments as to what is moral and our political judgments as to what can and should be embodied in law are related, but they are not the same thing. Their relationship is problematic even in a homogeneous religious setting. And in a country where multiple religious and ethical traditions flourish, we should move cautiously indeed in enshrining in civil law moral precepts that lack substantial support beyond a specific religious tradition. The U.S. Constitution, former New York governor Mario Cuomo acknowledged, "guarantees my right to try to convince you to adopt my religion's tenet as public law. . . . The question for the religious public official then [becomes] . . . *Should* I try?" Cuomo's suggested criterion for crossing that threshold was the presence of consensus, or the "plausibility of achieving that consensus," on the basis of convictions shared in the community at large.[16]

It is thus perfectly consistent, for example, for one who is convinced that abortion is always wrong to conclude that it is not prudent to embody a prohibition of abortion in civil law. Other criteria may also apply: For example, should religiously inspired disapproval of certain behaviors, such as same-gender sexual relations, be translated into laws that violate the principles of civil liberty, nondiscrimination, and equal opportunity—or into opposition to laws that would implement these fundamental and broadly shared democratic values? The answer, I believe, is no. Such judgments are partly prudential judgments, based on the necessary ground rules of a pluralistic society. But they are also theologically grounded judgments, based on an understanding of the voluntaristic character of religious obedience and of the limits and dangers—not least, to religious liberty—of placing the authority of the state behind any group's moral agenda.

This leads to my fourth point: that religious toleration and the separation of church and state are essential protections of the freedom of religious expression and practice. In the midst of the controversy over the use of religion in my first congressional campaign, a local minister allied with the incumbent was quoted as saying that my view represented that of a "pluralistic person in a pluralistic society." That statement is worth examining. I would readily acknowledge commitment to a pluralistic society, a society in which the expression of religious conviction is free and unimpeded. However, that does not mean that I am a "pluralistic person." In fact, the genius of a pluralistic society is its ability to combine a strength of conviction, a rootedness in tradition, with a respect for the convictions and traditions of others. And when we stand up for toleration and religious freedom, we're not suggesting that somehow our religious convictions are weak or indecisive. On the contrary, we're standing up for the strength of those convictions and defending our right to express them.

Governor Cuomo, a practicing Catholic, put it this way: "To assure our freedom, we must allow others the same freedom even if occasionally it produces conduct which we hold to be sinful. . . . I protect my right to be a Catholic by preserving your right to believe as a Jew, a Protestant or a non-believer or anything else you choose."[17] That states a basic truth, I believe, about American democracy.

The first amendment to the U.S. Constitution contains two complementary protections of religious freedom: Government is not to "establish" religion, but neither is it to prohibit "the free exercise thereof." There are to be no state-sponsored religious exercises and no religious tests, formal or informal, for political participation or election to office. Those precepts protect the freedom of religious expression we all possess. At the same time, the state is not to discriminate against religion or place undue burdens on religious practice. For example, the so-called equal access statute at the federal level, ensuring that religiously oriented school organizations will not be discriminated against because of their orientation, has been upheld by the Supreme Court.[18] After school hours, such clubs can use meeting rooms and school facilities on the same basis as other organizations.

Maintaining a delicate and judicious balance between the antiestablishment and free exercise principles is a continuing challenge for our country. Fortunately a serious threat in the form of the so-called Religious Freedom Amendment to the Constitution fell considerably short of the required two-thirds vote in the House of Representatives in 1998. This amendment, a project of the religious right, went considerably beyond the school prayer amendments of years past. It purported to improve on the first amendment in ways that would have broken down the barriers to state-sponsored religious exercises and government aid to sectarian institutions.[19] An impressive alliance of mainline religious organizations worked to defeat the amendment, and it was significant how many of the members opposing it spoke not only of protecting constitutional democracy, of which freedom from religious coercion is a cornerstone, but also of protecting freedom for the unimpeded expression of religious faith and conviction. What religious freedom is about, and what the proposed amendment threatened, is not only civil liberty but also religious faithfulness.

The boundary between establishment and free exercise was also at issue in the 2001–2002 debates over President Bush's faith-based initiative. Religious organizations and congregations had long utilized federal funding to build community centers in urban neighborhoods, provide housing for the elderly and disabled, shelter the homeless, deliver hot meals to elderly shut-ins, and provide other services. They normally carried out these activities through affiliated but legally distinct entities—often called 501(c)(3) organizations from the relevant section of the tax code—which prevented federal funds from being used for religious worship or proselytization and ensured nondiscriminatory practices in hiring and the choice of beneficiaries. This is what Bush sought to change. His legislative proposals and the executive order he ultimately issued weakened the barriers to the funding of sectarian activity and removed them with respect to discrimination in hiring. From the perspective of my district, where faith-based initiatives had flourished for years, this had the appearance of "fixing" a system that was not broken. In any event, it raised serious first amendment questions, which is why the initiative stalled in the Senate and the courts are still sorting out charitable choice issues.

My fifth point is that our religious traditions point up the limitations as well as the possibilities of politics and give us a realistic perspective on political power. These traditions reject cynicism and the placing of arbitrary limits on our aspirations, but they also provide a realistic view of human nature and the pervasiveness of sin and self-interest in society. We should have no illusions about the evils of which human beings, individually and collectively, are capable. Our task in politics therefore becomes not only to utilize power for the common good but also to check the inevitable abuses of power, to make the best of a sinful world. Reinhold Niebuhr's most quoted line is pertinent here: "Man's capacity for justice makes democracy possible; but man's inclination to injustice makes democracy necessary."[20] No policy or program, even the most well intentioned, can escape the taint of self-interest and self-seeking. Consequently the task of democracy is not only to realize our positive aspirations but also to provide a check against inevitable miscarriages of justice and abuses of power.

The framers of the Constitution believed that no governmental power could safely go unchecked. They therefore "contriv[ed] the interior structure of the government [so] that its several constituent parts [might], by their mutual relations, be the means of keeping each other in their proper places." James Madison's reflections on these arrangements revealed a persistent streak of Calvinism among these heirs of the Enlightenment:

> It may be a reflection on human nature that such devices should be necessary to control the abuses of government. But what is government itself but the greatest of all reflections on human nature? If men were angels, no government would be necessary. If angels were to govern men, neither external nor internal controls on government would be necessary. In framing a government which is to be administered by men over men, the great difficulty lies in this: You must first enable the government to control the governed; and in the next place oblige it to control itself. A dependence on the people is, no doubt, the primary control on the government; but experience has taught mankind the necessity of auxiliary precautions.[21]

Thus do we draw on our religious traditions in recognizing the distortions and dangers to which the exercise of political power is liable and in protecting ourselves against them.

It is important to distinguish this realistic view from the more simplistic antipower ideology that persistently rears its head in American politics. Government is hardly the only realm in which power exists or can be abused; political power can be used to counter or control economic or other kinds of power. Realism requires that we not only attend to the dangers of strengthening a given organ of government but also ask what powers and interests might fill the vacuum if it is weakened. There is nothing automatically efficacious about checkmated governmental institutions; a simplistic distrust of power is sometimes a poor guide to what is required to make institutions function accountably and effectively. What the realism rooted in our religious traditions offers is, rather, an awareness of the admixture of self-interest and self-seeking in all human endeavors, of the necessity to use power deliberately as we pursue the common good, and also of the need for checks and safeguards as we recognize the vulnerability of such power to distortion and abuse.

A final and related point is this: Our religious traditions warn against absolutizing anyone's political power or program, regarding this as a form of idolatry. The very worst kind of pride is often religious pride: equating our own point of view, our own interest or ideology, with the will of God. Here too Heschel spoke with eloquence:

> We must not regard any human institution or object as being an end in itself. Man's achievements in this world are but attempts, and a temple that comes to mean more than a reminder of the living God is an abomination.[22]

There is a story in the book of Samuel that, as far as I know, is unique in the ancient world. King David, at the height of his power and prestige, commits a grievous sin, and the lowly prophet Nathan visits him and calls him to account, pronouncing God's judgment: "Why have you despised the word of the Lord, to do what is evil in his sight?"[23] God's word stands above even David, king of all Israel. The conviction that no person or institution stands above or is to be identified with God's will is at the very heart of our religious traditions.

The American statesman who best understood this was Abraham Lincoln. Recall the words of his second inaugural address, all the more remarkable for being uttered after almost four years of civil war:

> Both [sides] read the same Bible, and pray to the same God; and each invokes His aid against the other. It may seem strange that any men should dare to ask a just God's assistance in wringing their bread from the sweat of other men's faces; but let us judge not, that we be not judged. The prayers of both could not be answered-that of neither has been answered fully.[24]

Niebuhr once wrote that this passage "puts the relation of our moral commitments in history to our religious reservations about the partiality of our moral judgments more precisely than, I think, any statesman or theologian has put them."[25] Lincoln expressed the moral commitment against slavery in uncompromising terms, along with his determination to "finish the work we are in." But there followed the religious reservation, the recognition that ultimate judgment belonged to God alone, the refusal, even in this extreme instance, to presume an absolute identification between his own cause and God's will.

On another occasion, responding to a clergyman who expressed the hope that the Lord was on the side of the Union, Lincoln reportedly said, "I know that the Lord is always on the side of the right. But it is my constant anxiety and prayer that I and this nation should be on the Lord's side."[26] We are too quick to claim that God is on our side, to claim divine sanction for the program that we are promoting or the power that we seek, and sometimes to demonize our opponents. "As all 'God-fearing' men of all ages," Niebuhr warned, we "are never safe against the temptation of claiming God too simply as the sanctifier of whatever we most fervently desire."[27] The crucial question is the one that Lincoln asked: Are we on the Lord's side? We ought never to lose that sense of God's transcendence and of the fallibility of all our human efforts, political and otherwise. This is the ultimate reason for rejecting the political pretensions and religious arrogance of those who equate their own program with God's will. Here too we look not only to the tenets of pluralism and the U.S. Constitution but to the deepest insights of our religious traditions themselves. For these traditions counsel a kind of religious humility, a sense that our own strivings are always subject to God's judgment.

The imperatives of faith will continue to require and inspire political action. The fact that others may put a religious label on policies too easily or quickly or opportunistically does not make the imperative of faith any less compelling. But there are good reasons (rooted not only in democratic experience but also in the theology of divine transcendence and human sinfulness) for refusing to identify any particular ideology or political program with the will of God and for rebuking those who presume to do so. "For my thoughts are not your thoughts, neither are your ways my ways, says the Lord."[28]

Notes

1. Seymour gives an account of his ministry, particularly as it concerned the struggle for racial justice, in *"Whites Only": A Pastor's Retrospective on Signs of the New South* (Valley Forge, Pa.: Judson, 1991).

2. Martin Luther King Jr., "Letter from Birmingham Jail," in Herbert J. Storing, ed., *What Country Have I? Political Writings by Black Americans* (New York: St. Martin's, 1970), p. 128.

3. King, "Letter," p. 127.

4. Rev. Jerry Falwell, "Special Memorandum to Pastors," March 7, 1988.

5. *Congressional Record,* daily ed., March 22, 1988, p. H1041.

6. Debate on this latter amendment occasioned the most vicious personal attack I ever witnessed on the House floor. Representative Steve Gunderson

(R-Wisconsin), who had acknowledged that he was gay, spoke in opposition to the amendment. He was immediately attacked by Rep. Robert Dornan (R-California): "He has a revolving door on his closet. He's in, he's out, he's in, he's out, he's in. I guess you're [now] out because you went up and spoke at a huge homosexual dinner." The manager of the bill, Rep. Bill Ford (D-Michigan), demanded that Dornan's words be "taken down" because of the personal and demeaning nature of the attack. As presiding officer, I was astounded by the viciousness of the attack and needed considerable guidance from the parliamentarian in handling the situation. After a few minutes, Dornan withdrew his words, stopping the process short. For this reason, the text remaining in the *Congressional Record* (March 24, 1994, p. 6560) does not reflect the full exchange.

7. *Congressional Record,* daily ed., September 29, 1994, pp. H10277–78; and *Congressional Quarterly Almanac* 50 (1994): 42.

8. 1 Samuel 8:20.

9. H. Richard Niebuhr, *Christ and Culture* (New York: Harper, 1956), p. 2.

10. See Harry R. Davis and Robert C. Good, eds., *Reinhold Niebuhr on Politics* (New York: Scribner's, 1960), chaps. 12–14. Quotations below are from p. 148.

11. W. L. Miller, *The Protestant and Politics* (Philadelphia: Westminster, 1958), p. 24. See Luke 10:29–37.

12. Amos 5:24.

13. Abraham Joshua Heschel, "On Prayer," in Susannah Heschel, ed., *Moral Grandeur and Spiritual Audacity* (New York: Noonday, 1996), p. 261.

14. Quoted in Arthur Waskow, "'My Legs Were Praying': Theology and Politics in Abraham Joshua Heschel," *Conservative Judaism,* Winter-Spring 1998, p. 144.

15. Thomas Aquinas, *Summa Theologica,* question 92, article 1. Reprinted in D. Bigongiari, ed., *The Political Ideas of St. Thomas Aquinas* (New York: Hafner, 1953), pp. 24–26. On the "clean heart," see Psalm 51:10.

16. "As I understood my own religion," Cuomo said of his Catholicism, "it required me to accept the restraints it imposed in my own life, but it did not require that I seek to impose all of them on all New Yorkers." See the exchange between Cuomo and Rep. Mark Souder (R-Indiana) and, among other commentaries, David E. Price, "Faith in Public Office, in E.J. Dionne Jr., Jean B. Elshtain, and Kayla M. Drogosz, eds., *One Electorate under God: A Dialogue on Religion and American Politics* (Washington, D.C.: Brookings Institution, 2004). Cuomo quotes from pp. 14–15.

17. Mario Cuomo, "Religious Belief and Public Morality: A Catholic Governor's Perspective" (paper prepared for delivery at the University of Notre Dame, Notre Dame, Ind., September 13, 1984), pp. 4–5.

18. *Westside Community Board of Education v. Mergens,* 496 U.S. 226 (1990).

19. The text of the proposed amendment was as follows: "To secure the people's right to acknowledge God according to the dictates of conscience: Neither the

United States nor any State shall establish any official religion, but the people's right to pray and to recognize their religious beliefs, heritage, or traditions on public property, including schools, shall not be infringed. Neither the United States nor any State shall require any person to join in prayer or other religious activity, prescribe school prayers, discriminate against religion, or deny equal asset to a benefit on account of religion" (House Joint Resolution 78, 105th Congress). My floor statement on the proposal may be found in *Congressional Record,* daily ed., June 4, 1998, pp. H4074–75; also see the statements of Reps. Vic Fazio and Bill Hefner, pp. H4093–94.

20. Davis and Good, eds., *Niebuhr on Politics,* p. 186.

21. James Madison, "The Federalist," no. 51, in Clinton Rossiter, ed., *The Federalist Papers* (New York: Mentor, 1961), p. 322.

22. Abraham Joshua Heschel, *God in Search of Man* (New York: Octagon, 1972), p. 415.

23. 2 Samuel 12:9.

24. Philip Stern, ed., *The Life and Writings of Abraham Lincoln* (New York: Modern Library, 1940), p. 841.

25. Quoted in William Lee Miller, *Lincoln's Second Inaugural: A Study in Political Ethics* (Bloomington, Ind.: Poynter Center, 1980), p. 8. I am drawing here on Miller's insightful exegesis. For further exposition of the Second Inaugural as "almost a perfect model of the difficult but not impossible task of remaining loyal and responsible toward the moral treasures of a free civilization on the one hand while yet having some religious vantage point over the struggle," with an application of the model to the post–World War II conflict with communism, see Niebuhr, *The Irony of American History* (New York: Scribner's, 1952), pp. 171–174.

26. Francis B. Carpenter, *Six Months at the White House with Abraham Lincoln* (New York: Herd & Houghton, 1867), p. 282.

27. Niebuhr, *Irony,* p. 173.

28. Isaiah 55:8.

12

Ethics Beyond the Rule Book

As a member who came to the Congress in 1987 from a teaching career that included work in ethics and public policy, it seemed strange to me to hear talk of an "ethics craze" in government and to witness a recurring preoccupation with ethical matters, centered around the troubles of House Speakers Jim Wright and Newt Gingrich but by no means limited to those episodes.

My first assignment on joining the Duke University faculty in 1973 was to devise an ethics course to be required as a component of the graduate public policy curriculum. Over the next decade, I worked with a growing group of academics and practitioners across the country, holding workshops, writing papers, attending conferences—promoting the study and teaching of ethics while developing its intellectual content and broadening its applications. I thus stepped into the swirling waters of ethical agitation and debate in the House with considerable background in the subject, but that background often seemed to have precious little relevance to what passed for ethical discussion there.

I say that not in criticism of the fields of political ethics and public policy as they have developed in academia. I am more inclined to be critical of prevailing public and congressional conceptions of ethics, what I will somewhat disparagingly term "ethics committee" ethics. This does not mean that the ethics committees and the congressional code of conduct should appreciably broaden their domain. The point, rather, is that the implications of ethical reflection and analysis for the Congress—for the policies it makes and how its members function—go far beyond what can or should be contained in a code or enforced by a watchdog committee. It is that broader conception of ethics and its relevance to legislative life that I will explore in this chapter.

Numerous colleagues and I had examined the ethical content of the legislator's role and the inherent limitations of ethics committee ethics as part of a major Hastings Center project in the early 1980s.[1] What I encountered as a member was an intensifying ethical concern in Congress itself, which was partly but not entirely a defensive reaction to the willingness of Newt Gingrich and others to wield ethics charges as weapons in partisan warfare. This concern led to the appointment of the House Bipartisan Task Force on Ethics and the passage of the Government Ethics Reform Act of 1989, which embellished ethics committee ethics considerably without significantly broadening the terms of discussion and debate.

A readiness to believe the worst about the motives and the integrity of public officials has characterized American political culture from the beginning. Historians like Bernard Bailyn and James Sterling Young documented the prevalence of a strong antipower ideology in the revolutionary and subsequent generations, a conviction that those with political power would invariably abuse it and that corruption and self-aggrandizement were endemic to government.[2] Young attributed the disabilities and demoralization of the early congresses in large measure to the tendency of the members to internalize the dominant public view of "power-holding as essentially a degrading experience. . . . The power-holders did not, in their own outlook, escape a culturally ingrained predisposition to view political power and politics as essentially evil."[3] Such cynicism and the mistrust of officeholders and public institutions have been heightened in recent years by highly publicized scandals and by the capacity and the inclination of the modern mass media to publicize and dramatize the foibles and failings of politicians.

For most of their first two centuries, the House and Senate had no written codes of behavior but dealt sporadically and often inconsistently with discrete acts of wrongdoing.[4] I came across one such instance in researching a brief bicentennial piece on those who preceded me in representing my district in North Carolina. I discovered that one of my predecessors, a Reconstruction congressman named John Deweese, had resigned his seat in 1870 one day before he and two other members were censured for selling appointments to the military academies. Progressive era reform sentiments and various election scandals led to a series of federal campaign practices statutes beginning in 1907. After World War II Congress finally moved to adopt more general codes of conduct for its members. The first was a government-wide aspirational code, adopted in 1958 in the wake of the Sherman Adams–Bernard Goldfine scandal in the Eisenhower administration. Widely publicized congressional scandals a decade later involving Sen. Thomas Dodd, Senate majority secretary Bobby Baker, and Rep. Adam Clayton Powell led both chambers to adopt their first formal codes of conduct. These were toughened considerably in 1977 and again in 1989.

The 1989 changes, passed after the resignation under fire of Speaker Jim Wright and packaged with a major adjustment in congressional pay, tightened limits on outside income and eliminated speaking fees (honoraria), strengthened financial disclosure requirements, enjoined members from converting campaign funds to personal use on retirement, and prohibited lobbying by members and staff for one year after leaving their positions. Most of these provisions were contained in the report of the Bipartisan Task Force on Ethics, accurately described by its cochairman as "the most sweeping reform of congressional ethics in the last decade."[5] But the proposals were comprehensive only in relation to the already defined domain of congressional ethics, and they did not break any new ground conceptually. The same was true of the tightened rules on the receipt of gifts that, along with lobbying reform, were brought down by Senate Republicans in 1994 but passed in modified form in 1995.

Dennis Thompson told of one instance in which a breakthrough did indeed occur. In Tennessee, in the wake of a 1977 political scandal, the leaders of the state senate decided they needed a tough code of ethics:

> Senators who did not want the code were reluctant to vote against it in the prevailing climate of reform, but when the code came to the floor, they thought they had found a way out. One senator proposed, as a substitute amendment, the Ten Commandments and the Golden Rule. The leaders knew that in Tennessee no legislator could vote against the Ten Commandments or the Golden Rule, and they scrambled to find a parliamentary compromise that would save the code. The substitute amendment became a regular amendment, and Tennessee became the only state to have a code of ethics that included, along with strong conflict-of-interest provisions, all ten of the commandments. From Article IV with its detailed procedural rules, the document jumped immediately to Article V, which read in its entirety: "Thou shalt have no other gods before me."[6]

But even Tennessee has now fallen into line; when the code was revised in 1985, Thompson reported, the Ten Commandments quietly disappeared!

The 1985 Hastings report acknowledged that a code of official conduct was only "one element in a well-rounded effort to inspire the conduct of legislators as well as to engender trust on the part of the public in those legislators." Nonetheless, it still was critical of the limits of existing codes: "They are generally narrow in scope, short on aspirational statements, and fail to deal with the full range of representative or legislative functions."[7] The report proposed three touchstones for legislative ethics: autonomy (the "obligation to deliberate and decide, free from improper influence"), accountability (the "obligation to provide constituents with the information and understanding they require in order to exercise responsible democratic citizenship"), and responsibility (the "obligation to contribute to the effective institutional functioning of the democratic legislative process").[8] Existing codes address the first two principles in their conflict of interest and financial disclosure provisions, but they still construe autonomy and accountability quite narrowly and barely deal with responsibility.

The Hastings authors suggested that a more adequate code of legislative ethics might, like the former code of professional conduct of the American Bar Association, contain aspirational elements and espoused ideals as well as precisely defined rules of conduct.[9] They probably underestimated the difficulty of reaching consensus on aspirational maxims and did not suggest what kind of enforcement mechanisms, if any, might be appropriate in this realm. But they were correct in noting the severe limitations of ethics committee ethics. Using that as my point of departure, I want to look beyond personal and official probity and ask what further ethical dilemmas and challenges confront legislators as they define and carry out their jobs.

Ethics and Policy

Members of Congress and other legislative assemblies continually make policy choices in crafting legislation for introduction, refining bills in committee, and engaging in debate at each stage of the process, as well as in hundreds of roll call votes. These policy choices are, among other things, choices of value. Legislators, like most citizens, value human liberty, feel that policies should be just and fair, argue for taking the public interest or the common good into account, and may speak of furthering human solidarity and community. They have varying degrees of awareness of the historical, philosophical, and theological grounding of such concepts, of how they might complement or contradict one another, and of the implications they might hold for specific questions of policy. But such concepts describe valued social states and help shape, however loosely, the process of deliberation and debate.[10] For years I taught a course called Ethics and Public Policy based on the assumption that policymakers and the policy process would benefit from more careful and critical reflection on our inherited notions of human well-being and the public good, coupled with more explicit efforts to discern the implications of these ideas for particular policies and institutions. Much of what I have experienced during my time in the U.S. House has strengthened that assumption.

This is not to say that the ethical assessment of policy among practicing legislators generally takes the same form that it does in the academy or that it should. Dennis Thompson argued persuasively that the demands of the role of the legislator, in particular the ethical demands, may conflict with the "generic requirements of ethics." "Ethics demands a general perspective, but legislators are also obligated to look after their own particular constituents. Ethics requires autonomous judgment, but legislators are also expected to defer to electoral decision." The perspectives members adopt, as broad or narrow as they may be, are often tied to the positions of responsibility they occupy within the institution, as I stressed in contrasting the "macro" and "micro" perspectives one adopts on the Budget and Appropriations Committees, respectively. Moreover, if members are serious about giving effect to their values and intentions, they must collaborate with and sometimes defer to colleagues whose values and goals they only partially share. Their roles may be partial or one-sided, depending on the opportunities they have and their expectations about what others will do. "The duties of any single representative depend on what other representatives do or fail to do, and thus the proper role of a representative cannot be determined without reference to the state of the legislative system."[11]

Still, as members develop, justify, and press their own positions, their notions of social value come into play. And one element in the viability of a legislative proposal—or in the credibility of a critique of executive or administrative policy—is its resonance with widely held notions of justice or the public good.

One of the few books that describe and characterize the process of valuation as it takes place among policymakers is *A Strategy of Decision*, by David Braybrooke and C. E. Lindblom. This volume has held up remarkably well as an account of how public officials cope with their environment, and my service in the House has led me to appreciate it anew. Braybrooke and Lindblom show that the process of social evaluation does not normally conform to the conventional (read: stereotypical) "rational-deductive" or "synoptic" ideal. Various features of legislative and other policymaking settings (the multiplicity of values and interests and the conflicts among them; shortages of time, information, and analytic capabilities; the multiplicity of decision points; the dominance of margin-dependent choices and remedial orientations) render synoptic decisionmaking impractical.[12] But this is not to say that normal practice—what Braybrooke and Lindblom describe as the strategy of "disjointed incrementalism"—is value free. Rather, they suggest that existing practice comports remarkably well with utilitarianism, the "family of theories" that "allows meliorative and distributive considerations a decisive role in confirming all moral judgments that are open to dispute, and . . . supposes that, among these meliorative and distributive considerations, social welfare and group happiness justify supporting an action or policy, while their opposites do not."[13]

Distributive considerations loom large in congressional policymaking, and distribution is often conceived in terms of the benefits or breaks sought by organized, active interest groups. But aggregative notions of utility (the sort of value we are getting at when we speak of "the public interest")[14] are also frequently considered and may serve as a standard against which narrower professions of interest are measured. This is true even on the Banking Committee, where the environment is replete with organized interests and policy deliberations sometimes seem little more than a pulling and hauling among them. For example, the committee's most ambitious legislative battle during my first term was an attempt to repeal the Glass-Steagall Act of 1933, expand bank powers, and bring financial services regulation into line with the evolving marketplace. On one level, the episode displayed familiar group conflicts: banks versus securities firms, banks versus insurance firms, money-center banks versus independent banks, and so forth. But persuasive public interest arguments were also developed and utilized. Proponents of Glass-Steagall reform were therefore not simply responding to the interests of major American banks; they were also attempting to increase the availability and lower the cost of capital in many regions of the country, enhance the competitive offering of financial services to consumers, bolster the competitive position of American financial institutions internationally, and move toward a rationalized system of regulation by function. These arguments did not immediately prevail. Interest group conflicts, plus a major turf battle between the Banking and Energy and Commerce Committees, killed the bill in 1988. But the broader economic considerations that gained currency in Congress and the executive helped move subsequent reform proposals forward, and in 1999 the Financial Services Modernization Act finally became law.

In housing, another major area of jurisdiction for the Banking Committee and my Veterans Affairs–Housing and Urban Development (VA-HUD) Appropriations Subcommittee, competing concepts of social value often arise with particular clarity. How, for example, should community development block grants be targeted? I used this issue as a textbook case in my class on ethics and public policy, and it is still debated from time to time in congressional committees. One's sense of justice (reinforced in my class with a reading of John Rawls's *A Theory of Justice*) might lead one to give priority to the poorest neighborhoods, to those most in need.[15] But the sort of utilitarian calculations described by Braybrooke and Lindblom might lead one to a different—and in my view more defensible—conclusion, at least as long as total community development (CD) funding does not go far beyond its present level. CD funding, which is mainly used to rehabilitate dilapidated housing and provide local infrastructure improvements, is modest. Yet it can halt deterioration and help turn a marginal neighborhood around, providing benefits that extend far beyond those persons directly assisted. In the poorest neighborhoods, by contrast, such funds might likely sink without a trace. Other types of housing programs are needed in the poorest areas, of course, but it would be a mistake to target CD funds too narrowly in this direction; the money should be used where it can be effective and do the most good for the most people.

A related dilemma in the area of public housing was addressed in the major housing bills of 1990 and 1997–1998. Ever-tightening federal preference rules in public housing had required that priority be given to those who paid more than 50 percent of their income in rent, were involuntarily displaced, or were living in substandard housing. "At face value," the director of the Greensboro Housing Authority told the Subcommittee on Housing and Community Development at the hearing we convened in Raleigh, "these rules suggest fairness, providing that scarce housing resources go to the most needy."[16] But she went on to describe how the rules were requiring the authority to replace working families who left public housing with multiproblem families and individuals who could not function independently. These were people who frequently placed a great strain on the inadequate network of community services (such as budget counseling, job training, and tutoring) and aggravated community drug and security problems. What was being lost was the socioeconomic mix that had given public housing projects stability and had provided indigenous role models and leadership. The obligation to assist the most destitute obviously stood in tension with the need to promote the well-being of those already in the project, ensure the viability of the project as a whole, and enable it to function as a community.

These difficult dilemmas call for a conscientious effort to balance competing values. In the 1990 housing bill, for example, I successfully pushed an amendment to allow up to 30 percent of the slots in public and assisted housing to go to persons who met the income eligibility requirements but fell outside the federal preference criteria (see Chapter 6). By 1997 the Republican leadership of the Housing Subcommittee proposed to abandon federal preferences and modify the income eligibility requirements for public housing as well, reducing the percentage of units reserved for the poorest (earning less than 30 percent of their area's median income) residents from 75 to 35. I thought this went too far in the opposite direction and voted accordingly. The bill the president eventually signed was better balanced, reserving 40 percent of public housing units for very low-income families but 75 percent of housing vouchers, which were normally spread over multiple locations.

The idea of community—to which I paid particular attention during my years of teaching and writing about the ethical foundations of public policy—often provides a perspective on policy questions distinctive from those formulated in terms of individual liberty, social utility, or distributive justice.[17] This notion gained currency in the 1990s with the founding of a "communitarian" movement, complete with a quarterly journal and a platform recognizing "both individual human dignity and the social dimension of human existence," under the leadership of sociologist Amitai Etzioni and ethicist William Galston, who later served as President Clinton's deputy assistant for domestic policy.[18] Communitarian ideas, which had some affinity with the "third way" (between individualist, laissez-faire approaches and those relying on central governmental direction) touted by the Democratic Leadership Council, helped shape National Service, welfare reform, community development, and other Clinton administration initiatives.

For two of the efforts described in Chapter 6, I framed much of my argument in explicit communitarian terms. The Teaching Fellows Act drew on the values of community service and reciprocal obligation and focused on collaborative learning and an extensive support system as means of strengthening professional identity. The attempt to roll back FCC media concentration rules was an even better fit. "The key value at stake," I told the unofficial hearing that Commissioner Michael Copps convened in Durham, "is *community*, a value partly but not entirely addressed when we speak of 'localism' as a public interest goal. . . . The term 'media' suggests . . . communication within or across a locality or region whereby isolated 'consumers' of media have their identities as members of the community strengthened, their knowledge increased, and their participation enhanced. . . . If the day comes—and I'm afraid it's fast approaching—when local media are merely a conduit for nationally generated information and entertainment, we will have lost a critically important component of community life."[19]

On questions of war and peace, the most familiar evaluative framework is "just war" theory, rooted in Catholic moral philosophy going back to Augustine and in secular seventeenth- and eighteenth-century systems of international law. In discriminating between the offensive against al Qaeda and the Taliban and the invasion of Iraq (see Chapter 9), I and others drew on and adapted just-war concepts such as the proportionality of means to ends and war as a last resort, whether we directly acknowledged it or not. I cited the eminent just-war theorist Michael Walzer in arguing against the rush to war in Iraq and aspired to the kind of moral discrimination that the tradition, at its best, exemplifies.[20] Walzer later elaborated his argument that the necessity of invasion was never established: "Even given the knowledge available at the time, the risks of war should have looked greater than the risks involved in sustaining the containment regime. And there were means available to increase the severity and forcefulness of [that] regime."[21]

In the context of the "Bush revolution" in foreign policy, with its penchant for unilateralism and preventive wars, just-war thinking is likely to counsel discrimination and restraint. But nations, like individuals, may commit sins of omission as well as commission, failing to do the good that they can and should do. (The Bush administration's disengagement from Middle East peacemaking can be critiqued persuasively in these terms.) As we consider recent history, the genocidal massacres in Rwanda in 1994 offer perhaps the most drastic and troubling example. One of the cardinal obligations in the just-war tradition is preventing the slaughter of innocents. Here too rational and prudential calculations are required; not all innocents can be protected nor all tyrannies removed. But it is impossible to justify the failure of the United States and other nations to intervene as the mass killing in Rwanda proceeded. Former secretary of state Madeleine Albright termed this failure her "deepest regret" from her years in public service. Effective action, she argued, "would have required a heavily armed, almost certainly U.S.-led coalition able to deploy quickly, intimidate extremists, arrest leaders, and establish security." While noting the likelihood that such a course would have been rejected by Congress and the public, she regretted her failure to advocate it and wondered aloud if the United States or the world would muster the political will to respond differently next time.[22]

In thinking about war and peace, the perspective offered by our religious traditions and expressed in Lincoln's Second Inaugural (see Chapter 11) is indispensable. Reinhold Niebuhr regarded just-war theory as vastly superior to pacifism, which he regarded as a simplistic application of the love ethic to politics, and to the moral skepticism he associated with Lutheran theology. But even just-war thinking, he warned, is susceptible to the distortions and blind spots of self-interest and the will to power. There is good reason to be wary of leaders who speak in absolute terms of good and evil or identify the nation's cause with God's will. We must recognize mass murder, dehumanizing ideologies, and brutal tyrannies for what they are, assess the threat they pose, and realistically consider the full range of means that may be required to stop them. We must realize that even peacemaking—if we seek durable peace that goes beyond the mere dominance of the strongest—sometimes requires coercive, violent means. But we must understand the limits and perils of military force and make discriminating judgments about the efficacy and morality of alternative means. And we must be acutely aware, for ourselves as for others, of the dangers of denying one's fallibility or absolutizing one's own cause.

What Sort of Member Shall I Be?

I now want to look at the legislator's responsibility from a different perspective, moving beyond the ethics of policy choice to the role he or she assumes as a member of an ongoing institution. Legislators must define themselves in relation to forces impinging on them from outside and from within the legislature and in terms of their responsibility for the institution's collective performance. Dilemmas of role definition and institutional responsibility depend, in the specific form they take, on the character of the legislative system and the possibilities it offers its members. I will therefore highlight some critical features of the U.S. Congress as it currently operates before focusing on specific dilemmas of role and responsibility that arise in this setting.

Portrayals by leading congressional scholars of members in their institutional environment shifted significantly after the 1960s. An emphasis on member adaptation to well-defined norms and procedures gave way to a portrayal of them as purposive agents in a fluid organizational setting. In the former category, Richard Fenno's landmark studies of the Appropriations Committees stand out, as does Donald Matthews's portrayal of the Senate, centering on the "folkways" of the institution, "its unwritten rules of the game, its norms of conduct, its approved manner of behavior," just like, as one senator put it, "living in a small town."[23] Consider, by contrast, the premise of David Mayhew's pivotal *Congress: The Electoral Connection* (1974). "I have become convinced," Mayhew wrote, "that scrutiny of purposive behavior [of individuals] offers the best route to an understanding of legislatures—or at least of the United States Congress."[24] Mayhew therefore assumed that members of Congress were "single-minded seekers of reelection" and found a close fit between the behavior such an assumption led one to predict and actual congressional performance.

Although this shift reflected changing fashions in social service research (from the use of functionalist or "sociological" models to assumptions more characteristic of the economist),[25] it owed much to changes in the institution being studied. A number of developments made an individualistic portrayal of Congress an increasingly plausible one. Folkways such as the expectation that members would serve an extended period of apprenticeship before taking an active role in committee or on the floor eroded significantly. Members still valued specialization and expertise, but they became less hesitant to get involved in areas beyond their committee assignments. Introducing bills and issuing pronouncements on a wide variety of subjects, formerly the hallmark of a few mavericks, became widely practiced and tolerated, and members were less concerned to maintain a facade of committee or party unity as they took their causes or their amendments to the floor.

These changes were rooted to a considerable extent in the altered electoral context outlined in Chapter 8: the decline of party as a determinant of public perceptions or assessments of politicians; reduced party control over the means of communicating with and mobilizing voters; and the rise of television, direct mail, and other technologies that promised unmediated contact with voters while offering opponents the same possibility. Increasingly on their own electorally and eager to gain visibility and leverage earlier in their congressional careers, members chafed at the traditional folkways and pressed for the dispersal of power and prerogatives within the institution. As already noted, this led to subcommittee proliferation and expanded opportunities for entrepreneurship and participation. It also prompted a strengthening of House party leadership, first as a counterweight to committee oligarchs and then as a corrective to the problems decentralization posed for mobilizing the chamber and realizing members' policy goals.

The centralization of leadership power since the mid-1980s, and particularly since the advent in 1995 of Republican control, has exceeded what most students of the "electoral connection" anticipated, leading to academic portrayals of the House as a party-centered institution. By most accounts, however, party government remains "conditional," dependent on homogeneity and agreement within the parties as well as disagreement and polarization between them.[26] The current electoral environment maximizes both of these factors, and party organizations in the House, particularly the majority Republicans, have found effective ways of reinforcing loyalty and discipline. Members nonetheless have numerous conflicting pulls in terms of electoral incentives, group and constituency pressures, and personal beliefs and preferences, and they have considerable leeway in determining what roles they assume.

What shape do decisions regarding role and responsibility take, and what is their ethical significance? I will focus on four questions every legislator must face. The electoral and institutional constraints on members vary considerably in character and severity. In posing these questions I do not assume that members can blithely disregard the profit-and-loss calculations related to maintaining their electoral viability and preserving their power base in the institution. I also assume, however, that a broad range of legislative strategies and activities are compatible with, and can be supportive of, self-interest in these senses. Most members of Congress, most of the time, have considerable latitude in defining their roles and what kind of job they wish to do. If they do not have the latitude, they can often create it, for they have a great deal of control over how their actions are perceived and interpreted. Consequently, I conceive of these ethical dilemmas as choices a politician makes within the bounds of political "necessity."

First, *to what range of values and interests should I be responsive?* I may believe that I am being properly representative and responsive if I give a respectful hearing to groups that present themselves on a given issue and then reach a reasonable accommodation among them. Such an assumption finds support in the pluralist school of political science. Braybrooke and Lindblom, for example, expect those most intensely interested and directly affected to make their voices heard on a given policy question: "Normally, people are not slow to protest when a policy looks like worsening their condition."[27] Public officials, such analysts conclude, generally feel constrained to be attentive to these groups and strike some sort of balance among them. Perhaps that is an acceptable operationalization of representative government under contemporary conditions.

But perhaps not. A number of analysts have argued persuasively that politically active organizations or constituencies that are prepared to press their views on a given question are likely to be a highly selective sample of all those whose interests and values are affected.[28] Furthermore, one cannot assume that all affected interests will find ready access to the political arena. Some lack the organizational or other resources to make their voices heard. Others may be frozen out by the ties that exist between dominant groups and clientele-oriented committees and agencies. Broader, more diffuse interests generally have more difficulty mobilizing their constituencies and developing effective organizational structures than more narrowly based interests whose stakes are more immediate and tangible.

A responsible legislator takes the initiative in looking to poorly organized or nontraditional interests that the system might exclude and to broad, shared public interests and values that are inadequately mirrored in the "pressure system." Many of the developments I have surveyed promote an uncritical particularism. These include the prominence of organized interests in lobbying and campaign finance, the growth of self-styled "grassroots" organizations that can jam legislators' phone and fax lines on a moment's notice, the fragmentation and clientele orientations of committees and subcommittees, and the parties' declining capacity to mediate between interest groups and public officeholders, because of either weakness or overidentification with group agendas. But taking a broader view of one's representative role need not be seen as self-sacrificial behavior, at least most of the time. Legislators often find it politically profitable to cultivate new constituencies or appeal over the heads of contending groups to a broader public concerned with one issue or another. Such strategies do not succeed automatically. Legislators must work at increasing the salience and attractiveness of their policy stances. To transcend the brokering role and make such moves politically viable and attractive to their colleagues, members must shore up supportive groups, cultivate the media, and otherwise attempt to "broaden the scope of conflict."[29]

Responsible representation does not require a dark view of any and all collaboration with "the interests." But neither does it permit a sanguine view of representation as a mere balancing of pressures or an expectation that competition among the interests that are best organized and most vocal in a given area will ensure an equitable outcome. It is important to take account of the biases and exclusions of the group system and of the full range of values and interests a policy question entails.

Second, *to what extent and in what fashion will I contribute to the work of the legislature?* It is often said, by both observers and members, that we legislators are very thinly spread. However, such complaints may miss the mark in accounting for institutional performance. The real problem is the erosion of inducements to engage seriously in the work of Congress. Pulling one's weight in committee and developing a substantial area of expertise are still serviceable strategies for members who desire the esteem of their colleagues. But weakening norms of apprenticeship and specialization, together with the pressures for self-promotion created by the media-dominated electoral environment, have made show horse behavior more profitable and less costly than it was in the past. Members today have stronger incentives to latch onto a piece of policy turf, gain control of a subcommittee, and cultivate an image of policy leadership. At the same time, their incentives to engage in the painstaking work of legislative craftsmanship, coalition building, and mobilization may actually be weaker. Such activities are more difficult under conditions of organizational fragmentation, and the pressures to do the homework are less compelling. Moreover, the public is only sporadically attentive, making the electoral payoffs for merely taking a position or introducing a bill as great as those that reward more extensive or conscientious efforts.

In stressing the importance of serious legislative work, I do not mean to denigrate the nonlegislative aspects of the job. I believe that constituent communication and service are worthwhile in their own right. Moreover, they can support the member's legislative efforts in important ways—enhancing the two-way, representative relationship and giving the member the kind of leeway he or she needs for flexible and cooperative legislative involvement.[30] But alterations in the electoral environment and the congressional ethos have made it thinkable, perhaps even profitable, for a number of members to engage almost exclusively in constituency-cultivation activities to the detriment of legislative and oversight tasks. And when members do turn their attention to policy, their involvement is too often superficial and fleeting.

This sort of position taking can be just as deceptive and manipulative as other forms of self-promotion. "Appearing to do something about policy without a serious intention of, or demonstrable capacity for, doing so," as Richard Fenno stressed, "is a corruption of the representative relationship."[31] Such behavior robs the legislative institution of the energy and persistence needed to make it work. Congress still contains many skilled and persistent legislators (more, I think, than Mayhew's model would lead one to predict), and some have managed to make their legislative power and productivity a substantial electoral asset. The institution still depends on members assuming such roles and adopting such priorities, but this behavior is currently more dependent on the choices and proclivities of the members themselves and less on institutional pressures and constraints than it was in the past.

Third, *what responsibilities do I bear for the functioning of the committee and party systems?* "Public duty," wrote Edmund Burke, "demands and requires that what is right should not only be made known, but made prevalent; that what is evil should not only be detected, but defeated. When a public man omits to put himself in a situation of doing his duty with effect, it is an omission that frustrates the purposes of his trust almost as much as if he had formally betrayed it." Such a demand for seriousness of purpose speaks directly to the superficial and symbolic gestures that too often pass for policymaking in the contemporary Congress. But what Burke specifically had in mind was the need for members of Parliament to associate, to cooperate under the standard of a party:

> No man, who is not inflamed by vain-glory into enthusiasm, can flatter himself that his single, unsupported, desultory, unsystematic endeavors, are of power to defeat the subtle designs and united cabals of ambitious citizens.

When bad men combine, the good must associate; else they will fall, one by one, an unpitied sacrifice in a contemptible struggle.[32]

Public duty, Burke argued, gives powerful ethical support to party fidelity. He was profoundly skeptical of the tendency of politicians to tout their own independence or to portray themselves as motivated by conscience; too often, he suspected, this was a cover for the pursuit of private advantage. Party operations, Burke believed, could and should leave room for occasional dissent, but the desire for concord and effectiveness would properly nudge fellow partisans toward agreement:

When the question is in its nature doubtful, or not very material, the modesty which becomes an individual and that partiality which becomes a well-chosen friendship, will frequently bring on an acquiescence in the general sentiment. Thus the disagreement will naturally be rare; it will be only enough to indulge freedom, without violating concord, or disturbing arrangement.[33]

This view squares imperfectly with individualistic notions of moral autonomy to which Americans typically repair—a "Lone Ranger" ethical bias. The late Sen. Jacob Javits anticipated his readers' applause as he wrote: "In this clash of loyalties—loyalty to constituents, loyalty to party, and loyalty to myself—my constituents and I had to prevail."[34] But we should be wary of imputing ethical superiority to the loner. If the committees and the parties play a legitimate and necessary role in developing and refining measures, aggregating interests, and mobilizing the chamber, should not the member who would violate the comity and the discipline necessary to their successful functioning bear a burden of proof?

This is neither to endorse mindless party regularity nor to deny that members should sometimes resolve conflicts with their party or committee in favor of personal convictions regarding constituency interests or the public good. In fact, with the shift from the 103rd Congress to the early months of the 104th, with Democratic disarray giving way to Republicans marching in lockstep to an almost unprecedented degree, contrasting ethical pitfalls became evident. But what was needed in both instances was a conscientious balance between autonomy and accommodation, between individual initiative and team play. More than most of the world's parliaments, the U.S. Congress places the responsibility for striking such balances on legislators themselves.

Fourth, *how should I present myself in relation to the workings of the legislature and the overall performance of government?* Former congressman Bob Eckhardt (D-Texas) suggested that every member of Congress performs three functions: lawmaker, ombudsman, and educator.[35] This last function, as I have shown, may be closely related to the first: Lawmakers who wish to do more than simply defer to the best-organized or most strident interests must give some attention to explaining their actions and educating their constituents, helping them place issues in broader perspective or even activating alternative bases of support. The extent to which a member is willing and able to undertake such explanations is ethically as well as politically significant.[36]

Here I turn to another facet of legislators' educative role: how they portray Congress and the government of which they are a part. Richard Neustadt, finding that American mistrust of government had reached proportions "truly and continuously damaging for timely innovation in governmental programs, for thoroughgoing implementation of them, and for realistic expectations about them," placed much of the responsibility on politicians themselves. They feed the mistrust, not only by their ethical lapses and policy failures but as a matter of deliberate political strategy: "Mistrust is of proven use in stalling or unraveling unwanted programs, and also in diverting public anxiousness from unmet needs. If mistrust were unfunctional from every point of view, contemporary politicians and reporters would be fighting it, not feeding it. And feed it they do."[37]

Richard Fenno, traveling with House members around their districts, found them constantly polishing their "individual reputation[s] at the expense of the institutional reputation of Congress":

> In explaining what he was doing in Washington, every one of the eighteen House members took the opportunity to picture himself as different from, and better than, most of his fellow members in Congress. No one availed himself of the opportunity to educate his constituents about Congress as an institution—not in any way that would "hurt a little." To the contrary, the members' process of differentiating themselves from the Congress as a whole only served, directly or indirectly, to downgrade the Congress.

This was in the mid-1970s, before Newt Gingrich began his systematic effort to condemn the institution as "corrupt" and "despotic," and when Congress bashing by advocacy groups and in the media was still relatively subdued. "We have to differentiate me from the rest of those bandits down there in Congress," Fenno heard a member say to a campaign strategy group. "'They are awful, but our guy is wonderful'—that's the message we have to get across."[38]

So much for the traditional norm of institutional patriotism! Opinion polls regularly reveal that public officials in general and Congress in particular rank low in public esteem. This evaluation has been reinforced over the years by ethics charges and countercharges and partisan showdowns, but it is rooted deeply in our country's history and political culture. We members reinforce such an assessment when we distance ourselves from any responsibility for the institution's functioning. This distancing helps produce a 30–40 percent approval rate for Congress and a 90+ percent reelection rate for ourselves.

My point is not that a member should defend Congress, right or wrong. Indeed, members have an obligation to assess the institution's workings critically and to press for improvements. That obligation falls especially on members of the minority party. But even when the abuses are as grave as the leadership tactics I detailed in Chapter 8, there is a line to be drawn between constructively criticizing practices and performance and undermining the legitimacy of the institution itself. Although it is often tempting to pose as the quintessential outsider, carping at accommodations that have been reached on a given issue as though problems could simply be ignored, cost-free solutions devised, or the painful necessities of compromise avoided, it is also deceptive and irresponsible. Responsible legislators will not only communicate to their constituencies the assembly's failings but also define fair and reasonable expectations, suggest what accommodations they would be well advised to accept, and so forth. In the past, institutional patriotism too often assumed that whatever the process produced must be acceptable. But self-righteous, anti-institutional posturing is no better. The moral quixotism to which reelection-minded legislators are prone too often serves to rationalize their own nonproductive legislative roles and perpetuate public misperceptions of the criteria that can reasonably be applied to legislative performance.

Although it may be politically profitable to "run for Congress by running against Congress," the implications for the institution's effectiveness and legitimacy are ominous. As Fenno concluded, "The strategy is ubiquitous, addictive, cost-free, and foolproof. . . . In the short run, everybody plays and nearly everybody wins. Yet the institution bleeds from 435 separate cuts. In the long run, therefore, somebody may lose. . . . Congress may lack public support at the very time when the public needs Congress the most."[39]

Legislative Structures and Legislative Ethics

Although the American founders regarded civic virtue—a willingness to forgo private advantage for the sake of the commonweal—as essential to the health of the new republic, they were unwilling to trust human nature to its own devices. On the contrary, they believed government must be structured in a way that not only anticipated self-serving behavior but turned it to good account. "Ambition must be made to counteract ambition," wrote James Madison in *The Federalist* (no. 51):

> This policy of supplying, by opposite and rival interests, the defect of better motives [is] particularly displayed in all the subordinate distributions of power, where the constant aim is to divide and arrange the several offices in such a manner as that each may be a check on the other—that the private interest of every individual may be a sentinel over the public rights.[40]

It can be argued, analogously, that certain organizational features of Congress have structured the pursuit of political advantage and turned it to the institution's account. The committee system, for example, accommodates the aspirations of disparate members but also represents a corrective of sorts to congressional individualism—a means of bringing expertise and attention to bear on the legislature's tasks in a more concerted fashion than the free enterprise of individual members could accomplish. The committee system channels members' desires for leverage and status into activity that serves the institution's needs and builds its policymaking capacities.

Members are not bound to defer to committee decisions any more than they are bound to contribute to their own committee work product, but in both instances they should give due weight, in assessing their own responsibilities, to what committees contribute to the institution. By the same token, it is a breach of institutional trust when a committee chairman behaves arbitrarily or short-circuits the deliberative process that gives members confidence in the committee's product. The breach can be particularly damaging if the committee is one, like Budget or Rules, that sets the parliamentary or fiscal parameters within which other members or committees operate. A striking example leaps out from Chapter 7: the way the leadership of the Budget Committee, often at the behest of the House GOP leadership, has since 1998 formulated budget resolutions on ideological grounds without regard to what was required to pass funding bills on budget or on time. The result has been an appropriations process in constant disarray, sacrificing the institutional capacity of the House and the work of the Appropriations Committees for short-term political considerations.

It is important to subject institutional structures and norms to ethical scrutiny. Despite Madison's expectation that the checking and balancing of power would protect the public interest, the constitutional system historically has advantaged certain types of interests at the expense of others. Similarly, the norms and structures that gave inordinate power to committee chairs in the 1950s (mainly southern Democrats) had a distinctive policy impact, inhibiting overdue changes in civil rights and other areas. As Roger Davidson contends, that period's folkways were promulgated by and served the interests of the conservative coalition that ran both chambers during the 1950s.[41] And there were powerful ethical arguments for modifying that particular pattern of institutional maintenance.

The present organizational arrangements in Congress may prove less durable because of the close and shifting division of Democratic–Republican control. The balance has shifted decisively toward strong party leadership in the House, giving the upper hand to the conservative forces dominant in the majority caucus. This bodes ill for most of the programs and constituencies on the domestic discretionary side of the budget. It creates discomfort among moderate Republicans, but nothing even faintly resembling the Democratic insurgency that eventually overcame the conservative coalition. The alteration of today's pattern of institutional maintenance will almost certainly await a shift in party control. Because of the divergent paths the parties have traveled since the Reagan years, the shift, when and if it comes, will not be a minor one in terms of the distribution of power or favored policy outcomes.

The effective, legitimate functioning of the Congress demands strong, resilient, and accountable party structures that are open to broad participation, responsive to member needs, committed to fair treatment of the opposition, and ultimately able to overcome fragmentation and govern. It calls for a credible budget process that is responsive in terms of policy priorities but free of deception and opportunistic manipulation. And it requires committees with the skill and the will to gather information, aggregate interests, foster initiatives, and build consensus in ways that produce effective and attractive legislation.

Strengthening the structures and norms by which Congress supplies "the defect of better motives" and protects its institutional capacities, however, will not dispense with the need for sufficient "slack" to accommodate the needs and circumstances of individual members or for a heightened sense of responsibility on the part of those members as to how they exercise the discretion they possess. For in today's Congress, members are largely on their own in dealing with the entreaties of interested groups, deciding what kind of contribution they will make to the work of the legislature, making the party and committee systems work, and shaping citizen perceptions and evaluations of the institution. Such challenges will continue to be central to legislative life, posing questions of value that members cannot help addressing in one way or another. How we deal with them will decisively shape the capacity of Congress for leadership and the quality of its performance.

Notes

1. Bruce Jennings and Daniel Callahan, eds., *Representation and Responsibility: Exploring Legislative Ethics* (New York: Plenum, 1985); and Daniel Callahan and Bruce Jennings, *The Ethics of Legislative Life* (Hastings-on-Hudson, N.Y.: Hastings Center, 1980).

2. Bernard Bailyn, *The Ideological Origins of the American Revolution* (Cambridge: Belknap, 1967), chap. 3; and James Sterling Young, *The Washington Community, 1800–1828* (New York: Harcourt, Brace, and World, 1966), chap. 3.

3. Young, *Washington Community,* pp. 56, 59.

4. A useful overview is provided in Richard Allan Baker, "The History of Congressional Ethics," in Jennings and Callahan, *Representation and Responsibility,* chap. 1.

5. Representative Vic Fazio, *Congressional Record,* daily ed., November 16, 1989, p. H8745.

6. Dennis F. Thompson, *Political Ethics and Public Office* (Cambridge: Harvard University Press, 1987), p. 10.

7. Callahan and Jennings, *Ethics of Legislative Life,* pp. 53, 55.

8. Callahan and Jennings, *Ethics of Legislative Life,* pp. 34–42. This framework was first developed by Amy Gutmann and Dennis Thompson, "The Theory of Legislative Ethics," in Jennings and Callahan, *Representation and Responsibility,* chap. 9; also see Thompson, *Ethics in Congress: From Individual to Institutional Corruption* (Washington, D.C.: Brookings Institution, 1995), pp. 19–24.

9. Callahan and Jennings, *Ethics of Legislative Life,* p. 55. Note the aspirational character of most of their suggested "next steps," pp. 60–62. For a more cautious view, see John D. Saxon, "The Scope of Legislative Ethics," in Jennings and Callahan, *Representation and Responsibility,* chap. 10.

10. The terms in which we conceptualize a problem may determine the solutions to which we are drawn. Consider, for example, the implications of conceiving of affirmative action policy in terms of social utility or the public interest rather than distributive justice; see David E. Price, "Assessing Policy," in Joel L. Fleishman et al., eds., *Public Duties: The Moral Obligations of Public Officials* (Cambridge: Harvard University Press, 1981), pp. 151–155.

11. Thompson, *Political Ethics,* pp. 96, 101.

12. David Braybrooke and Charles E. Lindblom, *A Strategy of Decision* (New York: Free Press, 1963), chaps. 3, 5, and passim.

13. Braybrooke and Lindblom, *Strategy of Decision,* p. 206. The authors also claim that the strategy conveniently compensates for some of the defects commonly attributed to utilitarianism (pp. 212–223).

14. See Brian Barry, *Political Argument* (London: Routledge & Kegan Paul, 1965), chaps. 10–11.

15. Rawls's theory of justice places a burden of proof on social and economic arrangements: Do they maximize the well-being of the "least advantaged" members of society? This might not always require giving first priority to those most in need, but assistance to other groups would depend on whether it improved the lot of those who were worst off in the long run. John Rawls, *A Theory of Justice* (Cambridge: Harvard University Press, 1971), chap. 13 and passim.

16. Testimony of Elaine T. Ostrowski, *Affordable Housing*, field hearing before the Subcommittee on Housing and Community Development, Committee on Banking, Finance, and Urban Affairs, U.S. House of Representatives, 101st Congress, January 26, 1990 (serial no. 101–75), p. 97.

17. Price, "Assessing Policy," pp. 155–167. See also Price, "Community and Control: Critical Democratic Theory in the Progressive Period," *American Political Science Review*, December 1974, pp. 1663–1678; and Price, "Community, 'Mediating Structures,' and Public Policy," *Soundings*, Winter 1979, pp. 369–394. I drew particularly on Robert Paul Wolff's idea of "rational community" in *The Poverty of Liberalism* (Boston: Beacon, 1968), chap. 5, and on John Dewey's concept of the democratic public, as developed in Dewey, *The Public and Its Problems* (New York: Holt, 1927).

18. See Amitai Etzioni, ed., *Rights and the Common Good: The Communitarian Perspective* (New York: St. Martin's, 1995); and Etzioni, ed., *The Essential Communitarian Reader* (New York: Rowman & Littlefield, 1998). For a comparative critique of Etzioni, Galston, and other communitarian thinkers, see Mac McCorkle and David E. Price, "Wilson Carey McWilliams and Communitarianism," in Dennis Bathory and Nancy L. Schwartz, eds., *Friends and Citizens: Essays in Honor of Wilson Carey McWilliams* (New York: Rowman & Littlefield, 2001), chap. 12.

19. David E. Price, "On Recruiting Teachers: A Communitarian Approach," *Responsive Community*, Fall 2001, pp. 4–8; and Sasha Polakow-Suransky, "When Corporate Media Giants Call the Shots: How New Rules from the FCC Will Squeeze Out Community," *Responsive Community*, Summer 2003, pp. 34–41.

20. See *Congressional Record*, daily ed., March 11, 2003, pp. H1739–41, citing Walzer, "What a Little War in Iraq Could Do," *New York Times*, March 7, 2003, p. A27.

21. Walzer, "Morality and Foreign Policy," in E. J. Dionne Jr. et al., eds., *Liberty and Power: A Dialogue on Religion in an Unjust World* (Washington, D.C.: Brookings Institution, forthcoming). Walzer also claimed a just-war defense for multilateralism: "In a system of sovereign states, multilateral action is preferable to the action of single states, since it protects those acted upon from imperial ambition and state aggrandizement. . . . On balance, over time, arrogance, zeal, and ignorance are more likely to be curbed than furthered by alliances, treaties, and international organizations."

22. Madeleine Albright, *Madam Secretary* (New York: Miramax Books, 2003), pp. 147, 154–155.

23. Donald R. Matthews, *U.S. Senators and Their World* (New York: Vintage, 1960), p. 92. Fenno likewise drew heavily on concepts from functionalist social science—role, function, integration, and adaptation—terms suggesting that members conformed to the institutional environment more than they shaped it. See Richard Fenno, "The House Appropriations Committee as a Political System: The Problem of Integration," *American Political Science Review*, June 1962, pp. 310–324; Fenno, *The Power of the Purse: Appropriations Politics in Congress* (Boston: Little, Brown, 1966).

24. David R. Mayhew, *Congress: The Electoral Connection* (New Haven: Yale University Press, 1974), p. 5.

25. See Brian Barry's exposition of "sociological" and "economic" modes of social analysis in *Sociologists, Economists, and Democracy* (London: Collier-Macmillan, 1970.)

26. For an account that explicitly references Mayhew's assumptions and predictions, see John H. Aldrich and David W. Rohde, "The Logic of Conditional Party Government: Revisiting the Electoral Connection," in Lawrence C. Dodd and Bruce I. Oppenheimer, eds., *Congress Reconsidered*, 7th ed. (Washington: Congressional Quarterly Press, 2001), chap. 12.

27. Braybrooke and Lindblom, *Strategy of Decision*, pp. 185–186. In chapter 10, these analysts proceeded to treat "disjointed incrementalism" as a tolerable substitute for (and in some ways an improvement on) utilitarianism's felicific calculus.

28. See, for example, Wolff, *Poverty of Liberalism*, chap. 4; E. E. Schattschneider, *The Semi-Sovereign People* (New York: Holt, Rinehart & Winston, 1960), chap. 2; Theodore J. Lowi, *The End of Liberalism*, 2nd ed. (New York: Norton, 1979), chap. 3; and Mancur Olson Jr., *The Logic of Collective Action* (New York: Schocken, 1968), chap. 5.

29. The phrase is Schattschneider's; see *Semi-Sovereign People*, chaps. 1–2.

30. On this latter point, see Richard F. Fenno Jr., *Home Style: House Members in Their Districts* (Boston: Little, Brown, 1978), pp. 240–244.

31. Fenno, *Home Style*, p. 243.

32. Edmund Burke, "Thoughts on the Cause of the Present Discontents," in *Works*, 3d ed. (Boston: Little, Brown, 1871), 1:526; emphasis added.

33. Burke, *Works*, 1:533.

34. Jacob K. Javits, *Javits: The Autobiography of a Public Man* (Boston: Houghton Mifflin, 1981), p. 134.

35. Norman J. Ornstein, ed., *The Role of the Legislature in Western Democracies* (Washington, D.C.: American Enterprise Institute, 1981), pp. 96–97.

36. For discussions of various techniques and difficulties of "explanation," see John W. Kingdon, *Congressmen's Voting Decisions*, 2d ed. (New York: Harper & Row, 1981), pp. 47–54; and Fenno, *Home Style*, chap. 5.

37. Neustadt, "The Politics of Mistrust," in Joseph S. Nye Jr. et al., eds., *Why People Don't Trust Government* (Cambridge: Harvard University Press, 1997), pp. 180–181.

38. Fenno, *Home Style*, pp. 164, 166. For an analysis of the behavior Fenno described and an account of historical antecedents, see Kenneth R. Mayer and David T. Canon, *The Dysfunctional Congress? The Individual Roots of an Institutional Dilemma* (Boulder: Westview, 1999), pp. 31–32, 57–59.

39. Fenno, *Home Style*, pp. 168, 246.

40. James Madison, "The Federalist" no. 51, in Clinton Rossiter, ed., *The Federalist Papers* (New York: Mentor, 1961), p. 322.

41. "Socialization and Ethics in Congress," in Jennings and Callahan, *Representation and Responsibility*, pp. 110–116.

13

Concluding Reflections

I have enjoyed eight terms of service in the House of Representatives. I feel they have been reasonably productive, and I am grateful to my constituents for making them possible. In this volume I have tried to convey some of the lessons I have learned—some joyfully, some painfully—about the resilience and resolve required in politics, the promise of policy entrepreneurship and the perils it entails, the necessity of team play and the dangers of partisan excess. My sense of personal satisfaction is tempered by the conviction that the collective response of Congress has often been inadequate to our country's needs. I am proud of the progress we made after 1992 in getting our fiscal house in order, energizing the American economy, and bringing public education to the top of the national agenda; I am appalled at Congress's complicity in the post-2000 fiscal reversal. I take satisfaction in the legislative and funding successes I have been part of, under varying political circumstances, in areas such as technical education, affordable housing, research, and transportation. But Congress's response to many challenges—ranging from the accessibility and affordability of health care to the future of major entitlement programs to our country's international role—has often been inadequate, inspiring more contempt than confidence.

This is not to say the public is of one mind as to what it expects from government. As E. J. Dionne noted, voters' response to the two most ambitious efforts of the 1990s to systematically take on the country's challenges, the Democratic experiment of 1993–1994 and the Republican experiment of 1995, was to create "two neat piles of rubble."[1] As one who participated in the first experiment and helped reverse the second, I am well aware of the shortcomings of both. I have an acute sense of missed opportunities with respect to the ambitions of the Clinton administration to reorient and revitalize the Democratic Party and to launch a new progressive era based on the values of opportunity, responsibility, and community. I share these objectives, which were significantly advanced in the 1990s. But much more might have been achieved had it not been for the deadly combination of presidential overreaching, weak discipline among congressional Democrats, and rule-or-ruin Republican opposition that hobbled Clinton's first term, and the Lewinsky scandal and impeachment that almost wrecked his second term.

While political and personal failings help explain the "piles of rubble" after 1994 and 1995 and Congress's erratic performance subsequently, the institution worked under constraints that even the most skilled, visionary leadership would have had difficulty in overcoming. Public opinion was divided and sometimes contradictory, demanding action but resisting the imposition of costs. Most people resisted unsettling change, whether it was revamping workplace-based health insurance in 1994 or Medicare in 1995; a strong, supportive consensus for major new departures in policy was difficult to come by. Popular divisions were reflected in not only divided party control of government but also the tenuous balance between the parties in Congress, making each susceptible to the threats of ideological or other intraparty factions to withhold support. The visible contentiousness this engendered and the barriers to concerted action it erected often fed public hostility and cynicism and made it that much more difficult to build support and confidence around serious or controversial policy initiatives.

Successful policy entrepreneurship in such an environment requires patience and persistence, akin, in Max Weber's memorable phrase, to the "strong and slow boring of hard boards."[2] I felt that way about several of my own initiatives (see Chapter 6) for reasons that had as much to do with institutional complexity and budget constraints as with political conflicts. And it certainly applied to numerous multiyear legislative ventures that eventually succeeded, such as the Americans with Disabilities Act, the Brady background-check gun law, the establishment of National Service, and the repeal and replacement of the Glass-Steagall Act. Modest initiatives that neither fired ideological passions nor required large budgetary tradeoffs often worked best. Clinton and congressional leaders of both parties demonstrated this when they reached compromises on such matters as health insurance portability, health coverage for uninsured children, community policing, and reducing class size, after their grander proposals had failed. Such incremental initiatives should not be dismissed. They were a rational adaptation to the political circumstances of the 1990s, chipping away at serious problems in ways that transcended the ideological polarities of "big government" and laissez-faire. But they left major challenges largely unaddressed.

The early 2000s offered a different model, one more in line with the prescription traditionally favored by political scientists—unified party government. Has it overcome the obstacles to decisive governmental action? Under the political conditions of 1993–1994, unified Democratic control proved no panacea, although it produced nonincremental budget changes in 1993 and facilitated numerous other initiatives. Unified Republican control has also facilitated nonincremental change, most notably in the realm of tax policy. This unsettling example is a reminder that party dominance can be used not only to take on stubborn policy challenges such as the deficit but also to finesse them, promoting the notion that ominous fiscal problems can safely be ignored. Republicans also used unified party control to pass their version of a Medicare drug benefit, advance the antiabortion agenda, and squeeze domestic discretionary spending. But partisan and ideological groupings in Congress and the country were still closely divided, and many of the familiar obstacles to concerted action remained.

Other critics have suggested that the answer lies in constitutional or institutional changes, particularly in the operations of Congress itself. In earlier chapters I touched on changes needed in the conduct and financing of campaigns, the budget process, and committee and party operations. I also stressed the importance of how members define their roles and responsibilities, suggesting that rules and structures can only go so far in supplying "the defect of better motives." I will revisit the topic here, not only to embellish my own reform agenda but to suggest that congressional reform is in danger of being oversold as well as taking some harmful turns. It would be ironic and unfortunate if, in responding to Congress's failings, we further weakened the institution and rendered it less capable of meeting the nation's policy needs.

Institutional reform is not an end in itself but must be part of a larger effort to revitalize American politics, to repair the frayed linkage between the needs and aspirations of the American people and the actions of their government. Faithful representation and effective leadership must be rooted in a renewed sense of common purpose in our communities and our country. We must find ways to articulate and communicate a vision of the common good and to act on its behalf. Reform efforts are likely to fall short, and they may even make matters worse, unless they are placed in this broader framework.

My work on the historical roots and policy implications of the idea of community during my academic years (see Chapter 12) convinced me that political ideals such as distributive justice and the public interest were apt to assume a rather abstract quality or become distorted amid the clamorings of self-interest unless they were underwritten by a sense of interdependence, common purpose, and responsibility for the community's well-being.[3] My years in public office have brought this theorizing down to earth and have convinced me of its practical significance. I do not believe that we will be able to solve our problems or get beyond the defensive maneuvering and unproductive standoffs that too often characterize our politics until we recapture a sense of common purpose, locally and nationally, and begin to think of ourselves and act more consistently as a community.

If this sounds hopelessly ambitious or even utopian, that is the measure of the challenge to both leadership and citizenship that we face. I cannot do justice to these matters here. But neither can I adequately convey the congressional experience without reference to this bigger picture. Accordingly, I will conclude this chapter with a discussion of two urgent needs facing our body politic. One concerns the quality of our public dialogue, particularly the dangerous gap that has developed between our political campaigns and the decisions and demands of governance. The second concerns the necessity, wherever we find ourselves within the political system, of acting on the imperatives of citizenship.

Reform Agendas

I decided not to call this book *A Political Scientist Goes to Washington.* In some ways, it would have been an apt title, for my training and work as a political scientist have helped shape my perceptions of my congressional experience and certainly my recounting of it here. But I did not like the connotations. "Political scientist" was only one of several identities I brought to Washington, and my primary purpose in coming was certainly not to study. Moreover, in bringing to mind *Mr. Smith Goes to Washington,* Frank Capra's famous film, the title might have suggested that I wished to perpetuate a stereotype of Washington as a den of conspiracy and corruption or that my academic background had prepared me poorly for the harsh realities I encountered. Neither was the case.

Being cast as a kind of academic Mr. Smith, however, is something I have occasionally had to endure. "I'll bet you're discovering it's not like they say in the textbooks!" people sometimes say, or they ask, "How are you finding things in the *real* world?" To such remarks I often think but seldom respond: "If you think academe is never-never land, you should try politics for a while!" The congressional studies of my generation, on which I was trained and to which I made a modest contribution, were based on close, sympathetic observation of the institution and provided an accurate picture of its workings—a view that went beyond the personality-centered, episodic accounts often rendered by journalists and members themselves. The experience of being a member is very different, in terms of what one learns and how one feels, from being an academic observer. But for an orientation to the place, I could have done far worse.

As a young political scientist, however, I found that the hands-on style of contemporary congressional research, often based on member interviews, along with the functionalist framework into which scholarly analysis was often cast, threatened a loss of critical distance from the institution.[4] The policy frustrations and failures of the early 1960s suggested the need for a performance-based critique of Congress—a need that was lessened but not removed by the post-1964 spate of congressional productivity. Books with titles like *Obstacle Course on Capitol Hill* and *House Out of Order* underscored the point.[5] It was therefore with a great deal of anticipation that I, along with a dozen other young academics, agreed to spend the summer of 1972 with Ralph Nader's Congress Project in Washington. As the scholarly arm of the enterprise, we were to combine solid research on the workings of congressional committees with a critical assessment of institutional performance and specific suggestions for reform. To some extent, we realized this goal, although I have never experienced as many frustrations and difficulties with a publishing project before or since.[6] What we received in the meantime, however, was an introduction to the kind of Congress bashing that came to full flower in the 1980s.

Nader apparently decided in midsummer that our studies were not moving fast enough and were not likely to attract sufficient attention. As a result, he put three of his in-house writers to work on a volume that, despite our protests to the contrary, presumed to anticipate and summarize our findings.[7] *Who Runs Congress?* dealt with Congress's substantive policy failings only incidentally and instead highlighted such topics as "Who Owns Congress?" and "Lawmakers as Lawbreakers." Some attention was given to the distribution of power within Congress, but the idea was to highlight instances of arbitrariness and abuse rather than distinguish dysfunctional concentrations of power from those that might enhance congressional performance. In one area—portraying Congress as "overwhelmed by the vastly greater forces of the presidency"[8]—the Nader critique differed from what was to come. In fact, it often seemed that a subservient legislative branch was precisely what the Congress bashers of the Reagan era, often highly partisan, had in mind. But in most respects, *Who Runs Congress?* anticipated the themes of modern congressional criticism and represented an unfortunate departure from the older but still important performance-based critique.[9]

The increasing din of Congress bashing powerfully reinforced the tendency of members to run for Congress by running against Congress. This mode of criticism, with its withering cynicism about all things congressional, encouraged a defensive detachment from the institution on the part of members, an exposé mentality on the part of the press, and increasing public distrust and alienation. What tended to get crowded out was any serious attempt to understand how Congress actually worked, as well as the sorts of proposals for change that could improve institutional performance. Indeed, the relentless trashing of the institution helped prevent positive change. Instead of considering what distributions and concentrations of power would make the institution work effectively, the critics tended to stigmatize all exertions of power as personal aggrandizement. Instead of asking what sorts of support services Congress needed to function efficiently, the critics often regarded such accoutrements indiscriminately as "perks." Although members' incentives to contribute to the work of the institution needed to be strengthened, the critics often viewed legislative dealings with a jaundiced eye and encouraged a righteous aloofness. All of this suggested that many of the critics were aiming (some deliberately, some inadvertently) not for a more assertive, competent institution but for the opposite.

Most critiques of the 1960s and early 1970s, by contrast, aimed at a stronger, more democratic Congress turning out an improved policy product. This strain of reform helped produce numerous positive changes: the House Rules Committee was reined in; leadership control over committee assignments, bill referrals, and floor operations was strengthened; a measure of accountability by committee chairs to the party caucus was instituted; and Congress's budgeting capacity was improved. These efforts were not an unqualified success, and some are still worthy of refinement, but the harsh institution bashing that arose in the 1980s took reform in other directions. Proposals such as the line-item veto and term limits, emanating from the most vociferous critics of Congress and masquerading as congressional reform, gained wide currency, as I often learned in my community meetings. It was an agenda that helped Newt Gingrich and the Republicans win control of the House, but it offered them little help (and sometimes proved a burden) as they actually tried to run the institution.

Some positive changes were made, in part as a reaction to the critics. Measures such as banning honoraria and restricting other outside income, prohibiting the conversion of campaign funds to personal use, controlling the frequency and the content of franked mailings, and clarifying the limits of appropriate advocacy on behalf of constituents before regulatory bodies were moves in the right direction, in some cases considerably overdue. Management lapses and abuses in the House "bank" and post office and the ensuing outcry led in 1992 to the appointment of a non-partisan, professional administrator, reporting to the bipartisan leadership, to run the support operations of the House. (Unfortunately, having insisted on this reform in 1992, Republicans reversed it once they took control, requiring the chief administrative officer to report only to the Speaker.) A law subjecting Congress to the same workplace laws and standards that govern the private sector was passed in 1995 as the first item in the Contract with America. Republicans were quick to claim credit, although an almost identical bill had passed the House 427–4 in 1994, only to be blocked by Senate Republican leaders.

The Contract with America featured both term limits and the line-item veto. In the first edition of this book, I gave considerable attention to these pseudo-reforms as manifestations of the Congress bashing mentality, likely to weaken the institution. I regarded that as unnecessary in the second edition, noting that the ideas had largely been discredited.[10] But some of the strongest former proponents of these ideas are still running the Congress, and President Bush revived the proposal for a presidential line-item veto when he submitted his proposed budget for Fiscal 2005.

The line-item veto, which would give the president the authority to veto individual items in appropriations bills, has more to do with institutional power than government spending. Presidents almost invariably ask for more overall spending than Congress is willing to appropriate (which was true over the Reagan-Bush years to the tune of some $61 billion, rhetoric to the contrary notwithstanding).[11] And given the leverage the line-item veto would give presidents in pressuring individual members to accede to their spending requests, the line-item veto might be expected to lead to more, rather than less, spending over time. An institutionalized line-item veto could radically alter the constitutional balance of power and the dynamics of congressional policymaking. Members would likely focus less on working together to craft a balanced legislative product and more on securing the acquiescence of the president, item by item.

The president already had the power to "rescind" individual items in appropriations bills, but the rescissions did not become effective without majority votes in both chambers, which Congress was under no obligation to schedule. I supported "expedited rescission" bills, pushed to passage by the House Democratic leadership in 1992 and again in 1993 but rejected by the Senate, that would have required Congress to schedule votes on proposed rescissions. This was quite different from the so-called enhanced rescission bill passed by Republicans in 1996, which put proposed rescissions in effect unless Congress explicitly rejected them and effectively required a two-thirds vote in each house to do so. President

Clinton, who as governor had found the Arkansas line-item veto serviceable, eagerly signed the enhanced rescission bill.

This experiment with the line-item veto was short-lived, however. Clinton used his new powers sparingly during the 105th Congress, but the
discussions I had with administration officials to ensure that several of
my research provisions were not deleted from the agriculture funding bill
gave me a glimpse of how appropriations might work in the future. Republicans began to regret handing this power to a Democratic president,[12] and both chambers voted overwhelmingly in 1998 to override his
veto of $287 million in military construction projects. Few objections were
heard from either side of the aisle when the Supreme Court struck down
the law as a violation of the "presentment clause" (Article 1, Section 7) of
the Constitution.[13]

Term limits, even more than the line-item veto, would weaken Congress, making its members—the one group of actors in the federal system
who regard themselves as representatives of local communities and ordinary citizens—less knowledgeable, less seasoned, less confident, and
hence more dependent on staff, lobbyists, and bureaucrats for information and guidance. Term limits proponents often seem to think that serving effectively in Congress requires no particular experience or expertise.
Perhaps I have said enough in this book to indicate otherwise. I have
heard members of the Intelligence Committee say that it took them four
years simply to know how to ask the right questions of career people who
were accustomed to revealing only what they wished, and I confess that I
sometimes felt the same way on the Banking Committee. To arbitrarily
expel all members after a short period of service would mean for the Congress, as it would for any business or other organization, a damaging loss
of institutional memory, stature, and staying power. The slack would
surely be taken up by the executive establishment, which makes term limits a particularly puzzling cause for conservatives (those erstwhile critics
of bureaucracy and concentrated presidential power) to embrace.

None of this is to deny that Congress, like most institutions, needs periodic infusions of new blood and needs to replace aging or ineffective
leaders. One does not always have to agree with voters' decisions (for
some members, as I often note in community meetings, *one* term may be
too many) to observe that they are owed deference in a democratic system and that they already produce substantial turnover. New members
normally come into the House at a rate of 10–18 percent (and sometimes
much higher) each election cycle. The 1992 and 1994 elections together replaced almost half of the House membership, accounting for much of the
loss of momentum experienced by the term limits movement. Republican

leaders dutifully trotted out the term limits constitutional amendment for House votes in 1995 and 1997, but both times it fell far short of the requisite two-thirds. In the meantime, the Supreme Court struck down attempts to impose term limits on members of Congress through state law.[14] Although some members of the class of 1994 who had come into office promising to leave after three terms kept their promise, others decided to seek reelection anyway, hoping not to fall victim to the voter cynicism that they had exploited six years before.

Is there a stronger case to be made for the imposition of term limits on committee leaders? Democrats have applied such a rule to the Budget and Intelligence Committees, where it has produced a sequence of high-caliber chairmen and ranking members and has helped keep the committees responsive to the leadership and the caucus. In 1995, implementing the Contract with America, Republicans imposed three-term limits on all their committee and subcommittee chairs. As 2001 approached, the date when most chairmanships were set to expire, unanticipated consequences became apparent, as some disestablished chairs elected to retire and others engineered swaps of committee and subcommittee positions in order to stay in power. In fact, given the authority Speaker Gingrich assumed to name chairmen, often bypassing seniority claims, it could hardly be argued that term limits were necessary to move along leaders who needed to be replaced.

On the Democratic side, rules in effect since the mid-1970s have given the caucus the power to disapprove sitting chairmen and then choose among possible alternatives, resulting in the replacement of several infirm and unresponsive leaders. Some strengthening of the process—perhaps providing for an initial balloting among several of the most senior members of a committee when a chairmanship comes open or empowering the Speaker (or minority leader) to nominate committee chairs (or ranking members)—is worth considering. Such procedures would remove barriers to change when needed and permit deliberate, rational choices, and they seem far preferable to simply turning all chairs or ranking members out on a fixed schedule, regardless of performance.

After 1994, Congress bashing became less prevalent in the media and campaign rhetoric, mainly because Gingrich and others who had fanned the flames were now trying to run the institution. The reform agenda, which had never been as coherent or compelling as that spawned by the critiques of the 1960s and early 1970s, fizzled. But important operational changes were nonetheless made, many of which picked up on earlier themes of congressional reorganization and reform. These changes had less to do with the institutional critique the Republicans had used to gain power or with the Contract with America than with their need to run the institution efficiently and effectively once in control.

Most of the Republican changes aimed to empower the Speaker and rein in the standing committees and subcommittees (see Chapter 8). Some involved changes in House or Republican Conference rules, but most were accomplished by Speaker Gingrich's assertion of control over the appointment of committee members and leaders and over legislative scheduling and strategy.

These were matters with which Democrats had previously grappled. The reforms of the mid-1970s devolved authority and resources from committee chairs upward to party leaders and downward to subcommittee chairs and individual members. A widespread feeling developed during Tom Foley's speakership (1989–1994) that the balance needed further adjustment in order to facilitate development of a unified Democratic agenda, early intervention to ensure that bills were reported by committees in a form that most Democrats could support, and improved party discipline. I participated throughout 1992 as a member of the Committee on Organization, Study, and Review (OSR) in discussions of reform proposals, many of which involved an enhanced leadership role in defining and coordinating the legislative agenda and to some extent anticipated the Republican changes of 1995. It became clear in the course of these discussions how resistant committee chairs would be to any process or structure that impinged on their authority and how disinclined Foley was to take them on. The sort of enhanced leadership many of us were looking for would be difficult to "legislate" through altered rules and structures and would rely more on the entrepreneurship and personal assertiveness of the leaders themselves. In any event, the package approved by the Democratic Caucus at the beginning of the 103rd Congress did not strengthen leadership prerogatives significantly, and the agenda-setting panel of members it established, the Speaker's Working Group on Policy Development, "quickly faded into obscurity, lacking the formal powers and political support to bind the committee chairs to a caucus- or speaker-driven policy agenda."[15]

Speaker Foley was probably correct in 1992 when he concluded that there was not a sufficiently strong consensus in the Democratic Caucus on policy issues or institutional reform to underwrite a major redistribution of power, particularly considering the opposition of the committee chairs and the anticipation of policy leadership to come from a new Democratic administration. But that same judgment need not and should not hold if and when Democrats retake the chamber. In retrospect, Foley expressed some envy for the freedom Gingrich had to direct legislation without facing "stiff-necked senior committee chairmen with strong personalities"; he "had the luxury of being King John without the barons."[16] The next Democratic Speaker may not have the same luxury, but neither will he or she face the same constraints Foley did. It will be a time to revisit the questions of leadership prerogatives and committee autonomy and to adjust the balance between them to ensure a coherent agenda and enhance collective performance.

Although Republicans hardly offer a model for emulation, Democrats can learn from Republican organizational successes just as Gingrich learned from Jim Wright. In his heyday, Gingrich also exemplified pitfalls to be avoided: the deterioration of deliberation and debate, particularly in committees; inordinate deference to favored groups and restricted opportunities for member input; bitter partisanship and interpersonal acrimony.[17] Republican leaders have applied some correctives since Gingrich's decline and departure, but in their abuse of the budget process and the tactics they have adopted to press their legislative agenda, they have gone even farther.

Both parties have also continued to grapple with what proved to be the most difficult and least successful reform effort of the 1970s: the simplification and rationalization of committee jurisdictions.[18] Defenders of the present system sometimes argue that its former defects have been addressed by the Speaker's enhanced referral and scheduling powers and that jurisdictional fragmentation has its virtues, getting more members engaged on key issues, providing alternative ways of developing measures when problems arise, and so forth. But even conceding such advantages, the present system's scattering of jurisdiction over key policy areas (particularly those that have come into prominence since the jurisdictional lines were last drawn, for example, energy and the environment), its generating of overlapping and competing claims, and its provision of multiple checkpoints for obstruction and delay have surely gone past the point of diminishing returns. And jurisdictional anomalies do have policy consequences. The long struggle to repeal the Glass-Steagall Act and reform the regulation of financial services, for example, might have proceeded quite differently had the House Banking Committee's jurisdiction matched that of its Senate counterpart. But the fact that securities regulation in the House was (until 2001) under the jurisdiction of the Commerce Committee virtually guaranteed unproductive turf battles and selective (as opposed to comprehensive or balanced) approaches to the problem.

Our OSR deliberations in 1992 shied away from committee jurisdictions, but we proposed and the caucus approved rule changes that would eliminate seventeen subcommittees. In 1993 Vice Chairman David Drier

(R-California) and other Republicans on the Joint Committee on the Organization of Congress proposed a comprehensive realignment of committee jurisdictions, but Democrats, pressured by their committee chairs, resisted any such changes. The House on its own, however, declined to reauthorize four select committees (Aging, Narcotics, Children, and Hunger). Drier then resurrected his plan after Republicans won control of the House, but he quickly ran into resistance from Republican chairs not unlike that mounted by Democrats two years earlier. Although Gingrich and other GOP leaders were willing and able to overrule the chairs on numerous matters of procedure and prerogative, with regard to committee reorganization they elected merely to eliminate three standing committees with mainly Democratic clienteles (District of Columbia, Merchant Marine, and Post Office) and to cut back further on subcommittee assignments and the number of subcommittees.[19] Hastert later made a major positive adjustment in shifting securities regulation to the Banking Committee, but that had more to do with resolving a difficult leadership contest than with policy considerations (see Chapter 8).

The case for a modest realignment of committee boundaries (e.g., to bring House and Senate committee jurisdictions into coincidence, a situation already present and demonstrably helpful on the thirteen appropriations subcommittees) is still strong. But the fact that Gingrich, like Foley, was unwilling to take it on suggests that committee jurisdictions are likely to remain one of the most difficult and contentious reform areas. Moreover, these questions have arguably been rendered less consequential by the larger difficulties the committees face, such as a loss of deliberative capacity and usurpation by the majority leadership.

The key litmus test for any congressional reform should be whether it will leave the Congress stronger and make it a more competent and effective institution, able to produce better policy. This suggests a couple of caveats, drawing on themes developed in Chapters 11–12. The first is to abjure a simplistic distrust of power. Congressional reform has reduced and should reduce the power attached to certain persons or positions when it is abused or when it hinders institutional performance. But it is not enough to scatter power and resources around and leave it at that; effective congressional reform will attend to the need for effective (albeit accountable) concentrations of power. The second caveat is to be wary of the Lone Ranger ethical bias, the tendency to idealize independence and autonomy. Congressional effectiveness requires strengthening the means of collective action and instilling in members a sense of responsibility not only for their personal integrity but for the performance of the institution.

It is important, finally, to recognize the limits of reform. This too is a critical lesson from earlier chapters. The strength and quality of the leadership of various Speakers was less dependent on their formal powers or the rules under which they operated than on their personal ambition, skill, and temperament. Policy entrepreneurship among members could be facilitated or hindered by conditions in committees, the chamber, and the external environment, but the main ingredients were the motivation, ability, and energy of the entrepreneurs themselves. Budget breakdowns and failures were often less indicative of flawed procedures or machinery than of an absence of public consensus, political will, and responsible leadership. Rules and structures do matter; the process changes in the 1990 budget agreement, for example, greatly facilitated later deficit reduction efforts. But the fact remains: The main concern of those who would move the institution forward should not be endless tinkering with rules and structures but rather mustering the leadership, discipline, energy, and initiative to take advantage of the opportunities the system already offers.

Governance, Trust, and Citizenship

Reforms made to the Congress and other institutions of government will accomplish little if they do not rest on a firm foundation of public understanding, confidence, and trust. Every indication is that this foundation is rather shaky nowadays and that one culprit is the quality of understanding conveyed through our political discourse. That, of course, is only one diagnosis. Republicans often portray the mistrust as a (largely justified) reaction to the inherent evils of government or Democratic/liberal misrule. Democrats often prefer to indict governmental "gridlock," citing policy failures such as those I listed at the beginning of this chapter. But much of our political discourse has little to do with the actual decisions of government, good or bad, and it is this separation that makes genuine accountability difficult and often provokes cynicism and distrust. I will focus in the following discussion on the nature of modern campaigns and on the image that Congress presents to the public—important facets of the problem over which candidates and members have at least some control.

Campaigning and governing are not the same thing; in Chapter 4 I discussed the transitions that any successful candidate must make from one to the other. However, a more radical discontinuity has developed in recent years. It is in the nature of political campaigns to polarize and oversimplify, but personal attacks and distortions have increased markedly. And the link between what candidates say in their campaign advertisements and the decisions they make once in office has become more and more tenuous. George H.W. Bush's 1988 campaign, which focused on furloughed murderer Willie Horton and the pledge of allegiance, demonstrated that even presidential campaigns can subsist on the manipulation of symbols, with scarcely a word about the major decisions the new president would confront. (Bush's "no new taxes" pledge was only a partial exception, for it offered no clue as to how he would reduce the deficit or what revenue proposals he would ultimately make.) "Scholars and political strategists say," reported the *Washington Post* early in George W. Bush's 2004 reelection campaign, that "the ferocious Bush assault on [John] Kerry this spring has been extraordinary, both for the volume of the attacks and for the liberties the president and his campaign have taken with the facts."[20] Often it seems that the campaign style we witnessed early in North Carolina, courtesy of Jesse Helms and other candidates of the National Congressional Club, has become the national norm.

This trend has been reinforced by the technology of campaign advertising and fund-raising. Thirty-second television ads and direct mail financial solicitations, for example, put a premium on hard-hitting, oversimplified appeals and symbolic hot buttons. The trend has been both cause and effect of the modern emergence of cultural and value issues, such as abortion, race, patriotism, and alternative lifestyles, which lend themselves to symbolic appeals and often enable candidates to divert voters' attention from economic and quality-of-life concerns. Institution bashing and personal posturing, likening oneself to the biblical Lot in wicked Sodom as virtually the only righteous person in the corrupt government establishment, are a potent part of the mix.

The growing gap between campaigning and governing both draws on and feeds public alienation and cynicism. Voters complain about the nastiness and irrelevance of campaign advertising, and such tactics can sometimes be turned against an opponent (see Chapter 2). My "Stand By Your Ad" provisions will help voters identify those responsible for tactics of which they do not approve. But voters who find little to encourage or inspire them in politics are tempted to vote in anger or protest, inclinations that modern campaign advertising exploits effectively. As E. J. Dionne suggests, the decline of the "politics of remedy" (i.e., politics that attempt "to solve problems and resolve disputes") has created a vicious circle.

> Campaigns have become negative in large part because of a sharp decline in popular faith in government. To appeal to an increasingly alienated electorate, candidates and their political consultants have adopted a cynical stance which, they believe with good reason, plays into popular cynicism about politics and thus wins them votes. But cynical campaigns do not resolve issues. They do not lead to "remedies." Therefore, problems get worse, the electorate becomes more cynical—and so does the advertising.[21]

If modern campaigns reveal a dangerous decline in democratic accountability, so does modern governance, but not always in the way one might think. Ironically, the result of the campaigning–governance gap often is not governance in disregard of the popular will but a failure of governance, based on an exaggerated sensitivity to opponents' anticipated use of difficult policy decisions. This accounted for much of the skittishness surrounding the 1990 and 1993 budget measures and is perhaps best illustrated by the difficulty of fending off "hang 'em high" amendments to crime bills. Members often support these amendments, even when they are constitutionally dubious and more temperate alternatives are available, out of a fear of being cast as supporters of anything less than the toughest possible measures. This kind of defensive voting is part of the price we pay for the deterioration of campaign dialogue and its disengagement from the actual issues of governance.

Members often feel stronger electoral pressures to avoid difficult tasks or votes than to be active and productive in areas of positive concern. This is not to say we must succumb to these pressures. All of us feel occasionally that "I'd rather vote against this than to have to explain it," but we should worry if we find ourselves taking this way out too often or on matters of genuine consequence. It is our job to interpret and explain difficult decisions, and with sufficient effort, we can usually do so successfully.

Responsibility for our descent into attack politics is shared by journalists, interest groups, campaign consultants—and the viewing, voting public. The media seem less and less inclined to cover serious campaign issues or relate candidate exchanges straightforwardly; recent analyses of presidential campaigns reveal more negative coverage, shorter candidate sound bites, and more reportorial commentary, much of it debunking or disbelieving in nature.[22] But members of Congress and other candidates are hardly helpless (or blameless) before these trends: We have choices about the kinds of campaigns we run. By making campaign tactics an issue, we can heighten public awareness of and resistance to distorted, manipulative appeals. And we can tighten the link between what we say in our campaigns and what we have done and intend to do in office.

This is not a plea for dull or soft-pitch campaigns; on the contrary, it is our duty to arouse people's concern and anger about areas of neglect, to convince them that we can do better, to inspire them to contribute to the solution. Most people believe that politics and politicians ought to have something constructive to offer in the realms of education, housing, health care, economic development, environmental protection, and other areas of tangible concern. Our challenge is to get to work on these major challenges in both campaigning and governing in a credible way that inspires confidence and enthusiasm, and, by so doing, to expose hot-button attack politics for the sham it is.

As important as the tone and content of campaign rhetoric are in fomenting public mistrust, they are not its only sources. People, after all, see Congress with their own eyes, and often they don't like what they see. This owes something to media coverage that features "self-interested officials and dysfunctional institutions," treats the legislative process in terms of its machinations more than its substance, and frequently attributes a manipulative or deceptive intent to politicians.[23] But it also applies to the mostly unfiltered medium of C-SPAN; one survey found regular viewers to be more critical of Congress than those who did not see the institution in action.[24] Some disapproval is rooted in disappointment at what Congress has done or failed to do in particular policy areas, but people more often express disapproval of the posturing and bickering and gamesmanship that seem to characterize congressional operations apart from specific policy outcomes. Congressional debates often seem as removed from a genuine search for "remedies" as do campaign broadsides.

What do citizens see when they look toward Washington? Political scientist Richard Neustadt answered:

> Warfare among elites, waged since the 1960s in the name of causes, not compromises . . . rousing supporters by damning opponents. . . . President and congressmen and private organizations, and their massive staffs, all swirl around one another, seeking to manipulate public opinion and the media and one another for the sake of scoring points. . . . Damn the torpedoes, full steam ahead, rouse your friends, trash the enemy, the long term's later, victory comes first.[25]

David King linked public dissatisfaction to what many people regard as excessive and unnecessary partisanship. The growing cohesion and polarization of parties in the Congress mirrors movement toward the ideological extremes among the strongest identifiers with both parties in the electorate. Yet most Americans have not moved in this direction. On average, they have become less partisan and only slightly more conservative, "creating a growing gap between the preferences of political elites [including members of Congress] and average citizens." As the parties have polarized, they have drifted farther from the centrist preferences of more and more Americans, and it is these Americans who express the strongest disaffection with government.[26] My own experience, particularly in mounting a comeback effort in 1996, suggested that King was onto something. Many voters let me know in no uncertain terms that the partisan pyrotechnics on C-SPAN had very little to do with them.

This leaves both parties in Congress with a dilemma. Their core voters and contributors tend toward the ideological poles. Winning the next election requires that those loyalists be energized; it also requires, particularly for the "out" party, a sharpened political message and a distinct defining of differences. But the dilemma is this: Most of the endangered members and pickup prospects in both parties are not in ideologically pure districts but in districts where moderation and subdued partisanship are often rewarded. Both parties face the necessities of governance and the need to be on the right side of the public desire for less polarized and contentious politics.

Both parties thus have incentives to eschew nonstop partisanship, avoid ideological rigidity, and go beyond tired orthodoxies in addressing policy challenges. They do not, however, always do so. The pressures in the contrary direction can be intense, particularly in a period like the 2003–2004 presidential nomination season, when it was often observed that the energy on both sides seemed concentrated at the ideological poles. The Republican congressional leadership under the George W. Bush presidency has often disdained compromise, even with Republican moderates, and the Bush White House, contrary to the expectations of many, has generally followed suit (see Chapter 8). This approach seems rooted in a determination to mobilize core voters and key conservative constituencies, a sense that adamant conservatives in the Republican Conference must be accommodated, and perhaps a belief that the conservative agenda can be packaged for broader appeal. But there is a potential price to be paid, not only in terms of how centrist voters respond to the president and his party but also in the level of confidence and trust in the political system those voters attain.

We should not suppose, however, that the current level of alienation from politics and government will be easy to dispel, even if the parties manage to present a less fractious image. Public mistrust often goes beyond a realistic perception of policy failures and flawed processes to invoke unrealistic expectations about how conflicts can be resolved and consensus achieved in a diverse democracy. John Hibbing and Elizabeth Theiss-Morse concluded in a landmark study that people often do not "distinguish between essential modern democratic processes and perceived abuses of those processes. . . . [They] want it both ways . . . democracy and no mess." As Hibbing further explained:

Even if Congress were reorganized and reoriented, even if the media covered issues, not fluff, in mind-numbing detail, even if Congress hired the best public relations firm on the planet, and even if people cared about substance more than scandals, the modern Congress would still be suffering

from public disapprobation. Why? Because the public does not like to witness conflict, debate, deliberation, compromise, or any of the other features
that are central to meaningful legislative activity in a polity that is open,
democratic, heterogeneous, and technologically sophisticated.[27]

This poses a tremendous challenge to the responsible legislator who
chooses neither to exploit public mistrust nor to be victimized by it but to
convey an honest and realistic sense of what constituents should expect
from the legislative process.[28]

Finally, a word about citizenship. In politics, we expect people and
groups to express their wants and interests vigorously, and public officials expect to be judged on how effectively they respond. But in a democracy we require something more. Joseph Tussman's account of the dual
roles citizens are called on to play is suggestive:

> Each citizen is a member, a subject, a private person free within the common
> limits to pursue his own ends. But each is also an agent of the body politic, a
> ruler, a manner of the sovereign tribunal with all of the duties, obligations,
> and responsibilities that go with that role. . . .
>
> The citizen, in his political capacity . . . is asked public, not private ques-
> tions: "Do we need more public schools?" not "Would I like to pay more
> taxes?" He must, in this capacity, be concerned with the public interest, not
> with his private goods. His communication must be collegial, not manipula-
> tive. He must deliberate, not bargain.[29]

Although some may regard such notions as unrealistic, they remind us
of the centrality of civic virtue—the ability and the willingness to make
the common good one's own—to democracy. As Bill Bradley put it, "the
language of mutual obligation has to be given equal time with the language of rights."[30] Unless we can strike a better balance between private
and public interests in our politics and until citizens and officials alike assume greater responsibility for the common good, our problems will continue to defy solution and our politics will continue to breed cynicism
and disillusionment.

This need was underscored by one of the unhappiest episodes of my
early years in the House, the passage and subsequent repeal of the bill to
add major medical (or catastrophic) coverage to Medicare. Enacted in
1988, this measure inspired indiscriminate attacks on the "seniors-only
surtax" by the National Committee to Preserve Social Security and other
groups and a firestorm of protest among senior citizens. I received some
3,000 letters opposing the bill, and the topic dominated my community

meetings during most of 1989. On one occasion, after hearing an especially long litany of complaints—some legitimate but others based on
wildly inaccurate notions of the insurance value of Medicare or of what
the new provisions would require—I turned to one particularly angry
questioner. Most people seemed to agree that the added benefits were
needed, I observed, but they objected strenuously to the supplemental
premium that would be imposed to cover the cost. As far as I knew, I told
my constituent, there were three—and only three—alternatives to choose
from. Would he have us impose an even greater payroll tax on younger
workers, which was already the way we were paying for part A of
Medicare (hospital coverage)? Would he have us turn to the depleted U.S.
Treasury, which was already the way we were paying for most of part B
(doctor coverage)? Or should we ask the beneficiaries, especially better-
off beneficiaries, to bear more of the cost themselves?[31] Instead of giving
an answer, the man bristled in anger: "You have no right to ask me that!
That's your job!"

Though I obviously erred tactically in this instance, I believe my constituent was profoundly wrong: I was justified in asking him how he
would solve the problem. Even if he owed no answer to me personally, he
had an obligation to think about the issue in terms that went beyond his
personal desire not to pay. But this larger obligation of citizenship escaped him entirely.

My senior citizens luncheon, held a few weeks later, offered a more encouraging example. After a series of largely negative questions and comments on the catastrophic coverage issue, one man arose to announce that
he was tiring of the complaints. What we really ought to be considering,
he declared eloquently, was why we as a nation were spending so much
more on older people than we were on the needs of the children who represented our future. The room fell into an embarrassed silence, and the
tone of the meeting was transformed thereafter. I felt relieved but also
moved, for I had witnessed the kind of civic virtue—the assumption of
responsibility for the commonweal—that is all too rare in our politics
nowadays.

The narrow perspectives that citizens, groups, and leaders often bring
to politics result in unproductive standoffs and block genuine solutions.
This is not a plea, I hasten to add, for removing all conflict from politics:
Good citizens still find plenty to debate about. But our country needs a
broader, more visionary debate about how all of our people are faring
and about how to secure our common future. We are unlikely to frame
that debate satisfactorily or meet our challenges decisively unless and until we recapture a strong sense of citizenship.

This need is especially acute for public officials. A central part of my job is to become aware of the interests of my variegated constituents and to respond in appropriate ways. I expect the individuals and groups who approach me to express their wants and interests unequivocally. They are especially likely to gain my respect if they show some awareness of legitimate competing views and formulate their requests with due regard for the good of the whole. But whether they do or not, that is the context into which I am obligated to place them.

The member of Congress is not entirely on his or her own in seeking and promoting this broader view. The various checkpoints through which a measure must pass may temper its biases and oversights; a major benefit of committee deliberation and strong party leadership should be the transcending of interest group or industry wish lists and an increased capacity to draft and pass legislation in the public interest. However, just as members have a wide latitude in how we define our jobs, so we are responsible for how we define and how vigorously we pursue the good of the community. The job has many satisfactions and challenges but none greater than the opportunity it daily affords to act on the imperatives of citizenship.

Notes

1. E. J. Dionne Jr., *They Only Look Dead: Why Progressives Will Dominate the Next Political Era* (New York: Simon & Schuster, 1997), p. 327.

2. "Politics as a Vocation," in H. H. Gerth and C. W. Mills, eds., *From Max Weber: Essays in Sociology* (New York: Oxford University Press, 1946), p. 128.

3. "The policies we implement in the name of justice, and the deliberations we undertake as to what the common good or the public interest requires, should be (and for most people, I believe, are) underwritten by a sense of social interdependence, of mutual sympathy and shared purpose, and of responsibility for one another's and the collectivity's well-being." David E. Price, "Assessing Policy: Conceptual Points of Departure," in Joel L. Fleishman et al., eds., *Public Duties: The Moral Obligations of Public Officials* (Cambridge: Harvard University Press, 1981), pp. 166–167.

4. I expressed some of this in an otherwise appreciative review of Richard Fenno's *Congressmen in Committees, American Political Science Review,* June 1977, pp. 701–704.

5. Robert Bendiner, *Obstacle Course on Capitol Hill* (New York: McGraw-Hill, 1964), is an account of frustrated efforts to pass aid to education legislation; Richard Bolling, *House Out of Order* (New York: Dutton, 1965), is a brief for reform by a prominent House member. See also Morris K. Udall's newsletters from the 1960s, reprinted in *Education of a Congressman*, ed. Robert L. Peabody (New York: Bobbs-Merrill, 1972), especially chapters 19–22.

6. The study that I directed, *The Commerce Committees* (New York: Grossman, 1975), although completed in a few months, was published almost three years later as one of a set of six volumes.

7. Mark J. Green, James M. Fallows, and David R. Zwick, *Who Runs Congress? The President, Big Business, or You?* (New York: Bantam, 1972).

8. Green, Fallows, and Zwick, *Who Runs Congress?*, p. 94.

9. The high (or low) point of the progression was reached in a 1989 *Newsweek* piece that Rep. David Obey (D-Wisconsin) dubbed "the worst example of institution trashing that I have seen in my twenty years here." In the space of six pages readers were informed, without benefit of documentation, that most congressional staff members were employed "to enhance re-election"; that it was now "theoretically possible for a lawmaker to spend virtually his entire working day on the air" (although admittedly no one had done it); that "trading votes for money or pleasure is just another day at the office"; and that campaign money "allows members to live a virtually expense-free existence" (my wife and I were especially intrigued by that one). The article simultaneously condemned Congress as a "fortress of unreality, its drawbridges only barely connected to life beyond the moat" and took members to task for "commuting home for four-day weekends!" Jonathan Alter et al., "The World of Congress," *Newsweek,* April 24, 1989, pp. 28–34. Obey's comments were made in an address to the Center for National Policy on May 10, 1989, p. 5. For a later elaboration of many of these themes, see Obey's extended comments on the House floor in the *Congressional Record,* daily ed., November 5, 1991, pp. H9377–83.

10. *Congressional Experience,* 1st ed., pp. 161–163; 2d ed., p. 249. Also see the discussions in Nelson W. Polsby, "Congress Bashing for Beginners," *Public Interest,* Summer 1990, pp. 15–23; and Kenneth R. Mayer and David T. Canon, *The Dysfunctional Congress? The Individual Roots of an Institutional Dilemma* (Boulder: Westview, 1999), pp. 126–130.

11. Net amount calculated from data prepared by the staff of the House Appropriations Committee. Figures include all discretionary spending plus entitlements incorporated in appropriations bills for FY 1982–1993.

12. As Rep. Mickey Edwards (R-Oklahoma) had warned his colleagues in 1990, Republican support for the line-item veto required "a bold gamble that no Republican nominee for president will ever lose to some future Michael Dukakis or Walter Mondale." "A Conservative Defense of Congress," *Public Interest,* Summer 1990, p. 83.

13. *Clinton v. City of New York,* 524 U.S. 417 (1998).

14. *U.S. Term Limits, Inc. v. Thornton,* 514 U.S. 779 (1995).

15. C. Lawrence Evans and Walter J. Oleszek, *Congress Under Fire: Reform Politics and the Republican Majority* (New York: Houghton Mifflin, 1997), p. 55.

16. Jeffrey R. Biggs and Thomas S. Foley, *Honor in the House: Speaker Tom Foley* (Pullman: Washington State University Press, 1999), pp. 187–188, 199.

17. "As a former Speaker," Foley concluded, "while I might have envied the new Speaker's ability to curb the independent agendas of committee chairmen relative to the leadership [the] price was too high." Biggs and Foley, *Honor in the House*, p. 270. For a more positive though mixed assessment and a prediction that reversion to Democratic control probably would not lead to "a systematic reversal of the Republican reforms," see Evans and Oleszek, *Congress Under Fire*, pp. 172–179.

18. See David E. Price, "The Ambivalence of Congressional Reform," *Public Administration Review* 34, November-December 1974, pp. 601–608, and Roger H. Davidson and Walter J. Oleszek, *Congress Against Itself* (Bloomington: Indiana University Press, 1977).

19. See Evans and Oleszek, *Congress Under Fire*, pp. 91–101.

20. Dana Milbank and Jim VandeHei, "From Bush, Unprecedented Negativity," *Washington Post*, May 31, 2004, p. A1.

21. E. J. Dionne Jr., *Why Americans Hate Politics* (New York: Simon & Schuster, 1991), pp. 16–17. Dionne borrowed the concept of democratic politics at its best as "the search for remedy" from Arthur Schlesinger Jr.

22. See Thomas E. Patterson, *Out of Order* (New York: Vintage, 1994), especially chap. 2.

23. Thomas E. Patterson, "Bad News, Period," *P.S.: Political Science and Politics*, March 1996, p. 19; also see Mark J. Rozell, *In Contempt of Congress: Postwar Press Coverage on Capitol Hill* (Westport, Conn.: Praeger, 1996).

24. Thomas E. Mann and Norman J. Ornstein, introduction to *Congress, the Press, and the Public* (Washington, D.C.: American Enterprise Institute/Brookings Institution, 1994), p. 10.

25. Neustadt, "The Politics of Mistrust," in Joseph S. Nye Jr. et al., eds., *Why People Don't Trust Government* (Cambridge: Harvard University Press, 1997), p. 187.

26. David C. King, "The Polarization of American Parties and Mistrust of Government," in Nye et al., *Why People Don't Trust Government*, pp. 173, 176.

27. Hibbing and Theiss-Morse, *Congress as Public Enemy: Public Attitudes Toward American Political Institutions* (New York: Cambridge University Press, 1995), pp. 147–148; Hibbing, "Appreciating Congress," in Joseph Cooper, ed., *Congress and the Decline of Public Trust* (Boulder: Westview, 1999), p. 53.

28. It also poses a challenge to civic education. "The public's distaste for the core features of any real-life democracy—disagreement, debate, compromise, all probably at a measured pace—must be addressed by a totally restructured educational process. Schooling on constitutional and institutional niceties desperately needs to be accompanied by schooling on unavoidable democratic realities." Hibbing and Theiss-Morse, *Congress as Public Enemy*, p. 160.

29. Joseph Tussman, *Obligation and the Body Politic* (New York: Oxford University Press, 1960), pp. 108, 118.

30. Bradley, "Civil Society and the Rebirth of Our National Community," *Responsive Community*, Spring 1995, p. 9.

31. The supplemental premium would have been paid by the 40 percent of beneficiaries who owed more than $150 a year in federal income tax. The maximum amount, $800, would have been paid by the wealthiest 5.6 percent of beneficiaries. Faced with massive protests, even by those who would have paid a minimal supplemental premium or nothing at all, and finding no supportive constituency, I said that I might be persuaded to repeal the program but never to shift the costs to the younger workforce. That, in effect, is what the House did on October 4, 1989.

Index